The Logic of Cooperation in Autocracies

Modern Intellectual and Political History of the Middle East
Fred H. Lawson, *Series Editor*

Select Titles in Modern Intellectual and Political History of the Middle East

For a full list of titles in this series,
visit https://press.syr.edu/supressbook-series/modern
-intellectual-and-political-history-of-the-middle-east/.

The Logic of Cooperation in Autocracies

Political Opposition in the Third Yemeni Republic

Jens Heibach

Syracuse University Press

For a listing of books published and distributed by Syracuse University Press,
visit https://press.syr.edu.

ISBN: 9780815638391 (hardcover)
      9780815638407 (paperback)
      9780815657101 (e-book)

Library of Congress Cataloging-in-Publication Data

Names: Heibach, Jens, author.
Title: The logic of cooperation in autocracies : political opposition in the third
    Yemeni Republic / Jens Heibach.
Other titles: Political opposition in the third Yemeni Republic
Description: First edition. | Syracuse, New York : Syracuse University Press, 2024. |
    Series: Modern intellectual and political history of the Middle East |
    Includes bibliographical references and index.
Identifiers: LCCN 2023053764 (print) | LCCN 2023053765 (ebook) |
    ISBN 9780815638407 (paperback) | ISBN 9780815638391 (hardback) |
    ISBN 9780815657101 (ebook)
Subjects: LCSH: Political parties—Yemen (Republic)—History—21st century. |
    Authoritarianism—Yemen (Republic) | Yemen (Republic)—Politics and government—
    21st century. | BISAC: POLITICAL SCIENCE / World / Middle Eastern |
    POLITICAL SCIENCE / Political Ideologies / General
Classification: LCC JQ1842.A979 H45 2024 (print) | LCC JQ1842.A979 (ebook) |
    DDC 324.2533—dc23/eng/20240104
LC record available at https://lccn.loc.gov/2023053764
LC ebook record available at https://lccn.loc.gov/2023053765

Contents

Illustrations

Tables

Acknowledgments

The topic addressed in this book has been with me for quite some time now. My interest in opposition cooperation under authoritarianism was initially sparked in early summer 2005. Still a student at Freie Universität Berlin, I was genuinely excited to see the cross-ideological Kifaya movement swelling and making alleged headway in challenging the Mubarak regime. In part, that excitement was owing to a previous stay in Cairo. I had spent two months there amid a climate that struck me, somewhat perplexingly back then, as both lively and asphyxiating at the same time. Granted, a fair bit of optimism—and perhaps naïveté—must have been at play as well.

Of that (for the most part at least) I would eventually be cured by the Syrian security apparatus: in one fell swoop in late 2007, almost the entire leadership of another opposition alliance I had been observing for a while, the Damascus Declaration for National Democratic Change, would be arrested. My confidence about the effectiveness of concerted opposition action in the face of the region's autocracies had been significantly curbed already before the December crackdown. Even so, right after learning about the events in Damascus, I rushed to fetch a copy of my final thesis—as it happens, a study of this very alliance—that I had defended just a few months earlier.

I still recall the mixed feelings encountered while thumbing through its pages. At first, I felt relief for having gotten it right after all. Considering the strength of the Assad regime, I had maintained throughout that the Damascus Declaration was fighting against long odds. But then I also felt an indistinct sense of remorse about my initial hunch in seeing the brutal repression of these activists, some of whom had spent years or, like Riyadh al-Turk, decades in prison already, often for no more than simply speaking their mind. It was the classic if simplistic good-guys-versus-bad-guys scenario, with me somewhere in between.

Slowly, it began to dawn on me that I had hitherto failed to sufficiently reflect on my own personal stance on these matters. My retrospective guess is that I had not been completely oblivious to my sympathies for figures such as al-Turk prior to this moment. Yet for some reason—and for all the years of training I had received in social science methods—I only then fully awoke to how seriously my sympathies, or antipathies for that matter, could interfere with my endeavor to provide sound and balanced scholarly analysis. Despite learning about the problem in my first semester at university, it seems that only after graduation had I come to really understand it. Shortly after, I set off to Yemen for the first time.

I by no means recount this episode to claim that I had become a better scholar on my arrival there in 2008. Frankly, fieldwork was not at the top of my agenda when I disembarked at Sanaa International Airport, at least to begin with; I had no concrete plans for conducting research there, and the only thing I knew of the Joint Meeting Parties (JMP) (this book's empirical case) at the time was that it existed. I give this context, rather, as I believe that the intricacies of doing research on the opposition in autocracies are only infrequently addressed by political scientists, that despite, more often than not, one interacting with individuals whose attitudes, values, and worldviews; whose demeanor and resolve; and whose living conditions and dependencies are quite different from one's own. In other words, one often meets activists about whom it is nearly impossible to not have strong opinions, or with interlocutors operating outside the realm of opposition politics who undoubtedly have particular opinions about the latter—even though they would usually present their expertise as impartial knowledge.

This finding is not groundbreaking, featuring indeed in every qualitative methods manual. Nor has my approach to handling these intricacies differed from the advice commonly given in such manuals. Still, I should briefly outline how I attempted to navigate the difficult waters of researching the (Yemeni) opposition, if only for the sake of meeting my own requirements.

Besides triangulation, which was key in several respects, I have tried to keep an intellectual and emotional distance to my research topic, including the people I talked to. Often doing so was not too great of a challenge, yet at times it was. Retaining (or establishing) such distance was then facilitated by granting myself sufficient time to digest and analyze what I had previously seen, heard, or read. Overall, the fact that several years had passed between my last interview and the drafting of this manuscript would be extremely beneficial. Also, I attempted to talk to as many people as possible and to include as many perspectives as deemed to exist and be feasible (needless to say, as a white researcher from western Europe you may not wish to meet representatives of all groups in a country that has been described as a hotbed of Islamic terrorism).

I failed with respect to the latter task. Because of, most notably, security concerns, I was not able to visit all governorates, and it is probably among the greatest weaknesses of this book that most formal interviews were conducted in Sanaa, even though my interviewees hailed from all over Yemen. Last, I have strained to be open-minded about almost everything I was told during the interviews, informal discussions, and qat chews, including rather dubious pieces of information. Many things I had surmised to be fiction later turned out to be just that, fabrications; other alleged cock-and-bull stories, however, shaped up to be increasingly reasonable ones and thus likely true.

Compiling a coherent account of the relationship between the regime of ʿAli ʿAbdallah Salih and the JMP, or between the latter and other collective actors, then posed the greatest challenge, requiring countless hours of consulting and reappraising a plentitude of additional sources. While I am positive about the results these efforts have yielded, I do not claim that the version of events I present in the following is the only valid one. Indeed, I look forward to learning how other scholars, Yemeni and international, will engage with my arguments.

One last remark concerning my interviews is in order. All the individual ones that this book draws on were conducted between 2008 and 2013. Since then, however, circumstances have changed in a way that few, if any, of my interviewees might have anticipated, myself included. To guarantee the safety of my interlocutors and their relatives amid the current war—and whatever might come thereafter—I have therefore decided to anonymize all interview data. Coming to this decision was hard, but I believe it is a necessary measure in these precarious times.

Many people have made this book possible—that is, in addition to my interlocutors in Yemen, whom I would like to cordially thank at the outset. The book started out as a doctoral dissertation, and I owe my supervisors, Rachid Ouaissa and Thorsten Bonacker, a debt of gratitude for the vital support they provided during its making. In Yemen, I am deeply indebted to ʿAbd al-Malik, ʿAbd al-Salam, Ahmad, Anwar, Hafiz, Mahmud, Nizar, Ramzi, and Yasir for their assistance and hospitality during my visits to the country. Large parts of the research for this book were done at the Center for Near and Middle Eastern Studies at Philipps-Universität Marburg, and I am still beholden to my former colleagues there, including Anne-Linda Amira Augustin, Julius Dihstelhoff, Farah El Shamaa, Verena Fibich, Albrecht Fuess, Pierre Hecker, Oliver Kahl, Ivesa Lübben, Walter W. Müller, Taoufik Rached, Karolin Sengebusch, Katrin Sold, Jaouad Tissouit, and particularly Christian Neugebauer with whom I had reams of professional discussions by day and less professional ones at night. I would also like to thank my students in Marburg for bearing with me whenever I wandered from our sessions' subject and ended up talking about Yemeni politics instead.

Following a longer interruption, I resumed work on the book at the German Institute for Global and Area Studies (GIGA) in Hamburg, where it took its final shape in a very stimulating work atmosphere. Many GIGA fellows and associates helped me to significantly improve the manuscript by commenting on earlier drafts or by lending their support in other crucial ways, notably Selman Almohamad, Sara Bazoobandi, May Darwich, Rim Darwich, Mira Demirdirek, Hayat Douhan, Julia Grauvogel, Maria Josua, Merouan Mekouar, Peter Peetz, Johannes Plagemann, James Powell, Miriam Prys-Hansen, Josef Richter, Thomas Richter, Christian von Soest, Jason Sumich, Hamid Talebian, Hakkı Taş, Nina Waßmann, Eckart Woertz, and especially André Bank, who has been a tremendous source of support ever since I came to the city. Beyond the GIGA, I owe thanks also to Gabriele vom Bruck, Felix Eikenberg, Gregory Gause, Marie-Christine Heinze, Jens Kambeck, Toby Matthiesen, Eckehard Schulz, Jillian Schwedler, Mareike Transfeld, and Atiaf al-Wazir.

Further, the book has also been greatly facilitated by the institutional backing received in the past few years. For a start, fieldwork assistance was provided by Philipps-Universität Marburg as well as by the Yemen Polling Center in Sanaa, which hosted me as a visiting research fellow in late 2012 and early 2013. The GIGA Communications Department, the GIGA Institute for Middle East Studies, and the GIGA Peace and Security Research Programme kindly agreed to fund the copyediting of the manuscript. For all this support, I am very grateful. In addition, I would like to thank the staff at Syracuse University Press, especially Laura K. Fish, who has been incredibly helpful and supportive herewith.

As is perhaps natural with a project that ran for years until its eventual completion, several bereavements occurred in the meantime. Some of my Yemeni interlocutors were killed before and during the current war, and while I was not personally close to them their deaths affected me all the same. During my last stay in Yemen, I shared a house with Luke Somers in the Old City of Sanaa. Luke was kidnapped by al-Qaeda just a few months after I had left the country and eventually killed during a failed rescue attempt by US Special Forces in December 2014. His death, too, had a deep effect on me for a number of reasons, not least because of the many hours we had spent together on our rooftop having enjoyable nighttime conversations. He truly was an amiable and astute character who had arrived in Yemen on the eve of the 2011 uprisings—an exceptional period in the country's recent history, and one during which almost everything seemed possible. I wonder what he might have thought about the war that unfolded in Yemen not long after his death. This war, for all intents and purposes, is a sequence of innumerable personal tragedies Yemenis are enduring to this day. Back in Germany and far away from the misery in South Arabia, however, I experienced my own personal tragedies when, within a relatively short while, my grandmothers and my mother died. I looked up to each of them, and I owe them very, very much, particularly my mother, Margit Heibach.

The last round of thanks goes to my friends and family. Much in contrast to the bulk of the other people mentioned thus far, I am thankful to Stefan Braun, Oliver Göbel, Christoph Koeberlin, Sebastian Metz, Gerrit Nanninga, and Oliver Ziegler for talking *not* about Yemen but about anything else instead. I am unable to list all the things I owe to my father, Axel Heibach, but also to my sister, Yvonne Heibach, and my parents-in-law, Erling and Rana von Mende, as well as their son, Tuğrul (whom I would have loved to ask for a review of this book, had he not been biased). Thank you all! Finally, my deepest gratitude goes to my wife, Leyla von Mende, and our son, Cenk. It is a blessing to know that you are around.

Abbreviations

AQAP	al-Qaeda in the Arabian Peninsula
AYU	Association of Yemeni 'Ulama'
CAUS	Center for Arab Unity Studies
DNP	Democratic Nasserist Party
EU EOM	European Union Election Observation Mission
FOY	Friends of Yemen
GCC	Gulf Cooperation Council
GDP	gross domestic product
GPC	General People's Congress
JMP	Joint Meeting Parties
MVS	majority-vote system
NDI	National Democratic Institute
NGO	nongovernmental organization
NUPO	Nasserist Unionist People's Organization
ODA	official development assistance
PCND	Preparatory Committee for National Dialogue
PDRY	People's Democratic Republic of Yemen
PPP	purchasing-power parity
PRS	proportional representation system
RAY	League of the Sons of Yemen
ROY	Republic of Yemen
SCCOP	Supreme Coordination Council of Opposition Parties

SCER	Supreme Commission for Elections and Referendum
SMO	social movement organization
STC	Southern Transitional Council
TOM	National Opposition Bloc
UNF	Union of National Forces
UPF	Union of Popular Forces
YAR	Yemen Arab Republic
YSP	Yemeni Socialist Party

The Logic of Cooperation in Autocracies

Introduction

This book's beginnings must be set in Taʻizz, a major urban center and cultural hub in the Southern Highlands of Yemen. Located near the former border between the northern Yemen Arab Republic (YAR) and the southern People's Democratic Republic of Yemen (PDRY), the city was perhaps the likeliest setting for a series of improbable yet momentous meetings launched in early 1996. By that time, the end of Yemen's civil war had not yet seen its second anniversary. Pitting North against South, the war of 1994 had resulted in a crushing defeat of the southern-based Yemeni Socialist Party (al-hizb al-ishtiraki al-yamani; YSP) that had striven to undo the Republic of Yemen (ROY)—itself established in a merger of the YAR and the PDRY in May 1990. While the civil war was ultimately short-lived, it was but the latest violent conflict in a rash of regular bilateral wars and cross-border skirmishes in South Arabia since the departure of the British from Aden and its hinterlands had engendered the emergence of the only Marxist state on Arab soil in 1967. Always embroiled in these conflicts in one way or the other were members of the northern-based Islamist Yemeni Congregation for Reform (al-tajammuʻ al-yamani li-l-islah, hereafter Islah) or its antecedent organizations who considered the southern atheists a direct menace to their beliefs about how the "two Yemens" ought to be constituted socially and politically. The same was indeed true of the YSP too, which, on unification, had anticipated the imposition of a "project of cultural renaissance"[1] on its northern neighbor to help it get to know the true promise of a progressive, secular order. In short, what made those meetings in Taʻizz remarkable was that representatives of Islah and the YSP got together to gauge the possibilities for joint future action despite a long history of mutual violence.

1

Unification in 1990 had coincided with the introduction of a liberal democratic system, which was swiftly celebrated as a harbinger of democratic change in the Arab world at the time.[2] The successful holding of the first all-Yemeni parliamentary elections in 1993 attested to the apparent success of the country's democratic transition. Yet while Yemen's unity had survived the 1994 war, albeit in tatters, its democratic consolidation came under heightened stress as the rule of the General People's Congress (al-mu'tamar al-sha'bi al-'amm; GPC) led by President 'Ali 'Abdallah Salih proceeded increasingly unchecked. Questioning the GPC's willingness to play by the rules, its political rivals were apprehensive about its conduct during the next parliamentary elections scheduled for April 1997. Against the backdrop of such suspicions, negotiations between Islah and the YSP in Ta'izz aimed to strike an agreement demanding the safeguarding of electoral integrity in the upcoming polls. Before long, they were joined by other parties and eventually published a common agreement on free and fair elections in August 1996.

Joint efforts did not come to a halt at this point. In the following years, cooperation between the opposition parties gained traction as political pluralism and democratic institutions in Yemen slid back to matching the Middle East's regional norm. Meanwhile, and reminiscent of those first joint encounters in 1996, the parties involved began to call themselves the Joint Meeting Parties (ahzab al-liqa' al-mushtarak). Notwithstanding serious setbacks, of which there were many, they built on the Ta'izz momentum and continuously pushed boundaries in pursuing a higher level of cooperation. Finally, in November 2005, altogether six parties (including Islah and the YSP) agreed to adopt a detailed set of rules regulating future interactions among themselves and vis-à-vis their external environment, notably the authoritarian regime that had been reinstalled in the meantime. In what appeared to be more of a founding charter than a political program, the parties concomitantly endorsed a broad plan for national reform. With their signing of these documents, the JMP became one of the strongest and most resilient opposition alliances in and beyond the Middle East, one whose analysis promises to be a fruitful and rewarding endeavor also from a more general perspective. This book seeks, then, to be as much an investigation of strategic cooperation among fellow opponents under conditions of authoritarianism as it is a study of this extraordinary Yemeni alliance per se.

The Joint Meeting Parties

When researching opposition alliances in autocracies, social scientists are commonly interested in their composition, durability, and success. If one takes that position as the benchmark, then the JMP appears to be an exceptional case here, given its values per each of those variables, and a deviant or extreme one when these three dimensions are considered in combination.[3] First, concerning its composition, the JMP consisted of five to six political parties for most of its existence. Given their leading position within the opposition camp and the breadth of their programmatic orientations, these parties can be seen as broadly representative of the dominant trends among those outside power in the ROY at the time. Among them, Islah was the strongest in terms of both party membership and resources. Officially founded in 1990,[4] it was Sunni Islamist in nature—although it also featured a powerful tribal wing whose actions were often motivated by more profane interests. Originating from the North, it quickly built a substantial grassroots base in the territories of the former PDRY after unification.[5] The YSP came in second when comparing its strength to that of other JMP members. As the former ruling party of the PDRY, it started out with sturdy Marxist-Leninist credentials on its formal establishment in 1978. With the passage of time, it became more ideologically pragmatic and eventually turned into a social-democratic force in the late 1990s. The party's power base lay in the South, where it remained a political heavyweight and largely uncontested in its claim to represent southern interests until roughly midway through the first decade of the new century.[6]

Throughout its existence, the JMP also encompassed two Zaydi parties, both of which were fairly insignificant with regard to membership numbers but still adjuvant to cooperation by way of their "political pragmatism":[7] the Union of Popular Forces (ittihad al-quwa al-sha'biyya; UPF) and the Party of Truth (hizb al-haqq, hereafter al-Haqq). Both parties sprang from Zaydi revivalism, an intellectual and political movement seeking to reassert Zaydi Islam in a post-imamate Yemen by, among other things, revising Zaydi doctrinal prescriptions and adjusting them to a republican setting.[8] As befitted their ideological orientation, they were firmly rooted in North Yemen, where the vast majority belonging to the Zaydi denomination live.[9] Yet unlike the most famous offshoot of Zaydi revivalism—that is, Ansar Allah (the Partisans of God, better known as the Huthi movement)—neither the UPF nor al-Haqq was able to garner significant levels of popular support, including in times of elections. It was only in the 1993 polls that al-Haqq managed to win two seats in the national parliament. One of its two members of parliament at the time was Husayn Badr al-Din al-Huthi, who, in 1997, left the party to establish the Believing Youth (al-shabab al-mu'min), Ansar Allah's predecessor organization.

In contrast to al-Haqq and the UPF, which were more of a unique feature of Yemen's political landscape, the JMP also comprised parties that had a number of siblings across the Arab world. To begin with, there was the Nasserist Unionist People's Organization (al-tanzim al-wahdawi al-sha'bi al-nasiri; NUPO). The latter was founded in Ta'izz in 1965 amid the civil war in North Yemen (1962–70), during which republican forces, with massive backing from Egyptian troops sent by President Gamal Abdel Nasser, would fight loyalists to the last Zaydi imam, Muhammad al-Badr—themselves supported by, most notably, Saudi Arabia.[10] Programmatically, NUPO offered a Nasserist blend of socialism and Arab nationalism, which, long past the heyday of Nasserism, had lost popular appeal when the party was legalized in 1990. Largely an urban phenomenon born of leftist intellectuals, the party—just as al-Haqq and the UPF also did—gained leverage over national politics mainly by dint of the JMP, of which it was a member throughout the alliance's life span. The latter was not the case with two other Yemeni branches of Arab nationalist parties. The Iraqi-oriented Arab Socialist Nationalist Ba'th Party (hizb al-ba'th al-'arabi al-ishtiraki al-qawmi), which traced its beginnings in Yemen back to the 1950s and was rather insignificant in terms of followership, was among the earliest members of the JMP. In 2006, it defected to the GPC. It was replaced by the Syrian-oriented Arab Socialist Ba'th Party (hizb al-ba'th al-'arabi al-ishtiraki), which joined the JMP in August 2008 on the grounds of the increasingly repressive nature of the Salih regime, as stated by its deputy secretary-general Mudhish 'Ali Naji.[11]

In a nutshell, there was a notable imbalance between the constituent parties of the JMP. Islah and the YSP were by far its strongest cogs: it has been argued that "as a practical matter . . . the JMP is and turns on Islah and the YSP."[12] This state of affairs did not change the fact that the alliance was an outstanding example of cross-ideological cooperation, and maybe an unprecedented one at that.[13] What is sometimes overlooked in studies focusing on Islamist-leftist cooperation, however, is that the JMP overcame not only deep ideological cleavages but regional ones too, being as they are particularly salient in Yemen to this day.[14] Given Islah's potent tribal wing, whose heartlands lay in the rural areas of Yemen's Highlands, the JMP additionally bridged the considerable urban-rural divide within the country. This reconciliation is interesting because cooperating parties' diverging social bases are, alongside ideological discrepancies,[15] assumed to be a key reason for the failure of alliances.[16]

Yet, and second, the JMP did endure despite multiple internal rifts—and did so in the face of recurrent regime attempts to unsettle cooperation by way of repression, co-option, or division. Such strategies are understood as another prime reason for the collapse of alliances,[17] which is the norm rather than the exception in and beyond the Middle East. Precisely because the premature disintegration of cooperation is such a widespread phenomenon, a case has been made for researchers to move beyond the failure-success nexus. Instances of cooperation, so the argument goes, merit scholarly attention notwithstanding their failure (or the absence of success),[18] with success often being defined in terms of cooperation endurance.[19] While this line of thinking is cogent, the reverse conclusion makes an even more compelling case for studying the JMP: it did maintain cooperation over an extended period. As noted, the alliance's beginnings reached back to 1996. In 2005, tactical cooperation turned strategic; only in 2011 did the JMP cease to be an *opposition* alliance. The sheer longevity of cooperation, particularly the prolonged formative period that also included instances of electoral coordination, is important as it allows us to analyze how and why strategic cooperation evolved, endured, and—in a more conventional sense—succeeded. After all, and third, the JMP ended up in government in December 2011 after months of massive popular protests—to which it had contributed significantly—led to Salih's eventual abdication. This latter achievement set the JMP apart from all other cases of strategic opposition cooperation in the Middle East.

The Research Problem

This book delves into the nature of such cooperation under authoritarianism. To this end, it explores three conceptual angles: Why are strategic alliances formed? What makes them last? And what makes them prevail? Based on the previous discussion, it considers the JMP to be a pertinent case study in seeking answers to these unresolved questions, whose empirical translations may read as follows: What gave rise to the emergence of the JMP as a strategic alliance? How did the JMP organize itself, and with what consequences? And why and how did the JMP interact with the principal relevant actors outside the alliance?

The ensuing analysis has profited from outstanding scholarly work on Yemeni politics, including some on the JMP, which has been heavily conducive to this book's own undertakings. Yet this scholarship has also come with certain limitations to it given the chosen analytical focus or the time period covered. Analyses of the authoritarian regime under Salih, for instance, investigate the JMP or its individual components, but they do so only to the extent to which this is necessary to scrutinize key characteristics of the incumbent government.[20] The same is true of those studies homing in on one of the JMP's most fascinating members, namely, Islah, including those scholars researching the alliance in order to assess, for instance, the impact of cooperation on the worldview of its Islamist members.[21] Another set of useful studies deal with the Yemeni uprising of 2011, in which the JMP was one important actor—but, indeed, only one.[22] Last, there has been some insightful scholarship directly examining the JMP; most of it, however, is either more empirical in nature or alternatively unable to cover the alliance's full life span given the year of publication.[23] In sum, while the subsequent analysis draws on a number of excellent works on Yemeni politics and the JMP, it could have scarcely been conducted had it been solely based on extant findings.

Another challenge this book has faced emerged from the relative dearth of theoretical discussions on strategic opposition cooperation under conditions of authoritarianism. This is not to say that it was necessary to start entirely from scratch. On the contrary, there is a rich body of theoretical literature on cooperation, including opposition cooperation in autocracies. While the corresponding works were rewardingly consulted, they fell short of providing satisfying answers to all the conceptual questions outlined earlier—let alone offering a coherent set of assumptions on strategic opposition cooperation under authoritarianism. Again, this situation owes to the divergent research problems they seek to tackle, their respective objects of investigation, and their individual scope conditions. There are, for instance, a substantial number of analyses discussing the causes behind the failure of alliances in authoritarian regimes. In addition to the ones already mentioned, which explore how internal divides, external encroachments, and structural problems all impede cooperation, other studies emphasize here the importance of a lack of trust or commitment.[24] These works are thus of only indirect use, as they inform us about what hampers cooperation but do not capture how parties (can) overcome the corresponding pitfalls.[25] However, to the extent that it was deemed conceptually sound—that is, capable of being reconciled with the general assumptions underlying this book (see below)—the core arguments put forth in those studies have been integrated here.

The same procedure was chosen with respect to other strands of the relevant literature, too. Besides the pieces discussing general trends and typologies of opposition alliances in autocracies,[26] these are primarily those studies researching the impact of cooperation on ideological moderation,[27] tactical cooperation (especially electoral coordination),[28] and the performance of alliances in times of political upheaval.[29] These analyses have yielded valuable assumptions on how and why alliances interact with their external environment, especially during elections and when popular protests arise. But they offer few indications of how (strategic) alliances behave in less exceptional periods, and fewer still of how the latter's external performance relates to internal processes—and, connectedly, vis-à-vis the issue of cooperation maintenance. Last, another source for making cautious inferences has been found in the broader literature on political cooperation. Unlike some seminal works in economics or political science that focus in on the micro level of cooperation,[30] the literature on social movement cooperation appears to be particularly pertinent in that the cooperating entities under scrutiny are also located at the meso level.[31] Still, one must take into consideration that political parties are not synonymous with social movements and that the bulk of those works' theoretical findings were arrived at chiefly by studying social movements in liberal, nonauthoritarian environments.

The upshot is that greater efforts need to be made to explain more systematically why strategic opposition alliances in autocracies come about, how they are maintained against the odds, and what (more) they can do to attain their goals. This conclusion is reinforced by the role these alliances are assumed to play during processes of social and political transformation, especially in times of democratization.[32] This book seeks to redound to such efforts. The following section outlines how it sets out to do so, briefly summarizing the key arguments that will be made in due course.

Conflict and Cooperation

What follows rests on two fundamental assumptions about human action and social change. First, and in line with the basic conjectures of structuration theory, it considers social structures to be principally the product of human action, which, in turn, is informed and shaped by the very social structures subsisting in the time and place in which a particular action occurs.[33] As a consequence, human agency is understood here as an actor's efforts to mold the social structures he or she is subject to, by seeking either to perpetuate or to change them. Once two or more actors hold diverging notions about how that molding should take place, human action breeds social conflict. The latter is, therefore, an omnipresent feature of social life.[34]

Yet, and second, conflict can be regarded as the main driver of social change, and not necessarily pathological per se.[35] Whether it becomes dysfunctional and threatens to destabilize a given social unit largely depends on how the conflict in question is dealt with. Important differences exist, for instance, between regime types in their approach to handling social conflict.[36] This is evident in the unwillingness of authoritarian governments to tolerate a "system of managing the major political conflicts of a society by allowing one or more opposition parties to compete with the governing parties for votes in elections and in parliament," which has been referred to as "one of the greatest and most unexpected social discoveries that man has ever stumbled onto."[37]

Further conclusions can also be inferred from these assumptions. For one, conflict and cooperation are intrinsically linked. If two or more actors share the same position or goal concerning a specific contradiction created by the social structures in place, they are essentially fit to cooperate vis-à-vis attaining the desired outcome, and the likelihood of them aligning their behavior increases in accordance with the degree to which their cost-benefit calculations and attitudes toward the contradiction in question correspond.[38] For another, regime type not only impacts the way political conflicts are handled but also sways cooperation in two major respects. On the one hand, the opposition in autocracies is seriously handicapped. Their incumbents dispose of significantly greater resources and define the legal boundaries within which the opposition is allowed to operate.[39] Given this structural imbalance and legal arbitrariness, opposition decision-making is bound to be conducted amid high levels of uncertainty.[40] Meanwhile, the opposition is exposed to regime strategies that are ultimately predatory in nature.[41] Altogether, this does not bode well for opposition cooperation, which, as a general rule, authoritarian incumbents seek to hamstring.

On the other hand, autocracies provide strong incentives for cooperation—most notably strategic forms thereof. If effective, strategic cooperation concentrates resources and thereby reduces the regime's competitive edge in relative terms. It thus provides increased shelter from the regime and boosts the prospects of success—as compared to tactical or single-issue cooperation, which mostly emerges in times of elections but is often unsuccessful.[42] In contrast, strategic alliances usually last longer than tactical ones,[43] thereby raising the odds of profiting from potentially favorable opportunity structures in the future.

This begs, finally, the question of what even qualifies as a strategic opposition alliance or as an instance of strategic opposition cooperation.[44]

Strategic opposition cooperation is here defined, first, in terms of at least two opposition actors—political parties, as concerns the JMP—working together for a common purpose.[45] Furthermore, and unlike tactical co-operation, it is characterized by the pursuit of multiple objectives, which must be clearly defined and mutually approved of.[46] Also, strategic coop-eration is formalized: its constituents delegate representatives to initiate and monitor joint action on a regular basis. Last, strategic alliances fall short of a merger, meaning their constituents remain independent entities and therefore organizationally and programmatically distinct from one another.[47] All opposition bodies meeting these criteria are here considered cases of strategic cooperation, regardless of whether they refer to them-selves, or are referred to by others, as alliances, coalitions, blocs, fronts, and so on.

Although strategic opposition cooperation appears to be longer lasting, more effective, and potentially more promising than tactical cooperation, it is a relatively rare empirical phenomenon regardless. This infrequency is because it is more challenging to sustain than tactical cooperation. This book, in fact, argues that strategic alliances come into being only once three conditions are met: the parties involved in the process of forging an alliance must settle on common goals, they must expect the benefits of cooperation to outweigh its costs, and they must hold balanced attitudes toward each other. In general, the process of alliance building is greatly facilitated by party elites being committed to the idea of cooperation. If, however, the notion of strategic cooperation is controversial within the ranks of would-be partners' organizations, it is only when those elites are at the helm of their parties' decision-making bodies that cooperation can ensue. Likewise, committed elites must retain those positions of authority if strategic cooperation is to continue.

These conditions are required for strategic opposition cooperation's onset. Importantly, they also form the basic requirements for its main-tenance. To disentangle the different layers of strategic cooperation—as well as the various tasks that need to be handled to make it last and, per-haps, prevail—the book suggests keeping the analyses of the internal and external performance of strategic alliances separate. The primary reason for adopting such a methodological approach is that those respective performances are driven by two distinct logics. In short, the internal logic of strategic cooperation is geared toward maintaining it. All corresponding assumptions arrived at suggest that the internal performance of alliances aims to uphold the basic conditions for cooperation, with it being posited that organizational structures are of crucial importance in this as they facilitate the reproduction of the latter and contribute to keeping external disruptive factors at a manageable level. This is not to say that internal performance is unconstrained by the domestic structures the alliance at hand operates within. Yet its organizational structures—however rudimentary they may be—function as a medium through which external factors are processed and measured. Hence, the cooperating parties can ultimately control the outcome of the alliance's internal performance.

This is not the case with its external performance, being directly swayed as it is by the wider environment. In other words, the cooperating parties cannot effectively control the outcome of the alliance's external performance; all corresponding assumptions in this book stress the extent to which the latter is impinged on by authoritarian structures and by the behavior of other principal actors (particularly the incumbent regime). This is not to question the agency of the cooperating parties, which crystallizes in the way the alliance approaches external actors and how it chooses to respond to related challenges. Yet it bolsters the previous claim that alliances' internal and external performances are best situated at different levels of analysis. Likewise, as noted, both follow two different logics. Whereas the internal logic of cooperation is geared toward sustaining cooperation, the external one is defined by goal attainment. As will be seen, both logics conflict with one another at times: it is the contradictions existing between them that significantly explain the often-perplexing overall performance of alliances.

The last three paragraphs have provided a roundup of the main theoretical arguments to come. The latter, in turn, are based on a set of interconnected assumptions about the formation of alliances and about their internal as well as external performance. In the following, these assumptions will be established from a hybrid process of both inductive and deductive reasoning: Some rest on the findings of extant works on (opposition) cooperation, which are discussed with respect to the empirical case at hand (Yemen). Others draw on related theoretical discussions that have not yet been included in the study of opposition cooperation. Still others are derived in an inductive manner from the empirical study. As an extreme case, the JMP is deemed to be particularly well suited to aiding theory building,[48] or—in words that more accurately capture the subsequent procedure—to helping blend confirmed theoretical assumptions and newly postulated ones into a novel theoretical framework for studying strategic opposition cooperation.

Several considerations are seen as supportive of this conclusion. First, theory building from case-study research stands to benefit from the original incorporation and combination of existing theoretical discussions.[49] Second, this book's underlying basic assumptions—particularly those of structuration theory—are conducive to taking such an eclectic approach. This is because they "allow for epistemological flexibility in tracing the interplay of agency and structure and of the material and ideal aspects of social action."[50]

The third and last consideration originates from the process-tracing method that is applied in the course of the subsequent study. As a "causal-process observation,"[51] process tracing attempts to dissect causal mechanisms operating between the independent and dependent variable and to detect any intervening variables (or hitherto unknown causal explanations) that can explain the outcome of the dependent one.[52] Process tracing is hence congenial to the tasks of theory building, although it cannot tackle the general flaw(s) of doing the latter via case-study research—in other words, the fact that theoretical inferences are necessarily less secure and must be tested in future research to prove their validity.[53] Also, process tracing "requires enormous amounts of data in order for causal mechanisms to be identified at every step of the process of interest."[54]

Two final remarks are in order concerning the applied method. First, while the JMP takes prominence here—that is, strategic opposition cooperation in conceptual terms—the study thereof is subdivided into three interlinked cases, or instances of "a class of events of interest to the investigator":[55] the formation of the JMP (or of strategic opposition cooperation; see chapter 1), its internal performance (or cooperation maintenance; see chapter 2), and its external performance (or cooperation success; see chapters 3 and 4). Strictly speaking, the ensuing chapters thus explore three distinct dependent variables by dint of the process-tracing method, although large parts of chapter 2 are based on the analysis of key documents (for instance, the JMP's bylaws). Second, as required by the process-tracing method, the analysis draws on voluminous data obtained from original expert interviews (see Appendix A); the bylaws, platforms, statements, and announcements of Yemeni organizations and parties, particularly the JMP and its constituent entities; memoirs as well as newspaper and journal articles written by key Yemeni protagonists; social media and participant observation; reports and statistics provided by Yemeni, regional, and international organizations as well as by Yemeni governmental agencies; and, last, a large amount of newspaper articles, mostly from Yemeni dailies. The latter are an indispensable source for the meticulous reconstruction of the causal mechanisms this book intends to uncover.[56]

Yemen under 'Ali 'Abdallah Salih

While the JMP represents a remarkable instance of opposition cooperation that invites further study, this is no less the case with the nation that bore it, too. Yemen is an intriguing and highly complex country, on the grounds of which it has been argued that its social and political processes are difficult to read—and are, in fact, often misread.[57] Yemen is the poorest Arab state to begin with (see table 1). Its populace is strikingly heterogeneous, being characterized by the existence of several denominations,[58] significant tribal segments,[59] profound regional identities,[60] as well as a number of other salient social categories.[61] It has thus been maintained that its society is "more socially fragmented than that of any other country in the region with the exception of Afghanistan."[62] Indeed, particularly North Yemen is often likened to the latter with respect to, for instance, its societal organization or its geographical features.[63] Also, just as with Afghanistan, Yemen occupies an important geostrategic position that, "combined with its large and impoverished population, renders it dangerously vulnerable to both internal upheaval and external influence."[64] External

Table 1. Poverty Indicators

Population	
Population (in millions)	25.39 (2013)
Population growth rate	2.5 percent (2013, est.)
Age structure	<15: 42 percent (2013) 15–65: 55.4 percent (2013) >65: 2.6 percent (2013)
Average of population living below poverty line (at USD 1.25 at PPP)	16.8 percent* (2010)
Number of poor at USD 1.25 a day (in millions)	3.53** (2005)
Number of poor at USD 2 a day (in millions)	9.39** (2005)
Economy	
GDP per capita (in USD)	1,494** (2012)
GDP growth (annual percentage)	0** (2012; 2010: -10)
Official unemployment (percentage of total labor force)	17.8** (2010)
Inflation, consumer prices (annual percentage)	17** (2012)
Health	
Health expenditure	5.5 percent of GDP (2011)
Access to health services	55 percent (2013)
Life expectancy at birth	64.47 years (2013)
Infant mortality (per 1,000 live births)	51.93 (2013)
Education	
Education expenditure	5.2 percent of GDP (2008)
Male literacy	82.1 percent (2013)
Female literacy	48.5 percent (2013)

Table 1. Poverty Indicators (Con't.)

Indices	
Global Gender Gap	136/136*** (2013)
Gender Inequality Index	160/186**** (2012)
Human Development Index	160/186**** (2012)

Sources: All data compiled from the CIA World Factbook, https://www.cia.gov /library/publications/the-world-factbook/geos/ym.html, in 2013 except: * World Bank, "MENA Quarterly Economic Brief," no. 2, 2014, 16; ** World Bank, https://data.world bank.org/; *** World Economic Forum, Global Gender Gap Report 2013 (Geneva, 2013), 378–79; **** United Nations, Human Development Report 2013, http://hdr.undp. org/en/data.

Note: GDP, gross domestic product; PPP, purchasing power parity.

interventions as well as more indirect means of exerting outside influence have therefore been recurrent phenomena in the country's contemporary history, ones continuing to this day.[65]

One of the main reasons for Yemen's vulnerability to outside interference, especially in recent decades, has been its notoriously weak statehood.[66] It is certainly accurate to say that low state capacities render Yemen ill-equipped when it comes to warding off external meddling. Often, however, also indirect mechanisms are at work. Jihadi terrorist groups such as, first and foremost, al-Qaeda, which usually favor fragile states over strong or failed ones as their base of operation,[67] have prospered in Yemen since the turn of the new millennium. This reality has not only led to regular if small-scale military interventions by, for instance, the United States but also resulted in the latter's granting of significant material support to the authoritarian Salih regime, which was long considered an indispensable ally in the "War on Terror"—up until a few months before his toppling in 2011, as a matter of fact. Then again, Yemen's weak statehood also entails favorable aspects too, as certain prominent features of its political culture—a significant consociational tradition,[68] a culture of dialogue and deliberation,[69] as well as a vibrant civil society[70]—all evolved owing to the absence of a strong state. In other words, "widespread political activism and lively public debates," for instance, may have come into existence "*because* state institutions [were] fragile."[71] However, these features, too, would be seriously affected by the authoritarian backsliding that gradually unfolded in the aftermath of the 1994 war.

As stated, the beginning of democratization in Yemen coincided with the unification of the YAR and the PDRY into the ROY in 1990. Unification took many observers by surprise,[72] including some with intimate knowledge of the state of rapprochement between North and South. Just a few years before, for instance, a leading northern representative in past bilateral summits between the YAR and the PDRY had predicted that unifying "the two parts of Yemen" remained a question of a "remote future."[73] Northern and southern interests seemed too far apart to reconcile, and the two political regimes too diverse to unite.

The YAR—created in September 1962 to overthrow the Qasimi dynasty that had ruled (North) Yemen since the early seventeenth century—was an ill-defined republican state whose government was repeatedly challenged by powerful societal groups, though it also featured important consociational elements to incorporate the centrifugal forces into policy-making (see above). While in no way satisfying the criteria for a liberal democracy, the northern leadership had to "play the game of democratic politics" at least to some extent because the central government was typically not sufficiently strong to dictate political terms to its constituencies, particularly the tribal ones.[74] The establishment in 1982 of the GPC—the sole "permanent 'political organization'" allowed to operate as a quasi-political party in the YAR[75]—did little to change this state of affairs in principle. That said, it was a "successful move by the state to co-opt the material resources and political reach of a network of civil societal organizations,"[76] notably the so-called Local Development Associations (hay'at al-ta'awun al-ahli li-l-tatwir)—that is, a set of community-based, elected nongovernmental organizations (NGOs) that had critically contributed to the construction of, for instance, local schools, irrigation systems, and streets and has been considered a fine symbol of both civil societal activism and early state-building efforts in the YAR.[77]

Unlike North Yemen, which—except for isolated periods of foreign rule (most recently by the Ottomans, 1872–1918)—was governed by a

Zaydi imamate whose foundations could be traced back to 897 CE, the South was no stranger to European colonialism. The British had occupied the port city of Aden in 1839, established a Crown colony there, and soon controlled South Yemen through the Protectorate of Aden.[78] Past experiences with European colonialism, however, were not the only marked difference between the YAR and the People's Republic of South Yemen (1967–70, hereafter renamed PDRY). After independence in 1967, the new leadership abstained from abolishing all structural remnants of colonial rule but deliberately took over many administrative structures the British had built, including a sophisticated financial-audit and -control system.

The southern bureaucracy hence "maintained a fair degree of professionalism that made it nearly impossible to exert overt influence over government spending."[79] The relative lack of corruption as well as a functioning system of government and of law and order in the PDRY were often highlighted by southern leaders before and after unification—and purposefully contrasted with northern lawlessness, chaos (*fawdha*), and backwardness (*takhalluf*) in general.[80] Another significant difference between North and South sprang from the state-led social modernization policies in the latter, which would result in notable achievements in education, employment, health care, and women's empowerment. Likewise, the PDRY made great efforts to eradicate tribalism and restrict religion to becoming "a private matter in an essentially secular state," also much in contrast to the YAR.[81]

Last, and yet again unlike the YAR, the PDRY featured a centralized one-party system of rule in which the YSP—emulating the Soviet Communist Party with its Presidium, Politburo, and Central Committee—possessed considerably greater means than the GPC to discipline disobedient party members and insubordinate societal groups.[82] Yet this is not to imply that the YSP was immune to factionalism and infighting. In fact, it was the January 1986 crisis—when a bloodbath during a YSP leadership meeting in Aden ushered in a short civil war going on to fracture the party and the armed forces—that "placed in jeopardy the whole future of the South Yemeni regime."[83]

The door to unification, something very popular in both Yemens, was gradually opened by the loss of political legitimacy the respective ruling parties—hence including the GPC in the YAR—had suffered in the course of the 1980s. Facing economic distress and the drying up of material support from the Soviet Union, the YSP was open to earnest unification negotiations toward the end of that decade. The YAR leadership led by Salih was equally willing to negotiate, being affected just as greatly by the international repercussions of the ending East-West conflict—in addition to being burdened by internal economic grievances, too. The factor that may have tipped the scales toward unification for both sides was the prospect of developing the oil deposits along the inner-Yemeni border.[84]

The founding of the ROY in 1990 may have come about unforeseen by many; however, few had anticipated witnessing it ride "Democracy's Third Wave" either.[85] While street banners raised in Sanaa on the day of unification—May 22, 1990—declared "Yemeni unity is an immortal victory for democracy, development and freedom,"[86] the underlying reasons for democratization on the part of the southern and northern leaderships were probably more prosaic in reality. Indeed, it has been suggested that their decision to introduce democracy was mainly informed by each side aiming to prevent the other from dominating.[87]

The ensuing transition period was secured by a power-sharing agreement struck between YAR president Salih and YSP general-secretary al-Baydh in December 1989. Although the PDRY encompassed only about 20 percent of Yemen's overall population, it was decided at the time that both parties would share power equally until the country's first parliamentary elections. By placing the two on an equal footing, the agreement facilitated the transition. Yet it also had a detrimental effect on the building of the ROY. Specifically, no consensus was reached regarding the integration of the political and administrative systems, and the two armies remained separate. Notwithstanding acute political and economic challenges, the power-sharing agreement between the GPC and the YSP initially remained intact.[88]

This situation would change, however, after the successful holding of parliamentary elections in April 1993, which resulted in a victory for the GPC and a defeat for the YSP (see table 2). The election returns gave rise to the formation of a tripartite coalition between the GPC, the YSP, and Islah—which, because of its close bonds with the GPC, critically

Table 2. Allocation of Seats in Parliamentary Elections of 1993, 1997, and 2003

	1993	1997	2003
GPC	123	226	230
Islah	62	53	45
YSP	56	boycott	7
al-Haqq	2	-	-
Arab Socialist Ba'th Party	7*	2	2
Arab Socialist Nationalist Ba'th Party		-	-
NUPO	1	2	3
UPF	-	boycott	-
Other parties	2	-	-
Independents	48	18	14
Total	301	301	301

Sources: Ri'asa al-Jumhuriyya—al-Markaz al-Watani li-l-Ma'lumat, "Nata'ij al-Intikhabat," n.d, https://yemen-nic.info/sectors/politics/detail.php?ID=9379; "The April 27, 2003, Parliamentary Elections in the Republic of Yemen," National Democratic Institute, n.d., 24.

Note: * The Arab Socialist Nationalist Ba'th Party, officially registered as a party in 1997, is a splinter group of the Arab Socialist Ba'th Party.

challenged the delicate balance of power between that party and the YSP.[89] Henceforth, the latter found itself frequently outmaneuvered by its northern partners and unable to enforce any of its core interests from within the coalition. A widening internal spat swiftly turned into a full-blown political crisis, prompting domestic and external mediation efforts—ones that ultimately proved of no avail.

While many observers, especially from North Yemen, attributed the subsequent civil war of 1994 to the YSP's unwillingness to accept the outcome of the 1993 elections, and thus democracy itself,[90] it was probably the GPC's and Islah's continued attempts to undermine the YSP's political existence per se via the politics of centralization that finally prompted the latter's leadership to forgo Yemeni unity and opt for secession instead.[91] Either way, the civil war was seen to denote Yemen's rejoining "the ranks of many other Arab states unable to rise above internal schisms and jealousies," as a former British officer in the Aden Protectorate would summarize the international—or rather Western—take on events back then.[92] From a southern Yemeni perspective, the South's surrender in July 1994 not only led to the demise of the YSP but also, and crucially, sealed northern domination over the South for many years to come—arguably up until today, as leading proponents of the Southern Movement would suggest. From an all-Yemeni point of view, however, the civil war marked the onset of a gradual authoritarian reversal.[93]

The regime that emerged in the years following the 1994 war has been given various characterizations, including "kleptocracy,"[94] "semi-authoritarianism,"[95] or "pluralized authoritarianism."[96] Most scholars agree that the Salih regime was "hybrid" in that it contained democratic elements—regular and free but not necessarily fair elections, for instance—while being staunchly authoritarian in nature. It thus met the definitional criteria of a competitive authoritarian regime in which "formal democratic institutions exist and are widely viewed as the primary means of gaining power, but in which incumbents' abuse of the state places them at a significant advantage vis-à-vis their opponents."[97] At the center of the postwar regime was Salih himself, a poorly educated Zaydi tribesman and former military officer in the North Yemeni army who had, somewhat unexpectedly, become president of the YAR in 1978 and, on unification in 1990, president of the ROY.

Salih's position vis-à-vis other domestic power brokers rested on formal and informal sources of influence. Apart from his chairmanship of the ruling GPC—a catch-all party bereft of any significant ideological underpinnings whose major role was to expand patronage[98]—Salih profited from the formal institutional powers granted to the president by the Constitution. As the head of the executive, for instance, he disposed of vast authority over the government, including via key portfolios such as the Ministry of Finance. Likewise, the military and security apparatus were firmly in his hands: as president, Salih was the supreme commander of the armed forces, the head of the National Defense Council, and in charge of controlling various intelligence branches, including the infamous Political Security Organization that was directly answerable to him.[99]

More important than those institutional powers, however, were the informal ones he had access to. Salih managed to establish a system of political loyalty and dependency that was entirely centered on his own person. Attempts to define the nature of the Salih regime therefore delineate it as a series of concentric circles emanating from the president, with the inner one chiefly comprising members of his family and of the president's Sanhan tribe; meanwhile, the outer circle encompassed select members of the country's tribal and religious elites. Beyond the rather indistinct confines of the regime, Salih also succeeded in securing sway over essential elite actors—including those from traditional Yemen dynasties, businesspeople, technocrats, and representatives of the country's political parties.[100] The key to this informal power base was patronage. While Salih's "style was always to encourage loyalty through patronage in jobs and pay,"[101] the potential for comprehensive patronage politics was critically boosted with the emergence of a profitable hydrocarbon sector in 1986, and once more with the discovery and exploitation of new oil fields and natural gas fields in the years that followed. With hydrocarbon revenues accruing directly to the state, and with the incumbent regime effectively controlling the budget as well as the distribution of posts and licenses, building rapport with the president became inevitable for the bulk of the country's elites particularly in the military and the tribes—meaning Yemen's traditional power centers, on which Salih focused his attention.[102]

Several additional remarks should be made at this point. First, informal institutions and mechanisms taking precedence over formal ones must be reiterated.[103] The constitutional rights and powers of the national parliament, for instance, were relatively strong on paper, but they were effectively annulled by Salih's informal mechanisms of rule.[104] Second, the patronage system he built was inclusive of those at the elite level, therefore also comprising members of the opposition—including the JMP's constituents. In fact, patronage under Salih was inclusive to the point that rejecting it was both delicate and dangerous "because it challenge[d] the very organization of power around the president." The implications of patronage politics for the JMP, and opposition cooperation as such, will therefore be discussed throughout the book, but especially in chapter 4. However, it is important to note that it was mostly the top party elites who were affected. Furthermore, not all of them were willing to be compromised by patronage, even though its nonacceptance often implied facing "the full gambit of regime retribution."[105] What has been asserted for Islah, which long had the closest ties to Salih, can hence be conferred on all other JMP parties: "Some Islah leaders remain in the closest circles of Salih's power, but these have little to do with Islah as a party and much to do with patronage, kinship networks, and personal relations."[106] Third, patronage politics blossomed in line with the growth of hydrocarbon revenues—just as it suffered from their eventual decline. During the first years of the new millennium, such revenues became increasingly volatile, shrinking on trend by the middle of the decade and dwindling soon thereafter (see table 3). In short, Salih's patronage system became progressively more exclusive toward the end of his rule.[107] How these developments impacted domestic-conflict dynamics and the opposition will be explored in greater detail in due course.

Salih's presidency was put to an end in November 2011 in the wake of popular protests during the so-called Arab Spring, though his leverage on Yemeni politics, and arguably his regime overall, would last considerably longer. As noted, the JMP joined the transitional government in December 2011, thereby ceasing to be part of the opposition. Consequentially, this study ends in December 2011 too. It is therefore, in a sense, an examination of a recently completed period of Yemeni history, though one that claims to be informative for subsequent periods as well, including the current war still ongoing at the time of writing.

Challenging the commonly used (international) periodization of Yemen's recent history, Stacey Philbrick Yadav states that the current war is usually seen as beginning with the onset of the Saudi Arabian–led intervention in Yemen on March 26, 2015. "With the benefits of hindsight, however," she asserts, "it is clear that the full decade since 2011 was marked by co-extensive armed conflict and civil action. . . . Does this mean that the war itself began in 2011?"[108] While the question is ultimately left unanswered, she convincingly argues that today's war might in fact have multiple beginnings, depending on the point of view of the various conflict parties.[109] For members of the Southern Movement, which came into being in 2007 to protest the South's political and economic marginalization, onset

Table 3. Structure of Public Revenues and Expenditure

	1999	2006	2007	2008	2009	2010
Crude oil production (1,000 barrels/day)	-	366	320	294	284	275
Marketed natural gas (billion cubic feet/year)	583*	646*	1,031*	1,059*	1,047*	1,153*
Hydrocarbon revenues (in USD million)	-	-	-	7,292	3,529	4,650
Hydrocarbon revenues, share of public revenues and grants (percentage)	-	-	-	73.6	56	61.8
Tax revenues, share of public revenues and grants (percentage)	-	-	-	26.2	26.2	26.2
Hydrocarbon revenues (percentage of GDP)	-	-	-	24.0	12.5	15.9
Public expenditure (percentage of GDP)	-	31.6	34.0	36.6	32.0	35.1
Net ODA (percentage of GDP)	6.01**	1.51**	1.12**	1.60**	2.22**	2.14**

Sources: Data compiled from the Arab Monetary Fund, The Joint Arab Economic Report 2011: Overview & Statistical Annexes (Abu Dhabi, 2011), 92–105, except: * US Energy Information Administration, http://www.eia.gov/cfapps/ipdbproject/iedindex3.cfm?tid=3&pid=3&aid=1&cid=YM,&syid=1999&eyid=2000&unit=BCF; and ** the World Bank, http://data.worldbank.org/.

Note: ODA, official development assistance.

might date back to the civil war of 1994, and many supporters of southern secession—spearheaded by the Southern Transitional Council (al-majlis al-intiqali al-janubi; STC) since 2017—would probably contend that the southern malady can be traced back to unification.[110] Citing another example, for members of Ansar Allah—a religiopolitical organization that originated in the Sa'da Governorate (bordering Saudi Arabia) as a religious movement, then oscillating between being a paramilitary and social movement before turning into a full-fledged political organization and, by 2014, a quasi-state actor[111]—the present war would likely be another continuation of the first Sa'da war (June–September 2004), whose roots they would deem to reach back to at least the early 1990s.[112]

In brief, the parties involved in today's war—perhaps one of the most complex and devastating conflicts since the fall of the Iron Curtain—are no dark horses to each other; it is, indeed, their record of past experiences, grievances, mutual hostilities, and instances of joint engagement that critically inform their respective stances and actions today. By analyzing the prior interactions of several of today's key actors—notably, the JMP parties (and Islah and the YSP in particular) as well as Ansar Allah or the Southern Movement—and the politico-economic structures they were (and still are)[113] operating in, this book may help the reader to better understand not only the conflicts predating the current one[114] but also today's war. The latter has, as such, been more aptly described as at least "three separate but overlapping wars."[115]

The Organization of the Book

This book can be read in two ways. The first—and recommended one—is to read it as it was devised, that is, as an investigation into the nature of strategic opposition cooperation achieved by analyzing the JMP in an exploratory case-study design. The second possible way of reading it arises from its peculiar composition. Instead of preceding each empirical chapter with a self-contained section featuring relevant theoretical arguments, I have chosen to embed the latter into the empirical analysis. In other words, all theoretical discussions will directly precede or follow the specific empirical event they seek to explain. Besides increasing readability, this approach allows for probing the phenomena of interest in a more focused and comprehensive way, and it meshes well with the inductive nature of many of the book's assumptions. Since the theoretical discussions are clearly demarcated from the surrounding empirical analysis, readers primarily interested in the politics of opposition under Salih may thus leapfrog the corresponding paragraphs (and vice versa). Both the theoretical and the empirical parts are intelligible on their own, although they will yield the most benefit when read in combination with one another.

The next chapter analyzes the genesis of the JMP, asking how Yemen's ideologically diverse parties managed to build a strategic alliance even against great odds. To illustrate the adverse circumstances under which initial contact between the prospective partners was made in 1996, the analysis begins with the direct aftermath of the 1994 war, during which two of the JMP's major forces, the YSP and Islah, had fought on opposite sides. It ends with the presidential elections of 2006, in the run-up to which the JMP had concurrently adopted bylaws and a joint program. While integrating extant findings on the conditions for cooperation's onset, chapter 1 also proceeds in an inductive manner and shows how committed party elites gradually found common ground, developed incentives for cooperation to increase the acceptance thereof among their fellow party members, facilitated attitudinal rapprochement, and eventually established themselves within their respective parties. It also discusses how internal factors such as stiff intraparty resistance to cooperation or defection and external factors like the growing authoritarianism of the Salih regime swayed the process of alliance building.

Chapter 2 asks how the JMP managed to maintain and consolidate cooperation. To this end, it explores the organizational structures built by the alliance to govern joint activities at the national, governorate, and district levels, and it places special emphasis on the issue of functionality by examining the extent to which, for instance, decision-making bodies, conflict-resolution mechanisms, and the established modes of internal mobilization or commitment building were able to cope with the horizontal and vertical challenges of cooperation. Another key element covered here is the ongoing attempts to obstruct cooperation on the part of peripheral elites such as the YSP's old guard or Islah's Salafi 'ulama'. Tracing the JMP's approach to dealing with such spoilers exemplifies the trade-offs between sound internal functioning and a loss of transformative power resulting from the (possible and actual) defection of key elites. Here is but one example of how the internal performance of the alliance was often at odds with its external one.

Chapter 3 is the first of two chapters focusing on that external performance. It provides an in-depth analysis of the conflict between the JMP and the regime, covering the period between the 2006 presidential elections and July 2010, when the alliance seemingly achieved a breakthrough in negotiations with those individuals in power. Highlighting the strategies implemented to rally the support of other opposition movements, the chapter explores the reasons for the JMP's shifting priorities, its oscillation between different modes of contestation, and its delicate relationship with regime renegades. Taking the example of the JMP-initiated Preparatory Committee for National Dialogue (al-lajna al-tahdhiriyya li-l-hiwar al-watani; PCND), which served as a major platform to coordinate opposition action with key Yemeni elites, Ansar Allah, and parts of the Southern Movement, it is shown how the JMP's external performance was critically swayed by internal considerations and necessities (and vice versa). Throughout the chapter, examples are provided that illustrate how the relationship between the JMP and the regime was impacted by the deterioration of the economic and security situation and, relatedly, by the interests of external actors, including the United States, the European Union, and Saudi Arabia.

Chapter 4 provides the second part of the analysis of the JMP's external performance, covering the period up until Salih's signing of the Gulf Cooperation Council (GCC) Initiative and the alliance's entry into the transitional government led by Hadi. It traces the gradual unfolding of the uprising against the regime, which, unlike in other states affected by the so-called Arab Spring, evolved from the unwillingness of elites in power to abide by the agreements struck with the JMP and the heavy-handed steps taken to introduce constitutional amendments in December 2010—leading to mass protests occurring at roughly the same point in time as the ones in Tunisia. It is shown how the JMP, which had by then emerged as the nearly uncontested leader of the opposition, spearheaded the uprising at first and then gradually lost the backing of major Yemeni groups, while concomitantly becoming a key player in the eyes of international actors. The reasons for these developments, as well as for the JMP's seesawing between the outright escalation and de-escalation of conflict in more general terms, are again explained against the backdrop of the trade-off between the internal and external requirements of cooperation. Furthermore, the alliance's initial reluctance to call for Salih's resignation and its first actions in government provide the opportunity for detailed discussion of how three decades of patronage politics impacted the JMP, as well as why reformers and rent seekers in its ranks ultimately managed to cooperate despite having different goals. These factors contribute significantly to explaining the imbroglio of the ensuing transition period.

The concluding chapter not only summarizes the main empirical arguments but also reflects on the general features of strategic opposition cooperation, as inferred from the preceding analysis. This evaluation is done by reviewing and contextualizing the previously established assumptions on the formation of strategic alliances and their internal as well as external performance. Crucially, the chapter discusses why it is expedient to conceive of strategic alliances as being driven by an internal and external logic of cooperation and how that may further our theoretical understanding of other strategic alliances elsewhere. In concluding, briefly discussed is whether the JMP can be seen as a role model for postwar conflict resolution in Yemen.

1

Launching Cooperation

The Emergence of the Joint Meeting Parties

In July 2001 the Center for Arab Unity Studies (CAUS) in Beirut, Lebanon, convened scholars from across the Arab world to discuss the calamitous state of the region's political opposition. Among the contributors to the concluding roundtable discussion were two Yemeni participants. In the course of it, Muhammad ʿAbd al-Malik al-Mutawakkil and ʿAbd al-Malik al-Mikhlafi focused their critique on the self-inflicted weaknesses of the Arab opposition. They opined that it was mainly the lack of internal democracy, the wanting transparency, and a totalitarian culture within most parties that together accounted for the opposition's severe crisis. Al-Mutawakkil also hinted at another factor: "Where political parties are concerned," he stated, "there is not only the tendency to mutually veer away from each other but also something that comes close to reciprocal enmity. I think that this results from secret defamations . . . and the absence of dialogue."[1] Al-Mutawakkil, a professor of human rights at Sanaa University, and al-Mikhlafi, who regularly authors op-eds on Arab and Yemeni affairs, were not speaking simply as political analysts. As high-ranking members of the Union of Popular Forces and the Nasserist Unionist People's Organization, respectively, they could also proffer important examples to support their claims about the difficulties facing opposition parties and, most notably, about the complex issue of cooperation. By 2001 they had, after all, gained some experience in this regard.

Since the mid-1990s, al-Mutawakkil's UPF and al-Mikhlafi's NUPO had been involved in opposition cooperation within the framework of the JMP; it would take the latter approximately another two years after the

Beirut workshop to evolve into a proper alliance. From 2003 onward, the JMP gradually became a serious challenger to the regime of 'Ali 'Abdallah Salih, and some Western observers began to deem it "an important—if un-paralleled—instance of Islamist-secular cooperation [in the Arab world]."[2] Consequently, in 2010, when commemorating the murder of Jarallah 'Umar al-Kuhali, one of the JMP's major architects, al-Mutawakkil reversed some of his earlier criticism. "Today," he said, "the Socialist Party no longer takes a tough stance against the Islamists, and the Islamists no longer take a tough stance against the socialists, democracy, and other [non-Islamist parties]. Today, there is an earnest rapprochement between them."[3] One year later, in December 2011, the JMP became part of the newly built government following Salih's abdication from power after months of mass protests in which the JMP would play a decisive role.

This linear portrayal of events ignores, of course, the serious internal problems and external blows the alliance had suffered since its inception. The history of the JMP is essentially one of ups and downs, of relations fraught with violence and reconciliation, of enthusiastic plaudits, and of outright disapproval, especially in the early years. The JMP's early life is of particular importance if one is to fully grasp the alliance's overall performance up until the toppling of the Salih regime in 2011. It is thus the aim of this chapter to provide an in-depth analysis of the JMP's formative period, which stretches from 1996 to 2005, even though this chronology is largely analytical. It remains up for discussion, for instance, whether opposition cooperation took on concrete form in December 2000, as retrospectively determined by the JMP,[4] or in reality later. As the following discussion illustrates, the process of forming and intensifying the alliance was never a smooth and steady one. Rather, it was a protracted endeavor undertaken by key individuals who literally crafted the JMP against great odds, transforming the nature and scope of cooperation in the face of both internal resistance and tightening authoritarianism. From a conceptual perspective, in turn, it is argued that the emergence of the JMP as a strategic alliance required not only the settling on common goals but also the establishment of positive cost-benefit calculations within, and balanced attitudes between, its constituent parties. Likewise, for the launching of strategic cooperation, it was crucial that those party elites committed to the prospective alliance prevailed over its critics within their respective party organizations.

The Prelude to the Joint Meeting Parties, 1993–1996

The beginnings of the JMP's piecemeal development fall into the first legislative period of the Republic of Yemen (1993–97). By all accounts, these four years—just as the three preceding ones had been—were eventful and unsteady, characterized by political and social changeovers that would suffice to fill decades rather than years. In this respect, the ROY shared the same fate as several other countries worldwide whereby the end of bipolarity had acted as a catalyst for the major political changes rapidly unfolding during the final decade of the twentieth century.[5] Still grappling with the ramifications of unification, Yemenis experienced the first contested elections in 1993, heightened political conflict and deadlock in the aftermath, prudent but failed subsequent attempts at political settlement, the devastating civil war of 1994, and an incipient but largely unnoticed return to authoritarian normalcy. Given such turbulence, it may be unsurprising in retrospect to find that this unanticipated chain of events produced unexpected effects. In the immediate postwar period, however, a political tête-à-tête between such unlikely partners as Islah and the Yemeni Socialist Party must have seemed absurd, especially as both parties were members of two antagonistic blocs: the ruling coalition and the Supreme Coordination Council of Opposition Parties (majlis al-tansiq al-a'la li-ahzab al-mu'arada; SCCOP), respectively. The former had emerged from the April 1993 parliamentary elections, with it initially including the YSP. This tripartite coalition came to a sudden end with the 1994 war, as a consequence of which many YSP elites were forced into exile. Bereft of meaningful financial resources and with their organizational infrastructure battered, the remaining party leaders found themselves part of the opposition. The downsized ruling coalition of the General People's Congress and Islah, however, was powerful enough to quickly spur counterbalancing efforts on the part of the opposition.

In fact, the first such endeavors had preceded the SCCOP's appearance on the scene by two years. On August 19, 1993, five parties—al-Haqq, the UPF, the Unionist Gathering (al-tajammu' al-wahdawi al-yamani), the League of the Sons of Yemen (rabita abna' al-yaman; RAY), and the Democratic Nasserist Party (hizb al-nasiri al-dimuqrati; DNP)—announced the launching of the National Opposition Bloc (al-takattul al-watani li-l-mu'arada; TOM) to coordinate opposition activities. By ordinary standards, TOM was a fairly weak alliance as, for instance, only four parliamentary seats were held by its member parties (Husayn Badr al-Din al-Huthi and Ahmad al-Shami for al-Haqq, 'Abd al-Rahman al-Jifri for RAY, and 'Umar al-Jawi for the Unionist Gathering). It thus soon coalesced with a group of two hundred oppositionists to form the Union of National Forces (ittihad al-quwa al-wataniyya; UNF).[6]

Despite its meager record, TOM was significant for at least two reasons. First, it provided the initial platform for opposition (party) coordination, and, with the exception of the GPC-fostered DNP, all of its member parties would later merge into the SCCOP. Second, together with UNF cofounder Sinan Abu Luhum as well as Mujahid Abu Shawarib, TOM was instrumental in pushing the GPC and the YSP to participate in the National Dialogue Conference in 1993–94, which was intended to avert the looming war.[7] Although these efforts ultimately failed, the conference's final text, the so-called Document of Pledge and Accord (wathiqa al-'ahd wa al-ittifaq), would continue to be invoked by the opposition afterward. This detailed plan recommended numerous reforms related to good governance and the overhaul of the security sector and the judiciary. Regarding the future polity, it first and foremost called for a limited executive, a bicameral parliament, and extensive political, administrative, and financial decentralization.[8] This latter point was of crucial importance for the largest force within the ensuing opposition alliance, the defeated YSP. In fact, the whole document constituted the prospective manifesto of the SCCOP.[9]

The 1994 war was a watershed moment in many respects; the political landscape was by now divided into two main camps. The first basically represented the continuation of the ruling coalition between the GPC and Islah, but without the YSP. Its existence was officially confirmed and renewed with the signing of the coalition agreement in October 1994. The formation of the second camp, meanwhile, was mainly motivated by the need to counterbalance the ruling coalition, which had set out to undo the ROY's democratic institutions. As the UPF deputy secretary-general recalled later: "Imbalance usually generates a totalitarian regime and arbitrary rule. If there were democratic remainders, then these would be little more than décor adorning the regime's face to the external world and misguiding public opinion at home. . . . After the war over power in 1994, the [political] equilibrium collapsed. The opposition parties had no choice but to embark on coordination to re-establish at least some balance."[10]

To this end, the SCCOP was formed on August 14, 1995. Altogether it comprised seven parties: the Zaydi parties al-Haqq and UPF, the left-leaning Unionist Gathering, the Arab nationalist (and Iraqi-oriented) Ba'th, the Nasserist NUPO, the tiny Liberals' Constitutional Party (hizb al-ahrar al-dusturi), and the YSP.[11] With the inclusion of the YSP, which irrespective of its decimation was still a political heavyweight compared to the rest of these parties, the SCCOP became a more potent alliance than TOM ever was. Parties such as al-Haqq, the UPF, and the Unionist Gathering had already acquired vital experience concerning opposition coordination, while the YSP had been on good terms with al-Haqq since the beginning of the 1990s and had purportedly formed a "tacit alliance" with the Zaydi party.[12] On March 19, 1996, the parties settled on bylaws that provided the SCCOP with a statutory framework stipulating, among other things, decision-making by consensus (ijma'). They also agreed to adjust the parties' platforms for the upcoming elections, with a focus on the implementation of the Document for Pledge and Accord, the protection of democracy, and the eradication of the remnants of war by peaceful means. All in all, the SCCOP was an alliance to be reckoned with. Although it could not rival the ruling coalition's power, it was acknowledged regardless as a force capable of balancing the increasingly authoritarian nature of the postwar regime.[13] Such were the political circumstances, then, when Islah initially made contact with the alliance in 1996.

Yemenis are said to change alliance quickly, and some features of the country's political culture are believed to contribute to the building of such coalitions across social and ideological cleavages. Furthermore, alliances in Yemen do not appear to be rare exceptions. In 1995, for instance, the Democratic Opposition Coalition (al-i'tilaf al-dimuqrati li-l-mu'arada, or Adam) was founded, comprising thirteen parties. After its disbandment, it was replaced by the National Opposition Council (al-majlis al-watani li-l-mu'arada) in 1997 and by the National Alliance Parties (ahzab al-tahaluf al-watani) in 2003. Moreover, the GPC can be said to be a catchall party—if not a coalition in its own right—encompassing members of various social strata and ideological inclinations. It could thus be argued that Islah's approaching of the SCCOP and the emergence of the JMP were somewhat trivial and commonplace in the Yemeni context. What, then, is the point of studying and theorizing on an opposition alliance that emerged and acted under conditions ostensibly somewhat unique to the country of Yemen?

Adhering to such an assumption would mean judging a book by its cover. The Democratic Opposition Coalition, the National Opposition Council, and the National Alliance Parties were alliances of pseudo-opposition parties close to, and dependent on, the Salih regime. Routinely complying with regime demands, they had been "cloned"[14] on the emergence of serious opposition alliances in order to take the wind out of the latter's sails and contribute to their ultimate disintegration.[15] The GPC, in turn, may be seen, as noted, as a catchall or big-tent organization rather than a party in the conventional sense, and it can hardly be considered a theater of earnest political contestation, as it was initially a transmission belt for the regime.

Yemen's political culture may, indeed, facilitate the forging of alliances that transcend ideological boundaries. However, such factors are not sufficient to account for alliance building per se, nor do they easily compensate for the profound and often violent conflicts that had occurred between the would-be partners within the JMP. In fact, overcoming past conflicts would prove to be one of the main obstacles to the JMP's birth, with not every party willing or able to go down this route. The issues at stake in past conflicts between the prospective allies were usually related to values—meaning they were "dissensual conflicts" involving differences in beliefs, ideology, and cognitive structure that were rarely amenable to compromise.[16] With a few exceptions, all of these conflicts were of a fundamental nature, mostly perceived as zero-sum and often lethal. Islah was almost always embroiled in them, even before its actual foundation as a party.

The Muslim Brotherhood, which today forms one branch of Islah, was established in 1970, predating the latter by twenty years. Unlike the case in later decades, when the Brotherhood constituted Islah's moderate, reform-minded wing, it was highly conservative and purist initially, unwilling to compromise on religiopolitical stipulations allegedly emanating from shari'a law.[17] Led by 'ulama' such as 'Abd al-Majid al-Zindani or Hamud al-Dharihi, both of whom are today among the party's Salafi wing, the early Brotherhood spotted its nemeses across the intra-Yemeni border. The elites of the People's Democratic Republic of Yemen, who were a byword for the YSP's Politburo, indeed made perfect enemies given their policy of rolling back religion and tribalism in public life. On various occasions, the Brotherhood, together with Jihadi elements, participated in violent clashes between the northern and southern armies. In 1979 it founded the Islamic Front (al-jabha al-islamiyya) to fight the YSP-sponsored National Democratic Front (al-jabha al-wataniyya al-dimuqratiyya). Combating these "Marxist guerrillas" provided a common cause for the Brotherhood, the Northern Highland tribal shaykhs, and YAR president Salih in the following two decades, and many Brotherhood members even joined the GPC, the founding of which they had assisted with in 1982.[18] Then again, it is often maintained that Islah was initially established as a GPC offshoot tasked with safeguarding the conservative, tribal northern regime against its progressive, socialist southern neighbors.[19] In any case, many Islahis rejected unification with the southern "infidels," and this rejection was mirrored by many YSP leaders, who held deep reservations about what they deemed the backward, tribe-dominated northern system.[20]

Southern apprehension about northern elites was not unjustified, particularly when it came to Islah. The latter was still a highly conservative and even radical force in terms of its social and political vision as of the early 1990s, although the advocates of this outlook were mostly outside the Brotherhood by then. Some authors suggest that tribal elites prevailed within the party at that time, whereas others consider the Salafi trend to have been majoritarian instead.[21] In contrast, Yemeni author Najib Ghallab argues that although the two currents need to be treated as separate entities, both shared (and still do) the goal of preserving conservative values and their traditional role in society. Ghallab thus speaks of a "project of the religious tribal current."[22] While this issue is discussed in greater detail later, it seems safe to assume here that Islah was overwhelmingly antiliberal and antipluralistic, pursuing policies that gave priority to Islamic reform in the judiciary and the educational sector.[23] The importance of the latter for Islah was embodied by the so-called Scientific Institutes (ma'ahid 'ilmi-yya). Founded at the beginning of the 1970s, these institutes were first run independently from the state and had grown to several hundred in number by the time they were integrated into the public education sector in 2002. They were operated under the tutelage of conservative scholars such as Yahya al-Fusayl, 'Abd al-Malik Mansur, and al-Zindani; formed the main-stay of the Sunni reform movement; and, allegedly with Saudi funding,[24] served as a major platform for the spread of anti-Zaydi and antisecularist teachings.[25] Predictably, the institutes—as well as Islah's overall approach to education in policy—were not well received by most SCCOP parties. The YSP and al-Haqq in particular considered them a direct menace.

More threatening, however, were the physical attacks on members of the opposition before, during, and after the 1994 war. It is estimated that there were approximately one hundred assassination attempts on southern politicians in 1992 alone (some successful, some not).[26] Such acts of brute force intensified during the war before abating following the armistice, but they did not cease completely thereafter. In most cases, YSP members were targeted; however, affiliates of other left-leaning, secularist parties such as the Unionist Gathering and Zaydi parties like al-Haqq were also preyed on.[27] The perpetrators were often either close to or full members of Islah. Even though all were from the rank and file, well-respected Islah scholars sanctioned the killings by issuing legal opinions (fatwas) pronouncing individual politicians apostates or infidels (*kuffar*). The most infamous fatwa of this kind was issued in May 1994 by 'Abd al-Wahhab al-Daylami, an influential Islahi *'alim* and minister of justice (1994–97), with it effectively constituting carte blanche for the justified killing of YSP members.[28] This fatwa remained the semiofficial position of Islah on *kufr* (nonbelief, blasphemy) through the middle of the following decade.[29]

Relations between Islah and the SCCOP were hence conflict laden in every respect. This state of affairs obviously begs the question of how best to explain their first tentative rapprochement in 1996. A multifaceted answer is in order here, and it begins with Islah's increasingly uncomfortable position as a junior partner in the ruling coalition after the war. With the YSP considerably weakened, the GPC was no longer in need of an ally, while Islah saw its influence on the wane. The first Islah ministers to hand in their resignation did so in 1995, after they had failed to enforce their position within the cabinet—many more followed suit through 1997.[30] Worse yet, in the run-up to the parliamentary elections in the latter year, the GPC refused to strike an electoral agreement satisfactory to Islah. According to 'Abdallah al-Ahmar, the GPC had informed the party leadership in the summer of 1996 that it wished to obtain a "comfortable majority" of votes.[31] Islah's returns, on the other hand, were not to exceed the seventeen seats the party—or rather its informal precursor—had held in the YAR's representative body. While rejecting electoral coordination was one thing, some Islah members had serious doubts about whether the GPC was committed to fair play at all. This concern was shared by the SCCOP, which had long called for an overhaul of the election law. The issue of free and fair elections thus formed the common basis for dialogue between the SCCOP and Islah. Al-Ahmar later recalled that he was not "positive about the dialogue," which he considered to be of a purely tactical nature aimed at counterweighing the GPC's "burlesque."[32] But not everyone in Islah was as calculating as him. Given the two parties' conflict-ridden past, it is also highly unlikely that the SCCOP would have approved of any talks if there had not been some trusted Islahis.

Oddly, such Islahis were located in the party's Political Section (al-qism al-siyasi), which had by then come to be dominated by the Brotherhood.[33] Yet compared to the 1970s and 1980s, the latter had changed significantly. It had tacitly bowed out of the slogan "Islam Is the Solution" and evolved into a political organization that endorsed the notion of democracy not as a means to an end but as a discrete form of government per se. While the Brotherhood had formerly perceived democracy as a Western import alien to Islam, it now regarded it as "a synonym for the [Islamic] concept of shura [consultation]." It had accepted the notion of a party system and political pluralism, and it began to conceive of the state as being "separate from religion, [while being] predicated on the incorporation of religion into politics."[34]

That is not to say that the Yemeni Brothers had turned into show-case democrats. Nor was the acceptance of democracy as a legitimate and preferable form of government shared by everyone within the party. The Brotherhood had actually failed to introduce its ideas to the Islah plat-form passed during the first party congress in September 1994.[35] It had nevertheless succeeded in having the congress issue a statement in which the party acknowledged the need to remove the remnants of the 1994 war. The meaning of this sentence was left open to interpretation. But for many Brothers, it implied the normalization of Islah's relations with the YSP since, as one such interlocutor put it, "one could not speak about democracy if the parties' relations with one another were conducted out of the trenches."[36]

Besides these shifts in orientation, which were to some extent reflec-tive of the ideological changes most of the Brotherhood's branches in the Arab world had undergone in this period at large, some leading Broth-ers had earned credit with the SCCOP—and with the YSP in particular. Shortly before the 1994 war, some Brothers had attempted to resolve the conflict between Sanaa and Aden, even though these efforts were ulti-mately in vain.[37] With one exception (al-Daylami), all the Islah ministers who resigned following the war were considered moderates associated with the Brotherhood. Some of them, such as Muhammad al-Jubari and 'Abdallah al-Akwa', had resigned in protest against the government's un-willingness to reform, while Islah's minister of supply and trade, Muham-mad al-Afandi, reportedly stepped down out of frustration with his party fellows, who were unwilling to make far-reaching reforms.[38] Nasr Taha Mustafa, another influential Brother who played a key role in bringing together Islah and the SCCOP, later left the party altogether, purportedly on the grounds of opposing its educational policy and its focus on the Scientific Institutes.[39] All these Islahis belonged to the Brotherhood and were from a younger generation that had begun to challenge the party's approach to politics in general and its alliance with the GPC in particular. All had obtained a certain degree of acceptance from the SCCOP owing to their past behavior. And as most Brothers originated from the Ta'izz Governorate, they knew to whom to appeal inside the SCCOP: Jarallah 'Umar al-Kuhali, the head of the local YSP branch.

The man who was chosen by Islah's leadership to forge ties with the YSP was Muhammad Qahtan, a Brother and the head of the Political Section. According to one interlocutor, Qahtan "had some friends in the YSP regional branch" whom he asked to help him make contact with al-Kuhali.[40] The two met for the first time at the beginning of 1996 after the YSP Politburo had given its blessing. These circumstances are indicative of the atmosphere of suspicion that dominated the first meetings, and Qahtan was well aware of the mistrust and the "oddity" (*gharaba*) of the situation: shortly after the war, which had seen many atrocities take place between Islamists and socialists, Islah was negotiating with the SCCOP parties and its main ideological contender, the YSP, about how best to achieve the aim of free and fair elections, something that Islah as a ruling party was actually supposed to safeguard against together with its coalition partner. Nevertheless, the negotiating parties had a vested interest in achieving this goal. Free and fair elections were indispensable to maintaining Yemeni parliamentarism, which all SCCOP parties were committed to; only their representation in parliament could secure vital resources, and they all anticipated the regime's unwillingness to play by the rules in upcoming elections. According to a senior YSP member involved in the talks, the SCCOP was convinced that under the given circumstances "free, clean, and equal elections would be impossible. This was the key issue we focused on."[41] It was clear to everyone in the SCCOP that a partnership with Islah on the issue would add greater authority to their demands.

Based on the theoretical literature, there are two fundamental conditions that need to be met for individuals, social groups, and states to cooperate: goal convergence and a surplus of benefits. Goal convergence—or, in this case, the necessity that the opposition parties mutually approved of at least one objective—is so obvious that it hardly merits any mention in the scholarship. In his seminal study, Robert Axelrod argues that, indeed, very few prerequisites beyond goal convergence are required to initiate cooperation at the micro level. Individuals must not be rational, committed, or altruistic, nor is there a need to assume trust or a central authority. What is essential, however, is the "opportunity for mutual gain . . . [that] comes into play when gains from the other's cooperation are larger than the costs of one's own cooperation."[42]

But in the case of opposition parties, or social entities operating at the meso level in general, the problem is that it is hard to determine what exactly constitutes costs and benefits, threats and opportunities, for them. To name but a few influencing factors, the organizational nature, the preferences, and the size or the strength of the entity in question will all have an effect on its choices when contemplating cooperation. Scholars of social movement theory have found that the costs and benefits have an internal and external dimension to them for cooperating movements,[43] a discovery that is largely corroborated by studies on opposition cooperation in the Arab world.[44] Cooperation can, for instance, induce internal costs owing to a loss of decision-making autonomy, or external costs if an organization's media visibility is diminished. Then again, cooperation can produce internal benefits if, for instance, the political efficiency of an organization increases. Potential external benefits can include enhanced prospects of success (see figure 1).

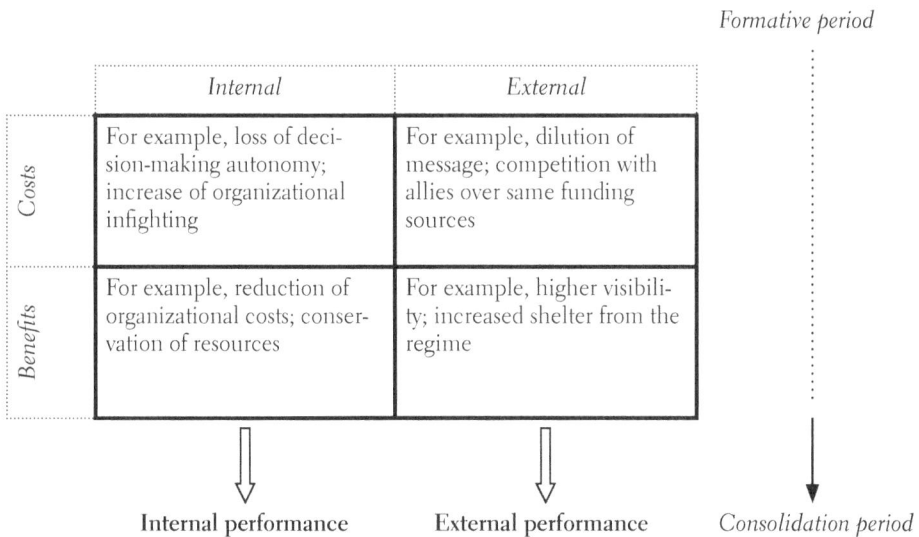

Formative period

	Internal	External
Costs	For example, loss of decision-making autonomy; increase of organizational infighting	For example, dilution of message; competition with allies over same funding sources
Benefits	For example, reduction of organizational costs; conservation of resources	For example, higher visibility; increased shelter from the regime

Internal performance   **External performance**   *Consolidation period*

1. The costs and benefits of cooperation

Such considerations did not put too much strain on the negotiators in the case at hand. Consultations between Islah and the SCCOP lasted for several months and suffered only minor setbacks. Their differences were negligible and settled without difficulty. According to interviewees, the mutually shared goal of free and fair elections was easily outlined and a draft declaration quickly agreed on. It should be noted here that the issue of forging an alliance was not on the table at this stage. What was at stake was merely the joint issuing of a declaration calling for free and fair elections: that is, an action of high mutual benefit and with virtually no costs—at least for the SCCOP, which had long since called for electoral reform, which had to make almost no compromises regarding content, and which could only stand to benefit if the upcoming parliamentary elections in 1997 were indeed free and fair. The gains from such a narrowly delimited form of cooperation were thus expected to outweigh the drawbacks by some distance.

For Islah, however, the situation was more complex. Not only were large segments of the party unconvinced by the talks with the SCCOP (in terms of both the contents of and the parties to the prospective deal), but the former also continued to consider the GPC as Islah's natural ally. As al-Ahmar put it: "President [Salih] always assured us and others that Islah was a strategic ally to the GPC. . . . We in Islah . . . felt that we were closer to the GPC than to the opposition parties. . . . Fateful bonds tied us to the president and to the head of the GPC. We were in accordance with him on fundamental questions."[45] To many in Islah, negotiations with the SCCOP were thus primarily intended to improve the party's bargaining position vis-à-vis the GPC. This strategy backfired. The negotiations with Salih instead became more acrimonious as he realized that the Brotherhood's talks with the SCCOP were serious and progressing. Despite this realization, he was not willing to make an offer that would have persuaded Islah to end negotiations with the SCCOP.[46]

On August 27, 1996, Islah and the SCCOP published the "Joint Meeting Program for Free and Fair Elections" (barnamaj al-liqa' al-mushtarak min ajl intikhabat hurra wa naziha).[47] Altogether, the negotiations had taken almost seven months. This duration was not because the views of the parties' delegates diverged significantly; nor were the SCCOP parties worried about possible negative effects among their grassroots base from

cooperating with Islah on the issue of electoral reform. Such delibera-
tions would surface at a later stage when actual alliance building was on
the agenda. Rather, given Islah's history and position in government, the
SCCOP feared being outwitted. Even though the split within Islah was
apparent and the intentions of the party's Political Section were deemed
sincere, no one in the SCCOP would have vouched for those Islahi factions that were not represented in the negotiations. The SCCOP delegates
therefore demanded a number of guarantees. At the very beginning of
negotiations, for instance, Islah's leadership was asked to submit a letter
of commitment to the principle of free and fair elections. Following the
signing of the declaration, the SCCOP required that it be published in the
Islah-affiliated *al-Sahwa* newspaper.

With all these steps successfully taken, most of the parties' negotiators
realized that there was still room to explore common ground. The tentative
rapprochement thus provided the opposition with a momentous window
of opportunity. This must have been immediately clear to characters such
as al-Mutawakkil or al-Kuhali, the latter of whom had reportedly already
said at an earlier stage: "I cannot and will not miss this opportunity. Even
if the other parties refuse to sign [the declaration] I will do so on behalf
of the YSP." Here he was addressing the skeptics among the SCCOP parties, and there remained many up until the very end of the negotiations,
namely, among the ranks of al-Haqq, the Unionist Gathering, and RAY,
the latter having joined the SCCOP after its head returned from the exile
he had been forced into following the 1994 war. Al-Haqq was eventually
cajoled into signing the declaration by al-Kuhali.[48] The Unionist Gathering and RAY, however, refused to do so until the last.[49] This intractability
can be ascribed to the intransigent attitudes the respective party leaders,
most notably al-Jawi and al-Jifri, held toward Islah.[50] Such depreciative
and hostile attitudes would form one of the biggest obstacles on the path
to the alliance's creation, as the next section will highlight.

Maneuvers in Narrow Spaces, 1996–2003

With the signing of the Joint Meeting Program for Free and Fair Elections
in August 1996, Islah and the SCCOP became a "partial alliance," as

Bilqis Mansur fittingly remarks.[51] This alliance would remain partial and highly fragile until December 2002. How, then, can the JMP's volatile development in the years after its formation be best explained? It is certainly true that Islah and the SCCOP were often in latent—and, on occasion, manifest—conflict over various issues, primarily regarding social and educational policies. But the parties had been able to settle on the goal of free and fair elections without great difficulty and subsequently managed to quickly agree on further goals concerning their shared vision of reforming the political system. That cooperation between Islah and the SCCOP was deemed purely tactical at the beginning was not an issue. If anything, this view was conducive to cooperation initially, since Islah's leadership could appease the party's radical fringes by citing the pragmatic nature of its relationship with the SCCOP and thereby substantially reduce the perceived internal costs of cooperation.

On balance, the parties' cost-benefit calculations neither militated against the unfolding cooperation nor hampered its subsequent intensification. With respect to the 1996 declaration, the potential benefits of jointly working against ballot-rigging were considered to outweigh the related costs, all the more so as the idea of containing the regime's nascent authoritarianism was still not wholly unrealistic in the mid-1990s.[52] Later in the course of alliance building, these calculations seemed to be paying off as well: the simplified formula read "shelter in return for legitimacy."[53] The JMP's smaller constituent parties such as al-Haqq, the UPF, NUPO, and the Ba'th were mainly granted protection from the regime. In addition, they were able to substantially increase their operational efficiency, enhance their public visibility, and gain access to various kinds of resources—above all from Islah. For the YSP and Islah, cooperating with the smaller parties also provided some shelter from the regime (and for the YSP, also from radical Islamist forces).

First and foremost, though, it meant an increase in strength.[54] While the YSP benefited from Islah's resources, the latter was able to prove its commitment to the opposition and thus increase its legitimacy in the eyes of large parts of the Yemeni public, particularly in the southern governorates. It was of no less importance for Islah to demonstrate its moderate Islamist nature via a willing alliance with leftist and Zaydi parties. The costs arising from cooperation, on the other hand, were deemed justi-fiable. The parties' potential loss of internal decision-making autonomy was limited because of the JMP's own regulations, though cooperation certainly came at a price in terms of an increase in intraparty quarrels and a soured relationship between the party elites and their grassroots bases. Nevertheless, the bottom line was that cooperation was worthwhile for all parties involved. One analyst with an intimate knowledge of Yemen's political economy would note: "Everyone grumbled equally. You would hear YSP people and Nasserists and so on saying 'We have to ask Islah for everything,' because they depended on the funding. The Islahis, on the other hand, were saying 'Why are we giving these guys so much? We do not really need them that much.' So, there was this tension. But there was always benefit. The benefits by far outweighed the costs. So, they kept chugging along."[55]

It is reasonable at this point to look at how the "chugging" began—or, rather, continued—in the aftermath of the August declaration. In the course of the preceding negotiations, Islah's and the SCCOP's represen-tatives had discovered the potential for pushing cooperation to a higher level. But despite common goals and a surplus of benefits on all sides, this intensification of cooperation soon led to the multiplication of intrica-cies, evoking among other things a steady reassessment of the parties' cost-benefit calculations—and not all would ultimately consider the benefits of cooperation worth the likely costs. The intensified cooperation finally unsheathed the parties' conflicting ideological agendas, their uneasy past, and the issue of mutual distrust. In other words, they soon had to engage in the attitudinal component of cooperation.

Attitudes can be defined as relatively enduring dispositions encom-passing a cognitive, affective, and behavioral dimension.[56] They have a considerable impact on how actors perceive situations of conflict.[57] Like-wise, they significantly influence these actors' decisions regarding coop-eration or noncooperation. Attitudes toward cooperation can be positive or negative, and past instances of violence between actors usually gener-ate hostile ones swayed by emotions such as anger, fear, and hatred that impede—or even completely foreclose—later attempts at cooperation.[58]

Al-Mutawakkil's statement, cited in the introduction to this chapter, that the relationship between opposition parties in the Arab world has often been characterized by "reciprocal enmity" clearly refers to the widespread and often violent clashes between Islamists and leftists in the recent history of the Middle East. Conflicting ideologies, rather than past experiences of violence, are in fact often assumed to be the main factor dividing the Arab opposition and forestalling cooperation.[59] In line with the literature, ideology, trust, and the parties' positions in conflict (more below) are thus regarded here as key criteria for assessing the attitudinal component of alliance building between Islah and the SCCOP parties.

To begin with, the ideological chasm between the prospective JMP partners certainly complicated—but did not preclude—alliance building, for obvious reasons. Indeed, the JMP is often highlighted as a remarkable—if not unique—case of cooperation across ideological divides in the Middle East, although there are studies on other countries of the region indicating that it is often reasons other than ideology that prevent Islamists and leftists from joining forces.[60] This is not to say that ideological cleavages do not matter, and it is widely believed that ideological proximity greatly enhances the chances of successful cooperation.[61] Nevertheless, it is important to note that ideology has only an indirect impact on cooperation:[62] conflicting perspectives may, at least theoretically speaking, be ignored, with focus instead placed on matters that are beyond dispute. Empirical evidence from the Arab world shows that past attempts at opposition coordination or alliance building have typically centered on noncontroversial issues in the foreign policy realm or on the extension of political liberties.[63]

The Yemeni opposition was no exception in this regard. When preparing the JMP platform that was finally published in 2005, for instance, settling on foreign policy issues was fairly unproblematic. The section "The Reform of Foreign Policy" thus constitutes 9.68 percent of the whole manuscript—a figure that is disproportionately high given that none of the topics discussed were ever made top priority in the JMP's public discourse, if raised at all.[64] The issue of political liberties, on the other hand, was also relatively easy to negotiate, being of particular importance in the direct aftermath of the August declaration. Senior members of Islah and the

SCCOP, who had been involved in the talks taking place between 1996 and 2002, spoke unanimously of a "common essence" (*khulasa mushtaraka*) to the topics they had been able to address, ranging from freedom of the press to detailed notions of how to prevent the regime from dominating trade unions or civil society organizations.[65]

Major ideological discrepancies between the parties remained visible, and there were many issues that Islah and the SCCOP—as well as the parties within it—were not (yet) able to agree on. However, it must be noted that, first, ideology is not congruent with attitudes. Ideology swayed the attitudes of the negotiating elites because it was a major element in their respective party's identity, often demarcating it from the other parties around the table. Yet it was just one aspect informing these elites' attitudes alongside, for instance, their regional pedigree or religious affiliation. In any case, the attitudes many party elites held toward each other were extremely negative at the beginning of the negotiations, with many disapproving of any form of cooperation at this stage.[66] One senior Islahi, a conservative *'alim*, recalled the adverse conditions of the first meetings: "The most complicated thing was overcoming the prejudices we held about each other. I meet you for the first time. You do not know me, and I do not know you either. Your image of me is based on what you have read about me. My image of you is based on what I have read about you. When we meet, many things will change. A meeting between the YSP and Islah: Who would have dared imagine!"[67] He suggests that attitudes may change, and, with respect to the JMP, would do so to some extent. Yet one should be careful to differentiate between elites and their grassroots bases, on the one hand, and between different factions within the parties, on the other.

Second, there is a difference between ideology and goals. Ideology informs a party's preferences, which then determine its goals in a given conflict. Ideology therefore does not translate directly into goals, and not all of the latter have ideological underpinnings. Islah's inclination toward a first-past-the-post voting system, for instance, stems from its strong constituencies in the bulk of Yemen's electoral districts rather than from ideological considerations. As such, this goal was probably easier to abandon in the negotiations over electoral reform than the ones derived more directly from Islah's ideological fundament. Yet although some conflicting ideological positions had already been abandoned prior to 1996,[68] the potential for conflict remained unabated—particularly concerning issues such as secularism, women's rights, or minority rights. How the parties dealt with the intricacies resulting from their modest ideological congruence once the JMP had become a proper alliance is discussed in the following chapter. At the stage of alliance building, though, contentious issues were simply ignored in a purposeful and transparent way. This deliberate practice of "putting away"[69] was considered a key to success by the negotiators, who also stressed the pointlessness of engaging in ideological quarrels in the face of an abounding overlap of common positions.

Yet even these seemingly common positions often turned out to be highly disputable. In this case, the negotiators underscored the "intellectual seriousness" and "responsibility" they applied when approaching the discussions. As one senior YSP member put it: "We did not deny the difference of opinions, but we approached them responsibly. If we were unable to reach an agreement, we would adjourn the issue. We would not let our frictions linger on." He also recalled how the discussion culture progressed in line with the growing intimacy between the party elites: "Our relationship improved the more we discussed the [possibility of forging a strategic] alliance. Due to our good relationship, we were able to avert political and intellectual clashes as well as public quarrels. We did not just freeze our intellectual disputes. Instead, we discussed the nature of these disputes, and we did not convert [our] intellectual seriousness into enmity, agitation, and bigotry."[70] Looking back at the JMP's lengthy formative period, one senior YSP member also recollected how "we did not put too much pressure on ourselves," a statement that echoes the other negotiators' frequent use of "patience" (sabr) as a crucial tool for confronting negative attitudes. Referring to the parties' later discussions about the exact contents of the JMP platform, a senior Islah member stated that all negotiators had expected the talks to be concluded much earlier. But they soon realized the need to decelerate the proceedings as "sharp turns are dangerous," especially if one is to get the skeptics on board.[71] Patience is, however, also used somewhat euphemistically in this context. It was certainly key in reducing negative attitudes arising from ideological differences. However, patience was also needed to ride out the multiple setbacks the would-be alliance suffered as a result of Islah's maneuvering back and forth between its prospective partners and the regime up until 2003. That is to say, the hostility between Islah and the SCCOP did not solely stem from conflicting ideologies. Attitudes were equally impaired by the undermining of trust via Islah's numerous acts of deception.

Trust is an essential component in the formation and maintenance of alliances, for it critically informs attitudes toward cooperation per se. There is ample empirical evidence that a lack hereof has often hampered opposition cooperation in the Middle East and beyond.[72] Trust can be defined as the willingness of one party to rely on, and make itself vulnerable to, the actions or inaction of another party.[73] It usually builds on past experience and is often understood in terms of reciprocity, particularly when it comes to cooperation.[74] Thomas C. Schelling aptly illustrates the relationship between trust and reciprocity: "Trust is often achieved simply by the continuity of the relation between the parties and the recognition by each that what he might gain by cheating in a given instance is outweighed by the value of the tradition of trust that makes possible a long sequence of future agreement."[75] If political actors do not have a record of past interaction that can help assess their counterparts' trustworthiness, they often resort to historical or international comparisons instead.[76] Once exchange then occurs on a regular basis, existing stereotypes and negative attitudes are likely to be reduced and trust ceases to be merely calculative, with it becoming relational instead—and, crucially, more resistant to noncooperative behavior.[77] However, given Islah's maneuvering between 1996 and 2003, this increased resistance to noncooperation would be gravely jeopardized. The trust that had been hitherto established between the negotiators was seriously put to the test.

Islah's maneuvering can best be described as a recurring series of cooperative and deceptive moves that crystallized around three concrete occasions: the 1997 parliamentary elections, the 1999 presidential elections, and the struggle over constitutional amendments as well as local council elections in 2001. In fact, the maneuvering started in the immediate aftermath of the August declaration in 1996 when, in October of that year, Islah's Shura Council announced that it wished to maintain its relationship

with the GPC. In December, Islah then acted in concert with the opposition, with the vast majority of Islahi parliamentarians boycotting the budget
vote. In January 1997, however, Islah in effect failed the August declaration
by striking a deal with the GPC for the upcoming parliamentary elections.
According to this agreement, Islah would run uncontested in 50 constituencies and the GPC in 100, while both parties could compete in the remaining 151. Even though the deal was not implemented, it led most of
the SCCOP parties (the YSP, the Unionist Gathering, RAY, and the UPF)
to boycott the April 1997 elections. Walking away had also been favored
by the Brotherhood, but Islah's decision-making bodies ruled differently.[78]
The latter participated in the elections despite the failed agreement with
the GPC, suffering defeat. With 226 seats going to the GPC and only 53
to Islah, the Shura Council decided to join the opposition.

Islah's formal alignment therewith was welcomed by many inside
the party, most notably the Brotherhood. The SCCOP also praised Islah's decision, though it would soon become bewildered by the latter's
peculiar understanding of what this meant in practice. In hindsight, al-
Ahmar coined the term *calm opposition* to describe Islah's infamous leni-
ency toward the GPC.[79] According to a senior YSP member, meanwhile,
"there was no clash with either the regime or the opposition." Rather,
Islah aimed to become a "balancing factor" between both sides.[80] Bilqis
Mansur summarizes what she calls Islah's "center position" as follows: it
would not be an opposition force on principle. The party would refuse to
topple the regime, just as it refused to oppose any of the latter's measures
on principle. Instead, Islah engaged in backing up and consulting the
regime. This idiosyncratic understanding of opposition raised concerns
among the SCCOP. Already alarmed by Islah's defection in January 1997,
the SCCOP surmised that the party had not actually rescinded its strategic alliance with the GPC but was instead indulging the latter in return
for posts and policy concessions. Many voices within the SCCOP, indeed,
questioned Islah's position on democracy altogether.[81]

Such suppositions were reasonable, especially as Islah's maneuvers
continued unabated. Despite ongoing negotiations between it and the
SCCOP, as resuming in 1998,[82] Islah was one of the first parties to officially back Salih's candidacy in the presidential elections of 1999, even

though the SCCOP had fielded its own candidate in 'Ali Salih 'Ubbad Muqbil, the secretary-general of the YSP.[83] Even more controversial was Islah's abandonment of the SCCOP in parliament when Muqbil had to meet a 10 percent threshold of parliamentarians supporting his candidacy in order to be admitted to run for the presidency. With its own candidate impeded, the SCCOP boycotted the elections, while Islah participated in favor of Salih. It was clear from the beginning that Muqbil would stand no chance against Salih. He was a difficult character and had declined to curry favor with those parliamentarians who might have assisted his candidacy.[84] Senior Islahi leaders justified the party's decision "as an act designated to secure the party's survival and continuing influence, even as it began to explore other options." Nevertheless, "[it was] viewed by many outsiders as a betrayal of the potential opposition bloc."[85]

Islah's behavior in February 2001, when local council elections and the conflict over constitutional amendments necessitated a concerted effort on the part of the would-be alliance, was as ambivalent as it had been in 1999. In the summer of 2000, Islah had approached the SCCOP to coordinate their positions on these elections: both sides agreed on a boycott if their demands for political and electoral reform went unmet.[86] The proposed changes included the separation of the ruling party leadership and the presidency, as well as the abolition of the Supreme Commission for Elections and Referendum (al-lajna al-'ulya li-l-intikhabat wa al-istifta'; SCER)—a public body for electoral supervision whose neutrality had long been challenged by the opposition.[87] In lieu of the SCER, a new and impartial entity to supervise the elections was proposed. In addition, Islah and the SCCOP agreed that the latter would vote for the former in those electoral districts where only Islahi and GPC candidates stood a chance of winning. In return, Islah promised to vote against the constitutional amendments bill in parliament.[88] These prospective amendments, encompassing a number of crucial articles, had been introduced by the GPC.[89] Most notably, they aimed to extend the president's time in office from five to seven years and the terms of parliamentarians from four to six years, respectively. If implemented, they would have also enabled the president to dissolve parliament without a referendum—the necessity of which was stipulated by Article 100 of the 1994 Constitution.

Things developed differently, however. Facing a united opposition, Salih attended Islah's annual congress in December 2000 and convinced the delegates to revoke the imminent election boycott. In return, he promised to comply with the opposition's request for electoral reform and, decisively, revision of the SCER and voter-registration procedures.[90] Islah did indeed revoke its decision, as did the SCCOP, since the issue of electoral reform had been of crucial importance to the alliance from its earliest days. However, the proposed constitutional amendments then became a source of controversy. Islah had been divided over this question from the very beginning. According to a senior Islah member, on this matter the party "partially agreed with the opposition, partially with 'Ali Salih."[91] While the SCCOP publicly declared its unmitigated opposition to the amendments, Islahi parliamentarians eventually helped secure the necessary formal support for them. Islah failed the SCCOP once more, with previous agreements on electoral coordination rendered meaningless. On February 20, 2001, the SCCOP participated in the local council elections on a common voting list independently of Islah. The constitutional amendments, on the other hand, were approved by referendum, also because the government had abstained from communicating their substance to the public in advance.[92] Ironically, by backing the amendments of 1994 and 2001, Islah directly contributed to Salih's tightening grip on power, which it would oppose soon after from within the JMP.

Islah's maneuvering is not easily explained or understood. Regarding, for instance, the constitutional amendments, its leadership argued that extending the presidential and parliamentary terms would make the country more stable. As for the local council elections, both Islah and the SCCOP had refrained from boycotting them but subsequently complained about voter fraud and refused to acknowledge the returns for some time.[93] Confusingly, even al-Ahmar accused the GPC—including Salih as its head—of ballot rigging and the rolling back of democracy. The SCCOP's reaction to Islah's behavior was also anything but clear-cut. Hence, it is not difficult to find analyses that hold Islah's defection in 1999 and 2001 "greatly strained"[94] the relationship between it and the SCCOP, as now "characterized by deep mistrust"[95]; others consider, meanwhile, the 2001 local council elections "an important step in the bridge building process."[96] According to a senior YSP member as well, the 2001 elections helped "improve the climate [between the negotiators]."[97] How, then, can these antithetical statements be reconciled? Why did Islah act as it did? And how did this affect the attitudinal dimension of cooperation?

Irrespective of the successful development the JMP underwent here-after, the high level of mistrust prevailing between Islah and the SCCOP at this stage cannot be dismissed out of hand. Yet one must also look closely at who caused that mistrust, and why. Most of the SCCOP participants involved in the negotiations with Islah must have been aware that the party consisted of at least three currents whose interests were difficult to align: the Brotherhood, the Salafi wing, and the tribal wing. Each of these segments had a long-standing relationship with the GPC. Both the tribal and the Salafi wings pursued ideological interests that corresponded more with the GPC than with the SCCOP. In addition, many Islahis at the top- and middle-leadership levels were still, and would never completely cease to be, part of Salih's patronage network. Some parliamentarians from Islah's tribal wing had even defected to the GPC following the 1997 elections,[98] and the party chairman and leader of that wing, al-Ahmar, retained the presidency of the parliament after 1997.

The head of the Salafi wing, al-Zindani, also had more than an ideological interest in preserving the relationship with Salih. It has thus been stated that "while Islah as a party was excluded from political access, individuals with strong family or personal ties to the President retained their favored positions. . . . In other words, many of Islah's top leadership remained well connected, even as Salih attenuated the potential influence of the party as an organization."[99] These individuals, however, had a purely tactical understanding of the negotiations with the SCCOP, and people such as al-Ahmar played an "inhibiting role" more than once during the period of alliance building and thereafter.[100]

The SCCOP's negotiators were aware of this fact, just as they were also aware of Salih's competence at appealing to the weak points in every party. In fact, Islah was not the only one that had failed the SCCOP. The 1997 elections are a case in point. Here, Salih was able to divide the SCCOP in that he persuaded the (Iraqi-oriented) Ba'th, NUPO, and al-Haqq to participate in the elections while the rest of the SCCOP went for a boycott. Following the elections, he appointed the secretary-general of al-Haqq, al-Shami, to the position of minister of endowment and religious affairs, even though the latter's party had previously opted for abolishing that ministry altogether.[101] These measures even led to a temporary split within the SCCOP,[102] and they prompted the secretary-general of the Unionist Gathering, al-Jawi, to ask his fellow oppositionists: "Do we really feel some sort of co-ordination between us?"[103] Hence, there certainly was mistrust between the parties, and even serious mistrust between Islah and the SCCOP. Yet this wariness was largely at the party level. Those elites who were negotiating the terms of cooperation had established a relationship of trust over time, partly as a consequence of the intentional confidence-building measures that accompanied the negotiations from the outset.[104] For instance, the negotiators regularly met for a *maqil*, or qat chew, which was held on a rotational basis at their private houses. To cite another example, joint prayers were held before, during, and after each meeting; sometimes these instances were photographed, with the pictures later distributed to the rank and file. Later, members of the grassroots base would report either positively or negatively on the close relationships between many Islah and SCCOP leaders,[105] and human rights attorneys for nongovernmental organizations affiliated with Islah would defend journalists connected to the YSP in court.[106] At this stage, however, trust was still a fragile commodity.

A more nuanced perspective on the issue of trust—as well as the ideological disputes arising between these prospective bedfellows—can thus help explain why attitudinal aspects did not distract Islah and the SCCOP from proceeding along the path of alliance building. This becomes even more evident when we look at another attitudinal component of cooperation, that is, the parties' positions in conflict. The latter refers to, and is often used synonymously with, status—if status is understood as the position of a given party in relation to others—and there are strong theoretical and empirical indications that actors of similar status are more likely to engage in cooperation than those individuals who are dissonant in this regard.[107] As the concept is again relational, two benchmarks are deemed to be particularly salient in assessing the parties' positions in conflict. First, it has been suggested that asymmetries in terms of party strength hold the respective camps back from cooperating.[108] Second, the regime's approach to handling the opposition is believed to be of key importance, as authoritarian incumbents often purposefully structure political conflict by allowing some opposition parties to participate in the formal political system while excluding others. Such a divided environment produces different costs for mobilization on the part of the opposition and, crucially, different basic interests between those parties that are, and want to remain, included in the political system and the ones that are excluded and thus effectively barred from cooperation.[109] In contrast, an undivided environment in which the opposition faces a shared enemy is believed to foster cooperation by providing common ground.[110]

Concerning Islah and the SCCOP, that common ground was steadily strengthened in the course of negotiations, as the former's position in conflict increasingly resembled that of the latter. Indeed, the gradual rapprochement between both sides accompanied, and was facilitated by, the GPC gradually shutting out its junior coalition partner. Islah's creeping exclusion from the political realm altered the party's cost-benefit calculations. It also left its mark on Islah's attitudes toward the SCCOP, and it unquestionably made it more hostile toward the GPC—and Salih in particular. Islah was not merely expelled from power but in essence repeatedly deceived. Its agreement with the GPC over voting coordination ahead of the 1997 parliamentary elections had been breached, leading to its defeat at the polls. Salih's promise to Islah (and the SCCOP) to reform the election law in the run-up to the 2001 local council elections was effectively reneged on with the GPC's amending of the General Elections and Referendum Law (no. 13, 2001) in parliament. Prior to the parliamentary elections in April 2003, Salih repeated his promise of electoral reform, only to retract it during a GPC conference in August 2003. On that occasion he also offended Islah by rescinding the invitations extended to the bulk of the party's leadership, thus contravening a custom established in the 1990s. More insulting besides was the fact that he addressed the only two representatives of Islah, al-Ahmar and al-Zindani, by their public positions as president of parliament and former member of the Consultative Council, respectively, thus ignoring their leadership roles within Islah.[111]

In short, the negative attitudes Islah and the SCCOP had initially held toward each other became more balanced between 1996 and 2003, especially as the parties' positions in conflict began to gradually resemble each other. Islah was still the strongest party by far. However, having been cut off from the state coffers after leaving government in 1997, the party deteriorated in strength, and its relationship with the SCCOP became less asymmetrical. Both sides now found themselves in an undivided environment where they were barred from participating in political decision-making and increasingly excluded from the state-sponsored patronage system.[112] Both now shared common grievances that brought them closer together. Their relationship with the GPC deteriorated between 2001 and 2003, while their enmity toward Salih grew accordingly, both at the party and at the personal level.[113] Most notably, perhaps, even key elites in Islah who had been highly skeptical of a potential alliance with the SCCOP now grew wary of the GPC, asserting that Islah should intensify its cooperation with the SCCOP given Salih's frequent deceptions. Such attitudinal changes accompanied, and indeed contributed significantly to, important shifts in the parties' elite structures, particularly within Islah. This factor was of special importance for the eventual founding of the JMP.

The Catalyzing Effect of Jarallah 'Umar al-Kuhali's Murder, 2003–2006

The analysis of the JMP's formative period has thus far outlined the alliance's checkered history, as characterized by recurrent cooperative and defective moves, respectively. Notwithstanding the previous arguments, it is puzzling to some extent that the parties involved continued their attempts to intensify cooperation. It is, indeed, baffling that they had embarked on this strategy in 1996 at all given the parties' past record of hostile interaction. As will be argued in the following, most of the credit for this endeavor can be attributed to a small number of opposition elites. Likewise, it will be reasoned that only decisive shifts in the elite alignments within Islah and the YSP enabled the prospective alliance to proceed despite a start that was hardly promising.

The crucial role of elites in all matters concerning cooperation has been stressed frequently in the literature. It is party elites who settle on, and justify, the initiation and upholding of cooperation, since it is they who define a party's official position on the scope of it and persuade other elites and grassroots members of its benefits.[114] Negative attitudes threatening to impede cooperation are most likely to be spread among small clusters of interacting individuals, and it is especially at the elite level that the inclination to cooperate can be increased by establishing mutual trust, tolerance, restraint, and accommodation.[115] The importance of elites in forging cross-ideological alliances has thus long been acknowledged;[116] it has also been asserted that under certain conditions, such cooperation can have a moderating effect on the ideological positions of the elites involved.[117] Yet it is Michaelle Brower's study on the JMP that illustrates why moderation is not only a consequence of but also a precondition to cooperation, at least concerning the elite level. Without a small number of moderate elites pushing for cooperation with their ideological rivals, an alliance will hardly be considered a viable option. In other words, "cooperation requires moderates,"[118] and such levelheaded, committed elites are often the product of "free spaces" such as professional associations or trade unions—that is, spaces that are unfettered by authoritarian encroachment and that allow for encounters between elites with opposing worldviews.[119]

The critical role that committed elites played in Yemen was evident in the previous account of the first meetings between Islah and the SCCOP. It is primarily al-Kuhali who is today acknowledged as the JMP's main "architect," to borrow Brower's designation. This assessment is shared by many inside and outside the alliance, including many Islahis who consider him to have been the JMP's "practical and ideational engineer."[120] On the Islah side, it is primarily Qahtan who is credited with advancing the alliance, as well as Nasir Taha Mustafa and other high-ranking Islahis such as Muhammad al-Yadumi, Islah's chairman following the death of al-Ahmar in 2007, and 'Abd al-Wahhab al-Anisi, Islah's secretary-general. Although these Islah and YSP elites were of particular importance—simply because the JMP stands and falls with these two parties[121]—key elites from the smaller parties such as Muhammad 'Abd al-Malik al-Mutawakkil (UPF) or 'Ali Sayf Hasan (NUPO) also contributed significantly to the successful development of the alliance.[122] These individuals' importance probably lies less in the act of recognizing and seizing their chance, a window of opportunity that would later be characterized as an "exceptional moment in the history of Yemeni politicians,"[123] than it does in their unique demeanors and in the personal links they built, which together enabled them to instill trust in the parties' distorted relations.

The case of al-Kuhali aptly exemplifies why committed elites were so important here.[124] Born in 1942, he was raised in the province of Ibb, which later became part of the YAR. In Dhamar, the capital of the adjacent, homonymous province, he studied Zaydi jurisprudence (*fiqh*). In the 1960s, al-Kuhali joined the pan-Arab movement and fought on the side of the republican forces in the northern revolution. He was imprisoned from 1968 to 1971, beginning to study Marx and Gramsci while sitting in jail. Further radicalized on his release, he became a leader of the PDRY-funded National Democratic Front, which engaged in an armed insurgency in the YAR seeking to create a unified socialist republic. It is worth mentioning that among those individuals fighting on the other side were many from the Brotherhood—including Qahtan, who was an officer in the northern army. However, the PDRY's "Bloody January" of 1986 turned the staunch socialist ideologue into an advocate for political pluralism and social democracy. In his own words, he "had become convinced that social democracy was the best way to solve people's problems because it combines both political freedom and social justice."[125] In 1988, he outlined these demands in an open letter to PDRY president 'Ali Salim al-Baydh.[126] After unification in 1990, he was appointed minister of culture and, in addition to running this portfolio, mainly committed himself to the transformation of the YSP into a social democratic party—and to reaching a settlement between the northern and southern elites, who were heading toward war. Like many other JMP elites, he participated in the National Dialogue Conference during 1993–94 to avert the looming military conflict.

Al-Kuhali was convinced of the necessity of bringing together a diverse set of parties to contain an increasingly authoritarian regime, and his personal traits and biography, indeed, enabled him to build bridges between political forces as diverse as leftists and Islamists. Given his intimate knowledge of the authoritative sources in Islam, he was capable of engaging Islahis in religious discussions, also demonstrating that socialists were not atheists per se. It appealed to the Islahis that he had relinquished a strict understanding of socialism. His ideological flexibility and political pragmatism were well known. Abu Luhum, for example, stated that "he was a well-versed politician, distinguished by his wisdom, rationality, and flexibility."[127] Yet as someone who had spent years of his life as a guerrilla leader combating northern Islamists, al-Kuhali could also claim credibility among those individuals in the SCCOP who were highly skeptical about the merits of cooperating with Islah. Finally, his regional background was conducive to building bridges, too. Both al-Kuhali and Qahtan stemmed from Lower Yemen: the former from Ibb, the latter from Ta'izz. As mentioned, Qahtan first approached the YSP's regional office in Ta'izz, which was run by al-Kuhali at that time. The Ta'izz Governorate was also a hub of the Yemeni Brotherhood, something that cannot be underestimated given the salience of regional identities in the country.

In short, al-Kuhali was the ideal oppositionist for facilitating cooperation between the SCCOP and Islah. He "was a Northerner but also a Southerner," just as he was "a student of religion and of revolution."[128] In the words of Abu Luhum, he was "one of those rare figures that were accepted by all political parties."[129] Yet he was not the only one; the initially small number of committed elites within Islah and the other SCCOP parties grew steadily over the course of negotiations. Some features of Yemen's political milieu, such as the culture of deliberation and dialogue or the consociational tradition of seeking to establish equilibrium between rival forces, were deliberately invoked by the committed elites to facilitate talks. This state of affairs certainly contributed to the rapprochement of party elites, although the impact of political culture is difficult to verify—to say nothing of its exact measurement.[130] What can be detected, though, is the repeated use of free-space interactions, which even predated the first negotiations in 1996. "Free" is somewhat misleading in the Yemeni context. The Salih regime was clearly authoritarian in nature, and undeniably the "forging of those interpersonal and conceptual relationships that initiated and bound together actors in the JMP . . . [took] place *in a context of constricted political space.*"[131] However, the regime rarely exercised outright repression vis-à-vis the party opposition and never overtly clamped down on meetings between opposition party elites. Thus, free spaces here refer not only to spaces free from authoritarian encroachment but also to ones that were, by and large, unfettered by the contentious intra-opposition narratives conventionally celebrated in Yemen's public discourse. Such free spaces could be found both within and beyond the ROY's national territory.

The first encounters under free-space conditions between those opposition elites who would later forge the JMP took place within the framework of the so-called National Islamic Conferences, as launched in 1989. They were held on an annual basis, mostly in Beirut, and aimed to bring together Islamist and leftist forces from across the Arab world.[132] They were partly successful, as participants did indeed manage to find some common positions while agreeing to disagree on issues such as religion and democracy, secularism, the status of religious minorities, and women. Some Yemeni participants played a considerable role in these conferences, with al-Mutawakkil acting as the general coordinator of four of them and al-Ahmar as the funder of two final communiqués. Others merely attended; inspired by the spirit of rapprochement between the region's Islamist and leftist forces, they realized that their frustration with the GPC's control of political life was shared by other ideological currents in Yemen, too. Apparently, the possibility of Islah's integration into the SCCOP was first discussed between al-Mutawakkil and al-Kuhali during the 1994 conference; meanwhile, those meetings held in 1997 and 2000, as well as a further conference in Washington, DC, in 2002, provided ample opportunity for participants from Islah, the YSP, NUPO, the UPF, and the Ba'th to take stock of and reflect on the state of cooperation between Islah and the SCCOP.

These conferences are but one example of free-space interaction, and it is worth mentioning that the travel expenses of the Yemeni participants were regularly covered by the National Democratic Institute (NDI), a US government-sponsored organization promoting democracy that had opened an office in Sanaa in 1993. The NDI also provided free-space facilities inside Yemen, with it hosting numerous consultative meetings between Islah and the SCCOP in early 2002—in addition to offering workshops on conflict resolution and techniques to foster cooperation.[133] Local institutions were also instrumental in increasing the number of committed elites. The necessity of issue-specific coalition building between Islah and the SCCOP in parliament, for instance, often prompted the parties' parliamentarians to contemplate a more substantial alliance.[134] Perhaps the most significant platform for free-space interaction, however, was provided by the regular "Joint Meeting *maqa'il.*" These qat chews were usually hosted by two members of the prospective alliance, at a later stage coming under the auspices of the Political Development Forum (muntada al-tanmiya al-siyasiyya)—a Yemeni NGO run by Hasan and al-Mutawakkil.[135]

To summarize, free-space interactions between members of Islah and the SCCOP gradually augmented the number of elites committed to intensifying cooperation. In addition, journalists who were affiliated with the parties in one way or another soon began to publicly support party elites' endeavors, thus positively influencing public opinion on those individuals advocating for the alliance.[136] Accordingly, some four to five years after the first encounters between Islah and the SCCOP, one could find a significant pool of committed elites within the parties as well as among those able to affect Yemeni public discourse in more general terms. However, the mere existence of committed elites was hardly sufficient for the partial alliance to transform itself into a sound strategic one. For the latter to materialize, it would be necessary for these committed elites to actually assume control over intraparty decision-making processes or at least be able to exert decisive influence within the parties' corridors of power. The case of the JMP's formative period therefore illustrates that cross-ideological cooperation requires not only moderates but also ones who wield significant power over their organizations.

Given the JMP's lengthy formative period, it apparently took some time until the latter condition was met. The smaller parties such as al-Haqq, the UPF, or even NUPO can be neglected in this context, not because the question of joining an alliance with Islah was beyond dispute in their case but rather owing to the fact that their party leaderships were small in number and more homogeneous. With some notable exceptions (RAY, the Unionist Gathering), most parties' leaders unanimously accepted a coalition that included Islah—albeit if grudgingly in some instances. As for Islah and the YSP, however, the situation was more intricate, simply because the elite constellations were more complex. The discussion about when "the JMP" became more than a hollow label one could resort to for the purpose of single-issue cooperation on isolated occasions is telling in this regard. As already indicated, there are contradictory statements on when exactly it became a strategic alliance, with the JMP officially indicating 2000,[137] some authors saying 2002 or 2003,[138] and yet others 2005.[139] To be sure, the confusion over this issue results to some extent from the discrepancy between the official founding date contained in retrospective and factual developments, as well as from divergence between public and academic perceptions, on the one hand, and those claims of the various parties involved on the other. Almost certainly, however, it is also owing to the fact that during the first years following the 1996 declaration, elite constellations within the YSP and Islah were in flux: for a long time it was all but clear which factions within both parties would prevail and whether the JMP was ultimately considered a tactical option, a strategic option, or indeed no option at all.

Within the YSP, a party claiming to have a total of three hundred thousand members, there was a long history of leadership squabbles. Different approaches can be taken to categorizing the rival party factions, with the divides mainly falling along regional and ideological lines. Concerning the former, the party leadership was composed of a southern military tribal group, a northern military nontribal group, and a Hadramawt group centered on al-Baydh.[140] Regional identities overlapped somewhat with the positions the elites took on Bloody January, on the one hand, dividing them into followers of al-Baydh (*tughma*) and 'Ali Nasir Muhammad (*zumra*), respectively, and with their ideological inclinations, on the other. In terms of thought, one can differentiate between reformers and the conservative "old guard"—at least during the 1990s and much of the following decade, with the reformist camp including, among others, al-Kuhali and Sayf Sa'il (from the North) and the old guard encompassing al-Baydh, Haydar Abu Bakr al-'Attas, Muqbil, and Hasan Ahmad Ba'um,

most of whom stemmed from the Abyan, Shabwa, and Hadramawt Governorates. The reformists had long been lobbying for the moderation of
the party's ideology regarding social democracy, the inclusion of younger
and female members in its decision-making organs, and the maintenance
of unity. The old guard, in contrast, strongly resisted any changes to party
ideology, overwhelmingly rejected participation in any elections post-
1994, and increasingly campaigned for secession and the reestablishment
of the PDRY.[141] Most important, the old guard vehemently opposed strategic—if not all—cooperation with Islah.

The conflict between these two wings predated unification and para-
lyzed the party long into the 1990s.[142] Although key figures such as al-
Baydh and al-'Attas had been forced into exile in 1994, the remaining
representatives of the old guard successfully hampered coordination with
Islah at first. A breakthrough was reached only with the YSP's fourth general congress, which was split into two parts. The first round in 1998 saw
a programmatic shift toward social democracy and the adoption of political pluralism and general freedoms. In the second round, held in August
2000, major shifts in the YSP's leadership took place. While Muqbil was
elected secretary-general, al-Kuhali and Sa'il were elected deputy secretaries-general, signaling that the reformers had gained the upper hand.
Although al-Baydh and al-'Attas were also voted onto the Central Committee, a largely symbolic gesture given that they were in exile, the bulk of
the old guard were forced out.[143]

The stage was set for the intensification of cooperation with Islah,
at least on the part of the YSP. Salih's response to these developments
foreshadowed what would be his favored strategy toward the JMP in later
years. In late 2000, as well as in May 2003, he pardoned roughly two
dozen old-guard socialists, encouraging them to return to Yemen. With
this move, he was not seeking merely to deepen the power struggle inside
the YSP. In his effort to divide northern and southern YSP leaders, he was
also trying to undermine opposition cooperation per se.[144] Although he ultimately failed to do so, the mere attempt at it displayed his conviction that
alliance building was proceeding apace and becoming a threat to his rule.

The case of Islah is more complex—and arguably more interesting—
as those factions objecting to cross-ideological cooperation remained with

the party, sabotaging such joint endeavors from within instead of leaving the party altogether, as the YSP's defeated old guard would soon do (see chapter 2). Islah was by far the largest opposition party, with an estimated nine hundred thousand members.[145] Although many of its elites dismissed the notion of their party consisting of various factions with diverging interests,[146] Islah was anything but an organic whole: it included, as noted, a tribal wing, traditionally represented by the al-Ahmar family; a Salafi wing, spearheaded by highly conservative 'ulama'; and the Brotherhood. Islah is often portrayed as an overwhelmingly northern party, particularly by its southern critics, but following unification it built a strong grassroots presence in the southern provinces, especially in Hadramawt. Yet the Brotherhood's power base lay in the Southern Highlands, while the tribal wing was firmly rooted in the Northern Highlands. Since most of the 'ulama' leading the Salafi wing also originated from North Yemen, the assumption of al-Haqq's secretary-general that "the party's leadership was firmly under the control of the North" was not too farfetched.[147] While the Brotherhood was the driving force behind alliance building,[148] the Salafi wing rejected cooperation with the SCCOP on ideological grounds from the very beginning. The tribal wing, in contrast, shared much of the Salafis' social conservatism but was rather opportunistic in terms of political allies. Yet most of its leading representatives were deeply entwined in the regime's patronage system and primarily placed stock in upholding their business interests,[149] something that was secured by the regime for a long time.[150] When Islah joined the opposition in 1997, the tribal wing was thus often in open conflict with the Brotherhood. It repudiated an alliance with the SCCOP, considering it a transient, tactical choice at best.

While much of this history has already been noted, albeit in a fragmented manner, it is important to recapitulate at this point in order to understand the inconsistent policies of a party that included individuals as dissimilar as Nobel Peace Prize laureate Tawakkul Karman and al-Zindani, the latter a "specially designated global terrorist" and alleged mentor of Osama bin Laden.[151] This point is even more important as, compared to the YSP, there was no concrete point in time prior to the formal establishment of the JMP—which, as argued here, coincides with the adoption of a shared platform and the passing of bylaws in 2005—when the Brotherhood visibly came out on top. Throughout the 1990s, Islah was dominated by its tribal and Salafi wings. The first indications of a shift in the party's balance of power became visible only at the 1998 party congress, when the Brotherhood managed to influence the party program and achieved acceptance for female participation in the party's executive committees.[152] However, only as of the 2007 party congress—when Muhammad 'Ali 'Ajlan replaced al-Zindani as the head of the party's Shura Council and thirteen women were elected to the same body—did the Brotherhood formally dominate the decision-making organs.[153] The passing away of al-Ahmar in December of the same year was of additional importance since, as one Yemeni commentator explained, it meant the end of the "Catholic marriage" between al-Ahmar and Salih—a statement insinuating that the bonds between the chairmen of Islah and the GPC could be undone only by the death of one of the two.[154] Al-Ahmar's death also meant the loss of the only influential Islahi elite capable of reconciling the Salafi wing with the Brotherhood; it also signaled the rise of his son Hamid, who had fallen out with Salih in 2006 and who would press ahead on the path toward open conflict between Islah and the regime.

Although the Brotherhood never achieved complete control over the party, it must have gained the upper hand in the latter's internal power struggles at some point between 1998 and 2007. In all likelihood, the Brotherhood's rise within Islah was ultimately linked to an event that sent shock waves through the Yemeni opposition—and especially Islah. In December 2002, al-Kuhali was shot dead shortly after delivering a speech at Islah's annual party congress. While the precise motives behind the assassination remained unclear, it quickly transpired that the culprit, 'Ali Ahmad Muhammad Jarallah, was a former member of Islah who had become disaffected with the party's development and its increasing closeness to the YSP in particular. He had studied at the ultraconservative al-Iman University in Sanaa, run by al-Zindani; Jarallah justified the murder—as well as his further attempts on the lives of al-Mikhlafi (NUPO) and Qasim Salam Sa'id (Iraqi-oriented Ba'th)—by invoking the infamous fatwa issued by Islah's former minister of justice al-Daylami sanctioning the killing of leftists.[155] Al-Kuhali's murder prompted a public outcry and, eventually, a revision of Islah's official position on the use of *takfir*, the act of pronouncing someone an apostate. Most notably, it forced the Salafi wing on the defensive and rallied support behind those individuals within the party advocating cross-ideological cooperation. It is therefore commonly assumed that the murder of al-Kuhali was a catalyst for change both within Islah's leadership ranks and vis-à-vis alliance building.[156] This assumption appears to be corroborated by the rapid intensification of cooperation thereafter, which, in turn, contributed to the Brotherhood consolidating its position within Islah.[157]

The following three years saw an unprecedented period of successful cooperation. During a commemoration for al-Kuhali held on February 6, 2003, Islah, the YSP, NUPO, the Iraqi-oriented Ba'th, al-Haqq, and the UPF signed an "Agreement of Principles" (ittifaq al-mabadi') that was to govern their first official and comprehensive election coordination in the upcoming April 2003 parliamentary ones.[158] The agreement also envisaged the intensification of cooperation in the aftermath of the elections and called on the signatory parties to renounce all forms of violence and to abandon fraudulent practices, the use of *takfir*, as well as other means of coercion. In the elections, Islah and the SCCOP parties abided by their arrangement. Although the returns were sobering, with the signatory parties winning a total of 57 seats (Islah, 45; YSP, 7; NUPO, 3; the Iraqi-oriented Ba'th, 2) and the GPC taking 230,[159] cooperation was deemed to have undergone "a qualitative change"[160] or was seen as "an important step . . . marking the beginning of intensified cooperation."[161] Interestingly, YSP representatives asserted: "We were defeated in some districts because we had failed to coordinate properly. This experience enabled us to reconsider some of our positions."[162] The Brotherhood's evaluation of electoral coordination was similar. "After we had successfully engaged in election coordination in 2003, we entered a new phase as we agreed to shift to more general topics of popular concern. [From now on, we would] no longer cover national issues at the party level but rather at that of the JMP."[163]

In the early summer of 2004, Islah and the SCCOP began negotiating a common platform. The parties also realized that the prospective alliance would need basic rules governing opposition interactions in the long run. Negotiations on the platform and the bylaws were reportedly difficult; however, the NDI facilitated the discussions, which ultimately bore fruit. In November 2005, Islah and the SCCOP concomitantly published the "JMP Plan for Political and National Reform" as well as the "Basic Bylaws Governing the Work of the Joint Meeting [Parties]" (al-la'iha al-asasiyya al-munazzima li-'amal al-liqa' al-mushtarak) and the "Bylaws Governing the Work of the Branches of the Joint Meeting [Parties] in the Governorates" (al-la'iha al-munazzima li-'amal furu' al-liqa' al-mushtarak fi al-muhafazat).[164] Both the platform and the bylaws are discussed in the following chapter. However, it is worth mentioning here that it was argu-ably the first time that the label "Joint Meeting *Parties*" appeared in an official document.[165] The founding parties—meaning those factions a sig-natory to both the platform as well as the bylaws—were the same ones that had signed the Agreement of Principles in 2003: Islah, the YSP, NUPO, the Iraqi-oriented Ba'th, al-Haqq, and the UPF. RAY, the Liberals' Consti-tutional Party, and the Unionist Gathering had already bowed out of cross-ideological cooperation. Shortly after publication, the Iraqi-oriented Ba'th abandoned the JMP and was replaced by the Syrian-oriented Ba'th.[166] The September Gathering (al-tajammu' al-sibtimri), a tiny and rather insig-nificant party, joined the JMP as well. In any case, by November 2005 Islah and the SCCOP had become an alliance with an "institutional character."[167]

The upcoming presidential elections, scheduled for September 20, 2006, offered the first opportunity for the JMP to topple Salih via the bal-lot box. Their chances did not appear to be too bleak given the president's legitimacy was in tatters among large swaths of the population, owing to the regime's idiosyncratic participation in the unpopular "War on Terror," unsatisfying political developments, and the worsening of the country's economic situation. When, for instance, the regime lifted subsidies on diesel and gas in July 2005, all of Yemen's major cities witnessed massive protests.[168] The JMP stepped up its activities. In December 2005, the first official JMP congress was held and alliance committees staffed; a second conference, partly broadcast by Al Jazeera, followed in April 2006. On December 8, 2005, JMP parliamentarians presented a common draft bill on political reform.[169] In March 2006, the JMP then published two memo-randa, introducing to the public therewith those immediate measures the alliance deemed necessary to solve the political crisis and to guarantee free and fair elections.[170] Facing a united opposition, the regime made concessions in June 2006 concerning the JMP's demands for electoral reform—so that the latter would subsequently renounce its idea of an election boycott.[171] Most important, though, the JMP managed to settle on a common candidate for the presidential elections: Faysal bin Shamlan, a widely known and well-respected southern politician who was not affiliated with any party.

These developments were remarkable. Within the space of fewer than ten years, former sworn enemies had come together to form and uphold a strategic cross-ideological alliance that would pose a serious threat to the Salih regime in the 2006 presidential elections. The latter elections were a harbinger of the ensuing escalation of conflict playing out between the regime and the opposition, as ultimately culminating in the 2011 uprising.

Conclusion

Alliance building must be considered to belong to the standard repertoire of the opposition, regardless of what kind of entity is in operation as part of the latter and no matter when, where, and under what circumstances so. This reality is so for the simple reason that it is an obvious way of increasing its strength vis-à-vis the incumbent regime. In an authoritarian setting where the opposition faces a high level of uncertainty, the incumbent's concentration of power, and regime strategies being employed to contain or even undo opponents, alliance building is even more essential, for it increases the chances of changing—or at least surviving—a hazardous environment. Despite this, opposition alliances under authoritarianism are rather uncommon. In fact, most attempts at opposition cooperation end up being nonstarters. The case of the JMP—a cross-ideological alliance of leftist and Islamist parties that emerged as the major challenger to the Salih regime in 2006 following a prolonged formative period—therefore represents a splendid opportunity for identifying what it takes to build a strategic opposition alliance.

The starting position for the launching of cooperation in Yemen was unfavorable, to say the least. The major components of the prospective alliance, the YSP and Islah, had been caught up in violent conflict for

decades. The attitudes the parties held toward each other were negative. Furthermore, Islah was still part of the ruling coalition when it approached the opposition in summer 1996. Although Islah and the alliance
that predated the JMP, the SCCOP, quickly agreed to take action against
ballot rigging, the parties—and Islah in particular—often initially failed to
comply with the coordination agreements finalized. What is more, on account of strong intraparty resistance to cross-ideological cooperation, cost-
benefit calculations did not allow for anything more than tactical forms
for a long time. Cooperation did not gain momentum, indeed, until after
Islah's increasing marginalization and repeated deception by the regime.
Most important, though, the murder of the YSP's deputy secretary-general
led to a shift in elite constellations. Only after al-Kuhali's premature death
did those committed elites who had long since advocated for cooperation
hold sway within the parties, and especially within Islah. Al-Kuhali's assassination was thus a watershed moment. In the three years after, the
JMP evolved into a strategic alliance with organizational structures and a
multiple-issue agenda, one that was capable—and indeed willing—when
it came to escalating the conflict with the regime.

Discussing the JMP's formative period in light of the theoretical literature on opposition cooperation allows us to arrive at some generalizable assumptions, though with certain reservations. For instance, the
scope and intensity of opposition cooperation may vary from case to case,
ranging from low-level to high-level cooperation—or, put differently, from
purely tactical to outright strategic cooperation. Opposition *alliances* are
thus only one form of opposition cooperation; the parties involved do not
necessarily intend to achieve the highest level of cooperation, nor are they
necessarily willing to bear the consequences arising from strategic forms
thereof. The case of the JMP suggests that four basic conditions need
to be met for opposition parties to engage in strategic cooperation: they
must settle on common goals (goal convergence), they must be convinced
that cooperating on certain issues is worth the costs accruing from overall
alignment with the other parties involved (surplus of benefits), they must
smooth over any attitudinal constraints (balanced attitudes), and those
party elites committed to cooperation must take up the helm in their party
organizations' internal hierarchy (central, committed elites). The extent to

which these requirements are met influences the scope and intensity of cooperation, and the time it takes to do so correlates with the length of an alliance's formative period.

The JMP also illustrates that political opposition in authoritarian regimes is a highly dynamic institution, receptive to stimuli arising from both inside and outside the parties involved. In the JMP's formative years, stretching from 1996 to 2005, the political environment changed considerably; so did the respective parties accordingly. Likewise, opposition cooperation between Islah and the SCCOP shifted from being tactical to strategic in nature, from volatile single-issue coordination to a resilient reform coalition. Such a sea change necessitated new institutional and organizational arrangements and gave rise to previously unseen forms of intraparty resistance. The following chapter now turns to how the JMP handled these formidable challenges.

2

Upgrading Cooperation

The Consolidation of the Joint Meeting Parties

By the early years of the new millennium, most symptoms of the crisis that Yemen was rapidly sliding into were already discernible to the attentive observer. The authors of the JMP's Plan for Political and National Reform were in no doubt about "the decline of the general situation," either. Altogether, they had dedicated nine pages to a root-cause analysis of the country's malaise, based on which they concluded that "there is no longer any room for illusion in the mind of Yemenis about the tragedy that is awaiting them." "In order to halt this decline and avert the most painful woes," they went on to say, some worried parties, experts, and intellectuals had gathered to search for a way out of the pending crisis. This endeavor, they stated, had yielded "a number of ideas, initiatives, and calls," inspiring the JMP to outline its vision for "comprehensive political and national reform." This vision—meaning the Plan for Political and National Reform—would constitute the "common denominator," necessitating "the unification of national efforts and the bringing together of [the JMP] in a historical struggle to rescue the country from collapse."[1]

This chapter explores how the JMP organized itself to win this "historical struggle," and what the latter was ultimately about. While the platform is in parts loftier in style than precise in content, it does provide insight into the alliance's goals, its ranking of them, as well as its basic approach to challenging the regime of 'Ali 'Abdallah Salih. The platform will thus be subject to brief analysis. The central argument put forth, however, is that the alliance's organizational structures were an indispensable wherewithal for the JMP as they critically shaped its internal performance and, in many ways, its one vis-à-vis the external environment, too—an argument, indeed, that is assumed to be applicable to strategic alliances in general. To assess the functionality of the JMP's organizational structures, and their meaning for strategic alliances overall, the focus will be on two key aspects. First, how the JMP set itself up so as to enable its member parties to reproduce the basic conditions of cooperation will be examined. Second, the extent to which the JMP's institutional setup facilitated internal mobilization efforts will be discussed. Connected to both issues is the question of how the alliance dealt with dissenters—or, put differently, with those peripheral elites who were highly critical of cross-ideological cooperation and, on this account, either left their party (Yemeni Socialist Party) or attempted to sabotage cooperation (Islah).

Joint Objectives

Identifying the JMP's objectives is no simple task. Judging from its Plan for Political and National Reform, which is but one—if central—document in this regard, a great number of objectives emerge. Yet it is up for discussion which ones we may consider of top priority or of secondary importance, respectively, the JMP's own indications notwithstanding. Beyond that, some objectives were certainly more relevant to one member party than to another. To complicate matters, there might have been objectives that were simply off the record. It has been argued that "contemporary Arab democratic discourse is less the ground of a national political consensus than a term used in political contestation."[2] Many Yemeni critics maintained, in a similar vein, that the alliance was little more than a rent-seeking coalition harnessing democratic discourse to mask base motives,[3] and significant segments of its leadership were said to be essentially competing "for a share of the political and economic pie."[4] This particular issue will be discussed in chapter 4. Here, however, those parts of the platform that arose as the main points of contention between the JMP and the regime are the ones forming the focus of inquiry. Contrasting these specific parts of the platform with the declarations published and actions taken by the JMP during its confrontation with the regime will shed additional light on the alliance's actual agenda.

The platform, which has been likened to the Document of Pledge and Accord,[5] comes with a lengthy preface (fifteen pages; 24.19 percent) and a short closing part (one page; 1.61 percent), being divided into six sections: The first lists the alliance's demands for "Political and Constitutional Reform" and is the largest in length (seventeen pages; 27.42 percent). Section 2 is "The Strengthening of the Yemeni Unity and the National Unity" (two pages; 3.26 percent) and is followed by a third section, "Administrative Reform and the Fight Against Corruption" (seven pages; 11.29 percent). The fourth section (eleven pages; 17.74 percent) is titled "Economic and Financial Reform." In addition, the platform features a three-page section (4.81 percent) called "Reform of Cultural and Social Policies" and a section titled "Foreign Policy Reform" (six pages; 9.68 percent). In view of the organization and length of the respective sections, it appears that the reform of the political system, good governance, and state building are the overall focal points.[6]

These three objectives were also rewarding in that they were unlikely to cause tensions among the alliance's ideologically diverse members—should their discussion remain at a more general level. Nevertheless, the sections dealing with these and connected issues are among the most persuasive parts of the platform. The question of state building is a case in point here. The platform begins by deploring the absence of state institutions and the "rotten" nature of existing ones. It blames the Salih regime for the miserable state of affairs, proposing that it had excessively "embezzled public funds" and availed itself of "public services and all public facilities for the sake of the ruling party." The platform then offers a list of measures deemed necessary for "the overhaul of the state's administrative structure," the implementation of good governance, and the building of a democratic polity. This list is both substantial and practical in nature. For instance, the section on administrative reform results in a list of eight corresponding laws to this end, the rapid enactment or amendment of which the JMP would ensure after its coming to power. A subsection called "Guarantee of Neutralism and the Independence of Public Administrative Bodies" specifies suggestions on how the JMP would guarantee the neutrality of state institutions. The platform, moreover, acknowledges the urgent need for "the removal of the negative relicts of past conflicts, wars, and disputes" and explicitly calls for national reconciliation, which is considered to be a "necessity for the building of a democratic and modern Yemeni state."[7]

The overall emphasis of the platform, though, is on the reform of the political system, which is considered the linchpin of all other reforms. The platform states that reform in other sectors could be preceded—and rendered possible—only by the reform of the political system per se: "Of course, there can be no guarantee for success . . . without political reform. The precedence of political reform . . . is an impartial necessity, not merely a desire, a mood, or a selective and bold assessment. It results from the nature of the incumbent regime, which dominates the political, economic, and social domain and poisons cultural and moral life. . . . It is thus impossible to reform other sectors if the political system remains unreformed." The primacy of political reform appears not only to be the lowest common denominator but also to spring from calculated conviction. The underlying rationale at least is repeated time and again, as is the way in which reform should be accomplished. The platform states that reform of the political system could ensue only gradually, via peaceful means, and within legal and constitutional frameworks. Moreover, it stresses an inclusive approach to procedural reform, calling on others to participate: "With this vision the JMP is appealing to the people, to individuals, parties, and organizations to build a better future and to establish a consensus on the necessity of these reforms. . . . [The JMP] encourages joint action so that these reforms can be perfectly realized."[8]

This procedural approach would meet with strong criticism, including on the grounds of its being "anodyne,"[9] "oversimplified and ordinary,"[10] and unable to win over the electorate—which was "much more concerned with issues that [were] directly related to basic needs such as poverty and unemployment."[11] While the latter was certainly true, the platform provides one compelling reason for the procedural approach envisaged by the JMP, that is, to avoid the complete breakdown of order. Right at the start, the platform admonishes the reader that Yemen would descend into the "abyss of collapse and breakdown" (hawiya al-fashl wa al-inhiyar) if it continued along the path taken by the regime.[12] The ensuing text is interspersed with notions of actual and imminent "chaos," "conflicts," and "clashes."[13] It stresses that such concerns were shared by external observers, too: "The warnings that are implicit in official international resolutions are a wake-up call alerting to the awful consequences [Yemen will face]."[14] Given such perils, the inclusive, procedural approach was deemed the only viable option to reform the country's political system.

One key demand repeatedly put forward is the introduction of a parliamentary system. Several justifications are given for this move, including, for instance, Yemen's historical parliamentary experience reaching back to the 1930s or the "guaranteed" end of arbitrary rule herewith. Again, the platform argues that "the installation of a parliamentary system [would be] a decisive step toward the realization of political reform," which would then "provide the framework for reform in other sectors." This demand constituted a major departure from the existing constitution, which stipulated a semipresidential system, and even more so from the de facto presidentialism under Salih. The platform proposes concrete amendments aimed at strengthening the role of the parliament and cutting back presidential prerogatives by granting parliament the sole right to form a government; strengthening the second chamber, the Consultative Council, through the election of its members (that is, not by presidential appointment); enhancing governmental accountability vis-à-vis parliament; strengthening parliament's rights to supervise public finances and state institutions; increasing parliamentary control over presidential authorities; and limiting the presidency to two successive quinquennial terms.[15]

The platform elaborates on a number of further demands such as the effective separation of powers or administrative decentralization,[16] all of which would later become points of contention between the JMP and the Salih regime in one way or the other. As will be seen in the following chapter, however, the most prominent issue continuously resurfacing in the JMP's struggle with the regime centered on reform of the electoral system. Given the alliance's procedural approach, this method was sensible. If reform of the political system was to be reached within constitutional limits, meaning via elections, reform of the electoral system in place—which the JMP considered to discriminate against the opposition—would be a natural precondition for the latter.[17] In this respect, the platform focuses on three demands. First, it calls for replacing the first-past-the-post system with a proportional representation one (*nizam al-qa'ima al-nisbi-yya*). Second, it postulates the reform of the electoral administration, and the Supreme Commission for Elections and Referendum in particular, the neutrality of which and of its local branches could be guaranteed only "by the equitable participation of [all] active and organized political forces." Pointing to the General People's Congress's misuse of public resources before, during, and after previous elections, the platform, third, calls for the strict "financial control of electoral campaigns."[18]

There are conflicting views regarding the exact imprint each member party may have left on the drafting of the platform. While this question cannot be answered conclusively, reflection on it furthers our understanding regardless of the internal logics operating within the JMP—and, indeed, within alliances in general. It has been convincingly argued that certain sections were of greater importance to some parties than to others. For instance, those sections criticizing sectarian, regional, and racial discrimination or the instigation of violence have been considered to indirectly address the Saʿda wars and, hence, to speak to Union of Popular Forces and al-Haqq constituencies.[19] Likewise, the section on administrative decentralization must have been particularly appealing to constituencies in the South. Decentralization had long been a central demand of the YSP. Scholars disagree, however, over whether the platform on the whole bears the signature of Islah or the YSP. While Stacey Philbrick Yadav posits that the platform was "crafted in response to Islah's priorities,"[20] others maintain that "much of the JMP agenda [had] been set . . . by its junior parties, and not by Islah."[21]

The source of these conflicting interpretations arguably lies in the platform's dealing with women's rights and secularism. To begin with, it leaves us in the dark about the JMP's position on Islamic law. In fact, there is no single mention of the future role of shariʿa. Yet it attests to the JMP's intention to maintain the Constitution, which accredits the shariʿa with being the unique source of legislation (Article 3). This ambiguity reveals the platform's extensive discussion of basic rights and freedoms in a different light. This point is particularly true with respect to women's rights, which are broached twice in the platform, with both passages being largely identical as well as equally ambiguous. The platform states that women shall be empowered "to exercise the rights that are warranted by the constitution and by the laws and to assume [their] positive role in public life."[22] The inherent vagueness in this phrase is replicated in the Constitution, which, on the one hand, guarantees "equal opportunities for all citizens in the fields of political, economic, social and cultural activities" (Article 24), while, on the other hand, asserting that women "have rights and duties, which are guaranteed and assigned by the shari'a and stipulated by law" (Article 31). Islah hence managed to keep the platform's treating of women's rights and secularism as vague as possible—if, indeed, there was to be any mention of them at all.[23]

This issue can be approached from different angles. If conceived of in terms of human rights or the supposed moderating effect of cross-ideological cooperation on the worldview of Islamists, the authors of the platform, and the JMP as such, performed badly. Seen from the perspective of the parties involved, and subscribing to the logic of cooperation, the JMP's handling of the matter becomes comprehensible, though. As will be discussed, it is mandatory for the parties involved in cooperation to maintain a certain degree of distinctiveness unless purposefully heading for a full merger of their parties.[24] Given that secularism and gender relations were—and still are—of key significance for the self-conception of Islah as well as the YSP or the Nasserist Unionist People's Organization, one can imagine how their representatives walked a tightrope when discussing the respective sections. While composing a joint platform did not work without compromise, too much of it would have led to the strengthening of the parties' radical fringes. The critics of cooperation within the parties could have torpedoed the alliance more easily, or they could have abandoned their parties for good, thereby weakening the JMP's overall clout vis-à-vis the regime. Either way, it would have been detrimental to the functioning of the alliance in the medium to long term. On that score, vagueness in the drafting of sensitive passages was conducive to cooperation.

The National Setup

The meaning of organizational structures for the maintenance of alliances is yet to be systematically addressed by the scholarship on opposition cooperation.[25] Indeed, only a handful of studies have dealt with the issue so far.[26] Among activists, there is even disagreement about the extent to which organizational structures foster or impede cooperation. Whereas, for instance, representatives of various Arab opposition parties have pointed to a lack of organizational structures being a factor contributing to the cessation of cooperation,[27] others have deliberately refrained from adopting them.[28] It is key in this respect to differentiate between low-level types of cooperation on a single issue and short-term basis, on the one hand, and more developed, sustained types thereof, on the other.[29] As to the latter, however, it appears that adopting organizational structures in at least some kind of basic form is imperative to keep cooperation going. Scholars of social movement research, in fact, have long stressed that "[for a] movement to survive, insurgents must be able to create a more enduring organizational structure to sustain collective action."[30]

In a similar vein, a classic strand of collective action theory argues that "hierarchy and organization are especially effective at concentrating the interactions between individuals," thus facilitating sustained cooperation. In what can be reasonably assumed to also apply to cooperating parties, organizational structures help to establish transparency about the past moves of cooperation partners, hence facilitating reciprocity; to make interactions more frequent and durable; and to "promote cooperation through the transformation of payoffs," thereby making "the longer-term incentive for mutual cooperation greater than the short-term incentive for defection."[31] In what follows it will be argued that organizational structures are vital to keeping strategic alliances alive and running. By analyzing the JMP's national setup, this section shows that they are essential to reproducing the basic conditions of cooperation if they allow for functional decision-making processes and sanctioning power—if only contingent—at the interparty level.

The Basic Bylaws, first adopted in November 2005 and encompassing a total of thirty clauses,[32] authoritatively organize the JMP's internal performance—defined here as the entirety of interactions between its constituent parties at the horizontal and vertical levels (see figure 2). They designate three main bodies to run the JMP's affairs at the national level: the High Council, the Executive Committee (al-hay'a al-tanfidhiyya), and the Secretariat (al-sikritariyya). Among these, the High Council—staffed with the secretaries-general of the member parties as well as their deputies and assistants—is the only organizational *body* that can be attributed exclusively to the horizontal (or interparty) level. It is here where fundamental decisions are taken, and it is here where those matters are discussed that ultimately lead the parties to stay within or leave the alliance respectively. The High Council is thus the top decision-making body, assigned to lead the JMP (12, 13.1), to define its direction and general policies (13.2, 13.4), and to "enact the plans and programs submitted to it by the Executive Committee" (13.3), whose operations are supervised by the High Council (13.5). The Basic Bylaws stipulate a monthly meeting (17), yet in times of heightened conflict with the Salih regime the High Council often met on a weekly—even daily—basis.

The Executive Committee—staffed by the heads of the parties' political and media sections and their deputies—is mainly tasked with implementing the High Council's decisions (19.1), as well as with preparing for the latter "visions, recommendations, and available options on various national political issues and developments" (19.2, 13.7). Besides that, it oversees joint media activities (19.3), arranges for joint election programs (19.4), and supervises the work of the Secretariat (19.6). The Executive Committee is also commissioned to "establish and monitor specific committees" (*lijan naw'iyya*; 19.5). It is hence in charge of organizing the alliance's functional division of labor at the national level. Up until 2012, numerous such specific committees were brought into being—ones both temporary and permanent. Among the latter, the Political Committee and the Media Committee were considered most relevant for the JMP's national performance. While some temporary committees—such as the National Dialogue Committee (see chapter 3)—performed tasks that were of central importance to the overall alliance, their primary function ultimately consisted of doing legwork for the Executive Committee (20). The Basic Bylaws stipulate official meetings once every fortnight (22), but in turbulent times they were held on a weekly basis.[33]

Finally, the Secretariat chiefly fulfills administrative functions such as inviting the members of the High Council and the Executive Committee to regular and extraordinary meetings (25.5) or taking the minutes of these meetings (25.1). Likewise, it is responsible for archiving the latter as well as other relevant documents and making them accessible to members of both bodies on request (25.4). Albeit hardly noticeable at first, the Secretariat therefore also plays a role in maintaining cooperation. This approach is because long-term cooperation can only be upheld if non-compliant behavior by any of the cooperating partners is sanctioned in some way or another. Yet the imposition of sanctions presupposes transparency. The Secretariat helps to establish it, for its archives contain all joint agreements, compromises, and declarations, thereby enabling the parties to disclose later infringements by one or more of the JMP's constituents.

Sanctioning defection requires, of course, more than just transparency. A mutually agreed-on set of rules is one such precondition, for it defines the act of noncompliance per se.[34] Moreover, some sort of authority is needed to implement sanctions; it is here where opposition cooperation is prone to flounder. One reason for this is that alliances can be understood as "inclusive, large groups," with them, in general, handicapping cooperation as they by their nature spur the free-riding behavior of members. In this case, cooperative action can be mobilized by dint of "selective incentives," as Mancur Olson puts it. Such incentives, however, can be provided only by groups that "have the authority and capacity to be coercive, or . . . have a source of positive inducement" they can offer to their members. Olson actually denies that (purely) political organizations have the capacity to be coercive.[35] The problem here is less that alliances cannot be proper organizations; many meet the standards of formalization indeed, such as developing formal membership criteria, introducing formal statuses and established procedures, and creating a formal leadership and office structures.[36] In other words, they often have institutionalized rules, hierarchies, and built-in authority structures—notably at the vertical (or alliance) level. The key challenge lies in enforcing the rules at the horizontal one, where authority must be contingent (see figure 2).

Horizontal/
interparty level

ability to sanction *contingent*

Vertical/
alliance level

ability to sanction *provided*

| Party | ⟷ | Party | ⟷ | Party |

Top
decision-making
body

Executive body

| Functional units | | Territorial units |

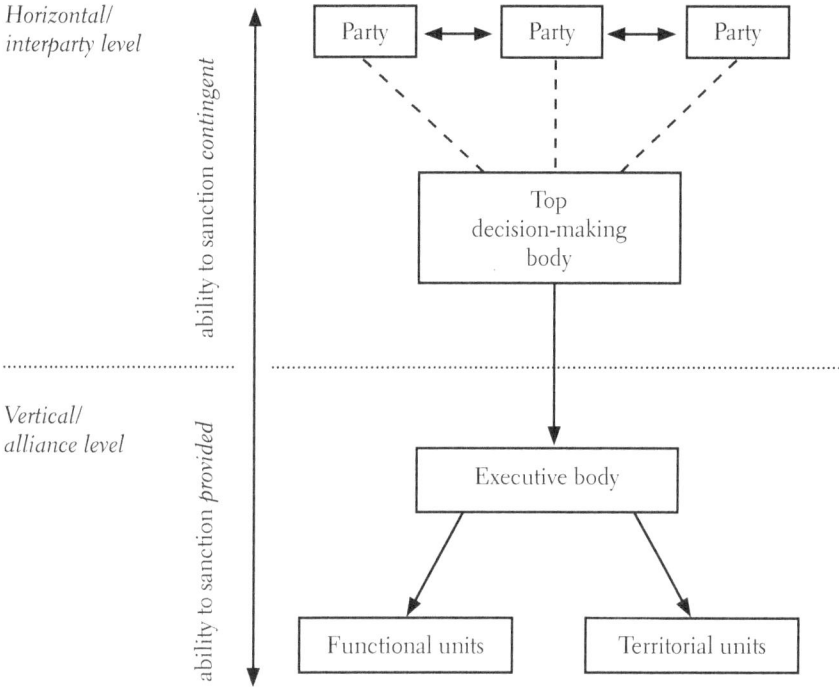

2. Contingent authority

As for the JMP, the Basic Bylaws feature a section defining the general rules of cooperation. Some of these resemble general appeals rather than strict rules, in the sense that their noncompliance hardly ran the risk of being sanctioned (5–7, 9). Other clauses were more likely to prompt sanctions in case of their breach. They enjoin constituents from entering negotiations with third parties in the name of the JMP without prior authorization (4), demand the coordination of activities during elections (8), or request members to meet their financial obligations, to attend joint meetings, and to participate in all previously agreed-on activities (10).

The body in charge of sanctioning is specified, too. It is the High Council, which makes fundamental decisions, including on the modification of bylaws (13.8, 28) or on the acceptance of new members (13.7). Seen from the horizontal level of cooperation, it could be no body other than the

High Council in charge of sanctioning defection. But its related powers were limited, and ultimately confined to the cancelation of membership. In theory, this tool is not an insignificant one. But it is disproportionate in the case of minor breaches, and never did the High Council expel a constituent prior to 2012. In the absence of an absolute authority, its sanctioning powers—like those of comparable bodies in other alliances—consisted of the capacity to withdraw the positive inducements that came with membership such as increased protection from the regime. Therefore, opposition cooperation is often a noisy business. Since the cancelation of membership is rarely a realistic option, threats and bluffs are used to discipline noncompliant behavior instead. This strategy works both ways: members can be threatened with expulsion, or they themselves can hint at withdrawal from the alliance. Whether either threat is successful depends on, first, the defector's importance to the alliance and, second, the alliance's environment—something that is beyond its control given, for instance, that the nature of the regime is ultimately what determines the costs of defection.

The following episode serves to exemplify the High Council's contingent authority. In 2008 and 2009, the conflict with the regime over electoral reform was at its height. The JMP had announced its boycotting of parliamentary elections scheduled for April 2009 unless the regime complied with its demands. But in August 2008, the conflict seemed to be on the brink of settlement. The GPC and the JMP had agreed on an amendment of the electoral law, to be passed by parliament on August 18. For it to happen, the JMP was to hand in a list of candidates for the SCER. For its part, the JMP had required the previous release of all political prisoners, most of whom stemmed from the southern governorates.[37] As such, this condition was particularly relevant for the YSP. Islah, in turn, was eager to get the amendment passed. It anticipated scoring well in the elections, and it would have been a delicate undertaking to convince those elites within the party critical of the JMP of the wisdom of missing out on this chance. To Salih, meanwhile, this constellation offered promising prospects for dividing both parties. In what in hindsight appears to have followed a hidden agenda, he ordered the prisoners' release on August 16.[38] While the YSP (along with the rest of the JMP) was waiting for it to happen—ultimately to no avail—Islah submitted a list of candidates at the eleventh hour, hence contravening the official JMP position.

The JMP had fallen into Salih's trap, now finding itself confronted with a number of different problems. For one, the GPC-dominated parliament refused to accept the list submitted by Islah, alleging that it had failed to meet the deadline.[39] Regardless of what had caused the lack of internal coordination, it put the whole alliance in an awkward position since Salih could now blame the JMP for the ensuing political stalemate vis-à-vis the Yemeni public and international donors.[40] Even worse, Salih had induced serious friction among the JMP's members. Rumors about earnest disputes were first discussed in the press on August 19.[41] Two days later, *Naba News* reported on an extraordinary JMP meeting without Islah.[42] The article was peppered with anonymous quotes from participants accusing Islah's secretary-general of conducting secret and unauthorized negotiations with the regime. It also reported that the YSP and NUPO were contemplating expelling Islah from the alliance. In short, the article suggested that the JMP was about to disintegrate. It was not to be, though. A few days later, the JMP rejected Salih's nomination of members of Islah and NUPO to the SCER and announced the escalation of its protests outside parliament.[43]

What can be learned from this? Since its formal establishment in 2005, rumors about the alliance's imminent collapse were far from an uncommon occurrence.[44] One can reasonably assume that reports about internal conflict were at times purposefully leaked to the press to discipline (potential) defectors. In the above case, the smaller JMP parties had to further pile on the pressure, excluding Islah from a de facto High Council meeting to add gravity to their threats. To be sure, the tactical considerations underlying such behavior were not openly acknowledged.[45] That aside, the Basic Bylaws did provide for the possibility of extraordinary meetings with a limited number of members.[46] Yet even if these meetings did conform with the legal requirements, they should still be considered as a quasi-sanctioning measure. In fact, only one such incident is known to the author. Such disciplinary action, however, was plainly a product of the JMP's contingent authority at the horizontal level. In this specific case, the smaller parties succeeded because Islah could not risk losing its allies at this juncture. The desired electoral reform had, after all, gotten nowhere after Salih outmaneuvered the alliance.

The episode suggests that strong mutual dependencies between co-operation partners help overcome the pitfalls emanating from the contingent-authority problem. As for the JMP, this state of affairs often meant that the YSP and the smaller parties had to work together to counterbalance Islah's dominance. Interestingly, the Basic Bylaws in themselves do not discriminate between the parties but treat them rather as equal entities. All member parties were, for instance, designated to take turns in chairing the High Council irrespective of their strength. This chairmanship was not an insignificant position, as it came along with the presidency of the JMP (16). The Basic Bylaws hence meticulously codify relevant procedures, stating that "the chairmanship of the [High] Council rotates [among the parties] for a period of six months in the alphabetical order of the JMP parties" (14) and that "in the event of the chairman's absence, the secretary-general next in line to follow the acting [chairman] shall chair all meetings for the period of his absence" (15). In addition, Clause 23 interdicts the chairmanships of the High Council and the Executive Committee being held concurrently by the same party. Evidently, these arrangements sought to facilitate the holding of similar status among the JMP's parties. They thus aimed to reproduce one core pillar of cooperation, something even more apparent regarding the JMP's decision-making structures.

The previous chapter showed that the JMP's official inception was rendered possible only once four related requirements had been met between its constituent parties: goal convergence, an expected surplus of benefits, balanced attitudes, and the ascension to power of the required committed elites. These requirements have been referred to as the basic conditions for strategic cooperation. For the latter to be maintained, then, these basic conditions must logically be reproduced, and organizational structures—particularly decision-making ones at the interparty level—are key in their continuous rebirth. This situation is so because authoritarian regimes are persistent, and rarely succumb to opposition demands alone. In the course of conflict, however, alliances may be compelled to redefine their goals or to settle on additional ones (see chapter 3). If so, decision-making structures must allow for the sound functioning of such procedures.

Likewise, cost-benefit calculations are not static. While, for instance, an alliance may still want to stick to its original goals or its ranking of them, one or more members may by unconvinced when a newly designed strategy to attain these comes along owing to an expected related increase in (internal or external) costs. Hence, decision-making structures must provide for controllable developments. If, moreover, strategic cooperation depends on balanced attitudes, decision-making structures must ensure a modicum of transparency so as to uphold trust, be capable of buffering against conflicts arising from disparate ideological preferences, and obviate dissimilarities in status. Finally, committed elites are scarcely likely to keep on prevailing within their parties' internal hierarchies if attitudes between camps deteriorate or if those individuals are frequently marginalized in the overall alliance's decision-making processes.

This all amounts to a comprehensive wish list for ideal decision-making structures. In practice, however, they are hard to come by, also because of the trade-offs between, for instance, majority and unanimity rule or equal and weighted voting systems. The JMP's modes of decision-making are a case in point here. To begin with, each party was allotted one vote in all JMP bodies (29). This rule in effect put Islah on a par with, for instance, the UPF, which had hitherto never gained a single seat in the country's parliamentary elections. From an attitudinal perspective, equal voting hence accommodated the smaller parties and probably strengthened their overall commitment to the alliance. Then again, it affected the cost-benefit calculations of the bigger parties, as one senior Islahi insinuated: "Sometimes . . . some of our members are not happy with the decisions we take. We try to ignore our size to maintain the movement [that is, the JMP]."[47] Not just the bigger parties were dissatisfied, though. Notwithstanding their disproportionately high leverage, the smaller parties, too, complained about Islah and the YSP dominating decision-making processes—for both would often coordinate their positions prior to a voting round.[48] This, state of affairs again, suggests that it is informal coordination processes within an alliance that can decisively sway its overall course.

Furthermore, the JMP formally adhered to a mixed voting system. Clause 27 of the Basic Bylaws states: "In the High Council, decisions are taken unanimously [*bi-l-tawafuq*]. In the Executive Committee, decisions are taken on a majority basis [*bi-l-aghlabiyya*] once it failed to decide unanimously." The principle of majority rule in the Executive Committee—responsible for the alliance's policy formation, after all—seems to have deprived members of the possibility of exercising control over decision-making processes in case of their being overruled. Given the High Council's sweeping control functions, however, defeated members could ultimately scrap adverse decisions if need be. This strategy had been a deliberate choice to safeguard cooperation at the horizontal level, as one of the alliance's architects would explain. "Concerning compromise, we say: unanimity rule for the High Council, majority rule for the subordinate bodies. For everything these bodies agree on will be forwarded to the High Council [for final approval]. . . . Unanimity rule . . . is a constitutive [element]."[49]

Yet the principle of unanimity rule also constituted the most obvious trade-off. One the one hand, it favored "the lowest common denominator of acceptable action" and put genuine limits on what could be achieved.[50] On the other, unanimity rule positively affected members' cost-benefit calculations, allowing them to veto decisions that were likely to increase their parties' internal costs vis-à-vis cooperation. In addition, it was often effective in regulating or preventing internal conflict.[51] However detrimental the principle of unanimity rule may have been to the JMP's external performance, it was in tune nonetheless with the necessity of reproducing the basic conditions of cooperation.

Besides, it is important to acknowledge that the JMP's decision-making structures did not foreclose the possibility of formally dealing with contentious issues. But for the alliance to cover as controversial a matter as its relationship with, for instance, Ansar Allah, the majority of members would need to be emphatic on its treatment and hazard the possible consequence of the JMP's ultimate disintegration. Reaching agreement on such sensitive issues between party elites would be particularly time-consuming, being facilitated by regularly held informal gatherings such as qat chews.[52] However, the greatest challenge would then be to attain acceptance of the agreement within the parties per se and to limit the damage done to the alliance's internal coherence. Challenges of that sort will be addressed in the following two sections.

The Local and Regional Setup

The previous section has suggested that organizational structures are indispensable to maintaining strategic alliances since they are instrumental in reproducing the basic conditions for cooperation. However, they serve yet another key purpose in that they facilitate—and, arguably, it is only they that render possible—mobilization processes both within the alliance as well as with regard to external actors (see figure 3). While the latter will be dealt with in subsequent chapters, the following two sections home in on the JMP's internal mobilization capabilities.

Mobilization is here understood as "the process by which a unit gains significantly in control of assets it previously did not control,"[53] and it is commonly believed that taking control over assets (or resources) and translating them into action "requires some minimal form of organization."[54] How efficiently resources can be mobilized by a unit, then, critically depends on the quality of its organizational structures and on the composition of the unit itself. In view of opposition alliances, it is thus expedient to recall that the relevant unit is, technically speaking, an assembly of preexistent, organizationally independent units. On these grounds, it is assumed here that an alliance's internal mobilization capabilities hinge on the extent to which its organizational structures at the vertical level allow for, first, the internal redistribution of resources and, second, the production of internal coherence (more below).

To grasp the interrelationship between internal mobilization and resource redistribution, for a start it is reasonable to assume that the basic amount of resources available to an alliance correlates with the share thereof every constituent party is willing to apportion to it—provided the nature of resources even allows for their assignment. That is, unlike property assets, labor, time, or expertise, resources such as the organizational

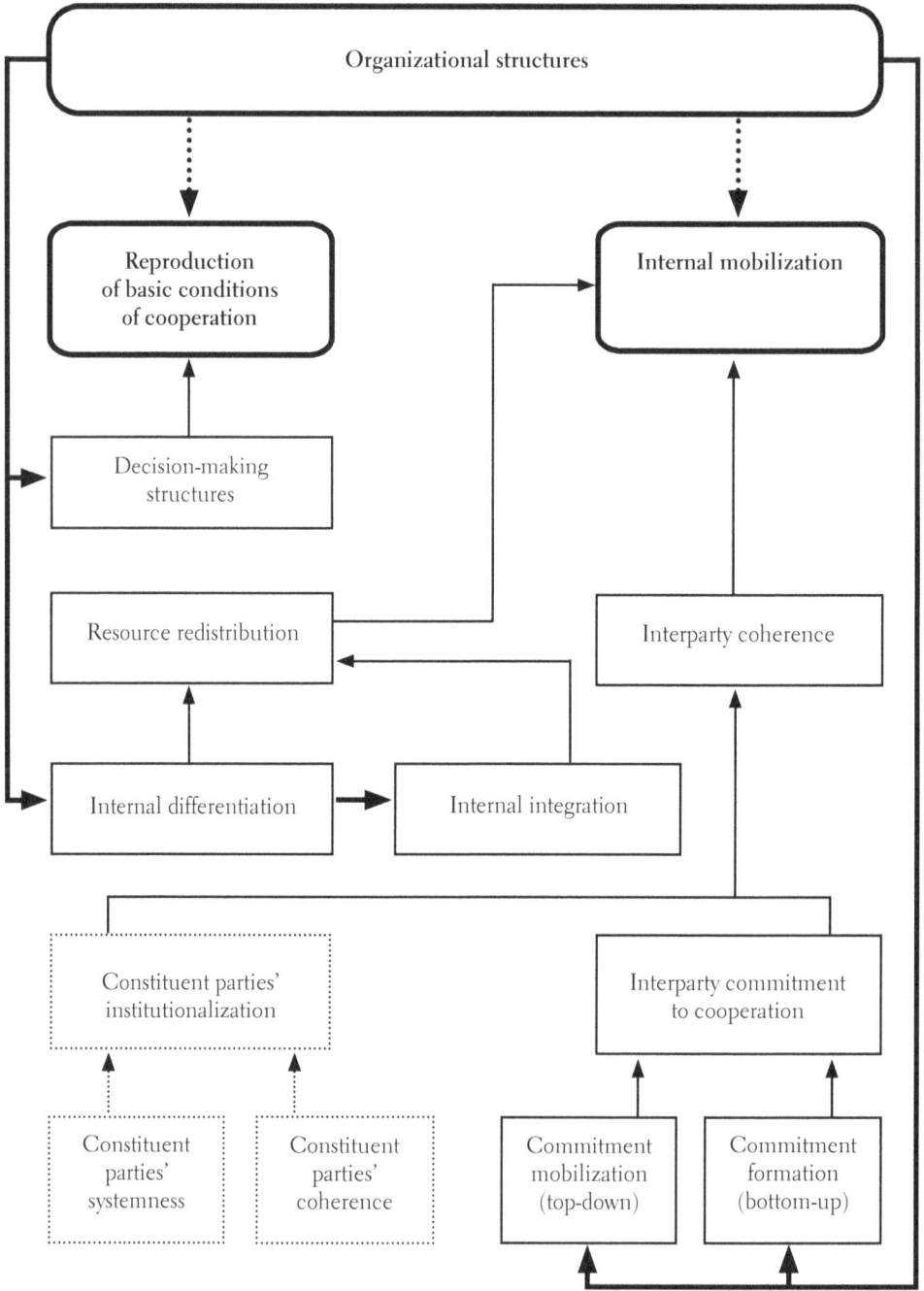

3. Determinants of strategic alliances' internal performance

infrastructure adopted by a constituent party—let alone the legitimacy it enjoys among the populace—cannot be easily transferred to the alliance. Yet even if the nature of resources principally warrants their transferal, constituent parties would usually shy away from placing them at the alliance's disposal unless they can expect an increase in effectiveness regarding resource deployment on the part of the latter. For that to happen, the resources provided to it must be internally redistributed and adapted to the newly established overarching entity.

There are two fundamental parameters useful in assessing the extent to which the internal redistribution of resources has been accomplished: First, one can explore the internal differentiation of an alliance, which concerns "the functional division of labor (task-structure) and the territorial decentralization (territorial subunits)."[55] In other words, the division of labor can be deemed functional if it is responsive to the alliance's task structure, which is mainly defined by the number and nature of its goals. It thus follows that there is an inherent upper limit to the number of functional units, whose expedience and usefulness can be assessed as the (empirical) case arises. In contrast, territorial units can—and should—grow in number. Indeed, the higher their number and the more evenly they are spread over the whole country, the more conducive it is to the alliance's well-being. This is because widespread collective action presupposes a decentralized mobilizing infrastructure that extends beyond the national level to include the regional (for example, the governorates) and local (for example, the districts) ones, too. Also, grievances often differ from region to region, and territorial units are well positioned to not only detect regional or local hardships and complaints but also develop local solutions that can be passed on to the pivotal bodies at the national, interparty level in requesting appropriate action.

These examples illustrate the need for connective elements facilitating coordination between the territorial and functional units of an alliance as well as its hierarchical structuration. The second parameter suggested to analyze the level of internal resource redistribution, meanwhile, hence concerns its degree of integration: that is, "the integration of the differentiated functional and territorial units," which is "achieved by horizontal coordinating mechanisms, and by centralization of decisions."[56] Put differently, the territorial and functional units must not act as isolated entities. If internal mobilization processes are to be effective, some sort of co-ordination between the differentiated units is in order. Exploring how this is implemented on the ground is, again, an empirical matter. Yet active channels of communication should allow for top-down and bottom-up exchange and enable coordination between the territorial and functional units. Moreover, to function as an organized whole, there must be an operative chain of command permeating the entire organizational skeleton of the alliance. This fact does not prevent the differentiated units from operating discretely, in principle. However, for the alliance to be competitive, it is imperative that the units act in concert whenever the top decision-making body mobilizes to a specific end.

So much for the pure theory of internal resource redistribution. But how did these considerations translate into the actual setup of the JMP? As an alliance that set out to reform Yemen's political system, it could not confine its operations to parliament but was often forced to take to the streets, too. Reviewing the previous section through the lens of the JMP's efforts at internal differentiation, one can assert that the two main functional units at the national, alliance level are the Executive Committee and the Secretariat that, in the broadest sense, support the High Council—meaning the top decision-making body at the interparty level. Further bodies at the national, alliance level include, for instance, the Political Committee or the National Dialogue Committee, making them functional units performing issue-specific tasks and ones that, as per internal provisions, are not directly concerned with maintaining the basis of cooperation. What is of interest here, then, is the JMP's setup at the local and regional levels, although it would only be partially correct to refer to these as territorial units. In fact, as was accentuated by senior members, it had been the shared aim of the party leaderships to replicate the JMP's central organizational structures at the regional level.[57] At first glance, the Regional Bylaws seem to validate these statements. But what do they tell us exactly?

The Regional Bylaws, made up of a total of nineteen clauses, closely resemble the composition of the Basic Bylaws.[58] The first section establishes essential requirements and designations. The following three sections then define the rights and duties of the three main bodies at the governorate (or regional) level: the Executive Council (al-lajna al-tanfidhiyya; 7–11), the Technical Office for Electoral Coordination (al-maktab al-fanni li-l-tansiq al-intikhabi; 12–15), and the Secretariat (16–17). Hereafter, Clause 18 regulates the JMP's organizational composition within the governorates (*al-takwinat al-far'iyya*)—that is, at the district (or local) level. The concluding four clauses (19–22) define general provisions. One can thus directly spot the Regional Bylaws' striking similarity to the Basic Bylaws in the organization of contents and division of sections. Indeed, some clauses appear to have been taken over verbatim from the latter, such as the ones defining the provisions for the Secretariats (16–17), regulating the Executive Councils' leadership functions (8–11), or stipulating voting equality (21). In other words, they are notably regulations addressing the attitudinal component of cooperation.

Notwithstanding some aberrations in terms of labeling, the JMP's national setup thus seems to have been largely replicated at the governorate level. In theory, one could find a tripartite arrangement of organizational bodies tasked to run the JMP's affairs in all twenty-one governorates.[59] Yet some reservations are merited. Not only are there substantial discrepancies as to the significance of the various governorates in demographic—and hence political—terms, but there are also major differences concerning the parties' strength in the governorates (not to mention the districts), begging questions as to how the smaller parties such as UPF or al-Haqq were actually capable of contributing to the JMP's activities in some governorates—particularly the southern ones. Also, a special note must be made of the Executive Councils destined to "lead the JMP in the governorate[s]" (7.1). The Regional Bylaws commission them to coordinate the actions of the JMP branches in the governorates (7.2), to design regional policies (7.3), and to supervise the regional secretariats (7.13). They are authorized to build and instruct subsidiary branches at the regional and district levels (7.11) and to form and control region-specific committees (7.12). They are furthermore obliged to coordinate regional media activities (7.8), to harmonize the actions of the JMP branches with regional and local nongovernmental organizations (7.10), and to "form and oversee a special committee for the coordination of joint gender activit[ies]" (7.9). Last, they are required to develop criteria for compiling lists of JMP candidates for the local council and parliamentary elections (7.5) as well as to actually do so (7.6).

Two conclusions can be drawn. First, while the Executive Councils were key to running the JMP's affairs in the governorates, their duties and prerogatives indicate that they were in fact designed as replicas of the national-level Executive Committee—and, as such, as some kind of hybrid combination of a functional and territorial unit. Importantly, the High Council remained the top decision-making body whose competencies reached far beyond the national level. This fact can be seen, for instance, in Clause 7.3 that calls on the Executive Councils to formulate policies "within the scope of the general political direction provided by the High Council." Second, the preparation and management of the local council and parliamentary elections are specified as one of the most significant spheres of action for the Executive Councils, as the Regional Bylaws make painstakingly clear. The composition of electoral lists falls into their domain (see above)—which is a thorny issue, as one can imagine. In addition, the Regional Bylaws authorize them to control the Technical Offices for Electoral Coordination (7.4; hereafter Technical Offices) and to establish new branches at the district level in the run-up to elections (18).

Both the initial Regional Bylaws of 2005 and the revised version of 2007 place great emphasis on the issue of electoral coordination in the regions. This importance is hardly surprising given the JMP's goal of reforming the political system from within, which inevitably requires scoring well in elections. While the bylaws do allow for various fields of action, electoral coordination must therefore be said to take center stage in view of the JMP's task structure. The responsibilities assigned to the Technical Offices are proof of this. They are enjoined to "support the [Executive] Council[s] in all matters connected to the electoral coordination between JMP members in the governorate[s]" (12). Clause 14.1–8 itemizes the kind of support the Technical Offices are to provide by developing concrete plans on how to technically facilitate electoral coordination; gathering, and commenting on, the topics to be raised during electoral campaigns;

monitoring joint activities in the electoral districts and consulting local NGOs about ways to guarantee fair and free elections; and forming and administering legal committees charged with prosecuting ballot rigging and pleading the JMP's case in court. All these activities are overseen and authorized by the Executive Councils, which must obtain approval from the High Council in turn.

The question that suggests itself when reading the bylaws is how the provisions were put into practice, and where. While the JMP swiftly managed to establish branches in all of the country's governorates post-2005, it is challenging to obtain reasonably robust data for its presence at the district level. After all, the Regional Bylaws compel the Executive Councils to found branches in the districts—that is, in both the administrative and the electoral districts—and to "define their tasks and responsibilities in accordance with local peculiarities" (18). Since the Republic of Yemen was divided into 333 administrative (*mudayriyya*) and 5,620 electoral (*da'ira mahalliyya intikhabiyya*) districts, however, it is feasible only to infer cautious guesses from past instances of nationwide JMP mobilizing campaigns. One example that lends itself to approximating the JMP's local clout is to be found in the context of the parliamentary elections planned for April 2009. To force the GPC back into negotiating electoral reform, the JMP called for a national boycott of the related voter-registration process scheduled to begin on November 18, 2008.

That day, the alliance mobilized massive demonstrations and sit-ins in front of registration offices across the country, especially in Dhammar, Hajja, al-Hudayda, Ibb, al-Mahwit, Ma'rib, Sanaa, and Ta'izz.[60] The boycott was also effectively implemented in the southern governorates. The latter offer a particularly revealing case insofar as, in 2007, the former territories of the People's Democratic Republic of Yemen had witnessed the rise of the Southern Movement, whose member organizations at that time were still undecided about the extent to which they could act in collusion with the JMP in opposing the Salih regime. The coverage of the Aden-based daily *al-Ayyam* of November 19, 2008, provides an illustrative picture of how the boycott unfolded. Altogether the newspaper featured twelve articles on the matter, with detailed reports on developments in

Abyan, al-Baydha, Lahij, and Shabwa.[61] Roughly half of the articles gave account of boycotts solely orchestrated by the JMP, while the remaining ones are suggestive of joint—if not coordinated—action between the JMP and local groups, including some affiliated with the Southern Movement. The boycott was sweeping and in some districts close to comprehensive. In al-Mahfad and Sirar, both in Abyan Governorate, it was reported, for instance, that seventeen and eighteen (both out of eighteenth) registration offices were incapacitated.[62] A few days after, the nationwide voter-registration process was officially suspended.

This incidence illustrates that by the end of 2008, the JMP had managed to build a broad network of regional and local branches fit to be mobilized for joint action across the country. It is also insightful in terms of the JMP's degree of integration. In early November of that year, the High Council had ordered the regional branches to prepare for the boycott; it was subsequently punctually and effectively implemented in the governorates and districts.[63] Such top-down instructions were also stipulated in the Regional Bylaws, with Clause 7.16 instructing the Executive Councils to "execute whatever tasks and operations the High Council and the Executive Committee commissions them to." These endeavors were frequently reported on in the press.[64] So, the JMP featured an active chain of command guaranteeing a centralization of decision-making at the alliance level.

Likewise, there were established mechanisms promoting coordination between its regional and local branches too, as well as between the latter and the JMP's national bodies. The alliance's annual conferences, which could be likened to the convention of a federal party, provided at least one such occasion per year for the JMP's national, regional, and local elites to physically meet and exchange information and ideas. More important, the provisions of both the Basic and the Regional Bylaws disclose a sophisticated organizational setup supporting an institutionalized flow of information between units, further to well-defined responsibilities, necessary procedural methods, and mutual dependencies. What remains controversial, however, is if, and when yes to what extent, the JMP's regional and local branches were able to operate discretely and how well they were positioned to engage in bottom-up exchange and consequently impact the decision-making of both the Executive Committee and the High Council alike.[65]

Generally, the Regional Bylaws state that the Executive Councils are free "to decide on various local (*mahalli*) issues." Since the meaning of this clause (7.7) to the overall performance of the alliance may not be immediately obvious, it is instructive to explore the regional and local branches' handling of the Southern Movement, which had been hovering between calls for outright independence and greater autonomy for the former PDRY territories since its emergence in May 2007. For reasons that will be detailed later, its rise mainly encroached on the interests of the YSP and Islah. While the YSP was vying with the Southern Movement for influence among its grassroots base, Islah—which also had strong constituencies in the South—not only dismissed the Southern Movement's core claims but also found itself regularly targeted by it for supposedly being the embodiment of northern backwardness. The YSP had thus been pushing for addressing southern grievances even more closely since May 2007, whereas Islah's stance on the matter was lukewarm—although the latter's own southern branches had long since warned the party leadership about the dangers of ignoring the southern case.[66]

The JMP's regional branches in the South, on the other hand, understood the seriousness of local grievances and the Southern Movement's popularity from the outset. In contrast to the High Council, the southern Executive Councils publicly—and in the name of the JMP—condemned assaults by security forces on the Southern Movement's activists,[67] paid visits to those detained,[68] demanded their immediate release,[69] and solidarized with the Southern Movement[70]—that is, long before the High Council could bring itself to do so.[71] Such examples reveal a considerable degree of discretion on the part of the regional branches, and they also suggest some sort of a vanguard role assumed by them in cases where the High Council had not yet taken a firm stance.

Things became more complex when the Executive Councils' position was openly inconsistent with that of the High Council. In such instances, their autonomy could be restricted. The Regional Bylaws grant the High Council the right to veto any decisions they took in breach of its directives (22). Still, there were numerous examples of the Executive Councils either overtly or covertly deviating from the course officially set by the High Council without any sanctioning on the part of the latter.[72] It appears that the High Council usually forbore interfering with the Executive Councils—so long as their actions did not compromise the member parties' interaction at the national, interparty level. The following examples may show that such considerations were indeed paramount in defining the High Council's stance toward the regional branches.

One of the main mechanisms built into the Basic Bylaws to ensure the reproduction of the basis of cooperation was, as noted, unanimity rule. To anticipate conflicts between constituent parties in the governorates, including their repercussions at the national level, unanimity rule was also codified in the initial Regional Bylaws. But in the revised 2007 version, the corresponding Clause 19 was eventually amended to allow for majority decisions in the Executive Councils after several regional branches had complained heavily about the impracticability of unanimity rule. While this example is also indicative of the leverage the Executive Councils could bear over the High Council, it is important to understand that the amendment did not undermine the latter's fundamental capacity to weigh in on the former's decisions when likely to cause friction at the national, interparty level. Clause 22 upholds the High Council's right to ultimately scrap such decisions. How seriously the latter took the potential reverberations of regional ruptures also emerges from reports about electoral coordination in the governorates. In several instances, the High Council intervened in the compiling of electoral lists, forcing the Executive Councils to replace promising candidates of one member party with less stellar ones from another to maintain equilibrium at the national, interparty level.[73]

In sum, the JMP's regional branches possessed a considerable degree of discretion, adding to the strong performance of the alliance in the governorates. This power, however, was curtailed as soon as regional developments threatened to jeopardize the basis of cooperation at the national, interparty level. In such cases, either the High Council would take corrective action against the Executive Councils, or the national party leaderships would intervene in the affairs of their regional branches. This takes us to the issue of internal coherence.

More than the Sum of Its Part(ie)s?

The bearing of coherence on effective opposition operation requires little elucidation. "The quality of forming a unified whole"[74] is commonly seen as a quintessential condition of opposition mobilization and even treated as ranking among the definitional requirements for opposition action.[75] It has been maintained earlier, too, that the internal coherence of an alliance, in addition to its related redistribution of resources, represents a second prerequisite for effective internal mobilization. The JMP, however, was often said to be lacking in this regard. Instead, it was portrayed as "a relatively loose coalition of opposition parties"[76] or as a "deeply fragmented"[77] alliance capable of operating smoothly "in a low-stress environment" but facing disintegration "as soon as [that] stress increased."[78] Such appraisals are far from astonishing given the number of controversial issues in play. The fault lines reported to be running between the constituent parties resulted from ideological discrepancies over issues such as secularism, women's rights, and the Saʻda wars,[79] but also from disagreements that could not easily be identified with their respective ideological stances such as Yemen's federal structure, political pluralism, and even electoral reform per se.[80] With regional cleavages putting additional pressure on its internal coherence,[81] the JMP struck many Yemenis and non-Yemenis alike as mainly a coalition of elites whose cordial but utilitarian ties hardly affected the parties' rank and file.[82] But still, as outlined previously, the JMP had proved its ability to mobilize its grassroots base on several occasions. It is thus worthwhile taking a closer look at the key matter of coherence.

If one takes for granted that alliances are assemblies of preexisting, organizationally independent units, two dimensions of coherence can be discerned that, despite being interconnected and potentially adding up to a comprehensive overall picture, should be kept analytically distinct. First, it is worthwhile to turn to constituents themselves, for an alliance is unlikely to act in a coherent manner if it consists of parties inherently incapable of acting as discrete units. The first dimension thus highlights the constituent units' degree of party institutionalization and treats the internal coherence of an alliance as consisting in the aggregated values of institutionalization on the part of its constituent units—which, as argued earlier, are bound together and more or less effectively managed via the alliance's organizational setup. The second dimension, in turn, focuses on the degree to which members of the constituent parties feel committed to the overarching entity, meaning the alliance, and thus asks whether the latter is more than the sum of its parts. While both dimensions will be elaborated on, it can be assumed that a high degree of institutionalization on the part of the constituent parties and a high degree of commitment to cooperation on that of their members bears positively on the alliance's mobilization capabilities, and vice versa.

Let us begin with a brief discussion of the first dimension, which rests on the following reasoning: To establish a modicum of coherence at the vertical, alliance level, constituent parties must pull together and implement the decisions made at the horizontal, interparty one. Accordingly, committed central elites in each party must see to these decisions being implemented in and by their own camps. The degree of their party's institutionalization, classically defined as "the process by which organizations and procedures acquire value and stability,"[83] informs us about the likelihood of this outcome happening. While the literature on party institutionalization is vast, two indicators are particularly salient regarding cooperation: systemness and (intraparty) coherence.[84] Systemness refers to "the increasing scope, density and regularity of the interactions that constitute the party as a structure," and it is important to note that "regularity . . . implies a degree of routinization, and the development of prevalent conventions guiding behavior."[85] Systemness thus inquires into the availability of mechanisms and rules governing, among other things, a party's decision-making procedures, internal elections, or conflict-resolution mechanisms—and, significantly, the degree to which these conventions are deemed authoritative and binding.

Put differently, the existence of peripheral factions critical of or hostile to cooperation is less problematic if they abide by the decisions made by the party leadership regardless. Yet while peripheral elites squarely opposing cooperation may temporarily fall in line and abstain from obstructing cooperation from within, they are prone to undermine cooperation in the medium to long run unless committed elites manage to win them over. If committed elites fail to do so, peripheral elites can be expected to sabotage cooperation or abandon the field altogether (more below). In any case, one can assume that the degree of (intra)party coherence interacts with that of intra- and interparty conflict. Several indicators for intraparty coherence are discussed in the literature, including the performance of the parliamentary group, the level of moderation characterizing relations between antagonistic factions, and the degree of tolerance vis-à-vis intra-party dissidence.[86] Often, though, the cases under scrutiny can yield more salient indicators helping to determine party coherence. Concerning the JMP constituents, for instance, ideological discrepancies and regional identities loomed large, at times backed up by the social backgrounds of faction elites.

For manifest reasons, party coherence was less of an issue for the smaller JMP parties—that is, the Syrian-oriented Ba'th, al-Haqq, NUPO, and UPF. These parties were too small to allow for the existence of significant, discrete factions. Even if they had had antagonistic factions, leaving the JMP would have scarcely been an option unless they had been prepared to resign themselves to political insignificance or being co-opted by the regime—as had happened with the Iraqi-oriented Ba'th in 2006. Parties such as al-Haqq or UPF were conscious of their powerlessness,[87] and they appreciated that the JMP enabled them to disproportionally sway Yemeni politics, albeit as part of an *opposition* alliance.[88] Regarding Islah and the YSP, the situation was profoundly different. Both featured a number of antagonistic factions, some of which seriously disapproved of cross-ide-ological cooperation. Yet while Islah's committed elites struggled with these factions until after the fall of Salih, the YSP leadership saw most of its peripheral elites abandon the party from 2005 onward (which is why Islah will be the main focus in this section). Developments in both cases had considerable ramifications for the two parties and the JMP. Questions pertaining to the YSP's and Islah's coherence, as well as the strategies their hostile factions embarked on to undermine cooperation, will hence be dealt with more thoroughly in the next section. Suffice to recall here that the existence of antagonistic factions in itself does not pose a challenge to cooperation, provided that an adequate degree of collective discipline exists within the alliance's constituent parties. This point brings us back to the issue of systemness.

One should consider most JMP constituents to be rather hierarchical organizations with a limited degree of internal democracy.[89] Only to a lesser extent does this statement relate to formal decision-making procedures within the parties' internal bodies or the conducting of ballots during their annual congresses, which were reported to meet democratic standards. Yet what was deemed increasingly problematic, especially by the parties' younger generations, was the lack of change in party leaderships[90] and the absence of a democratic culture that would have allowed for—or even helped foster—dissenting positions within the parties.[91] The latter point is worth commenting on for two reasons. First, intraparty dissent is often indulged to ultimately help reduce tensions and to strengthen interparty coherence in the medium to long term overall.[92] From this perspective, the party leaderships' continuing to suppress deviant positions constituted a repeated missed opportunity. Second, one must differentiate between the parties' rank and file and their peripheral elites. Even in cases of public dissent, the latter were treated leniently and barely had to face any disciplinary measures, because they were both too powerful and too important for the overall performance of the parties and, somewhat paradoxically, for the JMP as well (see chapter 4).

Concerning their grassroots members, however, the JMP parties were much less indulgent, usually insisting on strict obedience of leadership directives. Islah is a case in point here, with internal and external critics blaming Islahi elites—regardless of their belonging to the tribal, Salafi, or Muslim Brotherhood wings—of promoting a culture of "silence and compliance" (*al-samt wa al-taʿa*).[93] But such handling of internal dissent seems to have been more widespread inside the JMP, as the following comment of a high-ranking member suggests. Whenever the party leaderships noticed clashes among grassroots members, they would meet and "study the problem. . . . And they solve[d] it together. If we . . . found that our members were not right in their reaction to a certain issue, we told them so. And we express[ed] our apologies [to the other parties]."[94] Knocking grassroots followers into line was thus a common practice among the

JMP's parties. While such measures enabled the alliance to act in unison as the occasion demanded, the parties' systemness, and level of institutionalization at large, was but one dimension assumed to account for the JMP's overall coherence. The second was the degree to which members of the JMP's parties felt committed to the alliance.

A brief discussion of the term *commitment* and its implications in the context of alliance politics is in order at this point. To begin with, the notion of "collective identity" will be purposefully eschewed—notwithstanding its partial overlapping with commitment or the state of being obligated or emotionally impelled to support a given cause.[95] This is because the social construction of collective identity works by dint of differentiation, namely, by distinguishing between the in-group and its out-groups; it is here where alliances face serious challenges. First, their constituent units, meaning political parties, bring their own collective identity—with it having been built, potentially over a protracted period of time, by repeatedly stressing their being (ideologically, programmatically, morally) different from other parties, including their current cooperation partners. Second, for the sake of distinctiveness, the parties must keep on doing so to a certain extent even while in the process of cooperating. This situation is an impractical starting point from which to build an overarching collective identity. It is nevertheless expedient to incorporate key findings of collective identity approaches since they, too, explore how individuals and groups engage in processes of "'constructing' an action system."[96] That is, regardless of whether one speaks of collective identity, "imagined solidarities,"[97] the "capacity to act by drawing on a set of macroscopic normative bonds,"[98] or commitment: for an alliance to sustain coherent collective action in the medium to long run, it must comprise a critical number of members capable of identifying themselves with, or committing themselves to, the overarching entity to such a degree that collective action comes to acquire positive meaning. Commitment may not be a prerequisite here. But it considerably increases an alliance's capacity to act coherently and is at times treated as a resource in and of itself.[99]

The question, then, is how commitment to an alliance can be produced, and reproduced, in the case of constituent parties whose members' sense of political self was often formed in opposition to their current partners. One should first stress here that collective action is not the result of uniform actors working toward a common goal, given the mere fact that social actors are never homogenous. Rather, as Asef Bayat holds, "groups' interest may converge in some domains but diverge and contradict in others"—which is why interests and values can only be "partially shared," particularly regarding "deliberate coalition building." He therefore refutes the notion of "collective identity," maintaining instead that "the diverse participants tend to converge on the generalities, but are left to *imagine* the specifics, to envision commonalities." On that basis, an "imagined solidarity" emerges that is forged among different actors "who come to consensus by imagining, subjectively constructing, common interests and shared values between themselves." Such "imagining by the different fragments," he continues, "is by no means carried out in a homogeneous fashion." Rather, "fragmented actors . . . render imagined solidarity . . . a negotiated entity."[100] While Bayat fails to elaborate on how the process of imagining unfolds exactly, one can infer that it involves continuous negotiations between participating actors. This conclusion is supported by collective identity approaches, which state that actors must "contribute to the formation of a 'we' . . . [by] laboriously adjusting three orders of orientations: those relating to the end of actions; those relating to the means . . . ; and finally those relating to relationships to the environment."[101]

It stands to reason that commitment building, too, requires continuous internal negotiations, although it is still unclear how the latter are to occur so as to facilitate the desired outcome—and, indeed, at which exact levels. Here, it might be useful to draw on what Amitai Etzioni has suggested with respect to consensus building between diverse actors. He posits that consensus—like collective identity or commitment—"is not found but must be produced" and assumes that consensus building encompasses both upward and downward processes, with "consensus-formation" referring to the upward ones ("from member-unit to controlling layer") and "consensus-mobilization" to their downward counterparts.[102] In a similar vein, one can suppose that commitment building comprises both upward (that is, commitment-formation) and downward (that is, commitment-mobilization) processes. Likewise, one can presume that successful commitment building must focus on those factors that are most divisive, particularly concerning instances of cross-ideological cooperation—in other words, the attitudinal components of cooperation.

In this regard, the literature on ideological moderation sheds light on what must be incorporated in processes of both commitment mobilization and commitment formation. As to the former, it has been argued that party elites seeking to establish new practices—such as cooperation with ideological adversaries—must do so in terms of the party's central tenets. If party elites have hitherto repudiated another party on ideological grounds, they must recast their related reasoning and gradually redraw "the boundaries of acceptable practices" so as to include cooperation with the party in question.[103] However, "decisions on contentious issues that are put forth by small factions whose opinions do not represent the views of the group overall are unlikely to constrain what is justifiable to the group in the future." What is needed instead to effectively redraw the boundaries of justifiable action is room for inclusive debate and deliberation among both constituents and within the alliance per se.[104] For the purpose of commitment formation, then, it is again important that an alliance's organizational setup facilitates frequent interaction between members beyond the level of party elites, offering space for the exchange of views, the finding of common ground, and the establishment of mutual trust.[105]

What, then, did the JMP's efforts at commitment building concretely look like, and what can be said about grassroots members' commitment to the alliance? Although one can observe various instances of JMP elites concertedly touring the governorates to assure their congregated grassroots followers of a common position,[106] commitment mobilization was mostly confined to the party level. Here, it took various forms and, as regards ideological reshaping, worked in different directions. First, commitment mobilization encompassed instances of party elites deliberately withholding from grassroots members potential clashes between JMP policies and their original ideology.[107] Second, party elites also regularly attempted to offer ideological justifications as a way to convince their grassroots followers of the appropriateness and legitimacy of cooperation, including doing so across party boundaries.[108] Yet especially committed Islahi elites faced serious challenges here. As the following section will show, those elites holding the greatest authority in ideological matters within Islah, namely, the 'ulama', were highly critical of cross-ideological cooperation. Yet even though they frequently thwarted various High Council decisions, they ultimately refrained from publicly revoking the ideological justification for Islah's participation in the JMP. One could thus find highly conservative Islahi 'ulama' condoning cooperation on the grounds of their party's Islamic values being congruent with support for social justice, freedom, democracy, and the rule of law.[109] However, as the party's committed elites could not count on the support of the 'ulama', seeing them instead as a potential source of irritation, it became customary to corroborate the High Council's decisions by letting the Shura Council—dominated by the party's committed elites (that is, the Brotherhood)—approve of those decisions retroactively.[110]

Notwithstanding such challenges in terms of the commitment mobilization of a key constituent, the overall changes in the parties' ideological narratives were remarkable when compared to what they had been during the JMP's formative years. This conclusion can also be drawn in view of commitment formation. As outlined, the JMP's parties themselves provided little room for earnest deliberation and debate before decisions were taken by the respective party leaderships. At the vertical, alliance level, however, the situation shaped up differently. As highlighted in the previous section, the JMP's organizational structures at the governorate and district levels facilitated frequent interaction between regional and local elites, allowing for the exchange of views and the discussion of dissenting positions—if these did not endanger the parties' equilibrium at the horizontal level.

Still, for want of reliable survey data, it is virtually impossible to assess the degree of actual commitment to the alliance among grassroots members. One can assume, though, that it was not evenly distributed among the alliance's regional branches. Strained relations between the parties' grassroots followers were reported in Aden, Ibb, and Ta'izz.[111] Then again, the JMP's branches in Aden and Ta'izz had gone on to become the most active ones during the last years of Salih's rule.[112] It hence appears that, while grassroots members' commitment to the JMP continued to vary from governorate to governorate owing to regional peculiarities, commitment formation had gained momentum in the course of overall cooperation. Regular interactions, instances of mutual assistance,[113] and an emerging history of shared successes and setbacks assumedly had a positive bearing on the party members' commitment to the alliance. After all, by the time the so-called Arab Spring came around in Yemen, a decade of shared history had accumulated during which both party elites and grassroots members alike had weathered multiple critical situations.

The 2011 uprising is a splendid if rare example of how such critical junctures may impact commitment formation. This observation is particularly true of the JMP party youths, who, because of their exclusion from the constituent parties' main organs, had only had coincidental contact with the representatives of other JMP parties ahead of the uprising. Hence, their stance on the alliance was restraint and the image of their peers, from whom they had kept aloof, ill-conceived. Reportedly, relations improved substantially during the uprising.[114] A member of the Yemeni Socialist Youth Union (ittihad al-shabab al-ishtiraki al-yamani), for instance, recalled that "eventually, we got to know each other. We ate together, drank together, slept side by side. Initially, we considered each other as savages. [That changed] after we got to know each other."[115] A member of the Islah's Revolutionary Youth (majlis shabab al-thawra), seconded the latter assessment, holding that relations between the JMP's party youths warmed in this period and that their cooperation ran increasingly smoothly—at least concerning "youth elites."[116]

This supplementary distinction between the party youths and the party youth elites serves as a reminder that only cautious inferences can be made about grassroots followers' commitment to the JMP, on the one hand, and to its internal coherence, on the other. Despite the refusal to engage in cross-ideological cooperation by parts of the constituent parties' grassroots bases, however, one should acknowledge the alliance's notable record of mobilization up until 2011, conceding the case for a certain—albeit not exhaustive—degree of internal coherence. The sheer endurance of cooperation can be seen as supporting this claim. This point is even more true because the JMP had withstood a series of attempts by the Salih regime to undermine cooperation, the most promising of which were intended to divide the JMP along its inherent fault lines. To this end, the regime frequently banked on the parties' peripheral elites doing its bidding here.

Renegades and Saboteurs

Compared to its beginnings, the JMP's internal coherence would increase considerably in the process of cooperation. However, coherence building also had its limits, and arguably turned sluggish at some point in time. One key reason was the peripheral elites within the alliance's constituent parties who had never brought themselves to accept cooperation. To re-state one argument put forth in the previous chapter, strategic cooperation can come to fruition only after committed elites have managed to take the helm in their parties' top decision-making bodies. In other words, for cooperation to occur, those elites dismissive of it must be marginalized within key party organs. Following their intraparty defeat, peripheral elites have three basic options: First, they can resign from the party. Second, they can acquiesce to adverse conditions, follow the trail blazed by new party leadership, wait for the next opportunity to regain their former posi-tion, and attempt to steer the party's course anew. Third, they can remain with their party and attempt to thwart cooperation by undermining com-mitted elites' position within it and by delegitimizing the alliance in the eyes of grassroots followers.

As for the JMP, all member parties encompassed elites who were criti-cal of participation in the alliance. However, only in the case of Islah and the YSP did they head party factions powerful enough to seriously endanger the position of the committed elites and, by implication, the ex-istence of the alliance itself. These two parties' peripheral elites engaged in a combination of the previously mentioned options. On balance, how-ever, the YSP's peripheral elites tended to abandon the party, while Islah's peripheral elites chose to foil cooperation from within. Analyzing their selected moves thus sheds additional insight on the internal state of the JMP. Because the corresponding intra- and interparty conflicts were to some extent reflective of Yemen's ideological, regional, and social cleav-ages per se, this section can also be seen as preparing the ground for the subsequent turning of attention in due course to the JMP's capacity to mobilize external support.

As outlined in the previous chapter, the YSP had been affected by protracted intraparty conflict long before the official founding of the JMP. The party began to truly engage in alliance building only following its fourth general party congress in 1998 and 2000, respectively, which initiated a programmatic shift toward social democracy and political pluralism as well as major changes in the party's leadership. Former protagonists of its old guard such as 'Ali Salim al-Baydh, Haydar Abu Bakr al-'Attas, Hasan Ba'um, and others were either exiled or swept out of the party's top decision-making bodies, while the reformers around Jarallah 'Umar al-Kuhali and Sayf Sa'il gained the upper hand. There were isolated incidences of the old guard plotting against the reformers' engagement in cross-ideological alliance building in the aftermath of the party congress. Yet these were negligible in number and did not have the potential to imperil nascent cooperation. Until November 2005, when the JMP took on institutionalized form (and even several months later), it remained ambiguous whether cooperation would prove successful. The old guard may thus have believed that the latter would peter out anyway. After the 2006 presidential elections, however, they must have awoken to the fact that the JMP had become a serious platform for cooperation between their party and Islah—something they disapproved of not only in its own right but also on the grounds of its long-term potential to further weaken their position within the party's power structures regarding the reformers (much in the same way as cooperation weakened the tribal and Salafi wings' position vis-à-vis the Brotherhood inside Islah). Therefore, there was more than a temporal coincidence between the consolidation of the JMP as signaled by the 2006 presidential elections and the rise of the Southern Movement.

The latter emerged in May 2007 when the Supreme Coordinating Council for Southern Military Retirees (majlis al-tansiq al-a'la li-jam'iyya al-mutaqa'idin al-'askariyin al-janubiyin)—headed by Nasir 'Ali al-Nuba, a YSP Politburo member and retired brigadier—began to stage sit-ins in demand of higher pensions for all concerned. Given widespread grievances in the southern provinces, these sit-ins soon incited protests in large parts of the territories of the former PDRY that quickly evolved into a full-fledged social movement calling for "equal access to government jobs, services, and benefits; political and economic decentralization; establishment of the rule of law; and, finally, improved stewardship of the national economy, and particularly natural resources such as oil."[117] Instead of addressing these demands politically, the regime resorted to quelling the protests by means of the army and security apparatus. With the number of the Southern Movement's martyrs continuing to increase because of ongoing regime repression, its claims became more radical—with it gradually turning into a secessionist movement from 2009 onward.[118] Returning to an independent southern state was not a coherent demand until about 2011, though. One reason was the lack of a unified social movement organization (SMO). While the number of SMOs claiming to represent the Southern Movement had been steadily rising since its inception,[119] one striking similarity between them was that most were run by, or pledged loyalty to, members of the YSP's old guard.

This is not to say that the consolidation of the JMP directly led to the emergence of the Southern Movement. Grievances in the South abounded, indeed. But they could scarcely be ascribed to a coalition of parties that, except for al-Haqq, had been in opposition for more than a decade—unless the Southern Movement's elites were to frame the sources of the southern malaise accordingly. The JMP was, in fact, portrayed as part of the problem, and those individuals who were mainly in charge of offering such portrayals ranked among YSP peripheral elites who had become alienated on the grounds of the party's cooperation with Islah.[120] Besides their key contribution to the Southern Movement's framing processes, the YSP's peripheral elites further added to its gaining of a strong foothold in the South by bringing in vital resources such as their professional experience, established routines, and personal networks. Also, the Southern Movement often operated out of YSP offices and headquarters in many southern governorates.[121]

Bit by bit, it became apparent that the YSP had become a party divided. Soon after it transpired that the Southern Movement had turned into a viable political force, many peripheral elites resigned their YSP membership. Ahmad 'Abdallah al-Majidi, a member of its Central Committee, was one of the first to leave the party to campaign for southern independence, doing so in December 2007.[122] His membership had already been earlier suspended because he had refused to toe the party line when deciding to run for the presidency in the 2006 elections—that is, as a rival to JMP candidate Faysal bin Shamlan. Al-Majidi had also been at odds with most Central Committee members over the issue of cooperation with Islah.[123]

While only a handful of YSP elites followed al-Majidi's lead, the party suffered a more serious blow with the resignation of Salah al-Shanfara in October 2009. The latter was a prominent socialist member of parliament who had subscribed to the southern cause and founded the Movement of the Southern Peaceful Struggle (haraka al-nidhal al-silmi al-janubi). What made al-Shanfara's resignation particularly sensitive to the YSP was that it had been prompted by an order issued by former PDRY president al-Baydh, who had publicly demanded the South's secession in May 2009.[124] Al-Baydh had previously become involved with the Council of the Leadership of the Peaceful Revolution (majlis qiyada al-thawra al-silmiyya), a self-proclaimed umbrella organization for the Southern Movement; it was not universally accepted by all movement organizations, though. It was thus owing to power struggles inside the Southern Movement that still only a limited number of YSP peripheral elites followed al-Baydh's order. At that time, it had become clear that there was not only a "northern and southern Socialist party,"[125] namely, the YSP and the Southern Movement, respectively, but also that the latter itself was divided. [126] In January 2010, then, another influential umbrella organization, the Council of the Peaceful Movement to Liberate the South (majlis al-hirak al-silmi li-tahrir al-janub), emerged that enjoined its members to resign from the YSP shortly after its formation.[127] The first prominent ones to do so were the council's head, Ba'um; his son Fadi; and Ghalib al-Shu'aybi, paving the way for others to follow.[128] 'Ali Haytham al-Gharib, a former YSP Politburo member, explained the council's position as follows: "We refuse to allow the Socialist Party to interfere in the movements [sic]. It only tears us apart and creates disputes among us. You are either a member of the movement or of the party."[129]

Although the ties between the YSP and the Southern Movement were never completely dissolved, the latter gradually turned into a new political home for the bulk of the YSP's peripheral elites—most of whom had clearly dissociated themselves from the party prior to 2011. By the end of 2009, the dividing line between the YSP's leadership and the Southern Movement's major entrepreneurs had become the future status of the South, with the former opting for a federal solution over secession—as called for, conversely, by most of the Southern Movement's SMOs.[130] Cooperation with Islah had ceased to be a straightforward issue. However Islah, the JMP, and, by implication, the YSP kept being framed as the epitome of northern arbitrary rule; as part of an "occupying regime" (*nizam al-ihtilal*). The notion of the JMP being "the second sight of the regime in Sanaa," as propagated by former YSP elites, began to haunt both the alliance and the YSP.[131] Paradoxically, such accusations were usually substantiated by way of reference to high-ranking Islahis such as Hamid al-Ahmar or 'Abd al-Majid al-Zindani, representing Islah's tribal and Salafi wings, respectively[132]—namely, those factions that considered the JMP an opportunistic tool or as something to be opposed.

In a nutshell, the marginalization of the old guard was instrumental in fostering cross-ideological cooperation. But it came at a price. For the YSP, the rise of the Southern Movement resulted in an immense loss of strength in its former southern strongholds. For the JMP, the Southern Movement's emergence was accompanied by an increase in interparty conflict given the YSP was now less prepared to compromise on issues relevant to its southern constituencies. Also, it considerably constrained the alliance's mobilization power in the South. As will be seen in subsequent chapters, the JMP never managed to cooperate or join forces with the vast majority of the Southern Movement's SMOs when it came to taking on the Salih regime.

There is yet another aspect worth mentioning here. Rifts like the ones seen within the YSP provided an opportunity to disunite both the party and the alliance from the outside. The regime used a set of diverse strategies to weaken the opposition accordingly. Once the more subtle ones had proven ineffective (for example, "cloning") or impossible to maintain because of faltering resources (for example, the patronage system), the regime resorted to less sophisticated means—including administrative and legal measures,[133] defamatory statements,[134] threats,[135] and, indeed, outright repression.[136] Likewise, divide-and-rule strategies counted among Salih's standard repertoire in handling domestic adversaries. Attempts at driving a wedge between Islah's antagonistic factions were numerous (see later discussion and chapter 1) and, for a number of reasons, more common compared to those the other parties would be exposed to.

Yet the YSP, too, had to endure its share of enmity. Salih's pardoning of some two dozen exiled YSP elites in 2000 and 2003, respectively, most of whom were from the old guard, was presumably intended to undermine the strengthened position of reformers within that party—and hence the nascent cooperation between it and Islah. Although the returning exiles added to the degree of estrangement experienced between the YSP's antagonistic factions, Salih eventually failed to confound alliance building. In the case of one exile, Salih in fact assisted the latter—even if unintentionally so. Returning in 2003, former PDRY prime minister Yasin Sa'id Nu'man was appointed YSP secretary-general two years later. Instead of thwarting cooperation, however, Nu'man quickly became one of its most convinced, and convincing, advocates—"the only remaining YSP leader who seem[ed] to have the potential to appeal to all sides in the JMP." That said, Nu'man was declared an infidel by a group of students associated with al-Zindani shortly after his return.[137] Al-Zindani can in effect be considered the leading representative of Islah's peripheral elites, and the Salafi wing he headed surely constituted the one group inside Islah most assiduously working to hamstring cross-ideological cooperation. It was also Islah's Salafis—alongside the tribal wing—whom Salih most frequently attempted to manipulate to split the alliance.

In simplified terms, Islah encompassed, as detailed in chapter 1, a Salafi and a tribal wing as well as the Brotherhood. The latter formed the party's nucleus in terms of both ideology and origination. Compared to its beginnings in Yemen, the Brotherhood had undergone significant changes by the time cooperation took hold in the country in the mid-1990s. In terms of the religious, political, and social worldviews of most of its members, it had since become a relatively moderate force. Notably, it was the Brotherhood that had bred most of Islah's committed elites. On its establishment in 1970, however, the Brotherhood was far from moderate. Back then, it was led by Yasin 'Abd al-'Aziz al-Qubati and al-Zindani, both of whom would later be recognized as exalted 'ulama' inside and outside Islah. Often translated as "religious scholars," the term *'ulama'* (singular: *'alim*) denotes a loose categorization for a group of men specialized in religious and juridical functions, including scholars, jurists, preachers, and teachers. Contrary to the bulk of the literature on Islamism, which usually offers a clear-cut dichotomy between 'ulama', on the one hand, and lay Islamist activists and parties, on the other,[138] Islah featured a considerable number of the former in key positions—including the High Committee and the Shura Council, meaning Islah's highest governing and decision-making bodies, respectively.[139]

Except for some moderates such as Muhammad 'Ali al-'Ajlan, the longtime Shura Council chair, most Islahi 'ulama' could be characterized as Salafis in view of their literalistic approach to Islamic authoritative sources and their insistence on allegedly pure Islamic morals and legitimate political behavior. Hence, their positions regularly clashed with the Brotherhood's more progressive stances, particularly regarding women's rights, the Zaydiyya, or socialism. Consequently, many Islahi 'ulama' accepted the JMP on tactical grounds alone, while a critical mass was overtly or covertly working toward its abolition. Had they not been internally marginalized in the early years of the new millennium, the JMP would never have seen the light of day. Echoing events within the YSP, however, Islah's internal conflicts did not come to an end in 2005 but were aggravated herewith, in fact. As in the intra-YSP controversy over cooperation, ideological and attitudinal issues played a major role in the standoff between the 'ulama' and the Brotherhood. Yet what made the position of Islah's 'ulama' even more intransigent was that forfeiting their intraparty monopoly over interpretation concerning rightful moral conduct and legitimate political action also put at risk their religious and legal standing within the country's political system—not to mention their overall position in Yemeni society.[140] In the grip of the gradual shift of power toward the Brotherhood, Islah's 'ulama' upheld the claim of leading their lay party fellows.[141] However, after they had been dealt another defeat by the Brotherhood during Islah's 2007 party congress, rumors about the pending creation of a Salafi party headed by al-Zindani first popped up in the press.[142] Islah, it would be argued later, had become a party dominated by the Brotherhood, which was unwilling to approve of the authority of the 'ulama', a party led by politicians who had abandoned the core objective of introducing an Islamic state.[143]

Such a Salafi party was not ultimately founded until September 2012. But two months after their intraparty defeat in 2007, Islah's Salafi 'ulama' banded together with their peers outside the party and, in November of that year, created the Association of Yemeni 'Ulama' (hay'a 'ulama' al-yaman; AYU).[144] Corresponding to its main constituents—meaning Islah's 'ulama' as well as the two Salafi associations al-Hikma (jam'iyya al-hikma al-yamaniyya al-khayriyya) and al-Ihsan (jam'iyya al-ihsan al-khayriyya)—the AYU was headed by al-Zindani, while his deputies were from al-Hikma (Ahmad al-Mu'allim) and al-Ihsan (Muhammad b. Musa al-'Amiri). In the following years, Islahi 'ulama' would use the AYU to sabotage the JMP and help regain their position within the party. To this end, they also co-operated with the latter's tribal wing and the Salih regime, as evidenced by the creation of the—ultimately short-lived—Committee for Command-ing Right and Forbidding Wrong (hay'a al-amr bi-l-ma'ruf wa al-nahi 'an al-munkar).

Founded in the summer of 2008 under the aegis of the 'ulama' of Islah, al-Hikma, and al-Ihsan,[145] the so-dubbed Virtue Committee was modeled on the homonymous Saudi committee and formally designed to reinstate public morals—although political analysts suspected that the committee would not "be confined to treating the moral maladies of the *umma* but would involve the political, economic, educational sector, and so forth."[146] Officially, and seemingly innocuously, the Virtue Committee aimed to "activate the role of the 'ulama' and those campaigning for the distribution of the noble message in protecting the doctrine and the values of our Muslim Yemeni people."[147] In practical terms it meant that it was to assist the state in enforcing shari'a law, while its 'ulama' were to cooperate with the general state prosecutor.[148] In a joint statement, the JMP—includ-ing Islah that, as a party committed to the proselytizing of Islam (*da'wa*), had some difficulties in publicly dismissing the Virtue Committee—de-cidedly objected to the latter;[149] many within the alliance anticipated that it would be a means of their direct repression.[150] As a matter of fact, one *'alim* of al-Hikma had publicly insinuated that the Virtue Committee would become a tool in the hands of Islahi 'ulama' to be used against opponents.[151] However intended, it must have been clear to Islah's 'ulama' that its inception would incite open conflict within the JMP. Also, it can reasonably be assumed that the Salih regime initially supported the Virtue Committee on that account, with its distancing itself from the latter only once much mischief had already been done.[152] The damage inflicted on the JMP did not so much—if at all—concern its elites;[153] the Virtue Committee was too obvious an attempt by the 'ulama' to shipwreck Islah's cooperation with the "infidel" parties. At the grassroots level, though, the committee revealed deep fissures and induced open conflict in some of the country's governorates.[154]

The Virtue Committee, which ceased to exist a matter of weeks after its official establishment,[155] was also supported by high-ranking representatives of Islah's tribal wing, most notably Sadiq and Husayn al-Ahmar.[156] While the tribal wing shared much of the social conservatism propagated by the Virtue Committee, it did not, however, intend to harm the JMP per se. The interests of Islah's tribal representatives were more concrete. The founding of the Virtue Committee coincided with the fifth Sa'da war (March–July 2008), during which Ansar Allah was threatening to advance on al-Khamri village, the ancestral seat of the al-Ahmar family. Rallying with the Salafis, who had proved their preparedness to fight Ansar Allah in the past, was thus well calculated in that the closing statement of the committee's founding conference called on all Yemenis to join the tribal militia under Husayn al-Ahmar to contain Ansar Allah.[157] In doing so, Islah's Salafi and tribal wings again contradicted the official position of the JMP, including the Brotherhood, which at that time sought to settle the Sa'da conflict within the framework of a National Dialogue Conference, as the next chapter will show. For reasons that will be elaborated, the tribal wing cast its lot behind the JMP thereafter. But Islah's Salafi 'ulama' continued to challenge the Brotherhood in subsequent years and did not even shy away from excommunicating party fellows from the latter to this end.[158]

Some conclusions can be drawn from the above. Owing to strong intraparty resistance to cooperation, committed elites in Islah and the YSP had to be wary of their peripheral peers. This fact surely limited the scope for compromises to be struck within the framework of the JMP, and the peripheral elites' actions definitively hampered the process of commitment building inside the alliance. Most of the YSP's peripheral elites eventually abandoned the party. This clearly weakened it, the more so as they did not stop criticizing the YSP even after their resignation from it—even stepping up their criticism, indeed, to help bolster the legitimacy of the Southern Movement. Taking disciplinary measures against them was potentially counterproductive—and impossible in the case of those individuals who had resigned from the party already. Islah's leadership, in turn, could have done so but ultimately forwent this possibility. Later events, particularly those during the 2011 uprising, suggest that none of the other JMP parties had a keen interest in confronting Islah's Salafis. The 'ulama' might have been a constant source of irritation, but it was ultimately a predictable and seemingly controllable one. Why, then, expel al-Zindani and the like given they were individuals who not only had many followers among Islah's members but were also able to attract supporters in great numbers beyond just the JMP parties' grassroots bases? These considerations and others connected to the issue of external mobilization will be dealt with in the following chapter.

Conclusion

This chapter discussed the internal logic of opposition cooperation in an authoritarian setting. It proposed a set of tasks to be performed by involved entities to consolidate and upgrade such cooperation. Among them, the building of organizational structures is of eminent importance for multi-issue, strategic alliances such as the JMP. It is so for two reasons. First, organizational structures enable the involved entities to reproduce the basic conditions for cooperation, provided they are designed in such a way as to facilitate functional decision-making processes and provide some sort of sanctioning power—which must remain inherently contingent, however. This proposition relates to the interparty (or horizontal) level of cooperation. Second, and addressing the vertical (or alliance) level, organizational structures sway its (internal) mobilization capabilities. On the one hand, mobilization processes can be optimized if an alliance's internal setup allows for the efficient redistribution of resources—that is, if the alliance manages to establish differentiated *and* integrated units. On the other, the mobilization capabilities of an alliance critically correlate with its degree of internal coherence, which is, in turn, defined by both the degree of institutionalization on the part of its constituent parties and by the degree of commitment to the alliance on that of their grassroots members. Whereas party institutionalization homes in on the involved entities themselves, commitment building—and particularly commitment formation—is also a function of the organizational structures of an alliance, one that has proved especially difficult in the case of the JMP.

The analysis of its platform showed that the JMP was a multi-issue alliance pursuing three core objectives: good governance, state building, and the reform of Yemen's political system—including, most notably, electoral reform. In view of the task structure inferred from these objectives, the JMP can be characterized as a functional alliance, including on the grounds of its mobilization capabilities and organizational resilience. With the High Council, the Executive Committee, and the Secretariat, its architects managed to build bodies fit to govern joint action at the national level and, of no lesser importance, to reproduce the basic conditions for cooperation at the horizontal one, too. Given the strong mutual dependencies between the JMP parties, the contingent-authority problem was considerably alleviated herewith. Besides the Executive Committee and the Secretariat, the JMP established a variety of functional units at the vertical level and, partially overlapping with these, a comprehensive network of territorial units in the governorates and districts.

These functional and territorial units were well connected to one another. A centralized chain of command facilitated effective top-down mobilization, while the alliance's regional and local branches were allowed to retain a relatively high degree of autonomy—albeit subject to the condition that their actions did not compromise the JMP parties' relationship at the horizontal level. Although questions pertaining to the degree of actual commitment among grassroots party members cannot be conclusively answered, it can be assumed that it did increase appreciably over time. Moreover, wanting commitment was partially compensated for via the disciplinary measures taken by the party leaderships against grassroots dissent. In any case, various instances of successful mobilization between

2005 and 2011 suggest a sizable degree of overall coherence at the alliance level, notwithstanding the disruptive actions of peripheral elites.

Finally, the discussion of Islah's 'ulama' and the YSP's old guard showcased how these peripheral elites can impinge on cross-ideological alliances. These two examples, however, are also reflective of a basic phenomenon within (cross-ideological) cooperation. Despite their engagement therein, the parties must maintain a certain degree of distinctiveness all the same—not only regarding their organizational setup but also in terms of their ideological orientation. This state of affairs was one compelling reason that, for instance, Islah's central, committed elites refrained from taking distinct measures against the Salafi 'ulama'. Another was the expected accompanying loss in mobilization power. The conduct of Islah's Salafi 'ulama' undoubtedly led to the alliance losing much favor among party members and supporters of the Ba'th, al-Haqq, NUPO, the UPF, and the YSP. Yet given the strength of Islah's Salafi wing, including with respect to its potential to mobilize considerable segments of the Yemeni population, its leaving Islah would have caused an even greater loss of strength for the JMP. It is here where the internal logic of cooperation potentially conflicts with its external counterpart. In other words, a consolidated alliance operating smoothly internally is ultimately of little value if it is incapable of realizing its goals—and hence validating its raison d'être—in the foreseeable future. This outcome can only be brought about by challenging the regime. The following two chapters will thus now turn to the JMP's external performance.

3

Broadening Cooperation

Reaching Out to New Allies

Toward the end of May 2011, Yemen's Peaceful Youth Revolution (thawra al-shabab al-silmiyya) had long ceased to be so. The weeks following the Friday of Dignity (jum'a al-karama) on March 18, when dozens of protesters were killed by snipers in Sanaa, had witnessed military skirmishes of varying intensity all over the country, prompting the Gulf Cooperation Council to mediate between the warring parties. After 'Ali 'Abdallah Salih had refused to sign another GCC-brokered deal on May 22, massive fighting broke out between government forces and those groups loyal to Sadiq al-Ahmar, the head of the Hashid tribal confederation, putting at risk the lives of thousands of civilians in the capital. Yemen was thus close to being plunged into a full-fledged civil war when 'Abd al-Rahman Bafadhl (Islah) entered the Al Jazeera newsroom on May 29. Bafadhl's statements did not, however, center on the looming war. His central message was, rather, that the Joint Meeting Parties would be prepared to sign an antiterrorism agreement with the United States and the European Union "for one year minimum that can be renewed so that they can be sure . . . that we are with them against terrorism."[1]

It was little wonder that Bafadhl focused on the security concerns of Washington and Brussels who, despite the GCC's leading role in settling the 2011 crisis, were key external players in Yemen—most notably the United States. Nor were these concerns unfounded. Since the onset of the uprising, al-Qaeda in the Arabian Peninsula (AQAP) had attempted to exploit the emerging security vacuum, with it seizing control of Zinjibar, the capital of Abyan Governorate, on May 27. It was therefore only sensible for the JMP to reassure Western governments the security situation would not deteriorate further after Salih's ouster and that the JMP would be a reliable partner in the fight against AQAP.[2] But that the JMP felt compelled to do so via Al Jazeera suggests that communication channels between the alliance and Western capitals were provisional and its priorities were fundamentally different from those of the United States and the European Union.

It is not that the JMP had failed to make advances to Western governments previously. High-ranking members of the alliance had, indeed, reiterated time and again that they had no issue with cooperating with external actors,[3] and Muhammad 'Abd al-Malik al-Mutawakkil once nonchalantly conceded that "the Yemeni opposition [was] compelled to seek external support given . . . the impossibility of effective resistance without resources."[4] In fact, the JMP had sought to make the international community part of its strategy to take on the Salih regime.[5] Nor is it that the JMP's attempts at establishing ties beyond Yemen's borders had failed completely. There were sporadic meetings between representatives of the JMP and Western embassies and governments, not to mention the external support it received beyond just at the state level.[6] What constituted a serious problem for the JMP—and a major impediment to Yemen's further democratization for that matter—was, rather, that Western governments had come to see the Salih regime as the sole guarantor of stability over the course of the first decade of the new millennium.

These turbulent years would be characterized by rapid economic decline, the faltering of political processes, and a precipitous surge in popular grievances and regional conflict. The first Saʻda war was conducted in 2004. It was followed by further campaigns against Ansar Allah, with the sixth Saʻda war ending in February 2010. In 2007, violence erupted in the southern governorates when the Southern Movement emerged and subsequently met with a heavy-handed military response from the regime. The turmoil in the South swiftly evolved into a substantial threat to Yemen's overall territorial integrity. Abroad, however, greater heed was paid to al-Qaeda's reemergence in the country in 2006. Three years later, its Yemeni and Saudi branches would merge into AQAP, which significantly stepped up its operations in and beyond the Arabian Peninsula and ascended to become "the most active and dangerous affiliate of al-Qaʿida today."[7] Fearing that Yemen would turn into a safe haven for terrorist groups, Western governments boosted aid to the Salih regime—including substantial military and security assistance from the United States.[8] In doing so, they headed down a one-way street—even if unwittingly so. Doubts were growing about the likely end of Salih's rule, however, while Western donors became increasingly outspoken about their frustration with the regime— which would show appreciation for their aid but not their counsel on how to stabilize Yemen. But for all that, the suspension of payments was no longer deemed possible beyond a certain point in time as it would have led to "societal collapse," as one European diplomat put it. "Since the Yemeni government is aware of this, there are only limited options available to exert pressure toward the implementation of reforms."[9]

The implications for the JMP were twofold. First, since its formal establishment in 2005, the alliance had had to deal with a regime that was facing steadily shrinking popular support, on the one hand, but could rely on external backing to remain afloat, on the other. This is not to say that the regime would have imploded outright if external assistance dried up. But the support it received from abroad certainly had its role to play in keeping the regime from fraying at the edges, thereby contributing to keeping its relations of power and domination largely intact until the Friday of Dignity massacre on March 18, 2011. Second, the situation acutely affected the JMP's external performance. The regime's waning legitimacy and the abundance of national and regional conflicts—in part purposefully precipitated to sustain "a tenuous but enduring political order" and secure the flow of external assistance[10]—added authority to the demands of the alliance and provided an opportunity to appeal to new constituencies and to other persons hostile to the regime alike. Simultaneously, however, the soaring level of conflict nationwide gravely limited the JMP's latitude. Incremental disorder and the prospects of pending state failure set narrow boundaries to what its major protagonists deemed justifiably confrontational action, while simultaneously making a mockery of the alliance's procedural approach in the eyes of many Yemenis.

What follows addresses, then, the JMP's external performance, as taken up further in chapter 4 as well. It will discuss how the JMP set about broadening the opposition front, including with respect to its framing processes and modes of (external) mobilization, as well as examine more fundamental aspects underlying the external performance of alliances—notably the centrality of goal attainment. In addition, it will feature a discussion of what will be called the "ride-sharer problem" of cooperation that, albeit not necessarily present in every alliance, can be considered a pertinent phenomenon here. As in preceding chapters, the theoretical assumptions arrived at are embedded in the discussion of empirical events, which largely unfold in chronological order—stretching up until July 2010, when the JMP managed to seemingly wrest major concessions from the regime. Proceedings begin where chapter 1 left off, namely, with the presidential elections of September 2006.

The Centrality of Electoral Reform

The nearing 2006 presidential and local council elections had been a stimulus for the nascent alliance to expedite the drafting of a common platform and the building of organizational structures. Contrary to expectations, these tasks had been duly mastered by November 2005, providing the JMP ample time to canvass for its joint candidate, Faysal bin Shamlan. Its performance in the elections on September 20, 2006, however, showed room for improvement. In the presidential ballot, Salih won 77.2 percent of the vote and clearly outpaced Bin Shamlan, who merely received 21.8 percent thereof. The returns in the local council elections were worse again, yielding a landslide victory for the General People's Congress—which won 85 percent of governorate-level seats and 76 percent of district-level ones.[11]

The reasons for the JMP's sobering performance were at least twofold. First, it had stood in its own light. It had failed to mobilize the grassroots base in the run-up to the local council elections and had suffered from poor coordination and sporadic animosity between its constituent parties at the regional and local levels.[12] Then again, according to spokesman Muhammad al-Sabri, the JMP had deliberately disregarded the local council elections to focus its efforts instead on the presidential ones.[13] Whether this statement was retroactive whitewashing of the local council elections' returns is up for discussion. Yet what certainly added to Bin Shamlan's defeat in the presidential elections was the public lending of support to Salih by the heads of Islah's tribal and Salafi wings, 'Abdallah al-Ahmar and 'Abd al-Majid al-Zindani, respectively.[14] Second, the JMP complained of electoral fraud. It was partially supported in this assertion by the European Union Election Observation Mission (EU EOM) that, while eschewing the term *fraud*, pointed to serious irregularities and "a series of fundamental and systemic weaknesses within Yemen's political and administrative structures that undermined the democratic nature of key aspects of the electoral process."[15]

It was not just this external support that made the JMP broach the issue of electoral reform anew in the wake of the 2006 elections. The overhaul of the electoral system was a cornerstone of the JMP's procedural approach to reforming the political system—not to mention a crucial pillar of cooperation itself. The JMP had accepted the 2006 election results only because it feared doing otherwise would endanger the preagreed negotiations on electoral reform stipulated by the June Agreement.[16] What is easily overlooked in hindsight is that circumstances did appear promising and that the JMP had "never been better situated to focus calls for reform around the window of opportunity" granted to it in the aftermath of the 2006 elections.[17] These prospects for success were meaningful. The JMP's founding period had been wearisome for all parties involved, and committed elites had come under constant attack from their peripheral counterparts throughout these years. Settling on a joint candidate for the 2006 presidential elections had shaped up to be an equally challenging process, one during which the alliance was often on the verge of falling apart altogether.[18] Facing long odds in reaching one of the JMP's constitutive goals at that point in time would have been detrimental to—and probably a death knell for—continued cooperation.

This conclusion captures a fundamental—if manifest—function of the external performance of an alliance, here understood as the entirety of its actions directed toward nonmembers. It is the prospect of success, meaning goal attainment, that brings *and* keeps parties together. While the internal performance of an alliance may contribute its share hereto—with, for instance, its organizational structures boosting its internal mobilization capabilities—it is ultimately the external performance of an alliance that facilitates goal attainment. Therefore, such an entity will persist only if participating actors expect that its external performance contributes to goal attainment in the foreseeable future. It would not be altogether incorrect to replace *contribute* with *cause* in this assumption when strictly adopting an actor-centered perspective. Yet it is logically compelling, and empirically sound, to opt for the former, and there is little reason to believe that most real-world oppositionists are unaware of the inherent limits to their actions.

Why is it so? The simple answer is it takes two to tango. It is at least as much the actions of the regime as it is those of the alliance determining whether the latter achieves its objectives. The more complex answer, meanwhile, points to strategic reasoning and broadens the scope vis-à-vis the (f)actors typically influencing the outcome witnessed, namely, goal attainment or failure. To begin with a classical definition, "the *strategy* of opposition consists of the means it chooses to obtain . . . goals,"[19] and it can be inferred from this meaning that the difference in nature between the strategy of an alliance and its external performance is one between intention and actual implementation. Game theorists would add that the term *strategy* focuses on "the interdependence of the adversaries' decisions and on their expectations about each other's behavior,"[20] while seminal works on political opposition highlight the structural factors such as "system characteristics" affecting the strategic choices of the opposition regarding, for instance, which site or mode of engagement to pick in confronting the regime.[21] Again, it is helpful to consult social movement theory here. The latter holds that, before making a move, actors assess political opportunity structures along the following four dimensions: the degree of openness of the political system, the stability of elite alignments within the regime, the existence of elite allies, and the state's capacity and inclination for repression.[22]

In a nutshell, the choice of strategy can be controlled by an alliance, and those individuals in charge of steering its course will include assessment of the given structural features as well as the position of key actors both inside and outside the regime in their related decision-making. But the external performance of an alliance is the result of strategy meeting reality. This reality, in turn, is also—and critically—shaped by forces whose actions are ultimately beyond the control of the alliance, and it rarely produces quick, positive outcomes. Committed elites, who might have spent years already on launching cooperation, can be assumed to be conscious of the fact that goal attainment under authoritarianism is a marathon, not a sprint. Yet they must be convinced—and must, too, persuade others inside their parties—that the alliance can meaningfully contribute to goal attainment in the not too distant future. Failing this outcome, and all else held equal, the costs of cooperation will outweigh its benefits; cooperation must herewith run aground (see figure 4).

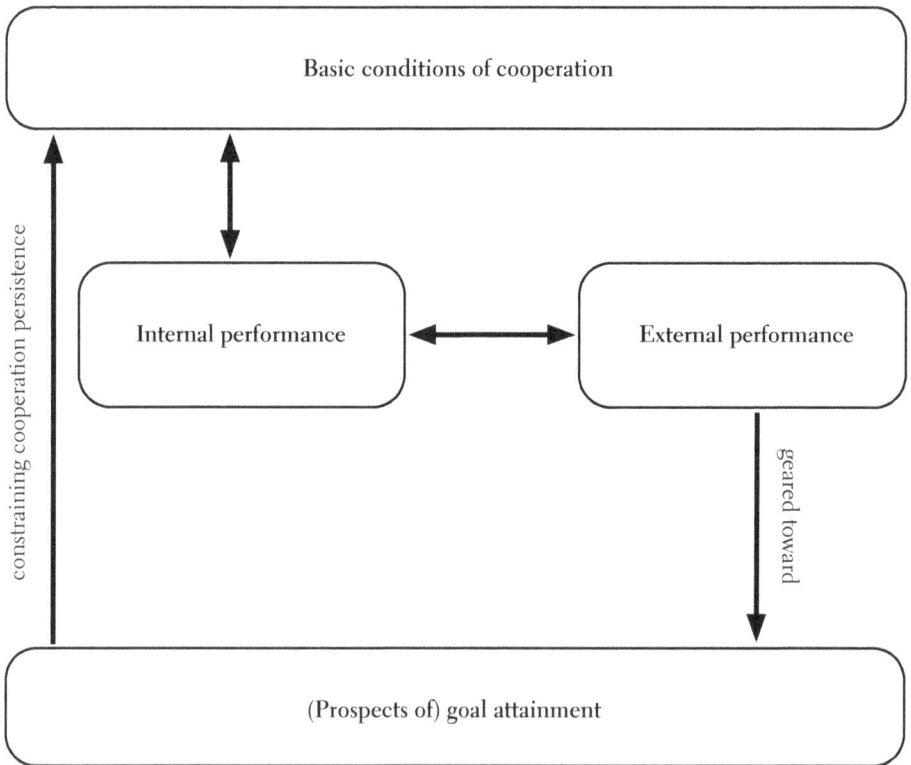

4. Goal attainment and cooperation persistence

In late 2006, however, the JMP must have been convinced that electoral reform was within reach, a belief that was certainly not without foundation. In the run-up to the elections of that year, the regime had yielded to the alliance and approved of electoral reform in the June Agreement. The EU EOM had taken up the issue, endorsed the June Agreement as a "cornerstone" of the parties' "commitment towards holding a credible and peaceful election process," and proposed thirty-five recommendations to improve future election processes—all of which underscored the validity of the JMP's demands.[23] The alliance could hence claim that the latter enjoyed the European Union's backing. In addition, already prior to the 2006 elections, key donors such as the European Union, the United States, and the World Bank had either cut back their assistance or threatened to do so unless the Yemeni government advanced political and administrative reforms and reduced rampant corruption.[24] Unlike in the subsequent period, during which donors' commitment was nearly unconditional, the regime still had to respond to such demands in 2006, that is, midway through the second tenure of US president George W. Bush, who had made global democracy promotion a major pillar of the "War on Terror" and the pursuit of American hegemonic primacy.[25] The June Agreement was one way of showing that reform was under way, and the Ministry of Planning and International Cooperation willingly emphasized the "significant agreement [that is, the June Agreement] signed between the GPC and the JMP" in preparation for the Consultative Group Meeting to be held in London on November 15–16, 2006.[26] On December 12, the GPC and the JMP signed an agreement "to fulfill the recommendations laid by the final report of the European Elections [sic] Observation Mission" in the presence of Baroness Nicholson of Winterbourne, the former head of the EU EOM.[27]

The prevailing mood among JMP politicians was thus one of optimism. Beyond public statements, senior figures even showed themselves content with the returns of the 2006 elections,[28] which some committed elites had considered a mere dry run for the parliamentary elections scheduled for April 2009.[29] The prospects of imminent electoral reform reinforced a sense of achievement, as did the consolidation the alliance had undergone in the course of the 2006 elections. The JMP had arisen herefrom "stronger and more unified, coherent and pragmatic than before, more able to speak and act as a single political entity than as a collection of separate parties."[30] There was yet another reason for positivity, too. Henceforth the JMP could count on the support of Hamid al-Ahmar, one of the sons of 'Abdallah al-Ahmar, who unlike his father was an outspoken adversary of Salih. Technically speaking, as a member of Islah (and of its Shura Council), Hamid al-Ahmar had been part of the JMP ever since its formation. Yet while not belonging to the regime's inner circle, he—as his father—had formed an integral part of the Salih camp regardless. For reasons that are not entirely clear, he had fallen out with the president and began to seriously campaign against him in the summer of 2006. His defection was a momentous development on a number of grounds. For one thing, it constituted a major rift within the incumbent regime.[31] For another, al-Ahmar could supply the JMP with much-needed resources. Most important, however, he must be seen as the JMP's first—and in fact major—ride sharer up until March 2011.

Ride sharers can be seen as symptomatic of the structural crisis facing the opposition in authoritarian settings, that is, of their competitive disadvantage vis-à-vis the incumbent owing to a chronic lack of resources. This imbalance applies to their financing in the first place, because opposition parties are normally incapable of deriving significant income from membership fees or public funds.[32] It is on this account that individuals with sizable sources of personal wealth frequently assume a dominant role within both individual opposition parties and alliances alike in the Global South,[33] with more recent examples including Sebastián Piñera in Chile, Mwai Kibai in Kenya, or Sa'd al-Hariri in Lebanon.

At times, resources other than money can also considerably strengthen the opposition and earn those individuals who bring them on board a pivotal position within the respective entity. The rise to power of the Syrian Ba'th Party in 1963, for instance, was greatly facilitated by its previous merger with the Arab Socialist Party (al-hizb al-'arabi al-ishtiraki), headed by Akram al-Hawrani. This union was a major step forward for the Ba'th, since it "had gained the adhesion of a first-class orator and political tactician, with a real power-base outside academic and cultural circles [let alone the] military strength which had accrued to it through Akram al-Haurani."[34] Systematic research on the meaning of such outstanding individuals for opposition alliances is still in its infancy. One recent contribution to scholarship hereon is the "theory of pecuniary coalition formation," which seeks to explain the role played by "coalition *formateurs*" as well as the conditions under which they can succeed in building electoral opposition alliances in multiethnic societies.[35] Yet while sharing some key features, ride sharers differ from such coalition *formateurs* in important ways, not least in that the resources they bring need not be confined to money.

The ride-sharer problem of opposition cooperation is another attempt to capture the precise meaning of outstanding individuals hereto. It is a problem that, for reasons pertaining to its repercussions for their internal performance, affects strategic alliances rather than electoral ones. By implication of the term, ride sharers do not acquire the vehicle but pay the owner-driver to get a lift from A to B. That is, they do not bother to initiate cooperation but join forces with an already-existing entity instead. Once they conclude the alliance has answered their purpose, they will disembark regardless of its condition or whether it has reached its destination. This outcome is because there is no goal convergence between the alliance and ride sharers. They merely accompany one another for one or more legs of the journey, envisaging that to include a number of stopovers. Ride sharers are generally defectors seeking to replace the incumbent ruler or to jack up the price to be paid for their acquiescence or loyalty. As such, they are not interested in the sweeping structural change that contrariwise spearheads the alliance's agenda. The latter is aware of this issue but still accepts ride sharers, doing so because these individuals are not mere free riders but rather people prepared to bring on board badly needed resources.

There is, however, an insidious downside to ride sharers' inclusion. On the one hand, the resources they bring grant them disproportionate influence over internal decision-making processes and shield them from disciplinary measures in case of misconduct, thereby jeopardizing the basic conditions of cooperation in the medium to long run. On the other hand, ride sharers negatively bear on the external performance of the alliance in that the inclusion of former regime members will alienate specific constituencies and, in general, undermine the credibility of the agenda seeking fulfillment in a given context.

Hamid al-Ahmar is a textbook example both of a ride sharer and of the challenges arising from their inclusion: his closer integration into the JMP's decision-making structures at first led to an increase in the alliance's strength but soon began to cause internal tensions and to derail its relations with key potential allies as well as large parts of the Yemeni public. This fact will be seen throughout what follows, and particularly in the next chapter.

Some background information here may help explain why Hamid al-Ahmar was such a controversial figure. The al-Ahmar family, most notably its longtime head 'Abdallah, had powerfully molded political developments in the Yemen Arab Republic and the Republic of Yemen.[36] For centuries, the family had led the country's biggest tribal confederation, the Hashid, hence commanding large contingents of tribal forces. Owing to this power base, its members held eminent posts in Yemeni politics and were included in Salih's patronage network—as well as, reportedly, also being on the Saudi payroll.[37] Skillfully using his family's position, Hamid al-Ahmar had managed to become a business magnate in his own right and oversaw major revenue sources coming in from, among others, his company Sabafon, the Saba Islamic Bank, as well as his involvement in the Yemeni power sector run by Siemens. He could thus provide the JMP with ample financial input. In addition, he maintained strong relationships with Salih's rivals in the president's Sanhan (Sanaa) tribe as well as with Saudi Arabia.[38] Although his brother Sadiq had followed his father as paramount shaykh, Hamid critically increased the JMP's power in terms of money, ties, and tribal backing.[39] Despite this, his influence went undisputed neither within the JMP nor, indeed, within his own party. Many complained about his claim to power within both Islah and the JMP, his unilateralist leanings, as well as his entanglement within Salih's patronage system.[40] Given the latter, his unpopularity in the South,[41] and in addition his family's antagonism with Ansar Allah, he quickly became a major impediment to the JMP's external performance.[42]

Hamid al-Ahmar's true political intentions remained a source of public speculation. Even though he repeatedly denied any aspiration to the presidency, he was notorious for his ambition. Few, however, took his scathing criticism of Salih's governance at face value. Hamid al-Ahmar failed to persuade the public of his alleged quest to change the very structures that had brought him to his current elevated political and economic position in the first place.[43] In any case, he had chosen the JMP as his personal vehicle via which to challenge Salih. His father had succeeded in softening Hamid's feud with the president prior to his death in December 2007. Hereafter, however, the conflict between the two intensified, as did the discord between the JMP and the GPC. While it was occasionally difficult to differentiate between the individual and the alliance, it is relatively uncontroversial to assert that Hamid al-Ahmar showed little enthusiasm for the JMP's platform across the board. Nor did he feign any particular interest in the details of electoral reform, which would prove to be the major point of contention between the regime and the JMP in the years ahead.

Barking Up the Wrong Tree?

Yemen's electoral law, last amended in 2001, had been a constant bone of contention ever since its adoption in 1992.[44] It is worth recalling that the conflict over electoral reform had preceded, and critically facilitated, the JMP's formation. Only to a lesser degree did this conflict result from manifest incidents of vote rigging, even though these were not uncommon.[45] The JMP's demand for electoral reform was of a more fundamental nature, encompassing the following elements: First, it called for the neutrality of state institutions before, during, and after elections. On several occasions, the opposition had decried the deployment of public resources in favor of the GPC—as exemplified by the disproportionally high coverage of the latter's campaigns in state-led media outlets or the intimidation of voters by members of the army and security apparatus.[46]

Second, the JMP demanded the overhaul of the voter-registration procedure. This demand included not only reforming legal provisions regarding related locations but also the transparent assembling of accurate electorate lists.[47] The update version of voter registers for the 2006 elections, for instance, had included up to 150,000 duplications and the names of ineligible or underage persons. Even more worrisome for the JMP was that the Supreme Commission for Elections and Referendum had refused the opposition's request that it verify these voter registers.[48] Hence, and third, the JMP sought reform of the SCER itself. By law, the SCER was supposed to be a nonpartisan institution in charge of administering and controlling electoral processes. In reality, however, its decisions were often biased in favor of the GPC, which ultimately decided on its staffing.[49] To establish equilibrium, the JMP therefore proposed either to replace its partisan members with judges or to augment its membership with opposition representatives.

All these demands were raised by the EU EOM, too, further to already forming an integral part of the June Agreement.[50] Yet the JMP had two further points on its wish list that found their way into subsequent negotiations. First, as penned in the 2005 platform, it advocated the strengthening of the second chamber, the Consultative Council, whose members should no longer be appointed by presidential decree but elected by the people. Second, the JMP lobbied for introducing a proportional representation system (PRS) in lieu of the majority-vote system (MVS) currently in place. The advantages of the former for the smaller JMP parties, which could scarcely command enough votes to win a majority in any district, were palpable. Also, a PRS promised to effectively counter the gerrymandering policies the regime pursued particularly in the southern governorates.[51] The extant MVS posed less of a problem for Islah.[52] It has been suggested that the YSP and the Nasserist Unionist People's Organization had dropped the issue of strengthening women's electoral participation in return for Islah subscribing to a PRS;[53] even though the June Agreement encompassed a rather vague passage on "the role of women in the democratic process," the JMP certainly did not champion the issue hereafter.[54] In contrast, despite the PRS *not* being mentioned in the June Agreement—and maybe not in the December Agreement either[55]—the JMP was continuously "pushing its claim to introduce proportional representation" in the negotiations, as one of the GPC's chief negotiators would recall.[56] For the JMP, the ensuing negotiations were full of potential pitfalls.

The first round of talks between the JMP and the GPC began on March 19, 2007; lasted until April 2, 2007; and were followed by a second round on June 13–16, 2007. The talks were somewhat pretentiously labeled a "national dialogue," as if both parties could claim to represent the full spectrum of relevant Yemeni actors, even though it was at around this time that the gist of negotiations did begin to also include the deteriorating situation in the southern governorates and in Sa'da.[57] According to another high-ranking GPC member, both sides settled on a new draft electoral law in October 2007 that failed to come to fruition owing to the JMP's ill will.[58] This assertion is inconsistent with the subsequent chain of events, as deducible on the basis of publicly available sources. In fact, both sides established a Technical Committee (lajna fanniyya) tasked with preparing the amendment only during the third round of talks, which took place November 2–8, 2007. It is indeed remarkable that talks had resumed at all given the difficulties arising during previous rounds thereof, including willful provocations.[59] On September 26, 2007, for instance, Salih had announced the introduction of constitutional amendments that the JMP considered a step toward the "complete presidentialization" of the political system. Shortly after, on October 2, Salih had publicly stated he deemed talks with the JMP "a waste of time."[60]

While it is unclear how often the Technical Committee met in the months that followed, negotiations between the GPC and the JMP soon reached a stalemate. On May 17, 2008, gubernatorial elections took place for the first time in Yemen, coming "at a time when relations between the GPC and the JMP could be best described as at an all-time low, primarily due to the stalled dialogue regarding the composition of the SCER."[61] The deteriorating situation in the southern governorates and in Sa'da was putting additional strain on relations. The JMP had come to understand the rise of the Southern Movement and Ansar Allah to have been facilitated by popular frustration at sweeping centralization and the lack of local say. Alarmed by the speedy growth of the Southern Movement in particular, the Salih regime had drawn similar conclusions and decided to make concessions on local government. On April 27, 2008, it hastily amended the Local Authority Law (no. 18/2008) to allow for governors—who had previously been appointed by presidential decree—now being elected by the provincial councils.

Still, the JMP decided to boycott the elections anyway, hence sticking to its earlier claim that provincial governors were to be elected directly by the people. Then again, the alliance also lacked control of provincial councils, most of which were firmly in the hands of the GPC.[62] Regardless of the true motives behind the JMP's boycott, the gubernatorial elections failed to ease local grievances. Rather, the regime's response to the continuing strengthening of the Southern Movement became increasingly repressive, with civilian casualties soaring especially in 2009.[63] In Sa'da the situation was tense, too. The fourth phase of the conflict had ended in January 2008, and it had involved intense military combat transiently spreading to adjacent governorates.[64] The cease-fire was short-lived, and fighting resumed in May of the same year. In June, as a consequence, Ansar Allah publicly appealed to the JMP to increase its efforts to end the war, even despite the resentment the group held toward the alliance's biggest member, Islah.[65]

Such was the state of affairs when the JMP, in early July, decided to set two preconditions to its continued dialogue with the GPC: first, the release of detained journalists and political prisoners affiliated with the Southern Movement and Ansar Allah; second, the adding of the conflicts in Sa'da and the southern governorates to the official dialogue agenda.[66] While these points were unconnected to the issue of electoral reform, the JMP could plausibly claim that they were directly linked to the upcoming parliamentary elections scheduled for April 2009: the alliance's leading representatives would argue henceforth that it was pointless—and virtually impossible in some places—to hold elections amid the escalating crises in the North and South.[67]

These preconditions were both essential and prudent for the alliance itself. For one thing, these conflicts acutely affected the core interests of several member parties: it had become impractical for the YSP, as well as for al-Haqq and the Union of Popular Forces, by this point to not give developments in the southern and northern governorates top priority without otherwise completely antagonizing their grassroots members and core constituencies. For another, these stipulations were a sensible move to help improve the alliance's external performance. For years, the JMP parties had struggled for electoral reform. This laboring had not amounted to much, also because it was hard to rally support for this technical and seemingly inconsequential issue from among other domestic players. In contrast, the conflicts in the North and South concerned millions of Yemenis, and they provided an opportunity to considerably broaden opposition cooperation. While it took the JMP some more months to fully embrace this strategy of reaching out to other domestic groups, it did eventually establish a Coordination Committee (lajna al-tansiq) on July 14, 2008, tasked with preparing a national dialogue that was to include a diverse set of actors at the governorate level.[68]

Unsurprisingly, the GPC declined to accept these preconditions, claiming they were not covered by the December Agreement. Although that was true, the GPC itself had breached the agreement just previously. On July 6, 2008, its parliamentary group had begun discussing an amendment to the electoral law without prior settlement in the Technical Committee. This amendment did encompass reform of the SCER but otherwise remained silent on most of the other demands raised by the JMP and the EU EOM. Lacking the means to effectively counter this maneuver, the JMP decided to boycott the session.[69] On July 14, the Technical Committee was dissolved;[70] the rhetoric employed by both sides became harsher hereafter. Salih, in turn, again switched over to driving wedges between the JMP's respective parties. Recounting an episode already depicted in the previous chapter, he feigned preparedness to release all political prisoners in mid-August. In return, the alliance agreed to resume negotiations. Playing on the constituent parties' differing priorities, Salih lured Islah into submitting a list of SCER candidates but ultimately abstained from releasing anyone from prison, thereby creating a major controversy inside the JMP. While it ultimately pulled through this and subsequent attempts at pitting one member party against the other,[71] none of it was in any way conducive to forging compromise between the GPC and the JMP.

Instead, the conflict would escalate slowly but surely. On August 26, Salih appointed new SCER members—who were promptly rejected by the

JMP[72]—and unilaterally proceeded to prepare for the upcoming elections. Ignoring the JMP's warnings, the SCER launched the voter-registration process on November 18, only to suspend it briefly hereafter. As outlined in chapter 2, the JMP as well as activists affiliated with Ansar Allah and the Southern Movement mobilized massive demonstrations and sit-ins outside of registration offices across the country, thereby successfully torpedoing the voter-registration process. The JMP's show of force did not, however, usher in a new round of talks with the GPC. The longer the deadlock lasted, the clearer it became that the holding of parliamentary elections in April of the following year would no longer be feasible. For months on end, there was no sign of the two sides earnestly talking to each other, let alone of a pending compromise. Even insiders were thus taken aback when, on February 23, 2009, the GPC and the JMP appeared before the public and announced they had come to terms on an agreement.

The February Agreement was treated as a hallmark of reform in the months that followed. It replaced the June Agreement and the December Agreement and would be invoked by both the GPC and the JMP in subsequent negotiations until way into the 2011 uprising. Despite this, the reasons for its coming about—and even more so its contents—remain mysterious. Its articles are not entirely known, and no official transcript has ever been circulated in public. Both sides had agreed to maintain silence on the grounds of "the higher national interest."[73] This secretiveness led some observers to surmise its articles were of a general nature,[74] while others even doubted the agreement constituted any content at all.[75] For all that is known, it must have encompassed the following elements, most of which were included as a concession to the JMP: a two-year postponement of parliamentary elections, the reform of the SCER, the compilation of accurate voter lists, and a shift from a MVS to PRS in 50 percent of the country's electoral districts.[76] It is also believed that both sides had agreed to introduce a bicameral legislature with an elected Consultative Council.[77] What would emerge as a major point of contention hereafter, though, was whether a settlement of the conflicts in the South and North within the framework of a national-dialogue conference had been included. Quarrels over this question began within days. Given the JMP's previous—and indeed subsequent—insistence on this issue, its omittance from the February Agreement would have been astounding. Yet this la-cuna cannot be spoken to conclusively.

Then there is the question of how the February Agreement even came into being,[78] and why it catered to the interests of the JMP to such an extent that it was interpreted as a major success for the latter.[79] To begin with, the timely holding of elections would have been virtually impossible in default of completed voter registration—to the prevention of which the JMP had certainly contributed its share. Moreover, the alliance had an-nounced its boycotting of the elections—which, had they been conducted even so, would have lacked any legitimacy among large parts of the popu-lace as well as the international community.[80] Adding to this state of affairs was the external pressure being exerted on the regime. In the second half of 2008, Western diplomats had met JMP representatives ostensibly to dis-cuss the issue of electoral reform.[81] In January 2009, the European Union and the National Democratic Institute had stepped up their efforts to me-diate between the GPC and JMP.[82] Toward the end of the same month, the US ambassador to Yemen, Stephen A. Seche, called on both sides to compromise, while the European Union refused to accept the regime's request that it assign election observers.[83]

However, it was not only accumulating external pressure that prompted the regime to acquiesce via the February Agreement but also the JMP's behavior—or, more precisely, its change in strategy is what made for the deal. Up until the early summer of 2008, the JMP acted as a coalition of political parties conducting negotiations with the ruling one despite an ongoing series of setbacks, thereby engaging in what has elsewhere been referred to as the "cross-party mode" of opposition.[84] Its dispute with the GPC at that time was largely settled by means of ordinary party politics re-sembling those found in polyarchic systems. However, this party mode—in which conflict between rivals principally took place within institutional confines and mostly by means of regulated parliamentary politics—was abandoned in mid-July 2008 when the JMP eventually realized the re-gime's inherent unwillingness to abide by the December Agreement. Tasked with conducting final direct negotiations with the president on behalf of the JMP, 'Abd al-Wahhab al-Anisi met Salih on July 9. After he reported negotiations to have failed, the JMP decided to take to the streets for the first time since the 2006 electoral campaign.[85] In its meeting on October 19–20, 2008, the High Council refined the JMP's strategy by coordinating the actions of its groups within parliament with those groups outside of it, too.[86] But after it was found that the JMP's actions in parliament—including the boycotting of sessions and voting—were to no avail, the alliance fully switched over to the "movement mode" of opposition, meaning it completely transferred its realm of action to the streets. The effectiveness of this strategy was validated during the voter-registration boycott on November 18, 2008, and later that month, too, when the JMP rallied tens of thousands of supporters in Sanaa.[87] Only after the February Agreement with the GPC was struck did the JMP return to the party mode of opposition.

Such oscillating between party and movement mode, which would continue up until Salih's abdication in late 2011, can be regarded a general feature of opposition entities operating in electoral (or competitive) authoritarian settings. Yet it is arguably one befalling alliances in the first place. This is because the latter can be assumed to be more prone to daring confrontational strategies than individual parties are; given their relative feebleness compared to alliances, such isolated entities are more vulnerable to regime repression. After all, and despite the liberal facade of most authoritarian states today, incumbent regimes do not shy away from resorting to repression if more subtle strategies have failed,[88] and they can be deemed predatory in the sense that their longevity ultimately depends on the neutralization of domestic opponents.[89] From the incumbent's vantage point, there is also good reason to allow for legalized opposition parties[90] as well as nominally democratic institutions in general. Electoral authoritarian systems shape up as being strikingly robust if they operate seemingly liberal institutions, including feckless legislative bodies, while concomitantly commanding vital external linkages as well as strong organizational powers and coercive apparatuses.[91] The domestic structures of such regimes, however, gravely bear on opposition behavior.

As outlined in the previous section, opposition actors factor various pieces of information into the process of choosing their course of action, including with respect to the apposite mode of contention. Concerning the latter, proponents of social movement theory point to the interrelation between regime type—as determined by government capacity and the extent of democracy—and the choice of "contentious repertoires," that is, the "arrays of contentious performances that are currently known and available within some set of political actors."[92] Decision-making is slightly more complicated here in the case of opposition parties, or alliances of such parties, in electoral authoritarian regimes. On entering parliament they become quasi-institutionalized entities that are, overtly or covertly, bound to prioritize official sites of contention such as legislatures, bureaucracies, courts, and so forth to avoid repression.[93] Yet all these institutions have previously been subject to "institutional gardening" or "institutional containment," namely, to the incumbent's conscious effort to keep "their adversaries in various institutional territories under control."[94] Opposition parties—including when forming alliances—are thus trapped in a participation dilemma.[95] On the one hand, there are the payoffs to being included. They can shun regime repression and expect a relative gain in power compared to excluded parties.[96] On the other hand, and despite the faint possibility of reaching one's end goal from within state entities, opposition parties are ultimately participating in institutional politics against long odds. In addition, they run the risk of alienating their constituencies since they cannot deliver on the promises they earlier made.

This dilemma can be softened only by embarking on seemingly inconsistent strategies, meaning by oscillating between the party and movement modes of opposition. This argument is, of course, not a completely novel one. Several studies have found political parties in authoritarian regimes adopt contentious strategies that are usually associated with social movements rather than parties per se,[97] while other scholars have argued more generally that political opposition in electoral authoritarian regimes is an intrinsically dynamic institution with concern to its shape, goals, and chosen modes of contestation.[98] The adoption of such a mix of conventional and unconventional strategies by opposition parties is a consequence of the domestic structures in place.[99] This fact does not, however, render the opposition an entity that is merely processing the stimuli emanating from authoritarian structures. While constrained, the opposition does still ultimately ponder over and choose the sites and repertoires it considers best suited to challenging the incumbent.[100] It lies within the agency of opposition parties to purposefully deliberate on whether, and when, the switching over to the movement mode promises to be a fruitful strategy. In this, alliances differ from single parties only insofar as their aggregated capabilities provide them with more room for maneuver.

It is crucial to note, however, that oscillation between party and movement mode is purely a function of the participation dilemma. Put differently, and all else being equal, this act does not in itself bring the opposition closer to goal attainment. When, for instance, in the summer of 2008 the JMP decided to abandon parliament to stage protests and organize countrywide boycotts as well as sit-ins instead, circumstances were auspicious. Against the backdrop of waning domestic legitimacy, the holding of parliamentary elections without the JMP would have had an adverse knock-on effect on the regime, the more so as it might have endangered vital external linkages—including the flow of dearly needed aid. The JMP's actions hence coincided with favorable both internal and external developments. These circumstances led to the conclusion of the February Agreement, which was, after all, still only that—an agreement. Its only manifest outcome was the postponement of parliamentary elections, and it is not farfetched to assume that Salih had consented to the February Agreement to play for time in the first place.[101] This possibility was not lost on the JMP, either. It hence expanded on its strategy of broadening cooperation to gain support from among other collective actors as well as the general public, the latter having become disenchanted with Yemen's political parties by now.[102]

Attempts at Broadening Cooperation

The February Agreement quickly shaped up to be a false summit for the JMP. Within less than a fortnight, a new controversy arose that would soon bring negotiations to a halt once more. Five days after the February Agreement had been reached, YSP secretary-general Yasin Sa'id Nu'man publicly expounded on his reading of it, claiming that the following two years would be used for the implementation of comprehensive political reforms and the settlement of the conflicts in Saʻda and the South.[103] He was supported in this endeavor by the other JMP parties, including Islah, whose local branches in the South were most vocal about the urgency of the matter at hand.[104] But the GPC gainsaid the JMP, vehemently traversing its claim that conflict settlement in Saʻda and the southern governorates formed part of the deal.[105] Given the nondisclosure of the document, it cannot be said conclusively whose claim was ultimately the correct one. Yet in the following months, the conflicts in the North and the South would become the all-dominant question for the bulk of the JMP parties, and indeed the major point of contention between the alliance at large and the GPC. While it would be incorrect to assert that the JMP's goal of electoral reform was abandoned in the subsequent period, it was certainly eclipsed by its demands for conflict settlement.

This shift in goals, or goal priorities, was not a unique feature of the JMP, and neither in the case of the latter nor in that of other empirical instances of strategic alliances should it easily be mistaken for an indication of opposition arbitrariness. Rather, it is a logical corollary of a number of assumptions on the external performance of alliances. The preceding section argued that alliances are prone to oscillating between the party and movement mode of opposition owing to the domestic structures of electoral authoritarianism. This oscillation is not conducive to goal attainment per se. Authoritarian institutions, including elections and legislative bodies, are designed to effectively constrain opposition performance; meanwhile, the success of extrainstitutional contentious action is largely dependent on the (external) mobilization capabilities of alliances, for only they may redound to altering the "relationships of domination" in place — or, put differently, "the relations among all the component parts of an authoritarian system."[106] Meanwhile, alliances must absorb the costs of cooperation—ones that from the very beginning continue to rise steadily until they have reached the point where cooperation ceases to be beneficial. Immediately on their establishment, in other words, alliances already find themselves in a downward spiral that is hard to escape from. This situation is so because the longer an alliance exists without delivering on its promises, the stronger resistance to cooperation will become within its constituent units. The viable prospect of reaching the goal state in the foreseeable future is, as such, of the utmost importance to keeping cooperation going.

In essence, there are only three ways to avert the pending disintegration. All of them may be found to empirically overlap but are nonetheless to be kept analytically distinct from one another: The first one, obviously, is goal attainment. Yet the latter would also entail the subsequent cessation of cooperation, since the alliance has come to fulfill its raison d'être—that is, unless it chooses to adopt a new goal. Besides, the key problem here remains the same. It is, as outlined, intrinsically difficult for the opposition in authoritarian regimes to achieve its core aim. Second, the alliance can replace one goal with another. This undertaking, however, resembles open-heart surgery performed in a nonsterile environment. It would be extremely challenging to not just settle on a new goal acceptable both within and between the constituent units but also convince the critics of cooperation inside those units that the prospects of hitting the new target are better than compared to for the old one. Almost certainly, the peripheral elites would prevail, and the patient would pass away. Last, and considering that strategic cooperation usually pursues several hierarchically ordered goals, the alliance can shift priority in terms of its goal ranking. Unlike in the previous case, it would be easier to maintain the basic conditions of cooperation herewith. Also, such a change of focus would be easier to sell to the outside world, and potentially even enlarge the alliance's support base.

While the JMP could exercise the third, less awkward, option, shifting goal priorities was by no means plain sailing. At the most basic level, the shift had to meet the interests of all member parties, which also had to evaluate the extent to which the corresponding decision (or nondecision) would embolden their radical fringes. Hereafter, the new goal ranking had to be made palatable to the parties' grassroots followers and core constituencies, thus requiring the adoption of new frames. Fortunately for the JMP, the former task proved to be viable. The latter one, in turn, did not seem overly complex, but would soon reveal certain intricacies to it.

To begin with the former, it is worth recalling that advocating for a peaceful settlement of the conflicts in Saʿda and the southern governorates was nothing new on the JMP's agenda. What was novel, rather, was the prominence now being attached to this issue by JMP organs at both the interparty and the alliance levels. This move was less an attempt to distract from the alliance's sobering performance on electoral reform; for some member parties, it was a question of vital importance, the ignoring of which would have seriously undermined—if not pulled the plug on—cooperation. In the South, the YSP's peripheral elites and grassroots followers had been flocking to the Southern Movement since 2008. Islah, too, had a strong presence in the South, with it equally threatened by the rise of the Southern Movement; its local branches repeatedly admonished Islah's headquarters in Sanaa about southern destitution. Likewise, the NUPO—and, to a lesser extent, the Syrian-oriented Baʿth, the UPF, and al-Haqq—had a vested interest in addressing the conflict. Hence, upgrading the southern issue was as uncontroversial as it was compulsory for an alliance claiming to represent the interests of all Yemenis.

The case of Saʿda was more of a challenge. Ansar Allah had come into existence to protest the marginalization of Zaydis. As Zaydi parties, al-Haqq and the UPF were thus directly affected by the conflict that had ravaged the heartlands of the Zaydiyya. With one notable exception, all JMP parties had spoken up for a just and peaceful settlement of the regime's conflict with Ansar Allah from 2004 onward. Contrariwise, Islah's attitude toward the latter was delicate. While the Muslim Brotherhood had ceased antagonizing Ansar Allah, the Salafi wing was overtly hostile to it—the latter's rank and file were said to have fought in Saʿda alongside the regular army. Likewise, Islah's tribal wing had been involved in fighting Ansar Allah, too.[107] Islah's approval of the peaceful settlement of the Saʿda conflict forming a core objective of the alliance was made possible only by the Brotherhood's dominant position within the party—as well as by the ambitions of Hamid al-Ahmar. In the public eye, he had come to be seen as the "head of the opposition."[108] This image presumably mirrored his own self-perception. Living up to this image necessitated a change in behavior and position, even if only superficially. He thus began to downplay his private feud with Salih, repudiating its being the major incentive for his joining the opposition.[109] Furthermore, he could no longer afford to not publicly encourage conciliation in the conflicts in the North and South, which were incrementally threatening Yemen's national unity—to say nothing of his own economic interests.[110] Despite corresponding efforts, he remained a highly polarizing figure for both Ansar Allah and the Southern Movement alike.

In a nutshell, for reasons of protecting its internal integrity and its relations with external actors, the JMP had begun to prioritize conflict settlement in Sa'da and the southern governorates in the aftermath of the February Agreement. At first, however, negotiations with the GPC continued. While both issues were officially excluded from these talks, the High Council seized every opportunity to excoriate the regime's use of violence to quell local resistance. If the strategy behind the issuing of public statements, as done on an almost daily basis,[111] was to bring the regime to either incorporate conflict settlement into the negotiations or desist from repressing Ansar Allah and the Southern Movement, then it failed. Consequently, the JMP resorted to the setting of preconditions again. On July 30, 2009, it suspended negotiations with the GPC for the first time since the February Agreement, insisting on the immediate cessation of violence and the release of political prisoners if talks were to resume.[112] Those demands fell on deaf ears. Only a few days later, on August 11, Salih announced the launch of Operation Scorched Earth.[113] The sixth Sa'da war had begun and soon spread into neighboring Saudi Arabia, prompting Riyadh to intervene militarily in early November that year.[114] Compared to the previous rounds, this war was particularly devastating, featuring heavy artillery and aerial bombardments with high civilian casualties and an estimated 250,000 internally displaced persons scattered across the northern governorates.[115]

It was not only the conflict in Sa'da that was by now getting out of control. Given the regime's intransigence on almost all fronts, its dispute with the JMP became increasingly menacing as well. A leaked US cable is indicative of just how tense the situation had become. According to it, Hamid al-Ahmar had informed the US Embassy in August 2009 that he was prepared to "organize popular demonstrations throughout Yemen aimed at removing President Saleh from power unless the president 'guarantees' the fairness of the 2011 parliamentary elections, forms a unity government with leaders from the Southern Movement, and removes his relatives from positions of power by December 2009." If Salih was unwilling to conform to these requirements—and al-Ahmar conceded that the president was "unlikely to meet any of his three conditions"—he promised to "begin organizing anti-regime demonstrations in 'every single governorate,'" modeled after the 1998 protests that helped topple Indonesian president Suharto. "We cannot copy the Indonesians exactly, but the idea is controlled chaos."[116]

The cable was also revealing in several other respects, notably regarding Hamid al-Ahmar's stance on the Sa'da issue. He maintained that "a lot of blood was shed to make Sa'ada Yemeni"—thereby implicitly suggesting Ansar Allah was alien to the Yemeni people—and that the "only solution in Sa'ada [was] to arrest Houthi leader Abdulmalik al-Houthi." This statement not only contravened the JMP's official position but was also telling of al-Ahmar's perspective on the conflict, which was probably shared by many others in Islah. In any case, the statement was perfectly in line with the position of the al-Ahmar family at large, which had organized and led tribal campaigns against Ansar Allah in the previous Sa'da wars, and so adds to explaining Ansar Allah's lingering reservations about banding together with the JMP.

Furthermore, al-Ahmar reported that the most recent Sa'da campaign was doomed to fail and that Salih had "given Ali Muhsin the impossibly difficult Sa'ada mission with the explicit intention of ruining his military career, and therefore his presidential ambitions, and hopefully have him killed in the process."[117] Back then, General Major 'Ali Muhsin Salih al-Ahmar was the commander of the First Armored Division and one of the most powerful men inside the Salih regime. While unrelated to Hamid's family, he stemmed from the president's Sanhan tribe and had been a close companion of his since the early 1970s. Rumor had it that 'Ali Muhsin was destined to succeed the president in office in return for his support during Salih's ascension to power. In the early years of the new millennium, their relationship had turned sour when Salih began to groom his son Ahmad for the presidency instead.[118] Al-Ahmar thus suggested a serious rift to exist within the regime and claimed that he would "work hard in the coming months to convince ['Ali Muhsin] to support the opposition." Salih, he went on to say, was "now at his weakest point politically, besieged by threats on multiple fronts and without the political support and counsel of key allies." The cable did not comment on this assessment, merely concluding that "Hamid al-Ahmar has ambition, wealth, and tribal power in abundance, a fiery combination anywhere but especially in Yemen."[119]

It is unclear whether al-Ahmar's plans had been coordinated with the leadership of Islah or the other JMP parties, notwithstanding his concession that "even members of the opposition [were] skeptical of the utility of mass demonstrations targeting Saleh personally." What we do know is that Salih, who had received the ultimatum via al-Ahmar's brother Sadiq, revealed himself to be unimpressed.[120] In October 2009, the SCER announced the preparation of elections to fill vacant parliamentary seats, causing an uproar among the JMP.[121] The following month, Salih threatened to legally ban the alliance,[122] which for its part disclosed it was contemplating henceforth pursuing the criminal prosecution of the president.[123] Against the backdrop of such alarming developments, regional and international actors increasingly called for restraint and dialogue. Already in July 2009, the Arab League had offered to mediate between the GPC and the JMP. This offer was turned down by the latter. Na'if al-Qanis of the Syrian Ba'th, JMP spokesperson at that time, asserted that this rejection was because "we [have not yet] exhausted, as Yemenis, our dialogue efforts."[124] He was not, however, solely referring to the dialogue between the JMP and the GPC, if indeed at all. His remarks were to add authority to the Preparatory Committee for National Dialogue, which the JMP had founded shortly beforehand as a way to reach out to other Yemeni actors.

There are two possible interpretations of the underlying rationale behind the creation of the PCND, both of which were, while not mutually exclusive in principle, widespread in Yemen at the time. As for the first, its founding in May 2009 was but a calculating move to augment pressure on the regime by superficially broadening the opposition front. That is, even if the JMP sought to address Yemen's ongoing crises—and, to this end, founded the PCND to coordinate with other individuals and groups beyond the alliance—the committee would be little more than adornment.

Real power rested solely with the JMP, which intended to negotiate all matters with the GPC alone. From this perspective, the PCND was a means to accelerate the JMP's coming to power in the first place, and the fact that Hamid al-Ahmar was elected secretary-general of the PCND was interpreted as supporting this claim.[125] Although Muhammad Salim Basindwa, a former presidential adviser to Salih, eventually became the president of the PCND, al-Ahmar was the dominant force therein—regarding the committee as his personal chiefdom, therewith antagonizing many of its participants.[126] As one YSP member put it: "[Hamid al-Ahmar] was the sole financier of the PCND. Well, as the one person providing all the funds you might at times feel tempted to manipulate decision-making."[127]

As per the second possible reading, the national dialogue had formed an integral part of the February Agreement.[128] It was to provide solutions on how to settle the conflicts in Sa'da and the South and to reform the political system—notably, solutions that were to be arrived at by dint of comprehensive and inclusive discussions involving all major social and political actors in Yemen, including Ansar Allah and the Southern Movement.[129] From this perspective, the JMP was convinced of both the necessity and the urgency of a national-dialogue conference. Since the regime proved unwilling to assume responsibility here, the JMP went it alone. The prevailing perception of being pressed for time was echoed in the motto "no time to lose" adopted by the PCND Working Committee (literally Downsized Committee; lajna musaghghara) on its establishment on May 25—in other words, three days after the founding conference of the PCND held on May 21–22, 2009.[130] Reportedly, twelve hundred representatives of all governorates and major political and social groups attended the conference and finally elected ninety delegates to the PCND.[131] The latter was dominated by the JMP and its affiliates—as was the case also with the Working Committee, whose seventeen members were elected by the PCND to represent all "popular groups."[132]

What the PCND was supposed to show to the regime was that the JMP's demands were supported by a broad range of relevant actors; Salih's reaction to this founding conference—with him being publicly scathing about the committee instead of simply ignoring it—revealed that the message had been well and truly received.[133] Also from this perspective the

PCND must be seen as an attempt to pressurize the regime by broadening cooperation.[134] This fact was later admitted by a leading JMP representative, who argued that it had become "necessary to enlarge the joint basis and step up confrontation."[135] As opposed to the first reading, however, the PCND was less an opportunistic move undertaken to facilitate the JMP's coming to power but rather a means to jointly work toward the solving of the country's most imminent crises.[136] At any rate, the PCND provided the JMP with an opportunity to communicate its interpretation of these crises to the outside world and to convince nonmembers to throw in their lot with the alliance.

In other words, the PCND enabled the JMP to canvass the support of external actors by improving its framing processes—which have been defined as deliberate efforts to "assign meaning to and interpret relevant events and conditions in ways that are intended to mobilize potential adherents and constituents, to garner bystander support, and to demobilize antagonists."[137] As such, framing processes can be understood as the discursive dimension of an alliance's external performance, and arguably the most decisive factor in the endeavor to broaden the scope of cooperation beyond the alliance. In fact, the external mobilization capabilities of an alliance hinge on the quality of its framing. However, high-quality forms—that is, framing of the sort that can mobilize a significant number of nonmembers, including other collective actors—are a complex matter. To be effective, an alliance must provide external actors with persuasive diagnostic, prognostic, and motivational frames, all of which are equally important.

To begin with, diagnostic framing centers on "problem identification and attribution."[138] Put differently, an alliance must point a specific problem out to the target audience, and it must convince the latter that it is indeed impinged on by the issue at hand.[139] Furthermore, it must credibly attribute blame and responsibility to those individuals it deems to have caused the problem in the first place, usually the regime. Prognostic framing, then, refers to the challenge of proposing a "solution, or at least a plan to attack, and the strategies for carrying out the plan."[140] In doing so, the prognostic framing of an alliance must center on reaching consensus regarding objectives, meaning the common goals of broadened cooperation, and define the way these goals can be attained best, namely, the common strategy of broadened cooperation.[141] Last, and crucially with respect to mobilization, motivational framing focuses on providing "a 'call to arms' or rationale for engaging in ameliorative collective action, including the construction of appropriate vocabularies of motive."[142] To this end, the motivational framing of an alliance must connect to the central values of a given society, provide a certain range of applicability, relate to key strands of the public debate, be credible and experientially commensurate, and possess narrative fidelity that relates to the empirical world of the addressees and ensures they are carried along by the proposed solution.[143]

It is not that the JMP had neglected to reach out to the outside world prior to the founding of the PCND. As discussed in the previous chapter, its framing processes had hitherto been informed largely by its platform. The latter provided a detailed list of major administrative, economic, political, and social problems, elaborately illustrating why the Salih regime was to blame for the country's deplorable condition. Such diagnosis had been complemented by a reasoned prognosis, according to which the reform of the political system—notably the electoral system—had to precede all other reforms. But with or without these clues to its platform, the JMP had thus far failed to generate large-scale external support. While it is disputable whether the alliance had intended to foment outright escalation vis-à-vis the regime by way of mass mobilization up to this point, it was certainly true that "the support for the coalition on the Yemeni street [was] not as high as many of its leaders [had] profess[ed]."[144] Seeing the core framing tasks outlined earlier, the JMP had underdosed—if not omitted entirely—key ingredients, notably with respect to motivational framing.

Since its formal inception in November 2005, the JMP had focused its strategic efforts almost exclusively on electoral reform. These endeavors might have been based on sound analysis regarding the modality and feasibility of political reform. But they were not actually palatable to nonmembers. Neither were larger segments of the Yemeni population interested in the minutiae of election law, nor were the technical issues about voting reform easy to understand.[145] Besides, it must have escaped the bulk of Yemenis why reform of the electoral system would in any way offer a realistic solution to their daily problems, above all the issue of more stable livelihoods.[146] Electoral reform simply did not move them to action. The same held true for the Southern Movement and Ansar Allah. The former was at best interested in issues pertaining to decentralization, and many of its leading figures had already ceased to call for political reform in demanding instead outright secession from the North. The latter, in turn, had little reason to pin its hopes on electoral reform either, being concerned with more imminent problems itself—notably the military conflict in Saʻda.[147]

Whether planned or not, the founding of the PCND brought with it revised framing processes on the part of the alliance, ones that did in fact contribute to the broadening of cooperation as will be seen. Several factors might explain why the JMP managed to appeal to a significantly greater number of external actors. First, the language employed by the alliance changed in that it became less technical, more belligerent, and now enriched with references to societal values and popular concerns. Proof of this can be found in the *Vision for National Salvation* (*ruʾya li-l-inqadh al-watani*), a sixty-nine-page pamphlet issued by the PCND on September 7, 2009.[148] The *Vision* itself appeared to have been modeled on a handbook on framing theory, beginning with "Diagnosis of [the] Current Political and National Crisis," followed by the section "Solutions," and ending with the "Mechanisms [for] Putting This Vision into Action."[149] Although the *Vision*'s contents greatly overlapped with those of the JMP's platform—something frankly admitted by leading representatives of the alliance—it shifted emphasis and priorities. Electoral reform was still dealt with,[150] but less prominently and detailed so compared to, for instance, the conflicts in Saʻda and the South—as the two most hotly debated public issues at the time.[151] Likewise, the *Vision* eschewed delicacy when charging Salih with responsibility for Yemen's miserable condition in now openly assigning the blame to him alone. The proposed solutions were more radical, too. For instance, the *Vision* demanded heavily reducing presidential powers, basically confining the presidency to protocolary functions, and banning members of the president's family (up to the fourth degree of kinship!)

from holding key posts in the political and administrative systems as well as the army.[152]

Second, the institution of the PCND itself helped to broaden cooperation, beginning with its appellation. The notion of (national) dialogue that the PCND carried in its name not only addressed what is commonly considered "a sublime value" deeply rooted in Yemen's central value system,[153] but also signaled to the populace that matters had become more urgent. The last national-dialogue conference in Yemen had been held shortly before the 1994 war, whereas the most well-known Arab examples had occurred in the context of the devastating civil wars in Algeria and Lebanon. Much in the same vein, it was to show the populace that what was at stake was no longer merely a conflict between the GPC and the JMP but a crisis concerning all Yemenis, thus claiming to be of centrality to their everyday lives. Another benefit of the PCND was that it could reasonably assert itself to have a higher degree of inclusiveness than the alliance, thereby facilitating the narrative fidelity of its statements and the quality of motivational framing. Right at the outset, the *Vision* avers the "diverse political and social figures, parties, organizations, businessmen, scholars and intellectuals, opinion leaders, women and youth leaders" who had contributed to its composition.[154] This claim of inclusiveness was further strengthened on December 26, 2009, when the PCND began to establish branches in the country's governorates and introduced several subcommittees that were to represent key societal groups, including religious scholars, tribal leaders, youth, women, workers, and nongovernmental organizations.[155] Representatives of these and other so-called expert committees as well as those individuals from the PCND's senior leadership would tour the country in the months that followed, hosting workshops to present the *Vision* to the general public and discuss the solutions at which they had arrived.

Third, such orchestrated attempts at dissemination were arguably as important to rallying support for the *Vision*—and by implication the JMP—as the new manifesto itself. During the 2006 electoral campaign aside, the JMP had hitherto largely failed to address bread-and-butter issues. Toward the end of 2009, however, the alliance stepped up its efforts to broach the daily problems of Yemenis via the PCND's local branches, which would organize public meetings or symposia to discuss the regime's calamitous economic policies,[156] the situation in the South and Saʿda,[157] the rise in commodity prices,[158] the absence of public safety,[159] and so forth. Doing so not only served to paint a broader picture of popular destitution and to demonstrate the interrelatedness of the various claims raised in the *Vision*, but by involving well-known experts and local dignitaries in such events, it also aimed to lend empirical credibility to the identified issues—another key aspect of motivational framing. As corresponding reports suggest, these activities attracted significant numbers of participants—although it remains inconclusive whether they were from among the JMP's core constituencies or indeed people newly recruited. Either way, the JMP's efforts did not go unnoticed by the Salih regime.

Success and Failure

While the JMP's making of headway in broadening cooperation was mainly the result of the self-induced changes in its external performance, conditions in Yemen around then did also abet the alliance. From 2009 onward, the Salih regime would face growing popular dissatisfaction. In the wake of the 2007–8 global financial crisis, the economy was rapidly deteriorating, belying Salih's campaign slogan, "New Yemen, Better Future," as used in the 2006 presidential elections. Meanwhile, the regime was running out of resources. From 2008 to 2009, hydrocarbon revenues—the regime's main source of income—had fallen from USD\$7,292 million to USD\$3,529 million annually, whereas Yemen's fiscal balance deficit had risen from USD\$1,143 million to USD\$2,552 million in the same period.[160] In contrast, the regime's expenditure on security was steadily rising. Although official figures must be taken with due caution, the 635 clashes between the army and Ansar Allah and the 445 protests by the Southern Movement reported by the Ministry of the Interior for the period between 2008 and 2009 are indicative of how seriously the security sector was straining the overall budget—and, indeed, how tense the situation in Saʿda and the southern provinces had become.[161]

Against the backdrop of such worrying developments and of stiffened opposition, Salih signaled his preparedness to make concessions to the

JMP. On December 14, 2009, he proposed entering a national dialogue, to be supervised by the Consultative Council.[162] Despite its skepticism concerning the sincerity of Salih's motives, the JMP approved on the condition that representatives of both Ansar Allah and the Southern Movement were allowed to participate.[163] Shortly after, Salih yielded to these terms, announcing on national television that both groups would be invited to partake, provided they renounce violence.[164]

It is a matter of speculation how things would have developed if Umar Farouq Abdulmutallab had not boarded Northwest Airlines Flight 253 to Detroit, Michigan, on Christmas Day 2009. Although Abdulmutallab failed to detonate the explosive device hidden in his underwear, this attempted act of terrorism drew international attention to Yemen. AQAP, which had masterminded the operation, was no longer considered a problem confined to the Arabian Peninsula, having just proven its ability to launch overseas attacks, too. International efforts to take down the organization were stepped up accordingly. On January 27, 2010, representatives of twenty-two states and five international organizations—including the European Union, the GCC, the United Nations Development Programme, and the United States—founded the Friends of Yemen (FOY) group in London and agreed to support the Yemeni government in combating what would soon come to be considered "the most aggressive branch of al-Qaeda."[165] This support meant a drastic increase in aid given to Yemen's incumbent regime, which was reckoned to be the most promising ally in the fight against AQAP.[166] The same year, the Barack Obama administration boosted its military assistance to Yemen from the previous less than USD$5 million to now USD$150 million.[167] Solely betting on the Salih regime, financial and military assistance from the United States and the bulk of the FOY's members was given now more or less unconditionally, uncoupled from any tangible progress being made on political and administrative reform.

These developments did not bode well for the opposition. Already on January 27, 2010, the JMP criticized the outcomes of the London conference, being scathing about its exclusive focus on security aspects and maintaining that the assistance promised by the FOY would in effect save the regime but not the Yemeni state.[168] The same day, the JMP also revoked its acceptance of entering a national dialogue under the auspices of the Consultative Council owing to Salih's failure to meet the conditions previously set out. Neither Ansar Allah nor the Southern Movement had been invited to participate, and many of their activists remained behind bars.[169] In the months that followed, Salih started playing cat and mouse with the alliance once more. Offers were made and withdrawn; arrangements were agreed but then breached; each party blamed the other for the ensuing political stalemate. Not even the cease-fire agreement in Sa'da—while welcomed by the both the JMP and the PCND—could break this deadlock.[170] Indeed, up until July 2010, hardly any episode is worthy of elaboration, with one notable exception: On May 22, 2010, Salih came up with an unexpected offer. In his speech to mark the twentieth anniversary of Yemen's unification, he announced the immediate release of three thousand political prisoners and invited the alliance to join a government of national unity.[171] The JMP acknowledged the prisoners' release as a major step toward the respecting of the February Agreement.[172] But it also insisted on its complete fulfillment, including with regard to the holding of a national dialogue; as such, it refused to accept the offer.

The JMP's reaction is interesting for a number of reasons, not least as it allows for assessment of its actual agenda. This topic will be saved for the next chapter. Here, it seems more apt to make conjectures as to Salih's own motives in making this offer.[173] For one thing, it might have been another attempt to split the alliance. For another, the offer might have been intended to woo the JMP into accepting the constitutional amendments the GPC was preparing to allow Salih to extend his term in office.[174] Last, and perhaps most relevant, Salih might have anticipated appeasing herewith the JMP, which had become increasingly powerful in the meantime as its efforts at liaising with the Southern Movement and Ansar Allah advanced apace.

To reconstruct how exactly those efforts unfolded, and what hurdles the JMP faced here, it seems expedient to briefly recall how difficult the alliance's relations with both actors had been up to this point, and why. Chapter 2 argued that the emergence of the Southern Movement can be partially explained by erstwhile power struggles within the YSP and the consolidation of the JMP midway through the new century's first decade. YSP reformists had managed to marginalize the party's old guard, which was strongly opposed to cooperation with Islah and used the nascent Southern Movement as a vehicle to regain political influence. The YSP's relations with key segments of the latter's leadership were thus strained and competitive in many ways.

This state of affairs was even more true for the alliance's other major constituent, Islah, which was a red rag to a bull for the bulk of the Southern Movement in attitudinal terms.[175] Likewise, Islah was considered a political rival given its strong grassroots base in the South.[176] Then again, the Southern Movement was far from unified itself, with most of its leaders at odds with one another. Not all of them had come to demand outright secession, and there was indeed a substantial overlap between the goals of the alliance and the goals of the Southern Movement concerning political and administrative reform. Still, the JMP was not completely disavowed as an opposition force to the Salih regime, given the former had dedicated much energy to the southern issue in recent times. Not only had the JMP's regional and local branches frequently campaigned for southern demands, but the High Council on numerous occasions also spoke up for the release of southern political prisoners, condemned the regime's use of violence against,[177] and rallied grassroots solidarity with the Southern Movement.[178] In addition, the JMP had repeatedly called for the latter's inclusion as a precondition for the alliance joining a national dialogue—most recently via the PCND.

Already during the committee's founding conference would Hamid al-Ahmar proclaim that he "wished to celebrate the [next] Unity Day together with 'Ali Nasir Muhammad, 'Ali Salim al-Baydh, Haydar Abu Bakr al-'Attas, Nasir 'Ali al-Nuba, Tariq al-Fadhli, Salah al-Shanfara, and Nasir al-Khubaji."[179] His wish was not to be granted, however. In late January 2010, while giving account of its activities, the PCND's Committee on the Southern Issue (lajna al-qadhiyya al-janubiyya)—founded only a few weeks earlier in December 2009—stated that it was unable to report any progress having been made concerning an agreement with the Southern Movement.[180] While the committee was enjoined to intensify its efforts, it must have been clear from the start that a rapprochement between the Southern Movement and the PCND—or the JMP for that matter—was impossible to reach without high-level talks between the two sides.

Tentative achievements concerning the latter were disclosed about four months later, when the head of the YSP's parliamentary group, 'Ayda-rus al-Naqib, read a letter by 'Ali Nasir Muhammad, the former president of the PDRY, addressing attendees of the PCND conference held on June 2–3, 2010. Meanwhile, al-Ahmar announced that the PCND had estab-lished contact with other southern leaders in exile.[181] Roughly three weeks hereafter, a Yemeni newspaper covered a meeting in Cairo between rep-resentatives of the JMP (Sultan al-'Atwani, NUPO; Nu'man, YSP; al-Anisi, Islah), the PCND (al-Naqib, YSP; Sakhr al-Wajih and Basindwa, both for-merly GPC), and a number of the Southern Movement's leaders. 'Ali Nasir Muhammad and Muhammad 'Ali Ahmad had attended, while al-'Attas, unable to participate in person, had conveyed his position in writing. The three had reportedly expressed their willingness to participate in an open-ended dialogue in which both the South's secession as well as its continu-ance in the ROY were equally possible outcomes.[182] The flip side to such positive news for the PCND, of course, was that the bulk of the Southern Movement's leadership had excused itself from proceedings, including al-Baydh—who was believed to yield considerable influence among those currents opting for renewed independence. In other words, those parts of the Southern Movement's leadership who had already previously refused to partake in the national dialogue pressed for by the PCND—indeed the majority[183]—could not be convinced to participate.

The JMP thus failed to align with the Southern Movement, includ-ing with its rank and file. Although there had been joint demonstrations between the JMP's and Southern Movement's grassroots followers,[184] they were but isolated incidents; they remained exceptional, in fact, even dur-ing the uprising of 2011. Relations between both sides were too soured, and the goals of the alliance versus the goals of the majoritarian seces-sionist wing were too divergent to allow for cooperation—even if only for the purpose of pressing Salih into indeed holding a national dialogue. It is certainly correct that many of the Southern Movement's leaders were put off from even considering joining in the latter—which was then still no more than a vague prospect—because they did not trust Salih to abide by any outcomes thereof.[185] This state of affairs was no less the case for Ansar Allah, either. Unlike the Southern Movement, however, Ansar Allah did at least contemplate subscribing to the PCND, despite its previous history of acute conflict between itself and Islah.

Notwithstanding the Brotherhood's prevalence over the Salafi and tribal wings within the party's top decision-making organs, there must have been strong reservations about liaising with Islah on the part of Ansar Allah regardless, and vice versa. After all, it would take years from the Brotherhood becoming Islah's dominant faction until the overall party could bring itself to not veto joint JMP positions demanding the cessation of violence in Sa'da, the release of detained members of Ansar Allah, and its categorial inclusion in the proposed national dialogue. Beyond such developments, other factors were likely to have facilitated the parties' harmonization. In contrast to the Southern Movement, Ansar Allah never contemplated secession. Making common cause with the country's most powerful opposition parties against Salih was thus consequential, the more so as the prolonged conflict with the regime, especially the last round of the Sa'da war, had cost them dearly. Last, and again unlike the Southern Movement, Ansar Allah was a unified movement under one leadership, on top of which sat 'Abd al-Malik al-Huthi—who was said to be on good terms with Hasan Zayd, al-Haqq's secretary-general who would facilitate negotiations between the two sides.

While it remains unknown when exactly these negotiations were stepped up, they must have predated the cease-fire agreement of February 2010 at least. In fact, Ansar Allah had called for the JMP's inclusion in the discussions over the latter with the regime.[186] Either way, on February 7, 2010, Islah's home page posted an official statement by Ansar Allah proclaiming that the movement was considering "the forging of a political alliance with Islah and the rest of the party opposition in the country on the basis of mutual respect." It directly referenced the PCND's Vision, stating that "there is a great convergence of positions regarding most of the key problems the country is suffering from."[187] This development was quite remarkable, and a major success for the PCND. Negotiations about Ansar Allah joining the latter advanced quickly. On April 8, a PCND delegation met with representatives thereof to negotiate the terms of their inclusion.[188] Some days later, on April 14, the two sides concretized their common position on the settlement of the Sa'da conflict and the general framework for the upcoming national dialogue; these unlikely outcomes can be interpreted as a validation of the PCND's *Vision*.[189] Ansar Allah was eventually accepted into the PCND, delegating three representatives to it.[190] Unlike in the case of the Southern Movement, the JMP had succeeded in broadening cooperation with Ansar Allah—which a short while later managed to renew the cease-fire agreement established with the regime.[191]

As the next chapter shows, the JMP's alliance with Ansar Allah soon began to falter and would finally crumble completely during the Yemeni uprising. A good deal of the explanation for this lies in the changed circumstances and unforeseen dynamics that came along with the latter, further to in Ansar Allah's own ambitions around power, too. Unmistakably, though, the JMP contributed to the breakup—as did the makeup of the PCND. Notwithstanding its seemingly undetermined nature, the PCND was dominated by the JMP. Soon, Ansar Allah would start complaining that it had been given only three seats in the PCND and was completely barred from both the Working Committee and the General Secretariat, two of its most significant bodies.[192] Likewise, internal decision-making processes were nontransparent, and PCND members often felt obliged to rubber-stamp decisions that had been made elsewhere already.[193]

JMP members, too, objected, some of whom even dropped out of the PCND altogether. In June 2010 future Nobel Peace Prize laureate and Islah member Tawakkul Karman together with Ahmad Sayf Hashid and 'Abd al-Bari Tahir resigned from their posts in the PCND, referring here to its lack of democratic and transparent structures. They also suggested that Secretary-General Hamid al-Ahmar was in effect bribing its members.[194] Criticism of the latter not only came from individual delegates; he was also the subject of controversy at the JMP's senior-leadership level, too. During a High Council meeting in the summer of 2010, for example, the NUPO took a swipe at al-Ahmar, whom it accused of having turned the committee into a "family project" that would harm the JMP given the rampant "monopolization of decisions" within PCND bodies.[195] Besides his inhibiting role within the committee, al-Ahmar also proved to be a major impediment to rapprochement between it and the Southern Movement. Leaders of the latter took offense at his very person, which also provided them with ample reason to uphold their grassroots base's belief that the JMP was part and parcel of the corrupt regime in Sanaa.[196] This belief was certainly true for the advocates of secession who regularly claimed Hamid al-Ahmar was no better than either Salih or the president's son Ahmad.[197] Yet even the Southern Movement's moderate leaders frowned on his role inside the PCND and questioned what his political ambitions ultimately were.[198]

In short, the ride-sharer problem began to haunt the JMP. Al-Ahmar had placed critical resources at its disposal, with these proving especially important during the 2011 uprising. Then again, his inclusion in the alliance also started to interfere with both its internal functioning and external performance. On balance, though, the JMP had significantly enhanced its external mobilization capabilities by the summer of 2010. While there was still much work to be done to better appeal to key popular segments such as youth and women,[199] it had engaged in framing processes that added to the delegitimizing of the regime and helped attracted more and more nonpartisan activists.[200] The demonstrations and other extraparliamentary activities occurring such as festivals, sit-ins, symposia, or workshops—organized under the banner of either the alliance or the PCND—drew in increasing numbers of Yemenis. After the alliance had aligned with Ansar Allah and continued to reach out to the Southern Movement, the regime had to concede some ground, thereby also feigning responsiveness to the advice of international donors.[201] On July 18, 2010, the GPC and the JMP signed an implementation accord regarding the February Agreement.[202]

On the face of it, the July Accord was another success for the alliance. In it, the GPC and the JMP had agreed to form a Joint Committee for the Preparation of a Comprehensive National Dialogue. The ensuing conference was to "provide political parties and organizations as well as civil society organizations the opportunity to discuss the required constitutional amendments to reform the political system and the electoral system, including a PRS."[203] The new agreement hence embraced the most vital claims the JMP had raised hitherto, yet doing so at a general, nonspecific level. And that was the crux of the matter. Hardly any specifics were mentioned in the July Accord, which left core questions unanswered. Most notably: Who would be allowed to set the concrete agenda of the national dialogue? Who exactly would be permitted to participate? And what was the future role of the PCND, or Ansar Allah and the Southern Movement, for that matter? Around six months ahead of the Yemeni uprising, the July Accord did little to alleviate tensions; the ensuing circumstances will be the focus of the next chapter.

Conclusion

Opposition cooperation is a means to improve the chances for goal attainment by increasing the overall strength of the cooperating entities. In other words, cooperation increases the strength of the opposition. Yet the quality of this strength hinges on the quality of cooperation. If cooperation is of a tactical kind, the resulting strength is but the sum of that of the parties involved; if it is strategic in nature and helped to endure, the resulting strength can reach a higher level as the overarching entity established to orchestrate cooperation optimizes the mobilization of the resources brought along by its constituent parties. Therefore, strategic cooperation has the potential to produce a strength that is ultimately more effective. But this form of cooperation is also more challenging.

Chapter 2 featured discussion on the internal performance of strategic alliances and explored what needs to be done from within to maintain the basic conditions for cooperation and improve their internal mobilization capabilities. This chapter here, in turn, was the first of two addressing strategic alliances' external performance. While its assumptions were developed by analyzing how the JMP set out to interact with external actors, and how it coped with the external structures constraining those interactions, it can be asserted that these assumptions are also applicable to other cases of alliances operating under authoritarianism—notably within electoral authoritarian regimes.

The latter permit the inclusion of opposition parties in institutional politics while concomitantly ensuring that those institutions cannot be used to undermine the incumbent's core interests. Since, ultimately, these regimes do not allow the opposition to operate as proper political parties, alliances tend to change the sites of contention and oscillate between the party and movement modes of contestation. Such mode switching, however, does not in itself increase the chances of an alliance reaching its goals. They must therefore be capable of adding new goals to their agenda or swap priorities in terms of goal ranking. This capability is critical, because the prospects for goal attainment are a key prerequisite for sustaining cooperation. Chapter 2 showed that the internal performance of alliances is important in this respect. It is their internal organizational setup that determines the extent to which they are able to alter goals and improve their internal mobilization capabilities. Yet it is mainly by means of their external performance that alliances can significantly increase their strength and draw nearer to their goals. That is, alliances are usually too weak to accomplish core goals on their own terms. Hence, they must attempt to mobilize other external actors, including collective ones, if they are to enlarge the opposition front and hence further add to their strength. Whether such attempts at broadening cooperation are successful hinges on the quality of their framing processes.

As the next chapter will suggest, the so-increased strength of alliances might then prompt other principal actors both inside and outside the regime to reconsider their positions and modify the relationships of domination in place. That said, shifts in the latter are a rare occurrence, empirically speaking. Given the centrality of goal attainment, it has thus been argued that an alliance will persist only so long as its members believe that its external performance will contribute to initiating these shifts—and hence to reaching the goal state—in the foreseeable future.

In view of the Yemeni case, there were indeed several occasions during the period under investigation in this chapter when the JMP must have been convinced that goal attainment was within reach. Between September 2006 and July 2010, the alliance managed to acquire three major agreements from the regime: the December Agreement, the February Agreement, and the July Accord. Owing to these pacts, the JMP's committed elites could continue to vindicate cooperation vis-à-vis grassroots followers while keeping peripheral elites at arm's length. But the

JMP also had to shift priority to keep cooperation a persuasive option. At first, electoral reform was the linchpin of joint efforts. This goal, however, was then eclipsed by demands for conflict settlement in Sa'da and the southern governorates within the framework of a national dialogue. Besides such shifts in goals, the JMP frequently changed its behavior, too. It took to the streets whenever engaging in institutional politics seemed but a futile endeavor, and it returned to the party mode whenever doing so showed greater promise with regard to goal attainment. While this dipsy-doodling did little—if indeed anything—to attract nonmembers and other opposition forces, the JMP had managed to significantly upgrade its external mobilization capabilities by 2010 even so.

The reasons were by and large twofold. On the one hand, the Salih regime had become increasingly unpopular. Yemen's economy had been in steady decline, leading to the impoverishment of large parts of its populace. Owing to dwindling resources, the regime's patronage network became more exclusive, thus reducing the number of loyal oppositionists. Cataclysmic developments in the North and South piled further pressure on the regime, although the worsening of the security situation led regional and international actors to support rather than challenge Salih's rule. On the other hand, the JMP skillfully played to these developments. By 2009, it had begun to alter its framing processes. They were now increasingly focused on bread-and-butter issues as well as on the country's most pressing local conflicts in Sa'da and the South. The introduction of the PCND buttressed the JMP's claim for an inclusive approach to conflict settlement and the reform of the political system, while facilitating its coming to terms with Ansar Allah, too. Despite its failure to align with the Southern Movement, the JMP thus succeeded in broadening cooperation—if only ultimately transiently.

There was yet another reason the JMP became a more potent challenger to the Salih regime. With Hamid al-Ahmar's joining of the alliance in 2006, the JMP was provided with the vital resources it needed to throw down the gauntlet to the incumbent. But al-Ahmar's inclusion was of ambiguous benefit. In keeping with the assumptions on the ride-sharer problem, his significant resources were at first conducive to the JMP improving its external performance. Before long, however, his overly

dominant position within the alliance came to hamper its internal functioning, gradually thwarting the JMP's attempts at broadening cooperation. By the time the so-called Arab Spring arrived in Yemen, al-Ahmar
had become a liability to the alliance in that his presence therein seriously
undermined its claim to be a credible alternative to the Salih regime.

4

Discrediting Cooperation

The Joint Meeting Parties in the Yemeni Uprising

Yemen's contemporary history has been truly eventful and conflict laden. Numerous reasons have been cited in accounting for the country's notorious record of violent conflict and social upheaval, including, among others, colonial legacies, tribalism, sectarianism, regionalism, proxy warfare, and, more recently, petro-aggression or global capitalism.[1] The Zaydi intellectual Muhammad Sharaf al-Din would offer yet another account of Yemen's sustained imbroglio:

> Since time immemorial, every Yemeni is inclined to compete for power. Power is an objective, but nobody profits from it except the leader himself. . . . The current corruption and disorder around us are like a mirror. Our mirror image reveals that all our interests center on gaining the money of those we cannot equal, laying bare the heavy weight of responsibility. Consider the quasi-fictional work of some Yemeni opposition parties which offer themselves as paragons, promising that they alone can bring justice and equality. In reality these are nothing but a means to help two or three persons to gain power. Once they have achieved this, all principles and slogans disappear; there is nothing left that guarantees the fulfillment of the promises. Human nature has been like that since time immemorial, and not just in Yemen.[2]

This passage is taken from Sharaf al-Din's "Advice to the Hashemites in Yemen," a polemic published just shortly before the formal establishment of the JMP in November 2005. Here, the author primarily sought to weigh in on an intra-Zaydi controversy, strongly advising the *sada*—that is, the Prophet's descendants—to abstain from politics in the name of the Zaydiyya. He therefore also addressed al-Haqq and the Union of Popular Forces directly, both of which would "not deserve mentioning for anything they have achieved. They have been accepted among the opposition parties because of their great political statements."[3] Whether this last sentence alluded to the emerging alliance is uncertain, and ultimately irrelevant. What Sharaf al-Din did appear to suggest, however, is that political parties in Yemen were little more than new pawns in an otherwise old game, namely, the perennial power struggle ensuing from being run by a tiny elite that was, in essence, bidding for power and money, notwithstanding the claims to public well-being.

Sharaf al-Din's supposition about the motives driving Yemen's political parties is nothing new. The rent-seeking tendencies prevalent among opposition elites have been discussed at various points throughout this book, and over the decades they have contributed considerably to the popular alienation felt from party politics—and, indeed, political parties altogether. It was thus little wonder that, during the Yemeni uprising of 2011, many key protagonists from among the so-called Independent Youth insisted on engaging in "revolutionary action" (*'amal thawri*), which they purposefully contrasted with "political action" (*'amal siyasi*). Party affiliation was deemed problematic at best, and prominent youth activists refused to launch their own parties since they believed doing so would be "the beginning of the end."[4] The picture was, of course, less clear than such statements suggest. Otherwise, it would be hard to explain the JMP's growing popular support from 2005 onward, notably in the first weeks of the uprising—during which the alliance managed to rally hundreds of thousands of Yemenis on multiple occasions.

For all that, rent seeking was an observable pattern also among the JMP's parties, and one that was difficult to reconcile with the alliance's official agenda as well as with those oppositionists who were earnestly striving for the latter's implementation. This chapter hence addresses the relationship between rent seekers and reformers under conditions of strategic cooperation. But it does not stop there. Beginning with the developments unfolding in the aftermath of the July Accord of 2010, it completes the analysis of the JMP's external performance in this critical period of

Yemen's recent history, and it attempts to make sense of the ambivalent behavior of the alliance—notably during the 2011 uprising. Empirically as well as with respect to the broader conceptual considerations driving this study, the chapter discusses why the JMP would seesaw between escalating and de-escalating the conflict with the regime of 'Ali 'Abdallah Salih, how it contributed to dismantling established relationships of domination, and why it was even important in the first place. Proceedings end with the signing of the Agreement on the Implementation Mechanisms for the Transition Process in Yemen in Accordance with the Initiative of the Gulf Cooperation Council—better known as the GCC Initiative Agreement—in November 2011.[5] Technically speaking, they must come to an end here. By the end of that year, the JMP had ceased to be part of the opposition, having now joined the newly formed National Unity Government (hukuma al-wifaq al-watani).

The Way into the Uprising;
or, The National Dialogue That Was Not

The July Accord constituted the fourth deal between the General People's Congress and the JMP within the space of little more than the same number of years. It was perhaps the best opportunity to settle the conflict between them and return the country to calmer waters. At the time it was signed, the regime seemed ripe for serious negotiations after all, and the July Accord also appeared to allow for a more inclusive approach being taken. How compendious negotiations were to ultimately become was still uncertain in July 2010, however. The July Accord called for the founding of a Joint Committee for the Preparation of the National Dialogue (al-lajna al-mushtaraka li-l-i'dad wa al-tahyi'a li-l-hiwar al-watani) that was to "prepare a schedule for the dialogue and establish the rules of conduct." Its resolutions were to be adopted unanimously and sessions held "openly and transparently so that the public, fraternal countries, and the Friends [of Yemen] could follow its course."[6]

The agreement detailed further practical issues, and one day into it 'Abd al-Rahman Bafadhl of Islah confirmed that the Joint Committee would "be authorized to draft suitable amendments" to be discussed and adopted by the prospective national-dialogue conference.[7] Yet the July Accord was also sketchy on detail regarding key questions, notably: Who was to be included in that conference, and in which capacity? And what was even to be negotiated? The document listed "the reform of the political system and the electoral system"; other than that, it merely referred to the February Agreement,[8] the contents of which remained secret. Ansar Allah therefore demanded being informed about the nature of the latter, stating it would be prepared to join in only if the Saʿda conflict was satisfactorily addressed.[9] This requirement was swiftly fulfilled. Apparently, the contours of the agenda for the future national-dialogue conference would also be determined by the strength of noncontracting parties—and whether they were admitted to the Joint Committee.

The technical side to this latter question was dealt with in the July Accord. The document stated that the JMP and the GPC would meet "as representatives of their partners and allies" to nominate their delegates to the Joint Committee. It also stipulated that neither side was entitled to veto the other's delegates. Accordingly, representatives of groups other than the JMP and the GPC were allowed to partake in the Joint Committee. Yet it was ultimately up to the JMP and the GPC to decide who would be on board *and*, as further determined in the document, take part in the national-dialogue conference, too. While it was not necessarily an impediment to inclusive dialogue—the document held that no party wishing to participate in the conference was to be excluded[10]—it added at least to the perception of some groups that the national dialogue would in effect be one merely between the JMP and the GPC—as particularly was the case among members of the Southern Movement. Whether the secessionists would have entered on different terms can be reasonably doubted. Yet under these circumstances they could easily justify their refusal to partake in the "northern dialogue" or "northern plot," as a number of secessionist groups would put it.[11] Even the Southern Movement's moderate leaders promptly objected to the Joint Committee, holding that the July Accord had taken them by surprise and that it contradicted their previous agreements with the JMP.[12] Several weeks later, they too would now call for southern independence.[13]

In contrast, Ansar Allah conveyed its willingness to continue cooperation with the alliance after it had been allowed to review the February

Agreement.[14] On July 29, 2010, spokesman Muhammad 'Abd al-Salam announced the group would delegate three representatives to the Joint Committee (himself, Yusuf al-Fayshi, and Salih Habra).[15] On the same day, the Joint Committee was officially established. Nine days later, on August 7, its two hundred members met in Sanaa; elected the vice president of the Republic of Yemen, 'Abd Rabbuh Mansur Hadi (GPC), and the president of the Preparatory Committee for National Dialog, Muhammad Salim Basindwa, as its heads; and assigned thirty persons chosen from among their ranks to join a steering group called the Working Committee (again, literally Downsized Committee, lajna musaghghara). In the presence of foreign diplomats, the Joint Committee announced its eagerness to address all of the challenges the country was now facing, from the southern issue and the conflict in Sa'da to the economic crisis and the threat emanating from al-Qaeda in the Arabian Peninsula.[16] The public statement following its second meeting, on August 26, sounded a bit more prosaic already, basically declaring its intention to contact the leaders of the Southern Movement and the southern-based League of the Sons of Yemen.[17] Its third meeting, on September 27, produced similarly meager results, although it was reported that several nongovernmental organizations had attended and henceforth decided to join the future national-dialogue conference.[18] This achievement was to be the last the Joint Committee would oversee. On October 1, the JMP announced putting its membership thereof on hold.[19]

Seeing the course of events from 2006 onward, the ending of negotiations two and a half months after the signing of the July Accord came as no surprise to political observers. Serious frictions between the alliance and the GPC had been reported long before the events of October 2010—in fact, only some seventy-two hours after the official establishment of the Joint Committee.[20] On that day, August 10, 2010, the Supreme Commission for Elections and Referendum was commissioned to launch the voter-registration process for the upcoming parliamentary elections even though that body—and the country's electoral law as a whole—had yet to undergo reform and despite the JMP having already announced that it would consider this step a breach of the July Accord.[21] By mid-September, the relationship between the two sides had become so strained again that the European Union suggested to relocate the dialogue to Cairo.[22] Quite a number of contentious issues had piled up for the JMP in the meantime.[23]

But when, on October 1, the GPC parliamentary group announced it was about to begin the process of amending the electoral law without having reached prior agreement thereon with the JMP, the alliance took measures. It called for an emergency meeting of the Joint Committee, appealed to the president of parliament, launched protests inside the latter, and eventually backed out of the Joint Committee altogether.[24] The regime at first appeared to backpedal and put the amendment on hold. But in November the GPC began the amendment process anew,[25] scheduled an election date,[26] and single-handedly announced that it would staff the SCER.[27] On December 13, the JMP terminated its participation in the Joint Committee for good. Two days earlier, the GPC had passed its proposed amendment of the electoral law, thereby "sounding the death knell for the national dialogue" in the eyes of the alliance.[28] In an effort to justify its chosen action, the JMP publicly reconstructed the course of the failed negotiations, detailed the multiple breaches of trust on the part of the regime, and called on the people to revolt.[29]

One may wonder in hindsight about the regime's intransigent position at the time. Of course, in early December it could not have predicted the regional uprising that would begin in Sidi Bu Zayd, Tunisia, on December 17, 2010. For all that, there were clear indications of how fragile its grip on power had become. Attempts have been made to account for Salih's misjudgment of the situation in 2010, including his excessive focus on the issue of presidential succession—that is, the passing of authority to his son Ahmed—as well as apparent conviction about unmitigated US support for his rule. It also appeared that he had lost touch with conditions on the ground and become increasingly isolated from reform-minded advisers.[30] Some of his long-standing confidants such as former prime minister 'Abd al-Karim al-Iryani continued their attempts to provide counsel despite Salih's sustained unwillingness to accept it. Others had already given up in this regard. Basindwa, for instance, had first approached the JMP in November 2008 while still one of Salih's top advisers. Purportedly drenched in tears, he had bemoaned the country's pitiable condition and Salih's refusal to accept any form of advice.[31] Such obstinacy continued up to the point that, in the second half of 2010, even GPC backbenchers dared criticize the president publicly.[32]

One high-ranking GPC member who had been involved in the current talks with the JMP offered another interpretation for the failure of negotiations. From his point of view, it was the JMP that had broken its word; only owing to the GPC's prudence could the Joint Committee still execute its work for a few weeks to come at least. But then, he maintained, "the crisis assumed alarming proportions when the JMP began organizing [protest] festivals in several governorates and districts."[33] It is true that, following the July Accord, the JMP had returned to the party mode of opposition and had refrained from mobilizing its grassroots members by and large.[34] Between July and December 2010, the alliance acted as a quasi-governing party within the framework of the Joint Committee. The JMP statements that were published during this period often focused on the technical aspects of legislative procedures. This approach changed, however, as doubts hardened on whether the GPC was indeed serious about putting through the electoral-amendment bill. Yet since it could not be entirely sure about the GPC's intentions, and because it was unwilling to take the blame for negotiations potentially failing, the JMP must have decided to first flex its muscles via its regional branches. This was the case, for instance, in early October 2010 when negotiations seemed on the brink of collapse for the first time,[35] or on December 7—meaning four days ahead of the enactment of the amendment—when the powerful JMP branch in Ta'izz, and not the High Council, organized protests in other governorates around the country, including Abyan, Aden, al-Dhali', Ibb, and Lahij.[36] Only after the amendment had been passed in parliament did the High Council take over again and directly call its members to action.

In the two weeks that followed, the JMP made extensive use of some well-tested repertoires of contention. JMP parliamentarians, together with many independent members of parliament, protested inside the assembly, either seeking to openly disturb parliamentary sessions or withdrawing ostensibly for prayer time.[37] They jointly boycotted the voting on the SCER's staffing and announced the same course of action would be pursued vis-à-vis the parliamentary elections scheduled for April 2011, too. Some JMP parliamentarians threatened to go on hunger strike.[38] Large numbers of

JMP members and affiliated human rights groups such as Women Journalists without Chains (sahafiyyat bi-la quyud, led by Tawakkul Karman) repeatedly formed crowds in front of parliament as part of holding sit-ins.[39] The High Council, in turn, called on the international community to intervene so as to thwart the regime's blatant attempt at abolishing democracy, appealed to national and international media to cover the worrisome developments in Yemen, and met with officials from the United States and the European Union.[40] Meanwhile, the JMP regional branches—one at a time—expressed solidarity with the High Council.[41] On December 12, 2010, the JMP also revived the PCND and thereafter forged another symbolic alliance with Ansar Allah by founding a Joint Coordination Committee (lajna al-tansiq al-mushtaraka). Four days later, this newly established entity reminded the public of the necessity of holding a national-dialogue conference.[42] Beyond doubt, it was also meant as a marker for the regime that the alliance between the JMP and Ansar Allah was still very much intact.

Despite these concerted efforts, it is important to understand that the JMP had still not fully exhausted its either internal or external mobilization capabilities. While it continued to incite public outrage over the GPC's misrule and incremental authoritarianism, it had hitherto refrained from seriously organizing mass protests. But it was now threatening to do so on an almost daily basis.[43] The GPC pretended to treat the JMP's corresponding announcements lightly. On Christmas Day 2010, for instance, its secretary-general shrugged off the JMP's threats to mobilize the streets, alleging that "the street of the GPC was incommensurably stronger than that of the opposition."[44] Despite the feigned equanimity, the regime had already begun deploying military units at strategic points in Yemen's urban centers, particularly in Sanaa, in anticipation of large gatherings and antiregime rallies.[45] Moreover, attacks on JMP elites proliferated at that time.[46] Although none of these were ultimately fatal, they were obviously intended to intimidate the alliance. But it was to no avail. On New Year's Eve 2010, the JMP abandoned its mobilizational restraint. That day, first reports about certain new constitutional amendments envisaged by the GPC were published. At their core was Article 112 of the Constitution defining the presidential term of office, the amendment of which would have removed the two-term limit and given Salih the "chance to rule for life."[47] One newspaper's headline fittingly read, "Eternal Presidency, Absolute Power."[48]

The GPC's announcement came at short notice—parliament began discussing the draft amendments the very next day, January 1, 2011—and at a critical point in time. Salih's brazen attempt at "setting to zero" (*tasfir al-a'dad*) his number of terms in office hitherto upset the JMP. But it also angered large parts of the population, too. All of these events happened at a time when Yemenis were curiously watching the unfolding of events in Tunisia via Al Jazeera.[49] Salih's popularity had waned substantially during his second term, and the prospects of the open-end presidency of a man who had ruled the country for more than thirty years now must have given the JMP another popular boost. In any case, the strength of the alliance had been steadily rising over the past four years: its internal mobilization capabilities had been considerably advanced, and its efforts at external mobilization had improved in much the same way. Despite the latest failure of the Joint Committee, at the turn of the year, the JMP's chances for goal attainment showed greater promise than ever before, including with respect to its coming to power per se. This possibility is because its clout had risen in both absolute *and* relative terms—and with it the JMP's transformative capacity, too.

While closely interlinked, the strength of an alliance must not be confused with its transformative capacity. That is, while both terms correlate with each other they must be kept analytically distinct. Strength is here understood to comprise the number of both tangible and intangible resources available to an alliance and, crucially, the way these resources are mobilized to a particular end. It hence significantly overlaps with resource-based understandings of power.[50] In contrast, transformative capacity refers to "agents' capabilities of reaching [desired] outcomes."[51] While not immediately obvious, transformative capacity has an intrinsically relational component to it. The latter is also closely related to the notion of agency prevalent in the structurationist school. Despite the diverse set of sociological theories put forth by its proponents, structurationists agree that social structures are characterized by their dual nature. In other words, they claim that social structures "are constituted by human practices, and yet at the same time they are the very medium of this constitution. Through the processes of socialisation . . . individuals draw upon social structure. But each moment they do this they must also reconstitute that structure through the production or the reproduction of the conditions of production and reproduction."[52]

In consequence, agency can be defined only via an actor's endeavor to mold the social structures they find themselves operating within—that is, by seeking to either reproduce or change them.[53] As such, agency and strength—or power for that matter—are very much interconnected. It has been argued that "the concept of action is *logically tied* to that of power."[54] This notion is generally true for all social actors participating in what Anthony Giddens, for instance, has called "the dialectic of control," which is "an intrinsic feature of regularised relations of power within social systems."[55] That the strength of social actors critically sways their interactions may be more perceptible at certain times than at others, depending on the kinds of interactions and of actors involved exactly. Yet it is usually a directly observable pattern, one characterizing the relationship between opposition and government in both liberal and authoritarian contexts alike. What sets the latter apart from the former, however, is that—from the opposition's vantage point—in authoritarian settings structural changes are hard to come by, particularly fundamental ones.

Several factors determine whether the opposition stands a chance in this regard, notably its resources and resource mobilization. In the case of opposition cooperation, this question pertains to an alliance's internal and external mobilization capabilities and, therefore, to things that it can control. Other (f)actors, in contrast, are beyond its reach and can be influenced only indirectly. This state of affairs is because transformative capacity, just as with power in a relational sense, "concerns the capability of actors to secure outcomes where the realisation of these outcomes depends upon the agency of others."[56] It is, however, not merely the agency of the regime that sways the outcomes seen. Rather, authoritarian incumbents rely on multiple actors to contribute to maintaining regime stability. This situation has been referred to as "relationships of domination" in the democratization literature, which posits that it is the task of the opposition "to change the relations among all the component parts of an authoritarian system in such a way as to weaken authoritarianism."[57]

The principal parties able to induce change in such relationships include the core group of regime supporters, the coercive apparatus, the regime's passive supporters, and both the active as well as the passive opponents of the regime.[58] The underlying rationale here is that any alteration in those relationships of domination, whether induced abruptly or evolving over time, may work to upend the whole constellation. Even subtle such changes may have repercussions for political stability and increase the involved actors' sense of insecurity, prompting them to cautiously reconsider the nature of their relations with the system in question's other constituent parts. However, a significant surge in the strength of the opposition—whether by way of the broadening of cooperative action or an increase in popular support—is likely to induce greater changes in those relationships of domination,[59] albeit ones not necessarily immediately detectable from the outside.

Such processes are neither unidirectional nor irreversible. But once they have gained momentum, the principal parties' decisions to abandon (or back) the authoritarian incumbent are mutually reinforcing. When, for instance, the tide is turning and a greater number thereof choose to sever ties with the regime, the last parties to flinch will be inclined to loosen their ties as well so as to not end up on the losing side. One can therefore assume an indirect relationship to exist between the strength of an alliance, on the one hand, and the transformative capacity of the alliance and that of the regime, on the other: the greater the strength of an alliance, the more extensive the changes will be within current relationships of domination; the more extensive the shifts within the latter, the greater the transformative capacity of the alliance—including vis-à-vis that of the regime. Of course, this state of affairs does not in turn imply that a potential loss in strength on the part of the regime directly accrues to the increased strength of the alliance in some sort of osmosis-like process. The latter may remain constant in absolute terms compared to its level at the point in time when alterations in those relationships of domination first set in. Once they have gained traction, however, the alliance's transformative capacity may rise in relative terms even so. Fortunately for the JMP, developments in Yemen from midway through the first decade of the new century onward worked in both directions: the JMP's strength would increase, while the regime grew weaker.

Some have maintained that the JMP and the regime had become almost equipollent on the eve of the Yemeni uprising.[60] Whether true or not, the regime had considerably weakened, with much of this being self-inflicted. As briefly outlined in the introduction, the Yemeni economy was highly dependent on the hydrocarbon sector. Peak oil in Yemen had been reached in 2001, and production had fallen ever since from 450,000 to 162,000 barrels per day as of 2011.[61] While Yemen's production of natural gas had doubled in about the same time period, climbing from 583 billion cubic feet per annum in 1999 to 1,153 billion cubic feet per annum in 2010,[62] it was not sufficient to make up for the overall losses in hydrocarbon revenues, which reached a trough in 2009 at just USD$3,529 million.[63] This loss was a serious problem for the regime, since such revenues had amounted to roughly three-quarters of the state budget on average in previous years. Owing to shrinking prices on the international oil market, the government had already cut most ministerial budgets by 50 percent in 2008, excluding only those ministries deemed to be of strategic importance for maintaining internal stability such as the Ministry of Defense.[64] The global recession of 2009, and the plunge in oil prices that came along with it, was hardly to be compensated for, though. One countermeasure taken was to drastically reduce fuel subsidies, which were debiting the state budget to the tune of USD$2.2 billion per annum,[65] three times in 2010 alone.[66] But doing so did little to alleviate looming troubles. Facing a budget deficit of USD$1.6 billion, then foreign minister Abu Bakr 'Abdallah al-Qirbi appealed to donors to increase their aid to Yemen by USD$6 billion over a five-year period.[67]

Such economic distress amplified grievances within the population, which had counted among the most impoverished in the region already prior to these events. Ebbing revenues also compromised the regime's ability to sustain its patronage system, which had long been a major pillar of regime stability. This state of affairs further added to that system becoming more exclusive, with Salih having already begun to channel greater resources to core family members previously, in fact.[68] Empty state coffers also led to the stalling of the growth in public wages—and often the stalling of salary payments altogether—prompting increasing numbers of state employees, including soldiers, to join JMP demonstrations.[69] Criticism could increasingly be heard from within the GPC, too, usually as levered by reform-minded party members who refused to comply with the regime's manipulation of democratic institutions.[70]

A more direct menace to Salih's rule came from within the coercive apparatus, meanwhile. Already in 2009, Hamid al-Ahmar had informed the US ambassador in a private conversation about the split between Salih and General Major 'Ali Muhsin al-Ahmar. By early 2011, the matter had become public knowledge, with newspapers discussing Salih's intention to reorganize the military leadership and disempower his erstwhile ally.[71] Such trends suggest that the country's relationships of domination had already undergone considerable revisions well ahead of the Yemeni uprising. Some of these shifts were apparent, like the JMP's aligning with well-known individuals from the GPC, tribal elites, or Ansar Allah. Others, such as the schisms within the armed and security forces, the ruling party, or the state bureaucracy, were more a matter of conjecture rather than manifestly obvious, with them becoming observable only in the early stages of the uprising. With hindsight, leading analysts would thus argue that "what created all of this [that is, the 2011 uprising] was the split in the elite, and the JMP had played a major part in it."[72]

There was yet another factor that would have a bearing on conflict dynamics in Yemen when, in January 2011, the GPC set about amending the Constitution. By then, people across the Arab world would be glued to their televisions, closely observing developments in Tunisia where the so-called Jasmine Revolution was now at its peak. On January 14, 2011, the Tunisian uprising finally culminated in the fall of longtime president Zayn al-'Abidin bin 'Ali. This watershed moment encouraged the opposition as well as aspiring youth activists in Yemen. It also jeopardized old certainties on the part of the regime. Still grappling with the potential implications of events in Tunisia for its regional security strategy, the United States would call on its Arab allies to reform. In a speech delivered in Doha, Qatar, during her five-day tour through the Gulf region, then

US secretary of state Hillary Clinton warned Arab potentates that "in too many places in too many ways the region's foundations are sinking in the sand," and that "those who cling to the status quo may be able to hold back the full impact of their countries' problems for a little while, but not forever."[73]

As a matter of fact, the Barack Obama administration had criticized Salih's plans for constitutional reform right on their announcement.[74] During her visit to Sanaa on January 11, 2011, then, Clinton unexpectedly met with the heads of the JMP's parties. This move might have been no more than a mere symbolic gesture. After all, the United States would continue to back Salih for some time thereafter. Yet the regime could no longer bank on enduring US support, and political observers such as 'Ali al-Jiradi openly speculated about the signal sent by the meeting—holding that the United States, as well as the European Union, would now consider the JMP a viable alternative to the Salih regime.[75] Such worrisome scenarios for the incumbent were aggravated by the fact that relations with Saudi Arabia—another major ally—had become strained, too. There were credible reports about Riyadh being extremely annoyed with Salih, who in the eyes of the Saudi ruling elite had exploited the last Sa'da war to amass Saudi funds without having actually broken Ansar Allah.[76] Such reports were impossible to verify. But as it happens, Riyadh would let go of Salih rather quickly in the upcoming months.

In the face of incremental regional upheavals and imminent domestic turmoil, it appears preposterous that the subsequent pattern of interaction between the regime and the JMP hardly differed from their previous one at first glance. Either anticipating or responding to JMP protests, Salih first feigned a willingness to compromise and back down. At least twice, on January 18 and February 2, 2011, the president announced he would cancel the proposed constitutional amendments, yet the GPC resumed preparations for their enactment in parliament shortly after.[77] And at least three times, on January 21, 25, and 28, 2011, Salih called on the alliance to return to the negotiating table but never extended an official invitation to them, nor did he meet any of the JMP's preconditions for talks to even take place.[78] To cite yet another example, the GPC and the JMP had agreed on postponing the parliamentary elections to be held on January

12, 2011.[79] Despite this agreement, however, it soon turned out that the SCER was preparing for the elections regardless.[80]

While this cat-and-mouse game seemed very familiar, there was one striking difference compared to their previous pattern of back and forth at least: the dimension of protests, as still exclusively orchestrated by the alliance at the time. Initially, they occurred on a regular basis but were limited in terms of the number of participants and their regional diffusion. On January 1, 2011, for instance, several hundred JMP members and supporters rallied in front of parliament. The following day, roughly two thousand protesters partook in another JMP demonstration in the capital.[81] Notwithstanding a number of interruptions, the alliance proceeded with this strategy of daily but restrained mobilization through the end of the month.[82] It was not until January 27 that the JMP would first organize mass protests across almost all of Yemen's provinces. Just as with the preceding ones, these demonstrations remained peaceful, too. But this time, one hundred thousand people or more took part. All participants wore pink slips, and preliminary calls could be heard for the regime to step back from power.[83] The turnout was higher still on February 3, when the JMP together with the PCND called for a nationwide Day of Rage (*yawm al-ghadab*). On that occasion, the alliance managed to mobilize several hundred thousand protesters.[84] The so-called Arab Spring had arrived, finally, in South Arabia.

The JMP during the Uprising; or, Making Sense of Its Ambiguous Performance

The Yemeni uprising is today widely referred to as the "Youth Revolution," a nomenclature used to stress that it was "initiated solely by young activists who . . . were acting with no guidance or involvement from the opposition Joint Meeting Parties."[85] This characterization is misleading, however, since it negates the key role played by the JMP early on. If one ignores the issue of when the uprising began—a highly disputed one given the very question of whether the latter was initiated solely by nonpartisan youth or not[86]—the fact that the insurrection evolved gradually from JMP-led rallies against the regime's projected constitutional amendments in

December 2010 should still be noted. These rallies attracted ever-growing numbers of people, including participants lacking any affiliation with the alliance, whose demands soon came to outrun the JMP's initial claims by calling for the toppling of the Salih regime per se.[57] Besides these JMP-led demonstrations, there were also smaller protests in January 2011 emulating more clearly the Tunisian model. Examples are those rallies at the University of Sanaa organized by the Union of Yemeni Students (ittihad tullab al-yaman)[88] or the rally in front of the Tunisian Embassy in Sanaa the day after Bin 'Ali had fled Tunis. In retrospect, the latter rally was seen as the onset of the Youth Revolution by some, although it comprised no more than twenty activists and also included JMP members as well.[89]

But until mid-February 2011, the JMP remained the main—if not sole—organizer of the mass protests joined by independent activists as well as other opposition groups such as Ansar Allah. The latter coordinated its activities with the alliance up until February 21, 2011.[90] One day prior to the JMP-organized mass demonstration that had been held on January 27, the pan-Arab al-Quds al-'Arabi hence noted that "many student bodies . . . had attempted to mobilize the Yemeni street ever since the collapse of the Tunisian regime. . . . These attempts remained limited to the area surrounding the campus. . . . Today, however, [the JMP] is trying to mobilize the entire Yemeni street against the authorities."[91] The outcome thereof would be one of the largest rallies the country had ever witnessed to date.

It is crucial to reiterate what the JMP was even mobilizing for at this stage: not (yet) regime change, but rather the abolishment of the planned constitutional amendments and the return to national dialogue under the terms of the July Accord. Muhammad 'Abd al-Malik al-Mutawakkil, the JMP's rotating head at the time, hence dwelled on the difference between those protests "following the prevailing seasonal pattern" and the ones "leading to dialogue."[92] The problem here was that the notion of dialogue had become unconvincing to many Yemenis in the meantime. The ouster of Bin 'Ali had boosted popular insurrections in other Arab countries, including in Egypt where a second long-standing Arab ruler, Husni Mubarak, would be toppled on February 11, 2011. It had also shown that one could do without opposition parties, which had come to be regarded as ineffective and corrupt. This perception was no different in Yemen, where reservations about the JMP's indulgent position toward the regime had become more concrete in recent years.

By mid-2010, also some of the alliance's prominent backers such as Basindwa or 'Ali Sayf Hasan had begun to challenge the idea of even negotiating with a regime that had breached earlier agreements so many times by now.[93] Ansar Allah, too, grew critical of formal talks and, from February 2011 onward, placed emphasis instead on its solidarity with protesters demanding the end of Salih's rule.[94] Even inside the alliance the High Council's position had become controversial. Some JMP branches had already joined in calls for overthrowing the regime,[95] while others warned of the potential consequences of returning to the negotiating table, holding that this step would be completely lost on the protesters.[96]

Such considerations may have contributed to the JMP's tardy response to the concessions Salih made in February 2011. On the second of that month, the president (again) announced the refraining from implementing the planned constitutional amendments and proclaimed that neither he nor his son Ahmad would run for the presidency in the country's next elections (scheduled for 2013).[97] Three days later, on February 5, the JMP received an official invitation to resume its work in the Joint Committee under the terms of the July Accord.[98] It took the JMP one week to think over its response, which was submitted on February 13 together with the reply of the PCND. In part, this delay must have owed to efforts at coordinating with allies and would-be partners. Senior JMP members had been heading to Arab and European capitals to convince the exiled leaders of the Southern Movement about the value of partaking in the proposed national dialogue.[99] But there were also reports about serious dissent inside the High Council on how to deal with Salih's request.[100] The stakes were high either way it chose to act. On the one hand, the JMP ran the risk of falling out with the youth activists who, on February 11, had organized the country's first mass protests independently of the alliance; they had left little doubt that they would not accept anything less than the outright fall of the regime.[101] On the other, Salih's offer perhaps provided the best opportunity to finally achieve substantial reform amid a very volatile and potentially dangerous situation. As Islah's secretary-general, 'Abd al-Wahhab al-Anisi, put it during a press conference on February 13, "Never before did we have a better chance to induce change by peaceful means."[102]

The same day, the JMP accepted Salih's request.[103] This decision soon shaped up to be a significant mistake. For one thing, it swiftly transpired that Salih had never intended to engage in serious dialogue. Already on February 19, the JMP withdrew its preparedness to speak with the regime owing to its use of brute force against protesters.[104] For another, and crucially, the JMP's acceptance of talks with the GPC was a turning point in its relations with other antiregime actors, for it marked the beginning of an irrevocable estrangement between the alliance, on the one hand, and youth activists as well as Ansar Allah, on the other.

As of February 2011, however, these opposition groups had not yet completely broken away from the JMP. For the time being, Ansar Allah stuck to its loose alliance therewith, and the High Council's endeavors to coordinate with the Southern Movement even seemed to pay off when some of the latter's moderate leaders challenged the need for secession in the event of successful regime change. This position—advanced by, for instance, Haydar Abu Bakr al-'Attas and 'Ali Nasir Muhammad—was echoed in several demonstrations by southern activists calling for the closing of ranks with protesters in the North.[105] The majoritarian secessionist strand, however, kept on rebuffing such calls as well as any rapprochement with the JMP. The alliance's relations with the emerging Independent Youth were no less delicate. On several occasions, JMP representatives met with youth activists to assure them of the necessity of negotiations with the regime.[106] Although some groups were temporarily persuaded, a clear majority refused to let go of their demand for regime change, calling instead on the JMP to abandon negotiations and unite against the incumbent.[107] The longer these requests remained unmet, the sourer relations between the JMP and the Independent Youth grew—not least in the face of the regime increasingly resorting to violence to quell the burgeoning protests.

From the regime's perspective, the opposition movement was swelling to perilous levels. In addition to the customary opposition spearheaded by Ansar Allah, the JMP, and the Southern Movement, nonpartisan youth activism was becoming a force to be reckoned with, as those individuals concerned set about organizing themselves into groups and umbrella associations.[108] In part, this self-organization was a response to the emergence of partisan youth groups such as the Youth Coalition for Change (i'tilaf shabab al-taghyir) founded by Islah members.[109] Moreover, a substantial number of parliamentarians, ambassadors, and ministers affiliated with the GPC began defecting to the protesters' camp in early March 2011, as did, too, key public figures widely known to be close allies of Salih such as 'Abd al-Majid al-Zindani of Islah as well as, crucially, the first army units. Already on February 26, many tribes inside Yemen's two largest tribal confederations, Bakil and Hashid, had thrown in their lot with the JMP, announcing their renouncement of violence but, if need be, willingness also to defend the peaceful protests at gunpoint.[110]

The regime's response to the growing opposition was familiar but menacing all the same. In January 2011 Salih had promised a boost in pay for state employees and members of the security forces, offered jobs to student protesters, and reportedly increased the bribes paid to loyal tribal shaykhs. Hereafter, on February 21 and March 1, respectively, he publicly called the protests a foreign plot instigated by the United States and Israel. When they continued to swell regardless, the regime incrementally resorted to repression: detaining activists, clearing protest hot spots on university campuses, and sending security forces, army units, and paid thugs to quash them. The first official casualty of the uprising in the North was reported on February 19. Leading public figures associated with the uprising and well-known renegades were purposefully targeted. Karman, for instance, was imprisoned a number of times; al-Zindani was said to have gone into hiding for weeks; and the son of Hamid al-Ahmar would be killed in an ambush on his father. The latter incident was to take place in early February, threatening to escalate the conflict even further.

Such prominent figures were provided at least some degree of shelter by their public standing, or by the tribal protection they enjoyed as in the case of Hamid al-Ahmar—who even succeeded in having his son's murder discussed in parliament.[111] But ordinary protesters were exposed to the full brunt of regime violence. This fact probably added to the Independent Youth's outright rejection of negotiations therewith, which was still the official position of the JMP when the first nonpartisan youth groups called for Salih's referral to the International Criminal Court.[112] The JMP kept on mobilizing its grassroots followers, tightened its preconditions to negotiations, and, on March 3, indirectly declared "the youth to be the supreme authority concerning . . . the modalities of regime change," as stated by PCND spokesperson Muhammad al-Sabri.[113] But in principle it was still prepared to enter talks with the regime. There was yet another source of irritation for the youth protesters, including those individuals affiliated with the JMP.[114] The alliance continued to refrain from calling for Salih's immediate resignation, merely demanding a "gradual transfer of power based on the announced presidential concessions concerning the non-inheritance of power, the non-extension [of the presidential term], and the noncandidacy for the elections in 2013."[115] This position was unacceptable to the overwhelming majority of nonpartisan youth protesters. When the JMP eventually joined in their demands for Salih's immediate resignation on March 18, it had already lost what was left of the authority it once held with them. On that day, the Friday of Dignity, snipers had wreaked carnage on peaceful protesters in Sanaa's Change Square, thereby altering the nature of the uprising for good.

The JMP's belated call for Salih's resignation is somewhat perplexing. It is difficult to understand why the alliance kept adhering to the mantra of negotiations amid this extraordinary and, from an opposition point of view, promising situation in early 2011, even though it cost the alliance dearly in terms of sympathies and external support. Then again, such de facto measures of de-escalation following episodes of intense escalation do correspond with some of the alliance's ambiguous decisions made in the past. On more than one occasion, the JMP had stepped up efforts to force the regime into meeting its requirements but backpedaled on gaining sham victories. Yet the latter's long record of breaching agreements—notably the June Agreement, the December Agreement, the February Agreement, and the July Accord—must have taught the JMP's leadership that paper never refused ink and that de-escalation was better only in the wake of tangible concessions. But if that was true, how can one best explain the JMP's past seesawing between escalation and de-escalation?

Escalation **can be defined** here as the "intensification of a conflict with regard to the observed extent and the means used,"[116] which is to suggest that the nature of the conflict in question by and large determines its potential degree of potency as well as the specific means deployed. Concerning government-opposition relations, the most fundamental conflict is the one over political power, as needed to authoritatively distribute the "rules and resources" that pattern political—and, arguably, all—social interactions.[117] In principle, this observation holds true for authoritarian settings as well, although the opposition therein often merely "struggle[s] for opportunities below the level of rulemaking, to influence, for instance, the diffusion of ideological orientations within society, the social implications of certain government policies, or the distribution of financial resources."[118] Such self-restraint owes to the imbalance of resources between authoritarian rulers and the opposition, which renders the conflict between them asymmetrical. The previous chapter outlined how such adverse domestic structures in electoral (or competitive) authoritarian regimes bear on the behavior of the opposition, including alliances. It was argued that such autocracies allow for the formal inclusion of the opposition in institutional politics while simultaneously ensuring that doing so does not seriously endanger the incumbent's own interests. Bereft of the ability to operate as proper political parties, the opposition is inclined to resort to contentious repertoires usually associated with social movements. This switching between the party and movement mode of contestation was assumed to be a phenomenon notably characterizing opposition alliances' behavior.

The switching between these two sharply divergent behavioral modes goes a long way to explaining the opposition's (here, the JMP's) seesawing between conflict escalation and de-escalation, for the sheer fact that any action taken outside of the institutional landscape of electoral autocracies may signal its nonacceptance of the extant polity and its politics, thereby undermining the legitimacy of the regime in place. However, there is another, communicative, dimension to be considered in this context, one that is closely connected with the latter modes of behavior. As already mentioned, the oscillating between party and movement mode is per se ineffective. Under normal circumstances, it does not bring the opposition closer to goal attainment, which is why chapter 3 argued that opposition alliances need to be able to adopt new goals, or shift priorities in their goal rankings, lest they face disintegration. Put differently, and ignoring the alliance perspective for the time being, the switching of behavioral modes does not result in any tangible achievements that could satisfy the opposition's grassroots members or the electorate. This condition is aggravated in regimes that can trump the opposition by distributing patronage rewards to the electorate. It was therefore posited that the most promising way for the opposition to cope with this structural disadvantage is by adopting narratives radical in nature, in that they aim at deep political change and, as such, are suited to attracting great numbers of activists.[119] However, and importantly, at the same time the opposition must remain mindful of the moderate narratives "preferred by the median voter."[120] In other words, to compensate for its structural disadvantage, the opposition must engage in discourses that serve to both escalate and de-escalate the conflict with authoritarian incumbents.

It is here assumed that such conflicting styles of communication complement the previously outlined modes of behavior and, in tandem, explain the opposition's seesawing between escalation and de-escalation. Before elaborating further, however, two remarks need to be made concerning the meaning of opposition communication. First, communication and behavior are here conceived of as two distinct categories, mainly so for analytical reasons and despite their inherent interdependence. This situation is so because what can be heard from the opposition does not necessarily align with how it actually behaves. Quite often, in fact, its communication and behavior are at odds with one another; this inconsistency might, indeed, even be by design. When, for instance, the opposition challenges the regime outside of the institutional landscape, official statements by the former can be used to signal accommodation so as to avoid full-fledged regime repression. Then again, individual public comments by leading oppositionists that are scathing about the authoritarian incumbent can occur in times of relative calm, when the opposition is assuming its intended role in institutional politics. Second, opposition framing is here understood as being part of, yet distinct from, opposition communication. As outlined in the previous chapter, framing processes are deliberate efforts at mobilization commonly designed and overseen by specific functional units within opposition parties or alliances. Opposition communication, in turn, encompasses the sum of all discourses emanating from within a given opposition entity, including its official framing. Hence, opposition communication also includes voices by, for instance, peripheral individuals or groups dissenting from the opposition entity's official position. In the case of alliances, such voices can be sanctioned when they threaten to undermine the overall basis of cooperation. Even then, however, they are often tolerated, since they help the alliance in its walking of a tightrope between recruiting radical and moderate constituencies.

If the above-described considerations on the behavioral and communicative modes of opposition action are taken together, one can classify the panoply of possible opposition interaction with the regime along a continuum possessing two extreme poles: escalation, as defined by highly contentious, extrainstitutional behavior or radical communication supportive of regime change, or both; and de-escalation, as defined by accommodating, intra-institutional behavior or conciliatory communication signaling the acceptance of the status quo, or both. The fact that these poles form two analytically distinct dimensions (communication and behavior) is conducive to establishing why the opposition might not only switch between modes of contestation within relatively short intervals but also why, indeed, it appears to be simultaneously both escalating and de-escalating the conflict with the regime. The resulting external performance is seemingly inconsistent and bewildering to behold from the outside. Yet it is a function of the domestic structures faced in authoritarian regimes, one that also allows the opposition to possess agency: it is the latter camp that ultimately decides whether, and when, to withdraw from institutional politics; what frames to adopt; and which dissenting statements are to be sanctioned. This assumption on the seesawing pattern of opposition performance can be applied to both single opposition parties and alliances. Crucially, it also corresponds to a core assumption on the relationship between reformers and rent seekers, as will be discussed in due course. Before turning to that issue, however, the assumption under consideration will first be briefly examined with respect to the JMP's external performance both prior to and during the 2011 uprising.

For reasons of organizational integrity, the JMP had little scope to break its seesaw pattern of escalation and de-escalation up until the end of 2010. The prospects of realizing political and, most notably, electoral reform had been the glue keeping the alliance together, and these goals were later supplemented by the conflict settlements in Saʿda and the southern governorates. Each time negotiations with the regime about these issues had come to a standstill, and whenever the JMP had exhausted all the legal means it had to hand within the narrow confines of institutional politics, the alliance had to crank up the pressure so as to not abandon these pivotal goals entirely—and, therewith, its raison d'être. The periods of de-escalation following the regime's make-believe compromises—as constituted by, for instance, the December or February Agreement—are, however, not to be mistaken for an indication of political naïveté on the part of the High Council or insincerity regarding its proclaimed goals. For one thing, even though the regime had previously reneged on its promises on a number of occasions, the High Council could not completely rule out that the former would abide by its word this time. For another, and importantly, up until the July Accord the relationships of domination seemed to be largely intact, rendering the continuation of escalation a highly venturous endeavor. Last, continued escalation would have also jeopardized the alliance from within. Particularly Islah featured substantial segments of its party elite were reluctant to rigorously challenge Salih, either because they were unconvinced of the necessity of fundamental political change or because they did not want to bite too hard the hand that fed them.

These rationales fostered internal conflicts that, in turn, had significantly contributed to the JMP's pursuing of contradictory modes of communication throughout its history. Deviations from the alliance's official framing processes could even be detected during the uprising. This state of affairs was notably so at its very beginning when, for instance, the JMP branch in Taʿizz began calling for Salih's ouster, while Islah's deputy secretary-general, Muhammad al-Saʿdi, publicly stated that an extension of the incumbent's presidential term was uncontroversial and could be used as a bargaining chip in upcoming negotiations.[121]

While the earlier reasons can soundly account for the recurring instances of de-escalation up until the beginning of the uprising, it is much harder to explain why the JMP refrained from full escalation hereafter when the relationships of domination started to rapidly crumble. Despite the regime's incremental vulnerability, the JMP in fact upheld its preparedness for a negotiated solution until Salih's announcement of his resignation in November 2011. The following factors can be considered to have informed the High Council's decision in the main. To begin with, key foreign actors had exerted massive pressure on the JMP to engage in negotiations with the regime. Ever since 2006, both the United States and the European Union had called on the parties to enter talks and, later, to partake in a national dialogue. Notwithstanding Clinton's meeting with the JMP in January 2011, the Obama administration had repeatedly announced it would cling to Salih even into the early months of the uprising—including after the Friday of Dignity bloodshed.[122] Prior to February, 13, 2011—meaning the date when the JMP agreed to resume negotiations and thereby alienated the protesting youth—its representatives had attended a meeting at the US embassy, which hereafter published a statement urging the alliance to respond to the president's initiative.[123] Reportedly, it was this "summoning" to the US embassy and the JMP's ensuing acceptance of further negotiations that irrevocably destroyed the alliance's reputation among the protesting youth.[124]

Even after the Obama administration and European governments had let go of Salih, they kept forcing the JMP down the road of negotiations. The same held true for the GCC states, notably Saudi Arabia, which had masterminded the United Nations–backed GCC Initiative that was to provide the framework for such talks. Hence, according to a senior European diplomat involved, "the international community had made it painstakingly clear to the JMP" that there was no alternative to the GCC Initiative. He went on to say that Saudi Arabia, which had not been too enthusiastic about the prospects of strengthened democratic institutions in its neighboring country, eventually accepted this development becoming a key pillar of the GCC Initiative on "seeing the consequences of the possible failure of a negotiated solution."[125]

These consequences would have presumably been dire indeed, something that did not escape the JMP either. It is therefore very likely that the latter abstained from full escalation also for fear of causing, or contributing to causing, a full-fledged civil war and the disintegration of the Yemeni nation-state per se. Such fears had swayed the JMP's assessment of the domestic situation long before the uprising began. The state of security had been worsening ever since the 2006 presidential elections, particularly in the South as well as in Sa'da and its adjacent governorates. Since 2009, meanwhile, AQAP had stepped up its activities in large parts of the country, thereby adding a sectarian dimension to its conflict dynamics at the national and subnational levels. In the face of this confluence of acute crises, there was hence little doubt among international scholars that Yemen was "on the brink"[126] or "teeter[ing] on the edge of becoming a failed state."[127] Protagonists on the ground, too, were painfully aware of the fragile context they were operating in: there is no shortage of preuprising statements to be found by senior JMP members cautioning about Yemen becoming a second Afghanistan or Somalia.[128]

Hence, the JMP did take the likelihood of civil war and state failure very seriously, particularly in late 2010 into 2011.[129] Its concerns were reported in the press,[130] and acknowledged by Yemeni analysts.[131] The majority of the country's political elite, too, realized the risk associated with the breaking off of negotiations. In a survey conducted in December 2010, two-thirds of the interviewed public intellectuals and politicians indicated that they strongly believed in the necessity of holding a national dialogue.[132] The following month, prominent public individuals, political organizations, and tribal associations took turns in attempting to bring the GPC and antiregime actors—including most notably the JMP—to the negotiating table.[133] Despite such broad elite support, the JMP's preparedness to talk also met with refusal, and it was not only the Independent Youth that looked blank on the issue of negotiations. In light of the nature of previous rounds of negotiations, one Yemeni political analyst would suggest that "what they were doing was political bargaining, and not even for the right price. There was an open dialogue, yet not about issues but about the . . . framework of the dialogue. . . . And these guys [that is, the JMP] were going back and forth, very obediently—despite the stupidity, the ridiculousness of the process."[134]

This fact was openly admitted by senior JMP representatives, though. In an interview in May 2010, for instance, the Yemeni Socialist Party's secretary-general, Nu'man, confessed that "whenever they [that is, the GPC] say come, we would go not because we like them but for the interest of the country. We go to the dialogue in order to preserve the last little thread between us."[135] In early 2011 that thread had worn even thinner, and, from the JMP's vantage point, the country's fate was hanging by it. Just two days before the JMP grudgingly accepted Salih's offer to resume negotiations, on February 13, al-Haqq's secretary-general, Hasan Zayd, for instance, stated that the protests had come to threaten both the regime and Yemen as such.[136] If the country was to avoid large-scale violent conflict, the JMP reasoned, it had to be poised to enter talks with the regime, despite the latter's incremental use of force and despite the alliance's consequential alienation of youth protesters. Notwithstanding multiple announcements about dropping out of the GCC Initiative, the JMP thus never sought to undermine it per se, as a senior European diplomat recalled. The GPC, for its part, never openly challenged the GCC Initiative but did attempt to thwart it time and again.[137]

There is yet another argument frequently made to explain the JMP's seemingly indulgent position toward the regime. The JMP, so the claim goes, had always been deeply enmeshed in Salih's patronage system and was not at all interested in subverting the very regime from which it had thrived for years. In other words, the JMP had never been striving for political reform but rather merely increased rents. The final section will address this popular allegation.

The Hijacked Revolution; or, Assessing the Rent-Seeking Claim

After the Friday of Dignity massacre in Sanaa's Change Square, the uprising continued for another eight months until Salih eventually agreed to resign from office.[138] During this tumultuous period, the JMP would forfeit its exalted position in the antiregime camp. The events of March 18 had set in motion dynamics that were extremely difficult for the High Council to influence—much less control—with the upheaval becoming both more militarized and internationalized. As such, the JMP was reduced to being but one in a group of multiple key actors affecting the trajectory of the uprising. The same could be said about the Independent Youth.

Unlike the latter, however, the JMP ended up as a contracting party of the GCC Initiative Agreement and, together with the GPC, formed part of the National Unity Government that was to steer the country through the subsequent two-year transitional period from December 2011 onward. It was also on account of this state of affairs that, in the immediate aftermath of Salih's signing of the GCC Initiative, the Independent Youth began referring to the uprising as the "stolen revolution" (*thawra masruqa*) or "hijacked revolution" (*thawra makhtufa*).

The Independent Youth's claim that "their revolution"[139] had been taken away by established elite actors, first and foremost the JMP, was both correct and simultaneously problematic. It was correct because the GCC Initiative acutely marginalized nonpartisan youth protesters—as well as other key members of the antiregime camp such as Ansar Allah or the Southern Movement—in those institutions that were tasked with shaping the post-Salih era, notably the government and the National Dialogue Conference initiated to prepare the new Constitution.[140] It was problematic, meanwhile, because it denied the JMP any credit for the toppling of Salih. The claim was furthermore based on a flawed dichotomy between the protesting youth, on the one hand, and the party opposition, on the other.[141] This dichotomy had been introduced by Salih in January 2011 to deepen the rift between what he called "the political forces" (*al-quwat al-siyasiyya*)—meaning the JMP—and "the revolutionary forces" (*al-quwat al-thawriyya*), that is, the nonpartisan (or independent) youth.[142] Yet this binary narrative did not take into account the fact that a large share of youth protesters were affiliated with the JMP's parties, or indeed that the latter, particularly Islah, had provided the country's revolutionary hubs—such as, for instance, Sanaa's Change Square—with valuable resources.[143]

Despite this, the nature of Islah's performance during the uprising would upset nonpartisan protesters and further added to the estrangement between them and the JMP. By mid-February 2011, the Independent Youth had become the driving force of the countrywide demonstrations and the actual face of the uprising. But Islah was set on making up ground on the nonpartisan youth, trying to reassert control over developments.[144] Particularly its conservative members would—together with Salafi activists from outside the party—start to impose their agenda on the country's Change

Squares, thereby challenging what the (nonpartisan) youth considered the fundamental characteristics of the Youth Revolution, namely, freedom of opinion, tolerance, individualism, and gender equality.[145] While Islah's partners in the JMP, as well as its Muslim Brotherhood wing, presumably disapproved of the Salafis' encroachment on the Change Squares, they abstained from publicly intervening. When, for instance, on April 16 a group of nonpartisan activists in Sanaa were assaulted by Salafis because men and women had protested side by side—thereby engaging in what the former deemed the unmoral mingling of sexes (*ikhtilat*)—the High Council failed to denounce the incident despite the public uproar it caused. Only al-Mutawakkil of the UPF apologized to the victims and in an open letter called on the other JMP parties to follow suit.[146] The fact that this expression of regret did not happen is indicative of just how important the conservative segments of the antiregime camp had come to be regarded by the High Council, particularly the tribes and the Salafis—who both had the capacity to introduce armed force to proceedings at a time when the uprising was already on the brink of violent escalation.[147]

The initial and indeed main reason for the Independent Youth's alienation from the JMP was the latter's sustained preparedness to negotiate, though. Further proof of this seemingly indulgent stance toward the regime was given on April 2, when the JMP published a five-point plan for Salih's transfer of power. This "last-chance offer" was to afford the president the opportunity for an "honorable withdrawal."[148] The five-point plan was coordinated with the United States, the European Union, and the GCC. It stipulated Salih's resignation but remained vague on the future of other key regime members—including the president's relatives. The plan thus matched the new position of the Obama administration, which was now prepared to let go of Salih, provided that the transfer of power "would enable the counterterrorism operation . . . to continue."[149] This development suggested that the counterterrorism file was to remain in the hands of officials who were members not only of the regime's inner circle but also, in part, of Salih's family, too. The five-point plan was instantly rejected by the Independent Youth—and by Salih himself. Immediately thereafter, the GCC took over. On April 5, negotiations were resumed under the leadership of Saudi Arabia and Oman. The following day, the

GCC Initiative was officially presented to the public and, shortly after, formally endorsed by the United States, the European Union, and the United Nations. Negotiations were facilitated by Jamal Benomar, who had been appointed UN special envoy to Yemen on April 2.

From April onward, the GCC Initiative provided the basic framework for all ensuing negotiations with the regime. At the most fundamental level, it granted Salih domestic immunity from prosecution in return for his resignation. It is important to note that the GCC Initiative was clearly a product of the Friday of Dignity massacre and, as such, an attempt to avert a looming civil war and the consequences thereof for regional security.[150] Also nicknamed "Bloody Friday," March 18 was a game changer. Within a few days, there were so many defections from the regime that then minister of water and environment, ʿAbd al-Rahman al-Iryani, commented on Facebook: "It is becoming silly that every member of the regime is now joining the revolution, when in fact they should render themselves to the revolution for crimes that they have committed against the people or looked the other way while these crimes were perpetrated."[151] Besides GPC officials, several of the military's top brass joined the uprising on March 21—including the commander of the First Armored Division, General Major ʿAli Muhsin al-Ahmar. Also, the head of the Hashid tribal confederation Sadiq al-Ahmar—brother of Hamid, but unrelated to ʿAli Muhsin—now declared his support for the antiregime forces. During an earlier JMP press conference held in mid-February, Nuʿman had used the term *baltajiyya* (literally "thugs, gangsters") as a synonym for widespread chaos and uncontrolled violence to warn the Independent Youth that "the country [had] entered a political vacuum soon to be filled by the *baltajiyya* on a bigger scale."[152] This scenario would turn real one month later.

Initial skirmishes between the troops of ʿAli Muhsin and the Republican Guard led by Salih's son Ahmad occurred just days after the former's defection.[153] Military combat and larger battles continued in the weeks that followed and became more intense after tribal fighters under the command of Sadiq al-Ahmar joined in on the side of ʿAli Muhsin. While these confrontations still fell short of outright war, they were often on the verge of turning into one—especially in May, September, and October 2011. Yet this standoff was just one theater of conflict. At the end of March,

Ansar Allah had taken control over Saʿda and thereafter began to expand its sway over adjacent governorates. In July, preliminary clashes between Ansar Allah and tribes affiliated with Islah were reported in al-Jawf Governorate, threatening to spur further violence. AQAP, in turn, attempted to take advantage of the situation in the southern governorates, from which the army had since withdrawn to engage with ʿAli Muhsin. In May, AQAP affiliate Ansar al-Sharia had captured the cities of Jaʿar and Zinjibar in Abyan Governorate. Although the army regained control over those cities in June, AQAP launched further successful offensives shortly thereafter. Amid such turmoil, the presidential palace in Sanaa was bombed on June 3. This attempt on his life left Salih seriously injured. For the next three months he would remain in Saudi Arabia, where he had headed for medical treatment. For all these developments, he still showed no willingness to compromise. When he returned to Sanaa on September 23, the situation would heat up once again.

It took Salih another two months until he could bring himself to accept the GCC Initiative. The magnitude and perseverance of resolute opposition to his rule from inside the country were factors that are likely to have finally forced him to capitulate. Presumably, another was external pressure, which had risen only further since his return to Yemen, too. Crucially in this respect, on October 21, the UN Security Council unanimously adopted Resolution 2014 that underlined "the need for a comprehensive, independent and impartial investigation consistent with international standards into the alleged human rights abuses and violations, with a view to avoiding impunity and ensuring full accountability." Somewhat contradictory, the resolution then "encouraged" Salih to "immediately sign the Gulf Cooperation Council initiative [sic]," hence suggesting that the latter was the last chance for him and other regime members to avoid prosecution.[154] Shortly hereafter, the European Union commenced discussion of the freezing of his and other regime members' assets.[155] All these developments must have shown the regime's inner circle that there was no returning to the status quo of before. After having failed to sign the GCC Initiative altogether four times in the preceding months, Salih eventually yielded to the relentless internal and external pressure—inking the agreement on November 23, 2011, in the Saudi capital, Riyadh.[156]

As mentioned, the other signatory party, the JMP, had never backed out of the GCC Initiative, despite Salih's multiple last-minute backtrackings—and even though it had won a powerful ally in 'Ali Muhsin by the end of March 2011. Since the latter had always had the reputation of being a staunch supporter of Salafism, few observers were taken by surprise in seeing him align with Islah and, by implication, the JMP. For many youth protesters, 'Ali Muhsin's joining of the uprising symbolized the end of the thitherto "peaceful revolution," and its alliance with him cost the JMP much sympathy again. How isolated the latter had become in the meantime could be seen in the fate of the National Council for the Forces of the Peaceful Revolution (al-majlis al-watani li-quwa al-thawra al-silmiyya) that the JMP had brought into being on August 17. Launched briefly after Salih had once more refused to sign the GCC Initiative, the council was supposed to act as a transitional government encompassing representatives of all major actors in the antiregime camp—including the Independent Youth, political parties, Ansar Allah, the Southern Movement, and tribes.[157] Yet many designated members declined to participate—most important, the representatives of Ansar Allah, the Southern Movement, and the Independent Youth.[158] The latter published a joint statement on August 20, as signed by more than 170 groups and organizations, justifying their rejection of "the entity fabricated by the JMP." They maintained that "the National Council [was] a body of the political forces which, while being supportive of the revolution, still believed in negotiations." The statement concluded by stressing the Independent Youth's flat refusal of the GCC Initiative.[159]

The reasons for the tough stance on the latter by the Independent Youth, Ansar Allah, and other antiregime forces were manifold and differed slightly from actor to actor. To name but a few shared ones: the reverberations from the Tunisian and Egyptian precedents, which had shown that one could get rid of longtime autocrats without negotiations; the prospects of impunity for regime members in general, as well as Salih and his relatives in particular; and the suspicion that external forces were imposing their will on Yemenis—especially Saudi Arabia and the United States, both of which had never been particularly popular in the country. While it is unclear whether greater inclusiveness would have softened this fundamental opposition to the GCC Initiative, it was a major flaw of the latter that key actors in the antiregime camp had been excluded from the list of negotiating parties from the outset. In fact, only the JMP officially represented that camp in the negotiations. Yet the alliance was not regarded as a "revolutionary force" by the bulk of the excluded actors, nor was it necessarily even seen as an antiregime force per se. Moreover, many of the JMP's critics did not even perceive the alliance as being the actual negotiator, pointing here to members of the al-Ahmar family and to 'Ali Muhsin instead. Many of its opponents thus looked on the GCC Initiative as either an attempt to broker a family feud (given 'Ali Muhsin's kinship ties with Salih), an intra-Hashid conflict (given that the president, 'Ali Muhsin, and the al-Ahmar family were all members of the Hashid tribal confederation), or an intraregime dispute (given that all major both official and unofficial negotiating parties were considered to be part of the Salih regime, including the JMP).[160] Although the latter view was not advanced by all members of the opposition camp, the JMP's loose alliance with 'Ali Muhsin—who had been an integral part of the Salih regime— did not improve its standing on Yemen's Change Squares. This point was also true for the JMP's relationship with Hamid al-Ahmar who, just like his brother Sadiq or 'Ali Muhsin, was seen as a major contender for power.

As outlined in the previous chapter, the JMP had long profited from Hamid al-Ahmar's presence within its ranks on the grounds of the crucial resources he would supply the alliance with. Although al-Ahmar began to hamper the internal functioning of the JMP soon after joining, the real price for his inclusion was to be paid in the alliance's external performance. Al-Ahmar had always strained the latter's framing processes. During the uprising, however, his person all but shattered its credibility entirely as a serious alternative to the Salih regime. To the Independent Youth, Ansar Allah, the Southern Movement, and even many youth activists associated with the JMP, al-Ahmar was the perfect embodiment of a corrupt regime renegade who intended to reinstate the old patterns under his own leadership. Yet now, the JMP was not only blamed for assisting his endeavors; rather, it was no longer seen as an independent institution but one that merely served his political ambitions. Already in January 2011, the PCND was thus being referred to as "the Hamid al-Ahmar Committee for Dialogue."[161] The same was said about the National Council for the Forces of the Peaceful Revolution, and non-partisan activists stressed the disproportionately high representation of the al-Ahmar family in it to make their point.[162] Even those JMP representatives who had been deemed most credible and upstanding such as al-Mutawakkil came to be regarded with the utmost suspicion. Indeed, one of the latter's daughters publicly expressed her disbelief about her father's participation in the above body, holding that she was unable to comprehend "how the name of my father, whose discretion had always struck me as the discretion of the heroes in the famous sagas, [could] be listed alongside the [names of those] warlords."[163]

Yet others found it less difficult to understand why JMP elites had allied with al-Ahmar and the like. To many of its critics in the antiregime camp, the JMP's elites had always been an integral part of Salih's patronage system. They would argue that the alliance had formed part and parcel of the regime ever since its inception, and the former's behavior during the uprising was seen as only further proof thereof. Some youth activists, for instance, maintained that "the opposition was the official partner of Salih for thirty years," and that "they were threatened by the revolution as much as Salih."[164] This assessment was also seconded by observers lacking any political affiliation, one of whom claimed that "in February 2011, they [that is, JMP elites] were not yet ready to stand in open defiance to Salih because then they lose their patronage payments."[165] From this perspective, then, the JMP was not an alliance for political reform but one of rent seekers—or, in more idiomatic terms, a coalition of "the corrupt" (al-fasidun) or "the self-interested" (al-maslahiyun).

While one should be cautious in dealing with such allegations—which were widespread in Yemen's political fray despite, or because of, their impossibility of verification—there is little reason to refute them outright. Major strands of research on contemporary Yemen have demonstrated that patronage was an established means of rule long before the advent of the Salih regime,[166] which, in turn, was shown to have operated an inclusive patronage system for most of its existence.[167] That is, patronage under Salih's presidency was inclusive at the elite level to the extent that its rejection prompted regime retribution since, for instance, the nonacceptance of bribes would have "challenge[d] the very organization of power around the president."[168] This fact also applied to the political opposition, and most notably Islah—which was not only the strongest opposition party but also a former longtime ally of the GPC. Many Islah elites, indeed, would remain on good terms with Salih long after the party's pulling out from government in 1997.[169] Only in the face of dwindling resources from the middle of the first decade of the new century onward would the patronage system become more exclusive.

This latter point, however, does not impugn the claim of the JMP being a rent-seeking coalition. On the contrary, its external performance can be reconciled with the contractions of the patronage system—if one conceives of the alliance's stepped-up efforts at mobilization as an attempt to increase once more its share of the regime's distributed rents.[170] The alliance started to engage in serious mobilization only in the aftermath of the 2006 elections, with rent distributions now shrinking. The more exclusive patronage became in the years that followed, the more contentious the actions of the alliance would come to be. As key JMP elites were still part of the patronage system, though, the alliance abstained from outright conflict escalation throughout.

The JMP's behavior in government after December 2011 did nothing to invalidate the claim. In contrast, roughly six months in, al-Mutawakkil, who had transformed into a critic of the JMP by then, would lament that "some [JMP] parties are still more interested in their own well-being than in the well-being of the country."[171] His criticism grew louder as more cases of nepotism on the part of the JMP became public.[172] One such incidence occurred in October 2012 in the Islah-led Ministry of Electricity, with nineteen friends and relatives of the minister in charge having been employed without meeting the required skills. As one source inside the ministry stated to the press, "It's like one mafia replaced another."[173] In December 2012, even the UN special envoy to Yemen, Benomar, publicly complained that the governing parties cared less about reform than they did about securing lucrative positions for themselves and others.[174]

Such examples—and, more significantly, the structural incentives facilitating rent-seeking behavior among members of the opposition—aside, the picture was never that clear-cut. Not all the JMP's high-level elites—let alone its mid- and low-level ones—formed part of Salih's patronage system, and there were certainly a substantial number genuinely committed to introducing political reforms that would fundamentally alter the system in place. This fact was not contested by observers either inside or outside the country. There was also agreement that opposition members representing specific social segments were particularly prone to rent-seeking behavior, notably those parts affiliated with the tribes and the business sector.[175] What was hotly disputed, though, was whether the rent seekers or reformers inside the JMP were in the majority and what the collaboration between both groups meant with respect to overall assessment of the alliance as such. Furthermore, and given that the JMP is far from being the sole empirical example of this phenomenon, how, then, can one best explain the cooperation between reformers and rent seekers within opposition alliances operating in patronage-based autocracies?

Initially, the concept of rent seeking was "designed to describe behavior in institutional settings where individual efforts to maximize value generate social waste rather than social surplus."[176] Originally developed by economists to analyze the behavior of a rational actor (*Homo oeconomicus*) in a nonmarket situation, the concept was soon adopted by political scientists for the analysis of group behavior in allocation or rentier states—meaning in "all those states whose revenue derives predominantly (more than 40 per cent) from oil or other foreign sources [that is, rents] and whose expenditure is a substantial share of the GDP."[177] To understand the assumed impact of rentier structures on collective action, however, one must first review the political assumptions underpinning rentier-state theory. Boiled down to its essentials, the latter holds that the incumbent regime in such states enjoys substantial political autonomy from its domestic society owing to the constant flow of external rent revenues, relieving them from the need to intensely tax their domestic populations. "[Because] an allocation state only spends and does not tax, its expenditure policy . . . will . . . usually be seen as benefiting everybody."[178]

In other words, allocation or rentier states provide little incentive for political participation and the formation of political parties representing the socioeconomic preferences of marginalized segments of the population. Parties that emerge nonetheless thus either have a "cultural or ideological orientation," meaning that "in practice, Islamic fundamentalism appears to be the only rallying point around which something approaching a party can form in the Arab allocation states."[179] Or it is expected that parties are affected by rentier structures to such an extent that the preferences informing their interactions with the incumbent regime can be reduced to but rent seeking, meaning that, in such settings, political parties—including opposition ones—by their nature solely endeavor to secure their share of rents by being included in the regime's patronage system.[180] It has even been emphatically argued that in rentier states, "there is always an opposition, but the opposition will not be any more democratic than the ruler."[181]

While this latter position might be theoretically overstretched, the impact of rentier structures on opposition preferences and behavior is empirically observable in the rentier states existing both in and beyond the Middle East. Also, it is likely that rent seekers often outnumber their reform-oriented peers in the opposition—that is, if one adopts a dichotomous understanding of rent seekers and reformers for analytical purposes. The problem with this assumed dichotomy is less whether reformers, too, can be conceived of as rational actors, which is plausible if one does not foreclose the possibility of preference formation being exogenous to prevailing structures and processes.[182] What one struggles to explain, rather, is how cooperation between these two kinds of actors even comes about given the inherent goal divergence between them: Rent seekers strive for personal material gain and, as such, for an exclusive good.[183] In contrast, reformers are interested in producing an inclusive good as they work toward implementing structural changes, or the reform of the entire (political) system, thereby benefiting everyone in society except the rent seekers. The goals of rent seekers and reformers are, therefore, not only incompatible but also potentially conflictive. Against this backdrop, there are two possible ways to account for the fact such cooperation does still happen regardless. The first is nescience. Neither rent seekers nor reformers know about the true intentions of the other camp when launching cooperation. This situation is improbable, though, since both groups would have been subject to the same structural incentives for an extended period of time and are likely to have gathered information about their prospective partners prior to the onset of cooperation.

Second, if both groups do know about their diverging respective goals and cooperate nonetheless, then they must expect to benefit from cooperation—even if transiently. In view of the anticipated increase in strength or transformative capacity resulting from such cooperation, this proposition is not too farfetched. Although their goals are disparate and the roads toward them might not entirely intersect, one could expect them to be able to cover long distances together regardless. The calculations of reformers in this context are easier to tease out. Since they are working toward producing inclusive goods benefiting large parts of society, they might assume that, with increased popular support, they will be capable of catching the rent seekers as they cross the finish line or even replace them with like-minded actors en route once the broadening of cooperation has gained traction.

Identifying rent seekers' calculations is a more complex endeavor, however. They must not cut ties with reformers too early on and should continue to support the latter—if only symbolically—in their attempts to challenge the regime until the right moment for a parting of ways has come about. In the meantime, however, rent seekers must not break with the regime entirely. This necessity is because they do not intend to change the existing system, nor do they want to topple the incumbent: the risk involved in the pursuit of either goal would be too high, jeopardizing the very system they profit from. Instead, by transiently cooperating with reformers against the incumbent regime, they either seek to jack up the price for their (future) loyalty or strive for their inclusion once more in the patronage system (should they have earlier been excluded from it).

As counterintuitive as it may seem, hybrid alliances between rent seekers and reformers are thus possible, and they can be assumed to remain viable so long as both camps envisage themselves to share more or less the same road toward their respective goals. Indeed, the JMP's external performance since its inception as a strategic opposition alliance can be neatly explained as being in line with this assumption, at least up until February 2011: From November 2005 onward, the alliance repeatedly escalated the conflict with the Salih regime. In doing so, the reformers sought to hustle the regime into introducing serious political change, whereas the rent seekers, depending on their position with respect to the patronage system, strove either for their readmission into it or for an increased share of its rents. Then again, the alliance recurrently de-escalated the conflict with the regime because both groups (rent seekers and reformers) were concerned about the potential consequences ensuing from prolonged, outright hostility. While the rent seekers feared for the continuance of the patronage system itself, or their future participation in it, the reformers worried about the outbreak of civil war. It is important to note here that this explanation for the JMP's seesaw pattern of escalation and de-escalation does not challenge but complements the one discussed in the previous section, since the behavioral and communicative modes of collective opposition action often coming into conflict with one another can be explained by the contradictory preferences of reformers and rent seekers, respectively. This point is no less true when stating that, empirically, pure reformer and pure rent seeker are both unlikely creatures. In Yemen, at least, "few prominent figures [were] squarely on one side or the other of this divide; instead, many [fell] into a grey zone."[184]

Also because of this last reservation, one is left to wonder whether rent-seeking tendencies did indeed dominate the JMP's agenda, as maintained by its critics. While a definitive answer cannot be given, certain clues seem to hint at this claim's dubious veracity. First, there was the relatively large number of JMP constituent parties as well as their differing strengths. As mentioned, rents are an exclusive good from which only a limited amount of benefit can be derived. Had the JMP thus been an alliance dominated by rent seekers, there would likely have been serious attempts to reduce the number of beneficiaries to its most powerful constituents, Islah and the YSP. Also, the weaker parties like the Nasserist Unionist People's Organization or the UPF would have had little incentive to join an alliance with overwhelmingly stronger partners that, as dominant rent seekers, would have lacked any motivation to abide by previous agreements regarding the spoils being equally shared. Yet those small parties were a core part of the JMP, remaining so even within the transitional National Unity Government.

Second, there were the JMP's elaborate platforms (the Plan for Political and National Reform and the *Vision for National Salvation*), its internal setup, and the significant efforts it undertook to accomplish both. Put differently, it is hard to imagine why an alliance dominated by rent seekers would have troubled itself with approaching either task in earnest. Had the JMP been such an alliance, it would have needed no more than one or two catchy slogans disguising its actual target. And since the cooperation of rent seekers can be deemed tactical in nature, there would have been no gain to be had from the complex organizational structures the JMP toiled to build. For that matter, it is also highly unlikely that any form of strategic cooperation is bestridden by rent seekers. Last, and importantly, had the JMP been dominated by rent seekers, it would have abandoned escalation and disbanded as an alliance once it had obtained (higher) rents. Contrary to this assumption, however, the JMP forewent this chance when Salih offered the alliance to join government and hence gain access to the state coffers. In fact, the JMP turned down such offers on at least four occasions between May 22, 2010, and February 28, 2011.[185]

For all these observations, when it joined the transitional government in December 2011, the JMP did give the impression that it was no more than a mere rent-seeking coalition. This outcome might have even become true by then, as forces other than the reformers appeared to have gained the upper hand inside the alliance in the eight months preceding Salih's approval of the GCC Initiative. In any case, the JMP's performance in government was utterly sobering when measured by its own standards (as formulated in, for instance, its platforms). To be sure, the challenges facing the National Unity Government in the transitional period were immense right from the start; also worthy of note is that the JMP was not the sole governing party, nor was the government the all-dominant actor in shaping the transition's trajectory. That notwithstanding, what the JMP did or did not do in government, and why, merits as much scholarly attention as the question of how its chosen courses of action contributed to the failure of the transition process—and, by implication, to the outbreak of civil war in

2014. While the latter will be briefly discussed in the concluding chapter, those key desiderata are beyond the scope of this book and so must be addressed elsewhere in due course.

Conclusion

This chapter completed the analysis of the JMP's external performance both conceptually and chronologically. Put differently, any study exploring the JMP as a case of strategic opposition cooperation must end in December 2011, being the point in time when the alliance joined the National Unity Government and as such ceased to be an opposition entity. The JMP can therefore be regarded as one of the few empirical examples of opposition alliances successfully challenging authoritarian regimes and turning into governing forces. It is true that the circumstances surrounding the JMP's ascension to power were extraordinary. The latter was greatly facilitated by a nationwide upheaval that itself was accelerated—if not altogether made possible—by the region-wide uprising that would come to be known as the Arab Spring. It would be flawed to assume that the JMP had merely scored a fluky success, though. Despite the seesaw pattern of conflict escalation and de-escalation characterizing the alliance's relationship with the regime from its formal establishment through deep into the 2011 uprising, its external performance had contributed significantly to changing the relationships of domination that had helped sustain Salih's rule for decades. Besides, and notwithstanding the harsh criticism that came its way during the uprising, the JMP ultimately also had a significant role to play in forcing him to finally abdicate.

These various contentions serve as a sound starting point for briefly rounding up the chapter's theoretical discussions. To begin with, the relational nature of an alliance's transformative capacity was stressed. That is, the strength of an alliance in itself—regardless of its scope in absolute terms—merely provides an indirect clue to its transformative capacity, or the likelihood of goal attainment. This state of affairs is because the relationships of domination hinge on the strength and decisions of all principal actors, including the regime as well as those actors bolstering the latter without belonging to its inner circle. The stronger an alliance becomes, however, the more likely it is to induce changes in those relationships of domination, which may then serve to undermine regime stability.

Second, the chapter sought to provide an explanation for the often confounding external performance of alliances vis-à-vis authoritarian incumbents. To this end, it differentiated between the behavioral and communicative modes characterizing the actions (or inactions) of the opposition, holding that what alliances do does not always match what they say. This situation owes to the domestic authoritarian structures constraining alliances, which prompt them to frequently swap the sites of contention, on the one hand, and attract disparate constituencies, on the other. One can therefore soundly reconstruct why such alliances switch between escalation and de-escalation within relatively short intervals, or why they may even simultaneously engage in both escalatory and de-escalatory courses of action.

Beyond doubt, internal factors may aggravate this seesaw pattern of conflict escalation and de-escalation. For one thing, and despite an even high degree of internal coherence, alliances consist of discrete actors (that is, political parties) that, while agreeing on an overall strategy, might subvert the common stance of a given cooperative endeavor in one or more fields of action, thereby adding to its ambiguous external performance. For another, alliances operating in patronage-based autocracies are likely to include significant numbers of rent seekers whose motives for engaging in escalation or de-escalation differ fundamentally from the aims of their reform-minded colleagues. In any case, the chapter argued that hybrid alliances between rent seekers and reformers not only are possible but also may prove to be a rather enduring phenomenon. In principle, and third, cooperation between reformers and rent seekers remains viable so long as both groups (consider themselves to) share the same path toward their respective goals.

It is by and large the latter two assumptions that help explain the JMP's severe decline in popular standing during roughly the final year of its existence as an opposition alliance. Before the advent of the Arab Spring in Yemen, the JMP had considerably broadened the opposition front, and its increased strength had helped alter the established relationships of domination. Corresponding processes had been progressively unfolding since midway through the first decade of the new millennium owing to, among other reasons, the growing exclusiveness of the regime's patronage system. While hardly discernible at first, these shifts gained momentum in late 2010, when the beginnings of the regional uprising in Tunisia coincided with the domestic uproar caused by Salih's announcement of further proposed constitutional amendments beneficial only to himself. The JMP-led popular protests against these amendments then gradually opened out into a more fundamental revolt emulating the emerging regional pattern of contestation. Notwithstanding the incrementally diverging demands between nonpartisan protesters and the JMP, the alliance remained the main organizer of mass demonstrations until mid-February 2011 when it decided to resume talks with the GPC. Although these and subsequent negotiations led to nothing, and despite the regime increasingly turning to outright violence to quell the protests, the alliance never abandoned its preparedness to pursue a negotiated solution in the months that followed. Yet the reasons for the JMP's unceasing readiness to talk with the regime during this period differed from previous instances of de-escalation. On the one hand, key international actors had pressed it to adhere to this path. On the other hand, key JMP elites had long argued that negotiations were the only way to avoid an impending civil war. Regardless of its public justifications, however, the alliance thereby antagonized other antiregime actors, notably the Independent Youth, Ansar Allah, and the Southern Movement.

It was, though, not only the JMP's stance toward the GCC Initiative or its attempts to dominate the Youth Revolution that led to its alienation from other key actors within the antiregime camp. Given the presence of prominent rent seekers in its own ranks as well as its aligning with renowned regime renegades in the aftermath of the Friday of Dignity massacre, the JMP was no longer seen as an eligible alternative to, but rather an essential element of, the Salih regime by most protest groups. While the reformers' cooperation with the rent seekers might have been profitable and maybe even inevitable in the past, it turned into a major liability during the uprising—and, indeed, on the JMP's later joining of the government, too.

Conclusion

This book set out to explore the basics of strategic opposition cooperation under authoritarianism. To this end, it has studied the Joint Meeting Parties, a Yemeni alliance that stands out in several respects when compared to other instances of opposition alliances both in and beyond the Arab world. Encompassing Sunni and Zaydi Islamist, leftist, and Arab nationalist parties, the JMP constituted a remarkable case of cross-ideological cooperation—and a highly unlikely one at that, seeing as its major constituents, Islah and the Yemeni Socialist Party, had shared a long history of violent confrontation prior to the JMP's formation.

Besides its peculiar composition, the JMP also made for an interesting case study because its sheer longevity allowed for analysis of the gradual evolution of opposition cooperation in Yemen per se. The JMP's roots could be traced back to 1996, when it started out as a tactical alliance. Despite a series of genuine setbacks, it was turned into a strategic alliance in 2005, having a comprehensive reform agenda and elaborate organizational structures fit to ensure its institutional upkeep and capacity to compete with one of the region's most enduring regimes. Another key incentive to study the JMP arose from its ambiguous external performance. For one thing, the JMP continuously drew in popular support from the 2006 presidential and local council elections onward, and it also aligned with other key opposition actors to challenge the regime of 'Ali 'Abdallah Salih. But in 2011, when the confrontation with the latter was at its height, its popularity declined severely and cooperation with its newfound allies came to naught. For another, its conflict behavior toward the regime was often inconsistent and contradictory, as were the assessments thereof by Yemeni elites and international scholars alike. Last, its success—or, more accurately, successes—provided a compelling reason to investigate the JMP. When it comes to opposition alliances, this state of affairs is often measured in terms of endurance. Yet the JMP not only persisted despite internal crises and multiple regime attempts to divide it but also ultimately managed to outlive the latter and become a member of the transitional government in late 2011.

Drawing on a variety of hitherto unused sources, including original interviews, platforms, bylaws, memoirs, social media data, and Yemeni newspapers, the book answers three interconnected questions whose discussion was also deemed conducive to our better understanding of other cases of strategic cooperation elsewhere: What gave rise to the emergence of the JMP? How did it organize itself as a strategic alliance, and with what consequences? And, finally, how did the JMP interact with the principal relevant actors outside the alliance, and why? In line with this set of key questions, substantial parts of the book have engaged in process tracing to discover the causal mechanisms at work behind the formation of the JMP and affecting its subsequent behavior vis-à-vis the regime.

One upshot thereof is that the JMP's overall performance cannot be explained without considering the internal limitations to cooperation, on the one hand, and the structural constraints as well as endeavors of other leading actors, on the other. By way of example, the JMP's behavior in 2006 differed from its conduct in 2010 since internal and external conditions had critically altered in the meantime. In the aftermath of the 2006 elections, its actions were geared toward electoral reform and remained within the confines of institutional politics. This chosen focus conformed with the primary interests of its constituent parties and met with support from Yemen's international donors. In contrast, in 2010 the goal of electoral reform had been eclipsed by the aim of conflict settlement in Sa'da and the country's southern governorates, while the JMP's actions now increasingly focused on hitting the streets. But this shift in strategy and orientation was not merely a consequence of the regime's intransigence on electoral reform. It also stemmed from a reassessment of the general political situation and changing interests on the part of key constituent parties. For instance, the rise of the Southern Movement in 2007 had affected the calculations of the YSP, which thereafter had to shift attention to the grievances of the South lest it lose its core constituencies. On top of that change came the increased flow of international aid to the regime in the wake of the "Christmas Bomber" incident, which reduced its willingness to compromise on the issue of electoral reform. All these events led to a change in the JMP's goals and behavior, in turn possible only because of the nature of the alliance's internal setup.

In other words, this book has produced a thick analysis of the JMP and its impact on Yemeni politics up until Salih's eventual abdication from power in November 2011. Not only has it homed in on the JMP's constituent parties and their interests, how these were accommodated within the institutional framework of the alliance, and sought their accomplishment via joint action. But the preceding pages have also scrutinized the Salih regime, its gatekeeping of Yemen's political economy, and how its corresponding policies impacted on both the JMP and the incumbent's other major critics—including Ansar Allah, the Southern Movement, and, later, the Independent Youth, all of which had been potential or actual allies to the JMP. Empirically speaking, and in terms of achievements, this book can hence be read as alternative political history of the third republic on Yemeni soil in that it adopts the perspective of pivotal opposition forces that were either (formally) established on the founding of the Republic of Yemen—such as the bulk of the JMP's parties—or had emerged before Salih's inking of the Gulf Cooperation Council Initiative finally marked the end of his decades-long rule and, by implication, a watershed moment in the recent history of South Arabia.

The book's second achievement lies beyond the domain of Middle East studies and thus spans, too, comparative research on political opposition, authoritarianism, and political transformation. To date, scholarship on opposition cooperation under authoritarianism has found itself compartmentalized. Extant studies have covered important aspects of the matter (notably with respect to the reasons for cooperation failure) but have thus far failed to provide a comprehensive analysis of the factors behind the formation—and, crucially, maintenance—of strategic opposition cooperation. The book has risen to this challenge. In what might be best described as a hybrid process of inductive and deductive reasoning, it has discussed a set of assumptions concerning the onset conditions of strategic opposition cooperation and the internal as well as external constraints strategic alliances face when challenging authoritarian incumbents. In the following section, these assumptions will be briefly recapitulated and contextualized.

The Logic of Opposition Cooperation

The book has been subdivided into four chapters analyzing the launching of the JMP (chapter 1) as well as its internal (chapter 2) and external (chapters 3 and 4) performance. Each chapter has featured theoretical discussions providing generalizable explanations for the empirical phenomena under scrutiny. At times, the ensuing assumptions have been formulated explicitly; more often, though, they have been stated implicitly. Appendix B thus gives an overview of all the major assumptions that have been discussed in this book. As highlighted in the corresponding chapters, some of those assumptions are based on previous work on (opposition) cooperation by other scholars; some draw on related theoretical discussions, yet ones that had thus far not been incorporated into the study of opposition cooperation per se; still others have been derived in an inductive manner from the case study at hand. While their relevance to other empirical contexts remains to be seen in future research, these assumptions are expected to capture several core rationales of strategic opposition cooperation. This outcome appears even more probable when the assumptions are boiled down to their essentials and put into context. This section therefore seeks to outline what might be called "the logic of strategic opposition cooperation under authoritarianism."

Any such venture must begin with a discussion of the conditions that give rise to opposition cooperation in autocracies in the first place. Given the imbalanced resource distribution between the opposition and authoritarian incumbents and the absence of binding rules governing their interaction, the former is seriously disadvantaged. One apparent way for opposition parties to compensate for these structural impediments is to concentrate their resources.[1] Yet despite its alleged benefits, opposition cooperation is a relatively infrequent empirical phenomenon, while instances of sustained cooperation are rarer still. Chapter 1 discussed why this situation is so and suggested four requirements that need to be ful-filled for cooperation to be initiated: goal convergence, a surplus of ben-efits, balanced attitudes, and central committed elites.

These requirements vary in complexity, and not all are situated at the same level of analysis. Goal convergence is so fundamental a requirement as to be almost tautological given that cooperation is commonly defined in terms of actors working together toward a particular end. Yet it is as quintessential as it is instructive, since the number of shared goals is in-strumental in differentiating between tactical (single-issue) and strategic (multiple-issue) forms of cooperation. Connectedly, multiple goals being in play affects the calculations of prospective partners. It complicates cooperation, requiring greater coordination efforts among and conflict-resolution mechanisms between parties—not to mention a heightened need to keep an eye on potential defections, too. In short, the existence of multiple goals entails the building of organizational structures—even if only rudimentary ones. These structures, in turn, affect the parties' cost-benefit calculations in that they raise the internal and external burdens of cooperation. For the latter to ensue, then, the benefits of engaging in it must be expected to outweigh the costs thereof. Likewise, attitudinal con-straints impact alliance building, and it has been argued that ideological discrepancies, a lack of trust, and dissimilar positions in conflict impede strategic cooperation, and vice versa. Just how important balanced atti-tudes are can be seen in those empirical cases where strategic cooperation did not materialize even despite its expected benefits.[2]

Whereas goal convergence, a surplus of benefits, and balanced atti-tudes are to be treated as key requirements—or necessary conditions—for the onset of strategic cooperation, a more parsimonious take on the mat-ter should dispense with central committed elites. This is not to question their overall relevance. However, when contemplating the chain of cau-sality between the above-mentioned conditions and the outcome, central committed elites are best conceived of as an intervening variable. It is they who facilitate the smoothing out of attitudinal constraints and convince their fellow party members of the benefits of cooperation; only after they have gotten the better of those peers hostile to cooperation, meanwhile, can their parties meet the conditions for cooperation. Put differently, central committed elites sway the necessary conditions, but it is the latter alone that ultimately affect the outcome of interest (the inception or not of strategic cooperation).

In this condensed form, then, only goal convergence, a surplus of benefits, and balanced attitudes form the necessary conditions for strategic opposition cooperation's onset. Crucially, they also form the basic conditions for the maintenance of cooperation, too. Chapter 2 discussed the extent to which organizational structures govern the internal performance of alliances, stressing the significance of decision-making ones at the horizontal, interparty level for the reproduction of the basic conditions of cooperation. For the sake of parsimony, however, the latter argument can be extended to organizational structures overall. That is, the primary task of organizational structures is to keep cooperation running. To elaborate hereon: chapter 2 maintained that the organizational structures of alliances not only serve to ensure these basic conditions' reproduction but also facilitate its internal mobilization capabilities by way of resource redistribution and commitment building. Ultimately, though, internal mobilization can and should be subsumed as a function of cooperation maintenance. This is because the malfunctioning of resource redistribution within the alliance would increase the internal costs of cooperation for its constituents and hence negatively impact their related cost-benefit calculations; underperformance in terms of commitment building within the alliance would negatively bear, meanwhile, on the attitudinal component of cooperation and hence strengthen those elites within its ranks who are deprecatory of—or even overtly hostile to—cooperation. In both cases, cooperation would be set to falter. In a nutshell, then, the internal logic of strategic opposition cooperation solely consists in perpetuating it.

Next, the assumptions put forth on the external performance of alliances need some contextualization. To begin with, if there is one overarching endeavor characterizing alliances' interactions with their external environment, it is goal attainment. It is the prospect of reaching mutually shared goals that makes for cooperation in the first place, and chapter 3 maintained that in order to uphold cooperation the members of strategic alliances must be convinced—and remain so, whatever the odds—that goal attainment is more than a pie-in-the-sky ambition. Achieving a common purpose is key, and all residual assumptions put forth in chapters 3 and 4 discussed how the external performance relates to goal attainment, in what ways the former can contribute to the latter, or how authoritarian structures impair the behavior of alliances regarding the pursuit of their core objectives. Therefore, and unlike its internal counterpart, the external logic of strategic opposition cooperation is geared ultimately toward goal attainment.

An alliance's internal and external performances are plainly interconnected. Neither empirically nor conceptually can one conceive of the former without taking account of its relationship to the latter. Yet since both abide by distinct logics—cooperation maintenance, on the one hand, and goal attainment, on the other—it appears expedient to treat them as analytically distinct categories. This state of affairs seems also to be necessitated by the fact that both logics may come into conflict with one another. Significant proof of such contradictions has been found throughout the course of this book. To cite just a few examples: In some critical passages of the JMP's 2005 platform, precedence was given to those formulations that safeguarded the interests of all constituent parties over ones that might have contrariwise met with more popular support. Also, the JMP's approach to electoral coordination demonstrates how the internal logic of cooperation maintenance interfered with the external one of goal attainment, with the High Council at times privileging less promising candidates from one constituent party over stronger peers from another for the sake of the alliance's overall integrity. Or there were the tardy efforts by the JMP to reach out to Ansar Allah. Allying with the latter would have increased the alliance's clout vis-à-vis regime contestation and would thus have been beneficial in terms of overall goal attainment. For long, though, going down this road was precluded by Islah's opposition to it. The party's de facto veto position was rendered possible by the principle of unanimity rule, which was otherwise highly conducive to sustaining cooperation.

These and other instances discussed in the book therefore suggest that considerations regarding cooperation maintenance usually outweigh those factors concerning goal attainment. In other words, whenever the internal logic of strategic opposition cooperation collides with its external one, the former tends to trump the latter. This proposition, however, must be treated with some caution. First, by way of an example cited previously that seems to point to the contrary being true: Confronted with Islah's peripheral elites, whose actions would repeatedly compromise the alliance's integrity, the High Council typically took a fairly lenient position toward these individuals. It has been argued that it did so because these peripheral elites not only headed powerful party wings but also were able to attract the key constituencies needed to genuinely take on the Salih regime. Considering the above-made proposition, though, an alternative and indeed complementary explanation could be that a tougher stance toward these peripheral elites would have endangered the integrity of Islah—and, by implication, the integrity of the alliance, too.

Second, this book falls short of providing robust explanations as to why that internal logic ultimately gains the upper hand over its external counterpart. One aspect thereof might lie in the core interests of the committed elites, whose power position inside their parties after entering the alliance is bound to either the continuity of the alliance or its ultimate success. Given this situation, and aware of the regime's competitive advantage, committed elites may lean toward playing it safe. That at least appears to be the most rationale approach to the politics of opposition in autocracies, at least until opportunity structures finally become more auspicious. However pertinent this tentative explanation might be, it is reminiscent of the fact that neither the external nor the internal logic of cooperation operates independently of the authoritarian structures that the alliance is embedded in—notably with respect to the relationships of domination.

Whereas this second reservation points to new potential avenues for future research, the third and final one must reiterate the general limits of this book per se. Theory building from cases is admissible and fruitful if several conditions are met. Yet given the exploratory research design underpinning this case study, the validity of its theoretical findings must ultimately be tested and further enhanced by future analyses—be they single- or multiple-case studies or variable-oriented research endeavors drawing on large-N designs. Since opposition cooperation is an important feature of modern-day politics, the universe of cases continues to expand apace. Interesting cases of opposition cooperation, including strategic ones, can be found both inside and outside the Middle East—and perhaps soon again in Yemen itself, too. After all, the JMP has been suggested as a potential role model for the country's postwar future, and even one that could help end the current armed hostilities. This idea will be now briefly discussed in closing.

Cooperation beyond the JMP

Symbols are deceptive creatures, not least because their referents can change over time. In 1996, when Ta'izz provided the setting for the initial meetings between Islah and the YSP that would eventually usher in the JMP's founding, the city—if only for a handful of Yemeni elites—stood for rapprochement between erstwhile enemies set to overcome their previous animosity for the sake of a more prosperous future.[3] Roughly twenty years later, it had come to signify quite the opposite. As the longest-running battleground in Yemen's latest war, Ta'izz by now exemplified the intractability of a multilevel conflict that had caused the world's worst humanitarian crisis.[4] In a conflict repeatedly labeled "the forgotten war" in the international media, the city was said to be the one place in Yemen that "feels most forgotten of all."[5] In a nutshell, within little more than two decades, Ta'izz had gone from being the embodiment of peaceful compromise to becoming a byword for the devastating war that unfolded in 2015 and, indeed, remains ongoing at the time of writing.

Effectively sidelined by the GCC Initiative,[6] Ansar Allah in 2014 profited from popular discontent with the political transition, still-rampant corruption, and soaring prices for basic commodities—which, in part, had been intentionally raised by the National Unity Government, led by interim president 'Abd Rabbuh Mansur Hadi, in compliance with the demands of the International Monetary Fund.[7] Ansar Allah's growth was also accompanied by the weakening of Islah, which had become Yemen's dominant political party following Salih's resignation. Yet from 2011 onward, Ansar Allah gradually extended its sway in the Northern Highlands, where local power dynamics are still pretty much a function of tribal politics. By the summer of 2014, the group had come to control the entirety of Sa'da Governorate as well as parts of al-Jawf, al-Mahwit, Dhamar,

Hajja, and Ma'rib Governorates too, thereby revealing that the balance of power within the Hashid confederation had shifted to the disadvantage of the al-Ahmar family and, by extension, Islah.[8] In September 2014, Ansar Allah eventually seized Sanaa. It was not without irony that the group was backed by Salih in this endeavor, as well as by considerable parts of both the army and the General People's Congress that were still loyal to the former president.[9]

While the National Unity Government was allowed to stay in office after it had been forced to sign the Peace and National Partnership Agreement (ittifaq al-silm wa al-shiraka al-wataniyya),[10] Ansar Allah would gain the upper hand vis-à-vis developments in the capital. After its rejection of the country's proposed future federal structure as established in the latest draft constitution was ignored, it could, in consequence, easily overthrow the government in early 2015,[11] advancing into South Yemen as far as Aden, where the Hadi government had taken refuge. Reportedly, Hadi fled Aden by boat after the initial skirmishes reached the outskirts of town in late March 2015. By the time he arrived in Riyadh on March 26, a Saudi Arabian–led coalition had already launched the military operation Decisive Storm to restore the Hadi government, return the country to the political transition in line with the GCC Initiative, and push back against Iran—which, according to representatives of the Hadi government and the coalition, had been offering Ansar Allah extensive support and in charge of its takeover. Crucially, the Saudi-led coalition was backed by key Western states, including France, the United Kingdom, and, most important, the United States—which, besides the delivery of arms, provided intelligence and logistical support to coalition forces.

Belying its code name, the operation turned out to be anything but decisive. Nor can the ensuing one, Restoring Hope—launched on April 22, 2015—be assumed to have instilled much hope for the bulk of Yemenis, let alone restored it. Rather, and as to be expected, the war brought despair and destitution across Yemen; it quickly evolved into a quagmire for Saudi Arabia as well, which, after years of intense but ineffective warfare, would end up the reluctant leader of a coalition that had been seriously downsized in the meantime. Despite the striking military imbalance favoring the coalition and Yemeni progovernment forces over Ansar Allah and its local allies, the former have been unable to attain any of their stated goals as of 2023. After initial setbacks, Ansar Allah has been able to sustain its position in North Yemen, where it has consolidated its rule in all but one governorate (Ma'rib). Furthermore, Iran's support for, and influence over, the group has been steadily rising since the onset of war in March 2015, having been deemed relatively marginal initially.[12] While its alliance with Ansar Allah might still fall short of the one Tehran maintains with Lebanon's Hizbullah, Iran and Ansar Allah have, on several occasions, proved their ability to seriously endanger regional security on the Arabian Peninsula by apparent coordinated action, most prominently in the Abqaiq-Khurais attack of September 2019. The costs of the war, on the other hand, are immense, especially with respect to the humanitarian and political situation in the ROY. In fact, Yemen's social fabric and state institutions—fragile and frail already prior to 2015—have literally been ripped apart in the course of the war.

As of mid-2023, Yemen resembles an ill-designed rag rug made up of three dominant colors demarcating the respective dominions of the competing political entities—that is, if one deliberately disregards the myriad of tiny quasi chiefdoms run by local strongmen, warlords, and terrorist organizations, including al-Qaeda in the Arabian Peninsula and the Islamic State. As mentioned, Ansar Allah controls the overwhelming part of the former Yemen Arab Republic, whereas the internationally recognized government—heavily dependent on Saudi Arabia and led by a newly formed Presidential Council after Hadi stepped down as president in April 2022—holds sway over roughly the governorates of Abyan, al-Mahra, Hadramawt, and Ma'rib. Besides, key southern governorates such as al-Dhali', Lahij, Shabwa, as well as large swaths of Hadramawt's coastal areas are under the control of the Southern Transitional Council, which nominally acknowledges the integrity of the ROY and delegates members to both the Presidential Council and the internationally recognized government, but ultimately strives for the rebuilding of an independent southern state within the former territories of the People's Democratic Republic of Yemen. The STC, in turn, is highly reliant on the material and political support of the United Arab Emirates—which, as critics maintain, is acting as a de facto occupying—or even colonial—power in South Yemen.[13]

Given this smorgasbord of domestic and external conflict parties, all of them pursuing different and often diametrically opposed interests, it is little wonder that international attempts at conflict settlement have thus far resulted in arranging or renewing cease-fire agreements at most. A more comprehensive approach to resolving the multilevel conflict—one that also involves meaningful negotiations between all major Yemeni conflict parties—is still as wanting as it is needed. As it happens, however, the JMP has been suggested as a potential role model here. The alliance's experience could guide contemporary Yemeni actors on how best to bridge existing divides, overcome past enmities, and cooperate on joint interests for the purpose of promoting the general good.[14] "Today," it has been argued, "Yemenis are facing a decisive historical moment in which it is imperative to create a sense of national awareness—that awareness that was once embodied in the experience of the JMP, notwithstanding all its negative features."[15] In the same vein, another analyst has reminded the Yemeni conflict parties that the JMP once managed "to break the barriers of fear and leeriness that had existed between the opposition. It left ideology and the legacies of history behind, searching instead for commonalities and ways to strengthen its joint action." Hence, today's Yemeni elites from all factions must continue along the path pioneered by the JMP if the country is to exit the current crisis "in defiance of the prevailing rivalry and petty political struggles."[16]

Although the JMP lends itself to being a good example here for obvious reasons, a number of reservations can still be expressed regardless. The first arises out of the history of the alliance itself. For one thing, as an essential component of the National Unity Government under Hadi, the JMP undoubtedly contributed its fair share to the unfolding of the current war. The alliance may have been just one component thereof alongside the GPC—which, with Salih having been allowed to stay inside the country and bring his influence to bear, acted more as a spoiler than a facilitator of the transition. The JMP may have also been restricted by the GCC Initiative's provisions regarding the shaping of the transition period as well as by a domineering—yet perhaps incompetent—interim president.[17] However, it did little to alleviate the looming conflict by, for instance, augmenting the power-sharing elements within transitional institutions and, in general, molding the period in question in a more inclusive way. Rather, it was particularly Islah's antagonism with Ansar Allah that, albeit mutually shared and nourished, set the course for the outbreak of civil war.

For another, the JMP's parties today are split themselves. Some such as al-Haqq or the Syrian-oriented Ba'th party are based in the territories held and partake in the political institutions controlled by Ansar Allah, with whom they now side; meanwhile, others such as, first and foremost, Islah are vital components in both the internationally recognized government and the anti–Ansar Allah military camp. Therefore, the JMP dealt with in this book effectively ceased to exist in 2015. Although its name is still used by former constituents now backing Ansar Allah—with "JMP statements" featuring prominently on its website to prove the alleged pluralistic nature of its rule[18]—other onetime constituents such as the YSP have publicly declared that the "original JMP" downed tools for good long ago.[19]

There are other reasons, too, for why living up to the JMP ideal may be easier said than done for present-day Yemeni actors. While it is impossible to gauge their exact impact on the making of the alliance, Yemen's consociational tradition and culture of dialogue certainly facilitated the parties' coming to terms with their past in the second half of the 1990s. Yet those features of the country's political culture would suffer dearly from Salih's authoritarian mode of governance, and the extent to which they have been further undermined by the current war—which arguably exceeds Yemen's previous ones in terms of ferocity—is unclear. What is quite apparent, though, is that many well-known bridge builders have become increasingly susceptible to attacks on their personal and physical integrity, including several leading JMP politicians. Already in November 2014, for instance, Muhammad 'Abd al-Malik al-Mutawakkil of the Union of Popular Forces was gunned down in Sanaa by unidentified assailants;[20] nearly six years later, in October 2020, Zayd of al-Haqq met the same fate.[21] To cite yet another example, Muhammad Qahtan of Islah was arrested in Sanaa in April 2015 and has been held incommunicado ever since. Although Ansar Allah has denied any involvement in Qahtan's abduction, Yemeni and international human rights organizations hold the group responsible nonetheless, calling on it to immediately release him—so far to no avail.[22]

The single biggest impediment to a rapprochement between Yemeni actors, however, is the ongoing heavy external involvement in the war. Yemen is certainly no stranger to outside interference, and attempts have been made to explain the sustained imbroglio there following World War II solely as the result of "a continued foreign effort to subordinate Yemenis," who kept defying global (financial) interests regardless.[23] To be sure, the Cold War and the superpower rivalry between the United States and the Soviet Union certainly left its mark on Yemen. The end of bipolarity, then, roughly coincided with the emergence of a profitable hydrocarbon sector, which attracted the attention of international companies, notably from France, Korea, and the United States,[24] which often succeeded in concluding contracts highly unfavorable to the country itself.[25] Hereafter, the terrorist attack on the USS *Cole* in the port of Aden in October 2000 and, more important, the events of September 11, 2001, significantly catalyzed US involvement in Yemen—chiefly to the benefit of Salih, who somehow managed to convince the George W. Bush and Barack Obama administrations that his regime was the sole horse to be backed in the fight against al-Qaeda. The Arab Gulf states, and Saudi Arabia first and foremost, would look after their own political and commercial interests in South Arabia, too, significantly stepping up their efforts at making inroads into Yemeni politics and the country's business sector during the GCC-sponsored transition process.[26]

However, the extent of past meddling—which was, after all, mostly indirect in nature—pales in comparison to the magnitude of the direct foreign interference the country has witnessed since March 2015. While Yemen's warring parties should not be conceived of as puppets whose strings are pulled in Abu Dhabi, Riyadh, Tehran, or Washington, the ongoing conflict has clearly exacerbated their dependency on external resources and, hence, critically reduced their agency. Interestingly, this state of affairs perhaps holds least true for Ansar Allah, which—despite being commonly depicted as an Iranian proxy and regardless of the significantly increased material support provided by that country since 2015—appears to still maintain considerable strategic autonomy.[27]

In contrast, the internationally recognized government's decision-making processes are heavily constrained not only by profound internal rivalries but also by the interests of its main external sponsor, Saudi Arabia. This reality is no less the case with one of its key components, Islah. The latter has to bank on Saudi Arabia as its major, if inconvenient, external supporter after Qatar reportedly terminated its backing for Islah.[28] One of the driving forces behind the containment of, if not crackdown on, Islah, in turn, is the United Arab Emirates, which also masterminded the region-wide suppression of the Muslim Brotherhood in the Middle East. It is thus unsurprising to find the United Arab Emirates patronizing Islah's natural challengers among Yemen's warring parties, namely, the STC and Salafi-aligned militias.

Last, little is known about the range of local partners (or the activities and extent of own ground forces for that matter) participating in US operations against al-Qaeda and the Islamic State in Yemen—arguably "the longest running of Yemen's three wars" and probably the most meaningful one for Washington.[29] What is known, however, is that the United States has kept supporting—decisively facilitating, in fact—the Saudi-led campaign since its inception and might thus be complicit in war crimes potentially committed by, for instance, the coalition forces' alleged targeting of civilians and Yemen's critical infrastructure.[30]

The extraordinary scope to foreign interference is likely to have caused a significant prolongation of internal warfare already,[31] and it stands to reason that the continuation of direct—as well as substantial indirect—external support for the Yemeni conflict parties will also impinge on their incentives to compromise going forward. Put another way, it might well be the case that "there exist no permanent friendships in politics, nor permanent enmities," as one Yemeni author commented on the improbable alliance that would be struck between the YSP and Islah in the second half of the 1990s.[32] Yet for today's enmities to end, a return to the primacy of politics would ultimately be necessary. With Saudi Arabia and the United Arab Emirates both increasingly bent on reducing their *direct* involvement in the war—as confirmed in the wake of the China-brokered reproachment between Iran and Saudi Arabia in March 2023—the stage for more politics might indeed soon be set once more. As a matter of fact, it has been maintained of late that "Yemen's elites, including those emergent and established, sense that the country is moving toward a new transitional phase where politics rather than war-making predominate," with them having induced more and more instances of cooperation between hitherto hostile parties in the meantime.[33] Still, even small doses of optimism seem to be premature given the sustained human suffering and the many setbacks encountered—including during the latest rounds of negotiations. All that said, however, as a prominent diplomat and veteran of Yemeni politics recently put it, "When Yemenis start talking anything is possible."[34]

Appendixes

Notes

Bibliography

Index

Appendix A

Cited Interviews

(Listed in chronological order)

Number	Position	Date	Place
1	Senior Islah member	07/22/2008	Sanaa
2	Senior al-Haqq member	08/02/2008	Sanaa
3	Senior UPF member	08/06/2008	Sanaa
4	Member of Yemeni NGO	08/09/2008	Sanaa
5	Political analyst	08/27/2008	Sanaa
6	Islah member	03/29/2012	Berlin
7	Political analyst	12/11/2012	Sanaa
8	Independent youth activist	12/13/2012	Sanaa
9	Journalist	12/18/2012	Sanaa
10	Journalist	12/19/2012	Sanaa
11	Political analyst	12/20/2012	Sanaa
12	Senior UPF member	12/21/2012	Sanaa
13	Senior Islah member	12/25/2012	Sanaa
14	Political analyst	12/25/2012	Sanaa
15	Senior GPC member	12/29/2012	Sanaa
16	NUPO member	12/31/2012	Sanaa
17	Islah member	01/01/2013	Sanaa
18	Senior Islah member	01/03/2013	Sanaa
19	YSP member	01/06/2012	Sanaa
20	Senior Islah member	01/07/2013	Sanaa
21	Head of international NGO	01/08/2013	Sanaa
22	Member of Ansar Allah	01/08/2013	Sanaa
23	Independent youth activist	01/09/2013	Sanaa
24	Independent youth activist	01/10/2013	Sanaa

Number	Position	Date	Place
25	Senior YSP member	01/14/2013	Sanaa
26	European diplomat	01/15/2013	Sanaa
27	Senior GPC member	01/16/2013	Sanaa
28	Feminist activist	01/19/2013	Sanaa
29	Islah member	01/21/2013	Sanaa

Appendix B

Synopsis of Assumptions

Assumption on	Reference
The Formation of Strategic Alliances	Chapter 1
The launching of strategic cooperation requires opposition parties that:	
First, agree on more than one shared goal (goal convergence);	p. 38
Second, expect the benefits of cooperation to outweigh its costs (surplus of benefits); and,	pp. 38–39
Third, have smoothed out attitudinal constraints (balanced attitudes).	pp. 43–44
The launching of strategic cooperation requires opposition parties to be presided over by elites who are committed to cooperation (central, committed elites).	p. 55
The Internal Performance of Strategic Alliances	Chapter 2
The maintenance of strategic opposition cooperation requires organizational structures fit to:	
First, reproduce the basic conditions of cooperation;	pp. 82–83
Second, facilitate internal mobilization.	p. 85
The reproduction of the basic conditions of cooperation requires organizational structures at the horizontal, interparty level to be furnished with a modicum of sanctioning power and functional decision-making structures.	pp. 78–79
The internal mobilization capabilities of an alliance correlate with the extent to which organizational structures at the vertical, alliance level facilitate:	
First, the redistribution of resources;	p. 85
Second, coherence building.	p. 85

Assumption on	*Reference*
The efficiency of internal resource redistribution correlates with the extent to which organizational structures at the vertical, alliance level facilitate:	
First, the building of differentiated units responsive to the task structure of an alliance;	p. 87
Second, the integration of those differentiated units into a cohesive whole.	pp. 87–88
The internal coherence of an alliance correlates with:	
First, the extent to which organizational structures at the vertical, alliance level facilitate commitment building;	pp. 99–101
Second, the scale of institutionalization on the part of its constituent parties.	pp. 95–97
The External Performance of Strategic Alliances	Chapters 3–4
The maintenance of strategic cooperation requires opposition parties to be convinced that the alliance's external performance contributes to goal attainment in the foreseeable future.	pp. 120–22
The likelihood of goal attainment correlates with the degree of transformative capacity on the part of an alliance.	pp. 168–70
There is an indirect relationship between the strength of an alliance and its transformative capacity: the greater its strength, the more extensive the changes occurring within the relationships of domination; the more extensive the latter, the greater the alliance's transformative capacity.	pp. 170–71
The strength of an alliance correlates with its ability to mobilize external actors. Its external mobilization capabilities, in turn, correlate with the quality of its framing processes.	pp. 144–45
Domestic authoritarian structures impact the external performance an alliance in that they:	
First, prompt it to oscillate between party and movement mode;	pp. 134–36
Second, prompt it to oscillate between conflict escalation and de-escalation; and,	pp. 180–82
Third, require of it the ability to change its initial goal(s), or goal ranking, lest it faces disintegration.	pp. 137–38

Assumption on	Reference
Domestic authoritarian structures give rise to nominal opposition actors who will strain the external performance of an alliance in case of their inclusion: ride sharers and, in patronage-based regimes, rent seekers. Despite this fact:	
First, reformers and rent seekers are capable of cooperation so long as they share the same path toward their respective goals;	pp. 195–97
Second, the inclusion of ride sharers increases the strength of an alliance in the short run but decrease it in the mid- to long run.	pp. 124–26

Notes

Introduction

1. See former YSP Central Committee member Ahmad Muhammad al-Harbi, *Al-Haraka al-Wataniyya wa al-Siyasiyya al-Yamaniyya*, 2:605–30.

2. Michael C. Hudson, "After the Gulf War: Prospects for Democratization in the Arab World."

3. Jason Seawright and John Gerring, "Case Selection Techniques in Case Study Research: A Menu of Qualitative and Quantitative Options," 301–3.

4. For general information on the parties discussed in the following, see Ri'asa al-Jumhuriyya—al-Markaz al-Watani li-l-Ma'lumat, "Ma'lumat Asasiyya al-Ahzab al-Siyasiyya fi al-Jumhuriyya al-Yamaniyya," n.d., https://yemen-nic.info/contents/Politics /detail.php?ID=8437; and Sheila Carapico, *Civil Society in Yemen: The Political Economy of Activism in Modern Arabia*, 140–51.

5. Stacey Philbrick Yadav, *Islamists and the State: Legitimacy and Institutions in Yemen and Lebanon*, 34; Jillian Schwedler, *Faith in Moderation: Islamist Parties in Jordan and Yemen*.

6. Noel Brehony, *Yemen Divided: The Story of a Failed State in South Arabia*; John Ishiyama, "The Sickle and the Minaret: Communist Successor Parties in Yemen and Afghanistan after the Cold War"; Volker Stanzel, "Marxism in Arabia: South Yemen Twenty Years after Independence."

7. Ludwig Stiftl, "The Yemeni Islamists in the Process of Democratization," 250.

8. Samy Dorlian, *La mouvance zaydite dans le Yémen contemporain: Une modernisation avortée*; Gabriele vom Bruck, *Islam, Memory, and Morality in Yemen: Ruling Families in Transition*.

9. Zaydis are a sect of Shiite Islam that today is almost exclusively found in the ROY, where they account for between roughly 30 and 35 percent of the population. North Yemen was ruled by Zaydi imams until the republican revolution of 1962. As concerns doctrine and ritual, the Zaydiyya is close to the (Sunni) Shafi'i school of law, whose adherents in Yemen constitute between approximately 65 and 70 percent of the population.

Therefore, the Zaydiyya is also referred to as the fifth school of Sunni jurisprudence. Paul Dresch, *Tribes, Government, and History in Yemen*, 11.

10. Jesse Ferris, *Nasser's Gamble: How Intervention in Yemen Caused the Six-Day War and the Decline of Egyptian Power*; Asher Orkaby, *Beyond the Arab Cold War: The International History of the Yemen Civil War, 1962–1968*.

11. See his interview with Khalid al-'Alwani in *al-Sahwa*, Aug. 14, 2008.

12. Robert D. Burrowes and Catherine M. Kasper, "The Saleh Regime and the Need for a Credible Opposition," 268.

13. Mona Yacoubian, "Building Momentum for Reform: The Islamist-Secular Alliance in Yemen," 59.

14. Stephen Day, *Regionalism and Rebellion in Yemen: A Troubled National Union*.

15. Maha Abdelrahman, "'With the Islamists?—Sometimes. With the State?—Never!': Cooperation between the Left and Islamists in Egypt"; Francesco Cavatorta, "'Divided They Stand, Divided They Fail': Opposition Politics in Morocco"; Dina Shehata, *Islamists and Secularists in Egypt: Opposition, Conflict, and Cooperation*.

16. Matt Buehler, *Why Alliances Fail: Islamist and Leftist Coalitions in North Africa*, 32.

17. Buehler, *Why Alliances Fail*, 32; Ellen Lust-Okar, *Structuring Conflict in the Arab World: Incumbents, Opponents, and Institutions*; Jennifer Gandhi and Adam Przeworski, "Cooperation, Cooptation, and Rebellion under Dictatorship."

18. Yasmine Berriane and Marie Duboc, "Allying beyond Social Divides: An Introduction to Contentious Politics and Coalitions in the Middle East and North Africa," 413; Vincent Durac, "Opposition Coalitions in the Middle East: Origins, Demise, and Afterlife?," 542–43.

19. For instance, see Buehler, *Why Alliances Fail*, 4–5.

20. Isa Blumi, *Chaos in Yemen: Societal Collapse and the New Authoritarianism*; April Longley Alley, "The Rules of the Game: Unpacking Patronage Politics in Yemen"; Sarah Phillips, *Yemen's Democracy Experiment in Regional Perspective: Patronage and Pluralized Authoritarianism*.

21. April Longley, "The High Water Mark of Islamist Politics? The Case of Yemen"; Stacey Philbrick Yadav, "Understanding 'What Islamists Want': Public Debate and Contestation in Lebanon and Yemen"; Philbrick Yadav, *Islamists and the State*; Schwedler, *Faith in Moderation*.

22. Laurent Bonnefoy, "The Shabab, Institutionalized Politic and the Islamists in the Yemeni Revolution"; Vincent Durac, "Yemen's Arab Spring: Democratic Opening or Regime Maintenance?"; Stacey Philbrick Yadav, *Yemen in the Shadow of Transition*.

23. Michaelle L. Browers, "Origins and Architects of Yemen's Joint Meeting Parties"; Vincent Durac, "The Joint Meeting Parties and the Politics of Opposition in Yemen"; Iris Glosemeyer and Hesham Sallam, "The JMP Alliance: New Political Pragmatism in

Yemen?"; 'Abdallah al-Faqih, "Al-Takattul 'ala Qa'ida al-Dimuqratiyya fi al-Jumhuriyya al-Yamaniyya, 1990–2009."

24. Jennifer Gandhi and Ora John Reuter, "The Incentives for Pre-electoral Coalitions in Non-democratic Elections"; Eugene Huskey and Gulnara Iskakova, "The Barriers to Intra-opposition Cooperation in the Post-communist World: Evidence from Kyrgyzstan."

25. See, however, Janine Clark, "Threats, Structures, and Resources: Cross-ideological Coalition Building in Jordan."

26. Berriane and Duboc, "Allying Beyond Social Divides;" Hendrik Kraetzschmar, "Mapping Opposition Coalitions in the Arab World: From Single-Issue Coalitions to Transnational Networks"; Ellen Lust, "Opposition Cooperation and Uprisings in the Arab World."

27. Michaelle L. Browers, *Political Ideology in the Arab World: Accommodation and Transformation*; Nancy Bermeo, "Myths of Moderation: Confrontation and Conflict during Democratic Transitions"; Janine Clark, "The Conditions of Islamist Moderation: Unpacking Cross-ideological Cooperation in Jordan."

28. David Armstrong, Ora John Reuter, and Graeme B. Robertson, "Getting the Opposition Together: Protest Coordination in Authoritarian Regimes"; Elvin Ong, "Opposition Coordination in Singapore's 2015 General Elections"; Nicolas Van de Walle, "Tipping Games: When Do Opposition Parties Coalesce?"; Michael Wahman, "Opposition Coalitions and Democratization by Election"; Adam Ziegfeld and Maya Tudor, "How Opposition Parties Sustain Single-Party Dominance: Lessons from India."

29. Vincent Durac, "Social Movements, Protest Movements and Cross-ideological Coalitions: The Arab Uprisings Re-appraised; Jack A. Goldstone, "Cross-class Coalitions and the Making of the Arab Revolts of 2011."

30. Robert Axelrod, *The Evolution of Cooperation*; Mancur Olson, *The Logic of Collective Action: Public Goods and the Theory of Groups*.

31. Nella Van Dyke and Holly J. McCammon, eds., *Strategic Alliances: Coalition Building and Social Movements*; Nella Van Dyke and Bryan Amos, "Social Movement Coalitions: Formation, Longevity, and Success."

32. Alfred Stepan, "Paths toward Redemocratization: Theoretical and Comparative Considerations," 79–81.

33. For an introduction, see Rob Stones, *Structuration Theory*.

34. Ralf Dahrendorf, "Toward a Theory of Social Conflict," 174.

35. Ralf Dahrendorf, *Gesellschaft und Freiheit: Zur soziologischen Analyse der Gegenwart* (München: Pieper, 1961), 127.

36. Edward Azar, *The Management of Protracted Social Conflict: Theory and Cases*, 10. See also Lewis A. Coser, *The Functions of Social Conflict*.

37. Robert A. Dahl, preface to *Political Opposition in Western Democracies*, xv–xvi. See also Ian Shapiro, "The Fallacies Concerning Minorities, Majorities, and Democratic Politics," 51.

38. To paraphrase Johan Galtung's "ABC" definition of conflict as a "triadic construct" consisting of a contradiction (C), assumptions and attitudes (A), and behavior (B). Johan Galtung, *Peace by Peaceful Means: Peace and Conflict, Development and Civilization*, 71.

39. Jean Blondel, "Political Opposition in the Contemporary World"; Juan J. Linz, "Opposition to and under an Authoritarian Regime."

40. Gandhi and Przeworski, "Cooperation, Cooptation, and Rebellion," 22; Andreas Schedler, *The Politics of Uncertainty: Sustaining and Subverting Electoral Authoritarianism*, 12.

41. Eva Bellin, "The Robustness of Authoritarianism in the Middle East: Exceptionalism in Comparative Perspective," 144–46; Margaret Levi, "The Predatory Theory of Rule," 438; Steven Levitsky and Lucan Way, "The Rise of Competitive Authoritarianism," 53.

42. Schedler, *Politics of Uncertainty*.

43. Kraetzschmar, "Mapping Opposition Coalitions," 288.

44. These two terms are used interchangeably throughout.

45. Kraetzschmar refers to domestic strategic alliances as "reform alliances." Kraetzschmar, "Mapping Opposition Coalitions," 291.

46. David S. Meyer and Catherine Corrigall-Brown, "Coalitions and Political Context: U.S. Movements against Wars in Iraq," 329.

47. Nella Van Dyke and Holly J. McCammon, "Introduction: Social Movement Coalition Formation," xiv–xv; Jillian Schwedler and Janine Clark, "Islamist-Leftist Cooperation in the Arab World," 10.

48. Todd Landman, *Issues and Methods in Comparative Politics*, 32.

49. Alexander L. George and Andrew Bennett, *Case Studies and Theory Development in the Social Sciences*, 73–88.

50. Rudra Sil, "The Foundations of Eclecticism: The Epistemological Status of Agency, Culture, and Structure in Social Theory," 379.

51. Jason Seawright and David Collier, "Glossary of Selected Terms," 283.

52. George and Bennett, *Case Studies*, 206–7.

53. Derek Beach and Rasmus Brun Pedersen, *Process-Tracing Methods: Foundations and Guidelines*, 269–79; Landman, *Issues and Methods*, 32; Andrew Bennett, "Case Study Methods: Design, Use, and Comparative Advantage," 39–41, 42–43.

54. Oisín Tansey, "Process Tracing and Elite Interviewing: A Case for Non-probability Sampling," 766; George and Bennett, *Case Studies*, 223.

55. Bennett, "Case Study Methods," 20–21. See also Charles C. Ragin, "Cases of 'What Is a Case?'," 8.

56. George and Bennett, *Case Studies*, 97.

57. Paul Dresch, *A History of Modern Yemen*, 211; Isa Blumi, *Destroying Yemen: What Chaos in Arabia Tells Us about the World*, 4–5, 27.

58. Besides Shafi'is and Zaydis, there are approximately one hundred thousand Isma'ilis in Yemen. The Isma'iliyya is a Shiite sect whose followers mainly live in the Haraz Mountains, falling under the Hajja Governorate.

59. The northern and eastern governorates are home to the majority of Yemen's roughly 185 tribes. The biggest tribal confederations are the Hashid, Bakil, and Madhhaj.

60. This issue applies not only to the North-South divide but also to distinct regional identities at the governorate level.

61. For traditional though still influential social hierarchies arising from descent, see, for instance, vom Bruck, *Islam, Memory, and Morality*, 44–48.

62. Fred Halliday, *Nation and Religion in the Middle East*, 68. See also Phillips, *Yemen's Democracy Experiment*, 41

63. Robert D. Burrowes, *The Yemen Arab Republic: The Politics of Development, 1962–1986*, 7–8.

64. Helen Lackner, introduction to *Why Yemen Matters: A Society in Transition*, 1; Ghassan Salamé, "Les dilemmes d'un pays (trop) bien situé," 37–60.

65. Blumi, *Chaos in Yemen*, 34; Robin Bidwell, *The Two Yemens*, esp. chap. 2–3.

66. This situation, at times, has also been purposefully invoked "only to justify external interventions that perpetuate regional-international domination over Yemen." Kamilia el-Eriani, "Mourning the Death of a State to Enliven It: Notes on the 'Weak' Yemeni State," 239. See also Kamilia el-Eriani, "Secularism, Security and the Weak State: De-democratizing the 2011 Yemeni Uprising," 1140–65.

67. Edward Newman, "Weak States, State Failure, and Terrorism," 463–88.

68. Nazih N. Ayubi, *Over-stating the Arab State: Politics and Society in the Middle East*, 431.

69. Lisa Wedeen, *Peripheral Visions: Publics, Power, and Performance in Yemen*, 103–47.

70. Carapico, *Civil Society*.

71. Lisa Wedeen, "Seeing Like a Citizen, Acting Like a State: Exemplary Events in Unified Yemen," 682 (emphasis in the original). See also Dresch, *History of Modern Yemen*, 211.

72. Robert D. Burrowes, "The Republic of Yemen: The Politics of Unification and Civil War, 1989–1995," 187.

73. Ahmad Jabir 'Afif, *Al-Haraka al-Wataniyya fi al-Yaman*, 181.

74. Abdo Baaklini, Guilain Denoeux, and Robert Springborg, *Legislative Politics in the Arab World: The Resurgence of Democratic Institutions*, 210; Burrowes, *Yemen Arab Republic*.

75. Robert D. Burrowes, "Prelude to Unification: The Yemen Arab Republic in Yemen, 1962–1990," 493; Helen Lackner, *Yemen in Crisis: Autocracy, Neo-liberalism and the Disintegration of a State*, 102.

76. Longley Alley, "Rules of the Game," 389.

77. Carapico, *Civil Society*, 107–8; Dresch, *Tribes, Government, and History*, 22.

78. The so-called Anglo-Ottoman Line, meaning the dividing line between the Ottoman and British spheres of influence, roughly demarcated what is today commonly understood as North and South Yemen.

79. Day, *Regionalism and Rebellion*, 75.

80. This trope of alleged northern backwardness proved to be so potent that even Saudi commentators—anticipating the social reforms that would be introduced by Saudi crown prince Muhammad bin Salman—later blamed North Yemen's geographical proximity to the Kingdom of Saudi Arabia as one of the root causes of Saudi social conservatism. See, for instance, the opinion piece "Hal al-Jumhuriyya al-Yamaniyya Dawla Mutakhallifa wa Hal Tu'aththir Dhalik 'ala al-Sa'udiyya?," by Sa'id al-Wahhabi, originally published by *Okaz* and republished by *'Adan al-Ghadd* on Jan. 13, 2016, https://adengad .net/public/articles/87448. For the rise of the Southern Movement (al-hirak al-janubi) and its perceptions of the YAR, the PDRY, and the ROY, see chapter 2 and Anne-Linda Amira Augustin, *South Yemen's Independence Struggle: Generations of Resistance*.

81. Noel Brehony, "From Chaos to Chaos: South Yemen 50 Years after the British Departure," *Asian Affairs* 48, no. 3 (2017): 431.

82. Brehony, "From Chaos to Chaos," 430–31; Day, *Regionalism and Rebellion*, 81.

83. Fred Halliday, *Revolution and Foreign Policy: The Case of South Yemen, 1967– 1987*, 52. The rival factions involved in the January 1986 crisis are still known today as *zumra* and *tughma* respectively, both of which can be translated as "group." The Politburo faction headed by then secretary-general of the YSP 'Ali Nasir Muhammad is called *zumra*. It lost to the *tughma* faction led by 'Ali Salim al-Baydh, who succeeded 'Ali Nasir Muhammad as secretary-general, and many of the *zumra* faction either fled Yemen altogether or migrated to the YAR, where they joined the GPC. Among the most prominent members of the latter group was 'Abd Rabbuh Mansur Hadi, who became vice president of the ROY in 1994 and then its president in 2012. The conflict between both factions still reverberates today; it is especially *tughma* members who are at the helm of the secessionist trend within the Southern Movement. See Jens Heibach, "The Future of South Yemen and the Southern Transitional Council," 8.

84. Burrowes, "Republic of Yemen," 190.

85. Samuel P. Huntington, "Democracy's Third Wave."

86. "2 Yemens Become One, and Celebrate," *New York Times*, May 23, 1990.

87. Jillian Schwedler, "Yemen's Aborted Opening," 48.

88. Burrowes, "Republic of Yemen," 193, 206.

89. For an analysis of the tripartite coalition government, see Jens Heibach and Tereza Jermanová, "Coalition Maintenance during Democratization: Comparative Insights from Tunisia and Yemen."

90. For instance, see 'Abd al-Wahhab al-Ruhani, *Al-Yaman: Khususiyya al-Hukm wa al-Wahda wa al-Dimuqratiyya*, 349–51.

91. Heibach and Jermanová, "Coalition Maintenance."

92. Michael A. Crouch, "A Post-war Democracy Turned Mirage," *International Herald Tribune*, May 12, 1994.

93. François Burgat, "Les élections présidentielles de septembre 1999 au Yémen: Du 'pluralisme armé' au retour à la 'norme arabe,'" 69.

94. Burrowes and Kasper, "Saleh Regime," 264–65.

95. Martha Brill Olcott and Marina Ottaway, "The Challenge of Semi-authoritarianism," *Carnegie Endowment for International Peace*, Oct. 1, 1999, https://carnegieendowment.org/1999/10/01/challenge-of-semi-authoritarianism-pub-142.

96. Phillips, *Yemen's Democracy Experiment*, 3.

97. Steven Levitsky and Lucan A. Way, *Competitive Authoritarianism: Hybrid Regimes after the Cold War*, 5.

98. Longley Alley, "Rules of the Game," 389–90; Carapico, *Civil Society*, 142; Lackner, *Yemen in Crisis*, 102.

99. Phillips, *Yemen's Democracy Experiment*, 67–88.

100. Sarah Phillips, *Yemen and the Politics of Permanent Crisis*, 87–104; John E. Peterson, "Tribes and Politics in Yemen," 10–11.

101. Dresch, *History of Modern Yemen*, 157.

102. Phillips, *Politics of Permanent Crisis*, 58–59.

103. Longley Alley, "Rules of the Game," 386.

104. Iris Glosemeyer, "The Development of State Institutions," 93.

105. Longley Alley, "Rules of the Game," 394, 403.

106. Schwedler, "Yemen's Aborted Opening," 51.

107. Longley Alley, "Rules of the Game," 393.

108. Philbrick Yadav, *Shadow of Transition*, 149.

109. For the examples provided in the following, see Philbrick Yadav, *Shadow of Transition*.

110. Heibach, "Future of South Yemen."

111. Abdullah Hamidaddin, "Introduction," in *The Huthi Movement in Yemen: Ideology, Ambition, and Security in the Arab Gulf*, 3. For Ansar Allah's religious and political ideology, see Bernard Haykel, "The Huthi Movement's Religious and Political Ideology and Its Relationship to Zaydism in Yemen."

112. See, for instance, Shelagh Weir, "A Clash of Fundamentalism: Wahhabism in Yemen."

113. One of the major sources of Ansar Allah's popularity was its sweeping anticorruption rhetoric before and during the transitional period. When the group ultimately took control of Sanaa in September 2014, however, its anticorruption purge within the state administration mainly targeted political opponents, while leaving its new ally—namely, Salih and his entourage—untouched. See "Beyond the Business-as-Usual Approach: Combating Corruption in Yemen," *Report* (Sana'a Center for Strategic Studies)

(Nov. 2018): 21–25. Patronage networks and corruption are still widespread in Yemen today, including in the territories under the control of Ansar Allah.

114. In fact, more recent contributions to the field of contentious politics attach great importance to studying the memories and practices featuring in past acts of contentious claim-making to better understand a given conflict. See, for instance, Jillian Schwedler, *Protesting Jordan: Geographies of Power and Dissent.*

115. Gregory D. Johnson, "Seven Yemens: How Yemen Fractured and Collapsed, and What Comes Next," 14.

1. Launching Cooperation: The Emergence of the Joint Meeting Parties

1. A transcript of the discussion is published in 'Abd al-Ilah Balqaziz, ed., *Al-Mu'arada wa al-Sulta fi al-Watan al-'Arabi: Azma al-Mu'arada al-Siyasiyya al-'Arabiyya,* 113–62, esp. 116–17, 136–37.

2. Yacoubian, "Building Momentum," 59. See also Glosemeyer and Sallam, "JMP Alliance," 157.

3. "Ra'is al-Mushtarak li-Niyus Yaman: Al-'Alaqa bayna al-Ahzab Mumtaza," *News Yemen,* Jan. 1, 2011, http://www.newsyemen.net/view_news.asp?sub_no=1_2010 _12_30_50486.

4. Al-Mutawakkil's latter statement was made on the occasion of the alliance's official celebration of its tenth anniversary, occurring during a JMP conference held Dec. 30–31, 2010. See "Ra'is al-Mushtarak."

5. In a sense, the ROY was one of the first states affected by the "New World Order," as heralded by George H. W. Bush in September 1990. In abstaining from formally condemning Iraq's invasion of Kuwait in the UN Security Council in August 1990, not only was the ROY diplomatically isolated internationally, but the bulk of donor countries, notably the United States and most Arab Gulf states, also withdrew their foreign aid to Yemen in the aftermath of that decision. Worse still, up to eight hundred thousand Yemeni migrant workers were expelled from the Arab Gulf states, causing high unemployment rates on their return home as well as a serious decline in remittances—as making up a significant portion of Yemen's gross national product at the time (and continuing to do so today). The ensuing economic crisis put a major strain on the unification process.

6. Carapico, *Civil Society,* 175.

7. Carapico, *Civil Society,* 178. Abu Shawarib and Abu Luhum are commonly referred to as "republican shaykhs," meaning tribal shaykhs who fought on the side of the republican forces during the revolution in North Yemen and later became important power brokers in the Yemeni Arab Republic. Abu Shawarib of the Kharif tribe (Hashid confederation) was a prominent member of the Iraqi-oriented Ba'th and personal adviser to Salih. He died in a mysterious car accident in 2004. Abu Luhum, a minor shaykh of

the Nihm tribe, became one of the most important tribal politicians in postrevolutionary Yemen and the head of the Bakil confederation.

8. For a detailed breakdown of the document, see al-Harbi, *Al-Haraka al-Wataniyya*, 715–38.

9. Bilqis Ahmad Mansur, *Al-Ahzab al-Siyasiyya wa al-Tahawwul al-Dimuqrati: Dirasa Tatbiqiyya ʿala al-Yaman wa Bilad Ukhra*, 368.

10. Muhammad ʿAbd al-Malik al-Mutawakkil, "Al-Afaq al-Dimuqratiyya fi al-Thawra al-Yamaniyya," 156.

11. Schwedler, *Faith in Moderation*, 113.

12. Samy Dorlian, "Zaydisme et modernisation: Émergence d'un nouvel universel politique?," 12.

13. Thaira Shalan, "Les organisations non gouvernementales et la société civil au Yémen," 297.

14. "Cloning" (*istinsakh*), meaning the reproduction of fake opposition parties or alliances, was a common regime strategy intended to confound the public and weaken the opposition. Dresch, *History of Modern Yemen*, 211.

15. Author interview no. 2, Aug. 2, 2008, Sanaa. When, for instance, the National Opposition Council was revived in July 2008, the JMP immediately stated that the coalition had been deliberately manufactured by the regime. See "'Uqb al-Tahaluf bayna al-Hakim wa al-Majlis al-Watani li-l-Muʿarada wa al-Baʿth al-ʿArabi al-Qawmi," *al-Shumuʿ*, July 26, 2008; and ʿAbd al-Fattah ʿAli al-Banus, "Istitlaʿ li-l-Balagh hawla Tahaluf al-Waṭani al-Dimuqrati," *al-Balagh*, July 26–29, 2008.

16. Jacob Bercovitch, Victor Kremenyuk, and I. William Zartman, "The Nature of Conflict and Conflict Resolution," 6.

17. For more on the early Brotherhood in Yemen, see François Burgat, "Le Yémen islamiste entre universalisme et insularité," in *Le Yémen contemporain*. On the early Islah party, see Schwedler, *Faith in Moderation*, 69–73, 89–92, 134–47, 176–91.

18. ʿAbd al-Karim Qasim Saʿid, *Al-Ikhwan al-Muslimun wa al-Haraka al-Usuliyya fi al-Yaman*, 79.

19. Phillips, *Yemen's Democracy Experiment*, 141.

20. Michael C. Hudson, "Bipolarity, Rational Calculations and War in Yemen," 22; Raymond Goy, "La réunification du Yémen," 259.

21. Michael Collins Dunn, "Islamist Parties in Democratizing States: A Look at Jordan and Yemen," 26; Dresch, *History of Modern Yemen*, 198.

22. Najib Ghallab, *Lahut al-Nukhab al-Qabaliyya: Taqdis al-Shaykh wa Laʿn al-Dawla*, 77.

23. Saʿid describes how large segments of the party refused to accept not only pluralism (*taʿaddudiyya*) but also the idea of party politics in general and how only ʿAbdallah al-Ahmar, Islah's preeminent figure at that time, could force critics to accept the notion

of *hizbiyya*. Note that on its foundation, Islah deliberately avoided the term "party" (*hizb*), instead calling itself a "gathering" (*tajammu'*). Sa'id, *Al-Ikhwan al-Muslimun*, 84.

24. Sa'id, *Al-Ikhwan al-Muslimun*, 79; Gabriele vom Bruck, "Regimes of Piety Revisited: Zaydi Political Moralities in Republican Yemen," 196.

25. Vom Bruck, *Islam, Memory, and Morality*, 197–98.

26. Day, *Regionalism and Rebellion*, 112.

27. Carapico, *Civil Society*, 172.

28. In 2011, Yemen Press released a facsimile of an Egyptian daily that had published al-Daylami's fatwa together with scathing criticism of Egyptian scholars, most prominently the shaykh al-Azhar Muhammad Sayyid al-Tantawi. "Sura Nadira li-Fatwa 'Abd al-Wahhab al-Daylami 'an al-Hizb al-Ishtiraki fi Sana 1994 wa Rudud al-'Ulama'," *Yemen Press*, Nov. 11, 2011, http://yemen-press.com/news-print4039.html.

29. Philbrick Yadav, *Islamists and the State*, 155–59.

30. Schwedler, *Faith in Moderation*, 218–19.

31. 'Abdallah b. Husayn al-Ahmar, *Mudhakkirat: Qadaya wa Mawaqif*, 309. Al-Ahmar, the paramount shaykh of the Hashid confederation, was one of the most influential figures in the YAR and the ROY. From 1993 until his death in 2007, he was the president of parliament and the head of Islah's highest governing body, the High Committee (*al-hay'a al-'ulya*). See 'Umar Ahmad Ghalib, *Al-Adwar al-Siyasiyya li-l-Shaykh 'Abdallah ibn Husayn al-Ahmar*.

32. Al-Ahmar, *Mudhakkirat: Qadaya wa Mawaqif*, 309.

33. The Political Section is one of the eight administrative divisions of Islah's headquarters.

34. 'Adil Mujahid al-Sharjabi, "Al-Tajammu' al-Yamani li-l-Islah: Bayna al-Barnamaj al-Siyasi wa Shi'ar al-Islam Huwa al-Hall," 150–51.

35. Al-Sharjabi, "Al-Tajammu' al-Yamani li-l-Islah," 148.

36. Author interview no. 20, Jan. 7, 2013, Sanaa.

37. Philbrick Yadav, *Islamists and the State*, 38–39.

38. Ludwig Stiftl, "Politischer Islam und Pluralismus: Theoretische und empirische Studie am Beispiel des Jemen," 261.

39. He then defected to the GPC and became the head of the state news agency SABA.

40. Unless otherwise stated, the ensuing portrayal of the JMP's formative period rests on interviews conducted with its leading representatives: author interview no. 1, July 22, 2008, Sanaa; author interview no. 13, Dec. 25, 2012, Sanaa; author interview no. 25, Jan. 14, 2013, Sanaa; author interview no. 2, Aug. 2, 2008; author interview no. 3, Aug. 6, 2008, Sanaa; and author interview no. 12, Dec. 21, 2012, Sanaa.

41. Author interview no. 25, Jan. 14, 2013.

42. Axelrod, *The Evolution of Cooperation*, 173–74.

43. Will Hathaway and David S. Meyer, "Competition and Cooperation in Social Movement Coalitions: Lobbying for Peace in the 1980s," 161; Meyer and Corrigall-Brown, "Coalitions and Political Context," 331; Suzanne Staggenborg, "Coalition Work in the Pro-choice Movement: Organizational and Environmental Opportunities and Obstacles," 374–75; Nella Van Dyke, "Crossing Movement Boundaries: Factors That Facilitate Coalition Protest by American College Students, 1930–1990," 228.

44. See, for example, Clark, "Threats, Structures, and Resources"; Abdelrahman, "'With the Islamists?,'" 52–53; Hendrik Kraetzschmar, "Electoral Rules, Voter Mobilization and the Islamist Landslide in the Saudi Municipal Elections of 2005," 519.

45. Al-Ahmar, *Mudhakkirat: Qadaya wa Mawaqif*, 312.

46. Author interview no. 20, Jan. 7, 2013.

47. A copy hereof could not be obtained, but all interviewees specified this name being the title of the first joint declaration. Many of its demands were probably included in the "Vision of the JMP Guaranteeing the Holding of Free, Fair, and Just Elections" (ru'ya ahzab al-liqa' al-mushtarak li-daman ijra' intikhabat hurra wa naziha wa 'adila), published shortly before the 2006 presidential and local council elections and reprinted in Ahmad Muhammad al-Kibsi, *Nizam al-Hukm fi al-Jumhuriyya al-Yamaniyya, 1990–2006*, 551–69.

48. Author interview no. 3, Aug. 6, 2008.

49. The August declaration was ultimately signed by Islah, the YSP, the UPF, NUPO, al-Haqq, the Iraqi Ba'th, and the Liberals' Constitutional Party.

50. An article by al-Jawi on the inability of Yemen's opposition to effectively coordinate among themselves is revealing, as it offers insight into his irreconcilable position toward Islah. See Omar al-Jawi, "We Are the Opposition . . . But . . . ," 85–87. Under the direction of Secretary-General 'Abdallah 'Awbil, the Unionist Gathering joined the JMP in the course of the 2011 uprising.

51. Mansur, *Al-Ahzab al-Siyasiyya*, 372.

52. Author interview no. 4, Aug. 9, 2008, Sanaa.

53. Phillips, *Politics of Permanent Crisis*, 109–10. See also Ghallab, *Lahut al-Nukhab al-Qabaliyya*, 203.

54. Author interview no. 13, Dec. 25, 2012.

55. Author interview no. 11, Dec. 20, 2012, Sanaa.

56. Bercovitch, Kremenyuk, and Zartman, "Nature of Conflict," 8.

57. Galtung, *Peace by Peaceful Means*, 71–72.

58. Oliver Ramsbotham, Tom Woodhouse, and Hugh Miall, *Contemporary Conflict Resolution: The Prevention, Management and Transformation of Deadly Conflicts*, 10.

59. Cavatorta, "'Divided They Stand,'" 142; Michele Penner Angrist, "The Outlook for Authoritarians," 226–27; Shehata, *Islamists and Secularists*, 2.

60. See, for example, Eva Wegner and Miquel Pellicer, "Left-Islamist Opposition Cooperation in Morocco," 320.

61. Michael Wahman, "Offices and Policies: Why Do Oppositional Parties Form Pre-electoral Coalitions in Competitive Authoritarian Regimes?," 643; Simon Hix, Abdul Noury, and Gérard Roland, "Power to the Parties: Cohesion and Competition in the European Parliament, 1979–2001," 215.

62. See also Van Dyke and Amos, "Social Movement Coalitions," 6.

63. Clark, "Conditions of Islamist Moderation," 547; Kraetzschmar, "Mapping Opposition Coalition," 291; Curtis R. Ryan, "Political Opposition and Reform Coalitions in Jordan," 378.

64. Mashru' al-Liqa' al-Mushtarak li-l-Islah al-Siyasi wa al-Watani (JMP Plan for Political and National Reform), 55–61. The platform is published as a small sixty-two-page booklet (DIN A6). The respective section contains eleven clauses, inter alia, on various vague points of criticism concerning the ROY's foreign policy (clauses 1–4); the Gulf Cooperation Council (5); further regional organizations (6); Palestine (3, 8, 10); North-South talks, a "dialogue of civilizations" (9); and a call to reform the United Nations (11).

65. Author interview no. 1, July 22, 2008; author interview no. 20, Jan. 7, 2013; author interview no. 13, Dec. 25, 2012; author interview no. 25, Jan. 14, 2013; author interview no. 2, Aug. 2, 2008; author interview no. 3, Aug. 6, 2008; author interview no. 12, Dec. 21, 2012.

66. Author interview no. 13, Dec. 25, 2012.

67. Author interview no. 18, Jan. 3, 2013, Sanaa.

68. Certainly, facilitating negotiations on alliance building with Islah was the fact that no party officially confessed to atheism. The YSP had altered its position on atheism in the run-up to the formation of the SCCOP, so as to accommodate al-Haqq. Stiftl, "Politischer Islam," 192.

69. This phrase was coined by a senior Islahi. Author interview no. 13, Dec. 25, 2012.

70. Author interview no. 25, Jan. 14, 2013.

71. Author interview no. 1, July 22, 2008.

72. Hesham Sallam, "Opposition Alliances and Democratization in Egypt," 2–3; Huskey and Iskakova, "Barriers to Intra-opposition Cooperation," 236.

73. Robin I. M. Dunbar and Alistair G. Sutcliffe, "Social Complexity and Intelligence," 111.

74. Axelrod, *The Evolution of Cooperation*, 139. On reciprocity and social movement cooperation, see Meyer and Corrigall-Brown, "Coalitions and Political Context," 331. While reciprocity is usually conceptualized in absolute terms (for example, the defection of one party will inevitably result in the defection of the other, thus immediately stalling cooperation), Andreas Schedler suggests that actors may feel responsible for maintaining cooperation despite previous defections by their counterparts in order to not jeopardize an overarching goal (in Schedler's case, the preservation of democracy). "Blending normative sensibility with strategic intelligence," he argues, "[preserving democracy] obliges them to heed the norms of reciprocity in ways that safeguard the entire system of

reciprocity." Andreas Schedler, "Democratic Reciprocity," 259. This sense of obligation may also explain why (nascent) opposition cooperation is at times continued even in the face of only partial compliance with reciprocity or the absence of trust (or both).

75. Thomas C. Schelling, *The Strategy of Conflict*, 134–35.

76. Nancy Bermeo argues that formerly antagonistic left- and right-wing forces in Latin America often took cues from the experience of their counterparts abroad, using these as cognitive and behavioral guidelines when pondering whether to pursue cooperation. Nancy Bermeo, "Democracy and the Lessons of Dictatorship," 284.

77. Andreas Zick, "Die Konflikttheorie der Theorie sozialer Identität," 416; Dunbar and Sutcliffe, "Social Complexity and Intelligence," 112.

78. Schwedler, *Faith in Moderation*, 114, 112.

79. Al-Ahmar, *Mudhakkirat: Qadaya wa Mawaqif*, 312.

80. Author interview no. 25, Jan. 3, 2013.

81. Mansur, *Al-Ahzab al-Siyasiyya*, 370–72.

82. Al-Faqih, "Al-Takattul," 162.

83. Author interview no. 7, Dec. 12, 2012, Sanaa.

84. Wedeen, "Seeing Like a Citizen," 687.

85. Philbrick Yadav, *Islamists and the State*, 46.

86. Author interview no. 20, Jan. 7, 2013.

87. Browers, "Origins and Architects," 570.

88. Mansur, *Al-Ahzab al-Siyasiyya*, 372.

89. The SCER website provides the full list of the 2001 amendments. See http://web.scer.gov.ye/.

90. Mansur, *Al-Ahzab al-Siyasiyya*, 382.

91. Author interview no. 20, Jan. 7, 2013.

92. Sarah Phillips, "Evaluating Political Reform in Yemen," 8.

93. Compared to the 2006 local council elections, Islah and the YSP performed well in 2001. At the governorate level, Islah won 77 seats (2006: 27) and the YSP 16 (2006: 10). At the district level, Islah won 1,391 seats (2006: 802) and the YSP 210 (2006: 172). In contrast, the GPC took 253 seats (2006: 319) at the governorate level and 3,703 (2006: 5073) at the district one. For further details, see the SCER website, http://web.scer.gov.ye/.

94. Glosemeyer and Sallam, "JMP Alliance," 331.

95. Philbrick Yadav, *Islamists and the State*, 46.

96. Laurent Bonnefoy and Marine Poirier, "The Yemeni Congregation for Reform (al-Islâh): The Difficult Process of Building a Project for Change," 54.

97. Author interview no. 25, Jan. 14, 2013.

98. These defections include Mansur 'Ali Wasil, 'Ali 'Ali al-Qasi', 'Abd al-Wahhab Hamud Ma'uda, and 'Abd al-Karim Muhammad al-Aslami. Al-Sharjabi, "Al-Tajammu'," 158.

99. Longley Alley, "Rules of the Game," 406.

100. Al-Faqih, "Al-Takattul," 163.

101. Browers, "Origins and Architects," 577.

102. Mansur, *Al-Ahzab al-Siyasiyya*, 374–75.

103. Al-Jawi, "We Are the Opposition," 87.

104. Author interview no. 1, July 22, 2008; author interview no. 20, Jan. 7, 2013; author interview no. 13, Dec. 25, 2012; author interview no. 25, Jan. 14, 2013; author interview no. 2, Aug. 2, 2008; author interview no. 3, Aug. 6, 2008; author interview no. 12, Dec. 21, 2012.

105. Author interview no. 29, Jan. 21, 2013, Sanaa.

106. Iris Glosemeyer, "Wo Islamisten für Rechte von Sozialisten streiten."

107. Conversely, social identity theory suggests that interactions between actors are likely to reduce conflict if they have a similar status. Zick, "Die Konflikttheorie," 416. Concerning Western democracies, Richard S. Katz and Peter Mair hold that shared professional experience among politicians smooths out attitudinal constraints, as "they come to regard their political opponents as fellow professionals." Richard S. Katz and Peter Mair, "Changing Models of Party Organization and Party Democracy: The Emergence of the Cartel Party," 23.

108. Shehata, *Islamists and Secularists*, 143; Sallam, "Opposition Alliances," 4.

109. Lust-Okar, *Structuring Conflict*.

110. Van Dyke, "Crossing Movement Boundaries," 230. Shared experiences of past repression are also believed to establish commonalities. Bermeo, "Democracy," 284.

111. Author interview no. 18, Jan. 3, 2013.

112. Exclusion from decision-making processes and resources as well as Salih's hegemony over the political realm were often mentioned by interviewees: for example, author interview no. 11, Dec. 20, 2012; author interview no. 2, Aug. 2, 2008; author interview no. 13, Dec. 25, 2012; author interview no. 16, Dec. 31, 2012, Sanaa.

113. The aspect of enmity was frequently mentioned by political analysts, JMP affiliates, and high-ranking regime members. Author interview no. 27, Jan. 16, 2013, Sanaa; author interview no. 20, Jan. 7, 2013; author interview no. 19, Jan. 6, 2013, Sanaa; author interview no. 10, Dec. 14, 2012, Sanaa.

114. Van de Walle, "Tipping Games," 85.

115. Robert A. Dahl, *Polyarchy: Participation and Opposition*, 37; Larry Diamond, "Introduction: Political Culture and Democracy," 2–3; Arend Lijphart, "Consociational Democracy," 216.

116. Schwedler and Clark, "Islamist-Leftist Cooperation," 11.

117. See, for example, Janine Clark, "Conditions of Islamist Moderation"; Jillian Schwedler, "Can Islamists Become Moderates? Rethinking the Inclusion-Moderation Hypothesis."

118. Browers, "Origins and Architects," 583.

119. Bermeo, "Democracy," 287. See also Carrie Rosefsky Wickham, "The Path to Moderation: Strategy and Learning in the Formation of Egypt's Wasat Party."

120. Author interview no. 17, Jan. 1, 2013, Sanaa.

121. As an editorial in the independent daily al-Shumu' argued much later that "the relationship between Islah and the YSP [acted as] an emergency valve [simam aman]," as only their alliance was able to counterbalance the regime. 'Abd al-Basit al-Shamiri, "Ijabiyya al-'Alaqa bayna al-Islah wa al-Ishtiraki," al-Shumu', July 26, 2008.

122. Jens Heibach, "Muhammad 'Abd al-Malik al-Mutawakkil: A Political Biography."

123. Author interview no. 17, Jan. 1, 2013.

124. The characterization of al-Kuhali that follows draws on Sheila Carapico, Lisa Wedeen, and Anna Würth, "The Death and Life of Jarallah Omar"; Brian Whitaker, "Jarallah Omar al-Kuhali," Guardian, Feb. 4, 2003, https://www.theguardian.com/news /2003/feb/04/guardianobituaries.brianwhitaker; and Ma'rib al-Ward, "10 A'wam 'ala Rahil Muhandis al-Liqa' al-Mushtarak," Alahale.net, Dec. 27, 2012, https://alahale.net/article /7885.

125. Jarallah 'Umar al-Kuhali, "A Short Autobiography," Al-Bab, n.d., http://www .al-bab.com/yemen/biog/jarallah.htm.

126. Al-Mutawakkil, "Al-Afaq," 150.

127. Abu Luhum, Al-Yaman: Haqa'iq wa Watha'iq 'Ishtuha, 169.

128. Carapico, Wedeen, and Würth, "Death and Life."

129. Abu Luhum, Al-Yaman, 169.

130. This point is made frequently, nevertheless. See, for example, Mohammed Bin Sallam, "Can Yemen's Opposition JMP Find Common Purpose after Saleh's Departure?," Yemen Times, July 27, 2011, http://www.yementimes.com/defaultdet.aspx?SUB _ID=36355.

131. Browers, "Origins and Architects," 566; italics added.

132. The following information is provided by Browers, Political Ideology, 77–86; Browers, "Origins and Architects," 577–78.

133. Yacoubian, "Building Momentum," 63.

134. Baaklini, Denoeux, and Springborg, Legislative Politics, 231.

135. Author interview no. 3, Aug. 6, 2008. Later, these qat chews would often be merged with the formal meetings of the JMP's highest decision-making body, the High Council (al-majlis al-a'la). See, for example, "Fi Maqil Qat: Al-Liqa' al-Mushtarak Yushakkil Hukuma Inqadh Watani," al-Haqiqa, Jan. 13, 2008.

136. Author interview no. 25, Jan. 14, 2013; author interview no. 18, Jan. 3, 2013.

137. The JMP officially celebrated its tenth anniversary in Dec. 2010. See "Ra'is al-Mushtarak." This date was confirmed by one senior Islah member; author interview no. 13, Dec. 25, 2012.

138. Sheila Carapico, "How Yemen's Ruling Party Secured an Electoral Landslide"; Faqih, "Al-Takattul," 156; Glosemeyer and Sallam, "JMP Alliance," 340; Mutawakkil, "Al-Afaq," 156; Phillips, *Yemen's Democracy Experiment*, 243–46; al-Sharjabi, "Al-Tajammu'," 152.

139. Bonnefoy and Poirier, "Yemeni Congregation," 55. Philbrick Yadav reports that while she "had interviewed a number of leading members of the JMP [she] was absolutely (and frustratingly) unable to derive from these interviews any kind of systematic history of the JMP." Philbrick Yadav, *Islamists and the State*, 225. Browers argues in a similar vein. Browers, "Origins and Architects," 569.

140. Ahmed A. Hezam al-Yemeni, *The Dynamics of Democratisation: Political Parties in Yemen*, 65, 67.

141. Ishiyama, "Sickle and Minaret," 19.

142. Walad al-Sadiq Milud, *Al-Inqisam al-Ijtima'i wa Atharuhu fi bayna al-Ahzab al-Qawmiyya*, 216–28.

143. Burrowes and Kasper, "Saleh Regime," 272.

144. Day, *Regionalism and Rebellion*, 210–11.

145. Phillips, *Politics of Permanent Crisis*, 107.

146. Author interview no. 13, Dec. 25, 2012; author interview no. 18, Jan. 3, 2013; author interview no. 4, Aug. 9, 2008.

147. Author interview no. 2, Aug. 2, 2008.

148. It is telling that a high-ranking member of the Salih regime would vilify only the Brotherhood—instead of Islah as a whole—in author interview no. 27, Jan. 16, 2013.

149. For instance, the case has been made that Hamid al-Ahmar's interest in upholding Yemeni unity was not only politically motivated but also the result of the "interest of a businessman seeking to enlarge his market area." 'Abdallah Hamuda, "Al-Yaman fi Muwajaha Azmat Qadima wa Mustajidda," 17. Hamid al-Ahmar, a son of 'Abdallah al-Ahmar, assumed key positions in Islah and the JMP as of the middle of the first decade of the new millennium (more below).

150. Although Islah must be considered a probusiness party that approves of privatization and economic liberalization, the notion of the existence of a business wing within the party has been challenged. Paul Dresch and Bernard Haykel, "Stereotypes and Political Styles: Islamists and Tribesfolk in Yemen," 422–23.

151. "United States Designates bin Ladin Loyalists," US Department of the Treasury, Feb. 24, 2004 (JS-1190), https://web.archive.org/web/20100314033922/http://www.treasury.gov/press/releases/js1190.htm.

152. Author interview no. 18, Jan. 3, 2013; author interview no. 13, Dec. 25, 2012.

153. Al-Sharjabi argues that the Brotherhood managed to defeat the Salafis during the 2005 party congress by introducing a committee responsible for overseeing dialogue with the Western powers, something the Salafis wholeheartedly rejected. Al-Sharjabi, "Al-Tajammu'," 152.

154. 'Arif 'Ali 'Umari, "Musa'ada al-Nazihin," *al-Balagh*, Oct. 19, 2009, http://www.al-balagh.net/index.php?option=content&task=view&id=8182&Itemid=.

155. Carapico, Wedeen and Würth, "Death and Life."

156. Philbrick Yadav, "Understanding 'What Islamists Want,'" 210; Glosemeyer and Sallam, "JMP Alliance," 332.

157. In addition, Salih was forced to prove his support for the George W. Bush administration's War on Terror in the aftermath of 9/11. The Yemeni president thus began removing mosque leaders in August 2003, most of whom were loyal to or members of Islah. This move again weakened those Islahis advocating cooperation with the GPC and strengthened the Brotherhood. Ludmila Du Bouchet, "The State, Political Islam, and Violence: The Reconfiguration of Yemeni Politics since 9/11," 159.

158. The agreement included seven clauses altogether defining the principal aims of electoral coordination (1–3), prohibiting coordination with nonsignatory parties (5), and outlawing other actions deemed detrimental to the signatory parties (4). Most important, it demanded that the parties not compete against each other in those districts where one signatory party stood a good chance of winning (6). Finally, clause 7 obliged the parties to commit to fair play in those districts where more than one of the signatory parties would field a candidate so as to not impede subsequent cooperation. The agreement is provided in Muhammad al-Qadi, "Ahzab al-Mu'arada al-Yamaniyya Tuwaqqi' 'Ittifaq al-Mabadi" li-l-Tansiq al-Mushtarak fi al-Intikhabat al-Barlamaniyya," *al-Riyadh*, Feb. 8, 2003, http://www.alriyadh.com/Contents/08-02-2003/Mainpage/POLITICS_72 50.php.

159. See the SCER website, http://web.scer.gov.ye/.

160. Author interview no. 3, Aug. 6, 2008.

161. Author interview no. 2, Aug. 2, 2008.

162. Author interview no. 25, Jan. 14, 2013.

163. Author interview no. 20, Jan. 7, 2013.

164. Author interview no. 20, Jan. 7, 2013. Both bylaws were later revised and newly approved on December 9, 2007 (Basic Bylaws), http://www.al-islah.net/print.aspx?pagename=gen&pageid=5570, and December 10, 2007 (Regional Bylaws), http://www.al-islah.net/details.aspx?pageid=5569&pagename=gen, respectively.

165. Mashru' al-Liqa' al-Mushtarak, 62. The 2003 Agreement of Principles used the term *Joint Meeting Bloc* (*takattul*), while the 1996 agreement was titled *Joint Meeting Program.*

166. The deputy secretary-general of the Syrian-oriented Ba'th, Mudhish 'Ali Naji, justified his party's alignment with the JMP on the grounds of the increasingly repressive nature of the regime. Interview by Khalid al-'Alwani in *al-Sahwa*, Aug. 14, 2008.

167. Author interview no. 20, Jan. 7, 2013. One senior YSP member remarked that from November 2005 onward, "one could begin to speak of an alliance." Author interview no. 25, Jan. 14, 2013.

168. "Dozens Dead in Yemen Fuel Riots," BBC, July 22, 2005, http://news.bbc.co.uk/2/hi/middle_east/4707145.stm.

169. A copy of the draft bill features in al-Kibsi, *Nizam al-Hukm*, 531–45.

170. For the text of the first memorandum, that is, the Plan of Challenges and Ambitions Guiding the JMP's Work in the Present Period (mashru' mahamm wa ittijahat 'amal al-liqa' al-mushtarak li-l-marhala al-rahina), see al-Kibsi, *Nizam al-Hukm*, 546–48. For the second memorandum, that is, the Vision of the JMP Guaranteeing the Holding of Free, Fair, and Just Elections, see 551–69.

171. Chapter 3 elaborates on the respective agreement, which was struck on June 18, 2006. For a first draft of the agreement, titled "Agenda of the Dialogue Held between the JMP and the GPC" (bunud al-hiwar alladhi tamm bayna ahzab al-liqa' al-mushtarak wa al-mu'tamar al-sha'bi al-'amm), see al-Kibsi, *Nizam al-Hukm*, 549–69.

2. Upgrading Cooperation: The Consolidation of the Joint Meeting Parties

1. Mashru' al-Liqa' al-Mushtarak, 1, 4–12, 1, 2—3

2. Aziz al-Azmeh, "Populism Contra Democracy: Recent Democratist Discourse in the Arab World," 112.

3. Riyad al-Adib, "Mahrajan bi-Ta'izz li-Rafdh Ta'jil al-Intikhabat," *News Yemen*, Jan. 5, 2011, http://www.newsyemen.net/view_news.asp? sub_no=1_2011_01_05_50674; Hakim Almasmary, "Corrupt Opposition Leaders Must Not Rise When Salih Falls," *Yemen Post*, Mar. 7, 2011, http://yemenpost.net/Detail123456789.aspx?ID=3&SubID=3251&MainCat=2.

4. Longley, "High Water Mark," 246.

5. Al-Faqih, "Al-Takattul," 167.

6. These points were also accentuated by individual JMP members from the top- and middle-level leadership during interviews conducted by the author between 2008–9 and 2012–13.

7. Mashru' al-Liqa' al-Mushtarak, 1, 4, 11, 5, 12–13, 29, 34, 40–41, 27–32, 33.

8. Mashru' al-Liqa' al-Mushtarak, 8–9, 61, 14–15.

9. Philbrick Yadav, *Islamists and the State*, 48.

10. Ghallab, *Lahut al-Nukhab al-Qabaliyya*, 209.

11. Glosemeyer and Sallam, "JMP Alliance," 341.

12. Mashru' al-Liqa' al-Mushtarak, 1.

13. Particularly, the root-cause analysis holds that "chaos is spreading at the expense of the rule of law" (Mashru' al-Liqa' al-Mushtarak, 11), that the regime was facilitating the "emergence of violent and extremist conflict" or "expansive conflicts" (Mashru' al-Liqa' al-Mushtarak, 12, 14), and that Yemeni history had been characterized by "violence and bloody clashes" (Mashru' al-Liqa' al-Mushtarak, 12).

14. Mashru' al-Liqa' al-Mushtarak, 1.

15. Mashru' al-Liqa' al-Mushtarak, 10, 16–18.

16. Mashru' al-Liqa' al-Mushtarak, 18–21, 22–24.

17. See also Burrowes and Kasper, "Saleh Regime," 277.

18. Mashru' al-Liqa' al-Mushtarak, 22, 18.

19. Mashru' al-Liqa' al-Mushtarak, 33–34.

20. Philbrick Yadav, *Islamists and the State*, 60.

21. Glosemeyer and Sallam, "JMP Alliance," 333.

22. Mashru' al-Liqa' al-Mushtarak, 25–28, 13, 53–54.

23. See also Browers, "Origins and Architects," 581.

24. Clark, "Threats, Structures, and Resources," 115.

25. Ellen Lust, "Opposition Cooperation," 432.

26. For example, Clark, "Threats, Structures, and Resources."

27. Sameh Fawzy, "What Is the Future of the Movement for Democratic Change in the Arab World?," 16–20.

28. Abdelrahman, "'With the Islamists?," 41.

29. On the different levels of cooperation, see Schwedler and Clark, "Islamist-Leftist Cooperation," 10. Kraetzschmar suggests a typology of opposition cooperation revolving around two parameters: the number of objectives (single or multiple) and the location of the actors involved (domestic and foreign), respectively. See Kraetzschmar, "Mapping Opposition Coalition," 291–300.

30. Doug McAdam, John D. McCarthy, and Mayer N. Zald, "Opportunities, Mobilizing Structures, and Framing Processes: Toward a Synthetic, Comparative Perspective on Social Movements," 13; Hathaway and Meyer, "Competition and Cooperation," 178; Staggenborg, "Coalition Work," 388.

31. Axelrod, *The Evolution of Cooperation*, 130, 139–40, 129, 134.

32. Al-La'iha al-Asasiyya. The Basic Bylaws that are referred to in this section date from December 2007. Note the flawed numbering. The original document lists twenty-six clauses, but the numbers for clauses 3, 8, and 9 are used twice. In the following, the correct, consecutive, numbers will be cited in brackets.

33. Author interview no. 2, Aug. 2, 2008.

34. Alfred Stepan, "On the Tasks of Democratic Opposition," 47.

35. Olson, *Logic of Collective Action*, 16–17, 51, 133. See also Schelling, *Strategy of Conflict*, 134–35.

36. Hanspeter Kriesi, "The Organizational Structure of New Social Movements in a Political Context," 154.

37. Aqeel al-Halali, "Parliament Likely to Approve Election Law Amendments, Choose SCER Candidate," *Yemen Times*, Aug. 18, 2008.

38. "Al-'Atwani: Nu'awwal 'ala Tawjihat al-Ra'is La 'ala Huwah al-Asmat bi-l-Mu'tamar," *al-Sahwa*, Aug. 16, 2008, http://www.alsahwa-yemen.net/view_news.asp?sub _no=1_2008_08_16_65392.

39. For conflicting reports on the above-mentioned incidence, see, for example, "Al-Mushtarak Yahnath bi-l-Qasam wa al-Barlaman Yarfudh al-Ta'dil wa Yushakkil Lajna al-Intikhabat," *Naba News*, Aug. 18, 2008, http://www.nabanews.net/news/15193; Mu'in al-Salami, "Bafadhl wa al-Zindani: Isqat al-Mu'tamar li-Ta'dilat al-Intikhabat Hadama li-l-Wifaq al-Watani," *al-Sahwa*, Aug. 18, 2008, www.sahwa-yemen.net/view_news.asp ?sub_no_2008_08_18_65431; "Ra'is al-Intikhabat Janubi wa Ajniha al-Sulta Tu'arqila al-Ittifaq bi-Tawjihat," *al-Ahali*, Aug. 18, 2008.

40. Official negotiations were put on hold until February 2009. The JMP referred to August 18, 2008, as a turning point here. See "Yasin: Dukhul al-Intikhabat Huwa Khiyarna al-Ra'isi," *al-Shari'*, Nov. 15, 2008.

41. Mohammed al-Kibsi, "Parliament Rejects Amendments, Votes for 2001 Elections Law," *Yemen Observer*, Aug. 19, 2008.

42. "Al-Ishtiraki wa al-Nasiri Yuqsiyan al-Islah min Ijtima' Mushtarak wa al-Azma Tatafaqam," *Naba News*, Aug. 21, 2008, http://www.nabanews.net/news/15236.

43. "Ra'is al-Jumhuriyya Yasdir Qiraran bi-Tashkil al-Lajna al-'Ulya li-l-Intikhabat," *Naba News*, Aug. 26, 2008, http://www.nabanews.net/news/15300.

44. Shortly before and after this incident, similar articles reported on its pending disintegration. See, for example, "Qiyadat Mu'tamariyya: Al-Anisi Mutashaddad Usuli Mutatarraf," *al-Balagh*, Aug. 5, 2008; "Khilafat al-Mushtarak Tansif Mubadara al-Fursa al-Akhira," *Naba News*, Oct. 26, 2008, http://www.nabanews.net/news/15869.

45. When asked to comment on this incident, one YSP member argued that such exclusionary meetings were a standard procedure used to carve out common positions among the participants that would subsequently be discussed with the excluded JMP member(s). Author interview no. 19, Jan. 6, 2013.

46. See clauses 17 and 22 for the High Council and the Executive Council, respectively.

47. Author interview no. 13, Dec. 25, 2012.

48. Author interview no. 2, Aug. 2, 2008. This point was conceded by a senior Islah member. Author interview no. 13, Dec. 25, 2012.

49. Author interview no. 20, Jan. 7, 2013.

50. Phillips, *Politics of Permanent Crisis*, 111.

51. Author interview no. 18, Jan. 3, 2013.

52. Philbrick Yadav, *Shadow of Transition*, 64.

53. Amitai Etzioni, *The Active Society: A Theory of Societal and Political Processes*, 388. See also Charles Tilly and Sidney Tarrow, *Contentious Politics*, 206.

54. John D. McCarthy and Mayer N. Zald, "Resource Mobilization and Social Movements: A Partial Theory," 1216.

55. Kriesi, "Organizational Structure," 154.

56. Kriesi, "Organizational Structure," 154.

57. Author interview no. 13, Dec. 25, 2012; author interview no. 25, Jan. 14, 2013.

58. Al-La'iha al-Munazzima, amended version as of December 2007. Note again the flawed numbering owing to the omittance of Clauses 4–6 in the original document.

59. Socotra, an archipelago in the Indian Ocean that had hitherto been part of the Aden and Hadramawt Governorates, respectively, became a governorate in its own right in 2013.

60. Mohammed bin Sallam, "Protests against Voter Registration in Many Governorates," *Yemen Times*, Nov. 20, 2008.

61. *Al-Ayyam*, Nov. 19, 2008.

62. See the reports by 'Abdallah Qardu' on al-Mahfad and Hatim al-'Amri on Sirar in *al-Ayyam*, same edition.

63. Mohammed bin Sallam, "Fears over Possibility of Postponing Upcoming Elections," *Yemen Times*, Nov. 10, 2008.

64. For example, "Al-Mushtarak Yad'u Kawadirhu wa Ansarhu ila 'Adam Musharaka fi Hiwar al-Sulta," *al-Sahwa*, Jan. 26, 2010, http://www.sahwa-yemen.net/view_news.asp ?sub_no=1_2010_01_26_75628; "Nass Bayan al-Mushtarak bi-Sha'n al-Tas'id al-Amni fi al-Muhafazat al-Janubiyya," *al-Sahwa*, Mar. 10, 2010, http://www. sahwa-yemen.net/view _news.asp?sub_no=1_2010_03_10_76646.

65. For conflicting statements in the literature, see al-Faqih, "Al-Takattul," 140; Sarah Phillips and Murad Zafir, "NDI Baseline Assessment of the Joint Meeting Parties (JMP)," 28–29.

66. For instance, Muhsin Basura, the head of Islah's Hadramawt branch, stated in August 2008 that "it is necessary to accept the issue of the South with all its demands." "Ra'is al-Intikhabat Janubi," *al-Ahali*, Aug. 18, 2008. For similar statements see "Qiyadi Islahi: Nata'ij Ittifaq al-Mu'tamar wa al-Mushtarak Tatawaqqaf 'ala Hall al-Qadhaya Kaffatan wa Minha al-Qadhiyya al-Janubiyya," *al-Ayyam*, Mar. 2, 2009, http://www.al-ayyam .info/default.aspx?NewsID=48cee7a1-1a51-404b-839b-9624c62f08b1; "Islah Ta'izz Yad'u ila al-Tawahhud wa Yaskhar min 'Askara al-Manatiq al-Janubiyya," *al-Balagh*, May 18, 2009, http://www.al-balagh.net/index.php?option=content&task=view&id=7479&Itemid=.

67. "Al-Mushtarak bi-'Adan: Awqafu I'tida'at 'ala Radfan," *al-Ayyam*, May 4, 2010, http://www.al-ayyam.info/Default.aspx?NewsID=21ccaf80-0602-438f-a9fa-96d276f12792; Samir Hasan, "Mushtarak 'Adan Yudin Qam' Tazahara 'Adan," *al-Sahwa*, May 23, 2009, http://www.alsahwa-yemen.net/view_news.asp?sub_no=1_2009_05_23_70674.

68. "Fi Balagh Sahafi li-l-Mushtarak bi-Hadhramawt: Ta'arradha Mu'taqilin fi Sijn al-Bahth al-Jana'i li-l-Dharb bi-A'qab al-Banadiq," *al-Ayyam*, May 4, 2009, http://www.al -ayyam.info/Default.aspx?NewsID=21ccaf80-0602-438f-a9fa-96d276f12792.

69. "Al-Mu'aradha al-Yamaniyya wa Ba'dh Ahali al-Mu'taqilin Yunafidhdhun I'tisaman Silmiyyan amam Idara al-Muhafizh bi-l-Mukalla," *Aden News Agency*, Mar. 15, 2010, http://www.aden-na.com/default.asp?page=1003&NewsID=937.

70. "Mushtarak Yastankir 'Askara al-Hayah wa Ta'kir al-Ajwa' fi Habban," *al-Sahwa*, Jan. 21, 2010, http://www.alsahwa-yemen.net/view_news.asp?sub_no=1_2010_01_21_75490;

"Mushtarak al-Mahra Yastankir Ahdath al-Ghaydha," *al-Sahwa*, Jan. 28, 2010, http://www
.alsahwa-yemen.net/view_news.asp?sub_no=1_2010_01_28_75691.

71. "Nass Bayan al-Mushtarak," *al-Sahwa*, Mar. 10, 2010.

72. See, for example, al-Faqih, "Al-Takattul," 28; Mohammed bin Sallam, "Ruling
Party Wins Majority of Governor Seats," *Yemen Times*, May 19, 2008; "Tawafuq Mabda'i
bayna al-Ra'is wa al-Mushtarak 'ala Muqtarah Amriki Yaqdhi bi-Ta'jil al-Intikhabat," *al-
Wasat*, Jan. 24, 2009.

73. Phillips and Zafir, "NDI Baseline Assessment," 20, 18.

74. *Oxford Dictionaries Online*, s.v. "coherence," http://oxforddictionaries.com/de
/definition/englisch/coherence.

75. Phillip Norton, "Making Sense of Opposition," 238.

76. Phillips, *Politics of Permanent Crisis*, 18.

77. Phillips and Zafir, "NDI Baseline Assessment," 16.

78. Author interview no. 11, Dec. 20, 2012.

79. Author interview no. 9, Dec. 18, 2012, Sanaa; author interview no. 1, July 22,
2008; author interview no. 19, Jan. 6, 2013; author interview no. 17, Jan. 1, 2013.

80. Author interview no. 15, Dec. 29, 2012, Sanaa; author interview no. 9, Dec. 18,
2012; author interview no. 19, Jan. 6, 2013; author interview no. 17, Jan. 1, 2013.

81. Author interview no. 5, Aug. 27, 2008, Sanaa; author interview no. 2, Aug. 2,
2008.

82. Author interview no. 4, Aug. 9, 2008; author interview no. 29, Jan. 21, 2013; author interview no. 20, Jan. 7, 2013; author interview no. 13, Dec. 25, 2012.

83. Samuel P. Huntington, *Political Order in Changing Societies*, 12, see also Vicky
Randall and Lars Svåsand, "Party Institutionalization in New Democracies," 12.

84. Note that institutionalization is often understood to have both an internal and
an external dimension, with the latter encompassing indicators such as autonomy from
external influence. See Matthias Basedau and Alexander Stroh, "Measuring Party Institutionalization in Developing Countries," 8–9; Randall and Svåsand, "Party Institutionalization," 12–14. See also Scott Mainwaring and Timothy R. Scully, eds., *Building
Democratic Institutions: Party Systems in Latin America*; Angelo Panebianco, *Political
Parties: Organizations and Power*.

85. Randall and Svåsand, "Party Institutionalization," 13.

86. Basedau and Stroh, "Measuring Party Institutionalization," 12.

87. Author interview no. 2, Aug. 2, 2008; author interview no. 3, Aug. 6, 2008.

88. While the Yemeni Unionist Gathering under 'Umar al-Jawi had refused to cooperate with Islah, the party joined the JMP shortly before Salih's resignation in November
2011. The party's new secretary-general, 'Abdallah 'Awbil, became minister of culture in
December 2011.

89. Note that most studies home in on Islah, but arrive at contradictory conclusions.
For instance, Hamzawy acknowledges "a high degree of both internal democracy and of

decentralization of decision-making powers" for Islah. Amr Hamzawy, "Between Government and Opposition: The Case of the Yemeni Congregation for Reform," 20. See also al-Faqih, "Al-Takattul," 140. Others point to the lack of internal democracy with respect to the JMP parties, particularly Islah. See, for instance, Phillips, *Politics of Permanent Crisis*, 114.

90. Author interview no. 17, Jan. 1, 2013; author interview no. 16, Dec. 31, 2012, Sanaa; author interview no. 19, Jan. 6, 2013. Irrespective of their party affiliation, these young party members maintained the "new generation" had not been integrated into the main party organs and that the situation was especially bleak regarding Islah. The YSP and NUPO, in contrast, were reportedly making progress on this issue. See also Longley, "High Water Mark," 255.

91. Author interview no. 16, Dec. 31, 2012.

92. Asef Bayat, "Islamism and Social Movement Theory," 902–3. On the JMP, see Phillips and Zafir, "NDI Baseline Assessment," 19.

93. One Islah member controverted this dictum. Author interview no. 6, Mar. 29, 2012, Berlin.

94. Author interview no. 13, Dec. 25, 2012.

95. *Merriam-Webster*, s.v. "commitment," https://www.merriam-webster.com/diction ary/commitment.

96. Alberto Melucci, "The Process of Collective Identity," 47, 43–44.

97. Bayat, "Islamism." See also Bayat, *Life as Politics: How Ordinary People Change the Middle East.*

98. Etzioni, *Active Society,* 98.

99. Gunter Schubert, Rainer Tetzlaff, and Werner Vennewald, *Demokratisierung und politischer Wandel: Theorie und Anwendung des Konzepts der strategischen und konfliktfähigen Gruppen*, 73.

100. Bayat, "Islamism," 902, 903.

101. Melucci, "Process of Collective Identity," 43–44.

102. Etzioni, *Active Society*, 470.

103. Schwedler, *Faith in Moderation*, 195; Melucci, "Process of Collective Identity," 49.

104. Schwedler, *Faith in Moderation*, 196.

105. For the meaning of interactions between middle- and lower-level elites at the governorate and district levels, see Wegner and Pellicer, "Left-Islamist Opposition Cooperation," 305.

106. Dhi'a Assoswa, "JMP Held an Open Symposium in Ibb," *Yemen Observer*, Dec. 24, 2009, http://www.yobserver.com/local-news/printer-10017808.html; "'Aydarus al-Naqib: Al-Hakim Yurid Khatf Mashru' al-Hiwar al-Watani," *al-Balagh*, Jan. 12, 2010, http://www.al-balagh.net/index.php?option=content&task=view?id=8617&Itemid=.

107. Author interview no. 20, Jan. 7, 2013. See also the subsequent section.

108. Philbrick Yadav, *Islamists and the State*, 53.

109. Mohammed bin Sallam, "Can Yemen's Opposition JMP Find Common Purpose after Saleh's Departure?," *Yemen Times*, July 27, 2011, http://www.yementimes.com /defaultdet.aspx?SUB_ID=36355; author interview no. 18, Jan. 3, 2013.

110. Author interview no. 20, Jan. 7, 2013.

111. Phillips and Zafir, "NDI Baseline Assessment," 42.

112. In December 2010, for instance, the JMP's Ta'izz branch—as such, not the High Council—orchestrated protests in many of the country's governorates, including in Abyan, Aden, al-Dhali', Ibb, and Lahij. See "Thousands of the JMP Members Protest in Taizz Province," *Yemen Post*, Dec. 7, 2010, http://www.yemenpost.net/Detail123456789. aspx?ID=3&SubID=2837&MainCat=3.

113. Iris Glosemeyer, "Wo Islamisten für Rechte von Sozialisten streiten," *Welt-Sichten*, Jan. 27, 2009.

114. Author interview no. 17, Jan. 1, 2013; author interview no. 19, Jan. 6, 2013; author interview no. 16, Dec. 31, 2012; author interview no. 24, Jan. 10, 2013, Sanaa; author interview no. 8, Dec. 13, 2012, Sanaa.

115. Author interview no. 19, Jan. 6, 2013.

116. Author interview no. 17, Jan. 1, 2013.

117. April Longley Alley and Abdul Ghani al-Iryani, "Fighting Brushfires with Batons: An Analysis of the Political Crisis in South Yemen," 2.

118. Stephen Day, "The Political Challenge of Yemen's Southern Movement," 69. See also Ariel I. Ahram, *Break All the Borders: Separatism and the Reshaping of the Middle East*, 111; Augustin, *South Yemen's Independence Struggle*; Susanne Dahlgren, "The Snake with a Thousand Heads"; Day, *Regionalism and Rebellion*.

119. For a list of the Southern Movement's main SMOs established through 2010, see Nicole Stracke and Mohammed Saif Haidar, "The Southern Movement in Yemen," 3.

120. The Southern Movement's leadership was mainly composed of elites such as, for instance, al-Baydh, al-'Attas, al-Nuba, Ba'um, al-Majidi, 'Ali Haytham al-Gharib, and 'Ali Mansar, who were members either of the YSP's Politburo or of its Central Committee. Author interview no. 19, Jan. 6, 2013; author interview no. 27, Jan. 16, 2013.

121. Author interview no. 19, Jan. 6, 2013.

122. For the reformers' response hereto, see "D. Sa'il: Li-l-Hizb Ijabiyyat wa Afdhal Kathira fi Hukm al-Janub wa Ahammuha Tahqiq al-Wahda al-Yamaniyya," *Yemenress .com*, December 11, 2007, http://www.yemeress.com/akhbaralyom/23168.

123. Muhammad al-Khamiri, "Al-Ishtiraki al-Yamani Yujammid 'Udhwiyya al-Majidi," *Elaph*, Feb. 23, 2006, http://elaph.com/Web/Politics/2006/8/171656.htm?section archive=Politics.

124. "Al-Shanfara Yuqaddim Istiqalathu min al-Barlaman wa al-Hizb al-Ishtiraki," *News Yemen*, Sept. 28, 2009, http://www.newsyemen.net/view_news.asp?sub_no=1_2009 _10_28_32837.

125. Author interview no. 15, Dec. 29, 2012.

126. See, for instance, Samir Hasan, "Mutalabat li-Mukawwinat al-Hirak al-Silmi al-Janubi bi-l-Qubul bi-l-Hiwar wa Nabdh al-Furqa wa al-Ikhtilaf," *al-Sahwa*, Jan. 13, 2011, http://www.alsahwa-yemen.net/arabic/subjects/1/2011/1/13/6290.

127. "Al-Za'im Ba'um Yu'akkid 'ala Jumla min al-Qirarat wa Yastaqil min al-Hizb al-Ishtiraki al-Yamani," *Aden News Agency*, Jan. 11, 2011, URL: http://www.adennews agency.com/index.php?page=article&id=1665.

128. "Ra'is al-Haraka al-Shababiyya wa al-Tulabiyya fi al-Janub Yuqaddim Istiqa-lathu min 'Udhwiyya al-Ishtiraki al-Yamani," *Aden News Agency*, Jan. 12, 2011, http://www.adennewsagency.com/print.php?id=1673.

129. Cited in Mohammed bin Sallam, "Southern Movement Leader Disagree as More Demonstrations Occur," *Yemen Times*, Dec. 13, 2010, http://www.yementimes .com/default.aspx?SUB_ID=35215. For an open letter by Gharib calling on the YSP leadership to stop dissuading party members from pursuing independence, see Gharib, "Risala al-Munadhil 'Ali Haytham al-Gharib ila Ikhwan al-Ishtirakiyin wa ila Sha'bna al-Sabir fi al-Janub," Southern Democratic Assembly—TAJ, Dec. 2, 2010, http://www.taj-sa .org/index.php?option=com_content&view=article&id=271.

130. "Amin al-Ishtiraki: La Tahima Mawaqif al-Baydh wa al-'Attas wa 'Ali Nasir Nad'u ila Dawla Ittihadiyya," *News Yemen*, Dec. 16, 2010, http://www.newsyemen.net /view_news.asp?sub_no=1_2010_12_16_49987.

131. See, for instance, "Bayan al-Tawdhihi min al-'Amid al-Nuba 'an Ma Yahsul 'ala al-Saha al-Siyasiyya fi al-Janub," *Muntadayat al-Dhali' Bawaba al-Janub*, Feb. 21, 2011, http://www.dhal3.com/vb//showthread.php?t=57021.

132. "Zahra' Salih Tudin Ibn Ra'is al-Nizam wa Abna' Shaqiqhu li-Irtikabihim Jara'id Dhidd al-Insaniyya fi 'Adan," *Sawt al-Janub*, Feb. 8, 2011, http://www.soutalgnoub .com/home/index.php?option=com_content&view=article&id=5999:----------------l-----&cat id=63:remarks&Itemid=133.

133. In 2009, for instance, the regime seized the assets of the Syrian Ba'th and out-lawed al-Haqq; "Ministry to Investigate Opposition Leaders after Conspiracy Statement," *Yemen Post*, Dec. 27, 2010, http://www.yemenpost.net/Detail123456789.aspx?ID=3&Sub ID=2917&MainCat=3.

134. See, for instance, the opinion piece titled "The Alliance of Culprits" published in the regime mouthpiece *26 September*, accusing the JMP of being an antidemocratic bunch of fundamentalists seeking to abolish Yemeni unity, of collaborating with Ansar Allah and the Southern Movement, as well as of indulging in harlotry (*fujur*). "Tah-aluf al-ashrar!," *26 September*, Apr. 29, 2010, http://www.26september.info/home/index .php?option=com_content&task=view&id=20849&Itemid=515.

135. In May 2010, Salih reportedly threatened to "cut off their [JMP members'] geni-tals." "Ra'is al-Yamani Yuhaddid Mu'aradh[-i-h, sic] bi-Qat' A'dha'hum al-Tanasuliyya," *Mubasheer.com*, May 4, 2010, http://mubasheer.com/news-action-show-id-8535. In No-vember 2009, he threatened to ban "the coalition of the devil," meaning the JMP, on

the grounds of its alleged support for, inter alia, al-Qaeda in the Arabian Peninsula. "It-tahama al-Mushtarak bi-l-Tawarrut fi al-Ta'yid al-Huthiyin wa al-'Anasir al-Infisaliyya," *al-Masdar Online*, Nov. 5, 2009, http://www.almasdaronline.com/index.php?page=news &article-section=1&news_id=2991.

136. Toward the end of Salih's rule, several JMP members were imprisoned: for instance, Muhammad al-Ghalib (YSP, April 2010) or Tawakkul Karman (Islah, January 2011). There were also attempts on the lives of, for instance, 'Abd al-Wahhab Mahmud (Islah, April 2010), who served as the JMP's rotating head at that time, Zayd (al-Haqq, June 2010), and Sultan al-'Atwani (NUPO, December 2010), or failed abductions of JMP elites such as Na'if al-Qanis (Syrian Ba'th, January 2011).

137. Browers, "Origins and Architects," 573.

138. Meir Hatina, "The Clerics' Betrayal: Islamists, Ulama and the Polity," 249–52.

139. For a detailed breakdown hereof, see Jens Heibach, "Contesting the Monopoly of Interpretation: The Uneasy Relationship between Ulama and Sunni Parties in Yemen," 567–68.

140. Heibach, "Contesting the Monopoly," 567–68.

141. Note that most Salafi 'ulama' both inside and outside Islah share the ambition to effectively control the government. 'Abd al-Malik 'Isa, *Harakat al-Islam al-Siyasi fi al-Yaman*, 183. See also Dresch and Haykel, "Stereotypes," 412; and Heibach, "Contesting the Monopoly," 575.

142. 'Abd al-Salam Muhammad, "Al-Zindani Murashshah li-Qiyada Hizb Salafi bi-l-Yaman," *Islamonline.net*, May 2, 2007, http://www.islamonline.net/servlet/Satellite?c =ArticleA_C&cid=1177156195156&pagename=Zone-Arabic-News%2FNWALayout.

143. "Ba'd Mukhawafa min 'Almana al-Dawla al-Shaykh 'Abd al-Majid al-Zindani Yuhadhdhir li-Qiyam Hizb Islami Yadhumm Shuyukh 'Ulama' Barizin," *Mareb News*, Jan. 20, 2012, http://marebnews.com/Detail123456789.aspx?ID=3&SubID=4502.

144. Muhammad Mustafa al-'Amrani, "Juhud Hay'a 'Ulama' al-Yaman fi Mu'alaja al-Ahdath," *Mareb Press*, Oct. 27, 2011, http://marib.net/articles.php?lng=arabic&id=12010.

145. Muhammad 'Ayish, "Tahrik Sa'udi li-Awraq al-Qabila wa al-Salafiyin," *al-Shari'*, July 19, 2008; personal observation during the founding conference held on July 15, 2008, in Sanaa.

146. Nabil Subi', "Al-Dharihi Laysa 'Sura al-Baqara' wa La al-Zindani 'Juz' 'Amm'," *al-Nida'*, May 29, 2008, http://www.alnedaa.net/index.php?action=showNews&id=1831.

147. Cited from a brochure distributed during the founding conference.

148. Nabil Subi', "Bada'at Nashathha Qabl Akthar min 'Amm – Hay'a al-Amr bi-l-Ma'ruf," *al-Taghyir*, May 22, 2008, http://www.soutalgnoub.com/vb2/showthread.php?p =82099.

149. The joint statement can be found in *al-Tajammu'*, July 14, 2008.

150. Author interview no. 1, July 22, 2008.

151. See the interview with Muhammad b. Muhammad al-Mahdi in *al-Balagh*, July 15, 2008.

152. Al-Zindani, Hamud al-Dharihi, and others had publicly stated that the regime was supportive of their plans, and the latter never refuted such claims. Minister of Awqaf Hamud al-Hittar was announced as being set to deliver a speech during the founding conference, but eventually failed to attend. Personal observation.

153. Author interview no. 2, Aug. 2, 2008; author interview no. 3, Aug. 6, 2008; author interview no. 19, Jan. 6, 2013.

154. Author interview no. 14, Dec. 25, 2012, Sanaa. While it is hard to determine the repercussions for grassroots members, anecdotal evidence provided by press reports corroborates there being many cases of local clashes. See, for instance, "Hay'a al-Amr bi-l-Ma'ruf Tudashshin Nashatiha fi Ta'izz bi-Tajnid Qawa'id al-Islah," *al-Nida*', July 9, 2008.

155. Salih revived the committee on September 30, 2010, issuing a presidential decree stipulating the establishment of a committee of 'ulama' to be "tasked with providing consultation and advice." See "Presidential Decree to Establish Islamic Scholars Committee," *SABA*, Sept. 30, 2010, http://www.sabanews.net/en/news225100.htm. On September 7, he had met with prominent 'ulama'—including many from the AYU—and used the occasion to promise that this "committee will be authoritative in *all issues*." "Al-Ra'is Salih Yuwajjih bi-Tashkil Marja'iyya Diniyya li-Kull al-Qadhaya wa al-Quwa al-Siyasiyya," *Mareb Press*, Sept. 7, 2010, http://www.marebpress.net/news_details.php?lng=arabic&sid=27366; italics added.

156. Husayn al-Ahmar, a prominent member of Islah's tribal wing, was elected a member of the Virtue Committee. The founding conference was promoted by mobile-phone provider *Sabafon*, owned by Hamid al-Ahmar, via a variety of text messages.

157. 'Ayish, "Tahrik Sa'udi."

158. Heibach, "Contesting the Monopoly," 573–77. For a history of Islah's "fatwa regime," see Philbrick Yadav, *Islamists and the State*, 39; and 'Abd al-Fuhaydi, "Islah . . . Ta'rikh Tawil min Fatawa al-Takfir wa al-Tahrim," *Shamsan*, Feb. 14, 2008.

3. Broadening Cooperation: Reaching Out to New Allies

1. "Yemen's Opposition 'Willing to Tackle al-Qaeda,'" *Al Jazeera*, May 29, 2011, https://www.aljazeera.com/news/2011/5/29/yemen-opposition-willing-to-tackle-al-qaeda.

2. "Yemen's Opposition 'Willing to Tackle al-Qaeda.'"

3. See, for example, the transcript of the 2001 workshop at the Center for Arab Unity Studies in Balqaziz, *Al-Mu'arada wa al-Sulta*, 116–17, 136–37.

4. "Al-Duktur Muhammad 'Abd al-Malik al-Mutawakkil Yushakhkhis al-Wadh' al-Siyasi fi al-Yaman," *al-Masdar Online*, Apr. 21, 2010, http://www.almasdaronline.com/index.php?page=news&article-section=1&news_id=7401.

5. Glosemeyer and Sallam, "JMP Alliance," 337.

6. See, for example, chapter 1 on the National Democratic Institute's role during the formation of the JMP.

7. White House, "Letter from the President: War Powers Resolution," June 13, 2006, https://obamawhitehouse.archives.gov/the-press-office/2016/06/13/letter-president-war -powers-resolution.

8. It was at times diverted from its intended use, namely, combating AQAP, and employed against, for instance, Ansar Allah instead. See "Yemen's Counter Terrorism Unit Stretched Thin by War against Houthis," US Cable 09SANAA2230, Dec. 17, 2009, https://wikileaks.org/plusd/cables/09SANAA2230_a.html.

9. Cited in 'Abdallah Hamuda, "Hall Tahsim al-Musharaka al-Sa'udiyya Harb al-Yaman?," 21.

10. Wedeen, *Peripheral Visions*, 185. See also Blumi, *Chaos in Yemen*.

11. "Report on the 2006 Presidential and Local Council Elections in the Republic of Yemen," *National Democratic Institute*, n.d., 11.

12. Longley, "High Water Mark," 251–53.

13. Cited in Duraid al-Baik, "Opposition Must Reform Programme, Say Yemen Analysts," *Gulf News*, Oct. 2, 2007, http://gulfnews.com/news/gulf/yemen/opposition-must -reform-programme-say-yemen-analysts-1.258857.

14. Day, *Regionalism and Rebellion*, 221.

15. "Final Report on the Presidential and Local Council Elections: Yemen 2006," *European Union Election Observation Mission*, n.d., 1.

16. Burrowes and Kasper, "Saleh Regime," 276.

17. Sarah Phillips, "Yemen: The Centrality of Process," 246; Yacoubian, "Building Momentum."

18. Burrowes and Kasper, "Saleh Regime," 269.

19. Robert A. Dahl, "Patterns of Opposition," 341.

20. Schelling, *The Strategy of Conflict*, 3.

21. Dahl, "Patterns of Opposition," 347; Blondel, "Political Opposition," 463.

22. McAdam, McCarthy, and Zald, "Opportunities," 10; Sidney G. Tarrow, *Power in Movement: Social Movements and Contentious Politics*, 164–67.

23. "Final Report," *European Union Election Observation Mission*, 6, 34–40.

24. Gregory Johnson, "Salih's Road to Reelection," *Middle East Report Online*, Jan. 13, 2006, https://merip.org/2006/01/salihs-road-to-reelection/.

25. See Robert G. Kaufman, *In Defense of the Bush Doctrine*, esp. chaps. 5–6. It is worth mentioning here that in the direct aftermath of the events of September 11, 2001, "Salih had genuine fears that he might be targeted by a U.S. military assault soon after the invasion of Afghanistan. . . . If Salih had not pledged full cooperation in America's newest war, then Yemen might have been attacked even before Iraq in March 2003." Day, *Regionalism and Rebellion*, 203.

26. "The National Reform Agenda: A Progress Report (Draft for Discussion at the Consultative Group Meeting in London in November 15–16, 2006)," *Ministry of Planning and International Cooperation*, n.d., 10.

27. "Political Parties Sign Agreement to Strengthen Democracy," *SABA*, Dec. 12, 2006, https://www.saba.ye/en/news123605.htm.

28. Author interview no. 20, Jan. 7, 2013; author interview no. 7, Dec. 11, 2012. The latter interlocutor stated his bafflement at Qahtan's expressed contentment with the 2006 returns immediately after their public announcement.

29. Stacey Philbrick Yadav and Janine Clark, "Disappointments and New Directions: Women, Partisanship, and the Regime in Yemen," 81.

30. Burrowes and Kasper, "Saleh Regime," 271.

31. Author interview no. 11, Dec. 20, 2012; author interview no. 9, Dec. 18, 2012.

32. Yemen's Party Law (No. 66/1991, here §17–27), for instance, states that parliamentary parties are entitled to receive public funds. §19 defines the share of allowances but does not determine the total amount of public funds to be distributed. Mansur, *Al-Ahzab al-Siyasiyya*, 275, thus insists that opposition parties are subject to regime arbitrariness.

33. Randall and Svåsand, "Party Institutionalization," 18; Leonardo R. Arriola, "Capital and Opposition in Africa: Coalition Building in Multiethnic Societies," 234.

34. David Roberts, *The Ba'th and the Creation of Modern Syria*, 38.

35. Leonardo R. Arriola, *Multiethnic Coalitions in Africa: Business Financing of Opposition Election Campaigns.*

36. Dresch, *Tribes, Government, and History*, chap. 7.

37. While impossible to verify, it was common knowledge that Saudi Arabia ran a "Special Committee" that, established in 1962, was charged with paying Yemeni elites so as to meet Saudi interests. In 2012, *al-Shari'* published a list of receivers of such "stipends." See "Exposed: Secret Committee of Yemen Chiefs Getting Million Dollar Pay-offs from Saudi," *al-Bawaba*, June 12, 2012, http://www.albawaba.com/editorchoice/yemen-bribes-saudi-arabia-429308. In 2008, the US embassy in Sanaa detailed that a "number of our contacts . . . have suggested that [Hamid] Ahmar, like his father, receives generous cash payoffs from the Saudi Government." See "Hamid al-Ahmar Sees Saleh As Weak and Isolated, Plans Next Steps," US Cable 09SANAA1617, Aug. 31, 2008, https://wikileaks.org/plusd/cables/09SANAA1617_a.html.

38. Phillips, *Politics of Permanent Crisis*, 102.

39. Longley Alley, "Rules of the Game," 401–2.

40. Author interview no. 10, Dec. 19, 2012; Phillips, *Politics of Permanent Crisis*, 115.

41. Hamid is said to have played a major role in the 1994 looting of Aden and to have illegally acquired land in the South following unification. Nasir 'Ali al-Nuba's and Zahra Salih's refutation of the JMP, cited in the previous chapter, directly refers to Hamid.

42. Even Islah was thus interested in reducing Hamid's public appearances as a party representative. Author interview no. 6, Mar. 29, 2012.

43. Phillips, *Politics of Permanent Crisis*, 102.

44. Carapico, *Civil Society*, 172–73; Browers, "Origins and Architects," 569.

45. Steven Heydemann, "Upgrading Authoritarianism in the Arab World," 11; Day, *Regionalism and Rebellion*, 222.

46. For more examples, see "Final Report," *European Union Election Observation Mission*, 2–3.

47. According to the amended General Elections and Referendum Law No. 13/2001, voters could also register at their place of employment, encouraging the GPC to relocate whole battalions of supporters to selected electoral districts to make up for its unpopularity in them.

48. "Report," *National Democratic Institute*, 10, 5–6.

49. Mohammad al-Mihklafi, "The Electoral System in Yemen," 104–6.

50. An English version of the agreement is replicated in "Report," *National Democratic Institute*, 23–25.

51. Marsha Pripstein Posusney, "Multiparty Elections in the Arab World: Election Rules and Opposition Responses," 100–101.

52. In January 2009 Hamud al-Dharihi stated that Islah would not insist on a PRS, thereby prompting uproar within the JMP. See "Buruz Khilaf bayna al-Ishtiraki wa al-Islah bi-Sabab al-Dharihi wa al-Qa'ima al-Nisbiyya," *al-Shari'*, Jan. 24, 2009.

53. Phillips and Zafir, "NDI Baseline Assessment," 20.

54. "Report," *National Democratic Institute*, 25.

55. It probably did, however, as the December Agreement was reportedly based on the "Final Report" of the EU EOM, which recommended a PRS for the parliamentary and local council elections. See recommendation 14 (i), 37.

56. Author interview no. 27, Jan. 16, 2013.

57. "Al-Taqrir al-Istratji al-Yamani," *Al-Markaz al-Yamani li-l-Dirasat al-Istratijiyya* (2008): 35–37.

58. Author interview no. 15, Dec. 29, 2012.

59. See "Al-Taqrir," *Al-Markaz al-Yamani li-l-Dirasat al-Istratijiyya*, 37–42.

60. François-Xavier Trégan, "Saleh für immer," *Le Monde Diplomatique*, Jan. 2008, 10–11.

61. "Briefing Note: Elections of Governors," *National Democratic Institute*, May 17, 2008, 1.

62. Day, *Regionalism and Rebellion*, 237.

63. "In the Name of Unity: The Yemeni Government's Brutal Response to Southern Movement Protests," *Human Rights Watch*, Dec. 2009, 25–39.

64. Barak A. Salmoni, Bryce Loidolt, and Madeleine Wells, *Regime and Periphery in Northern Yemen: The Huthi Phenomenon*, 143–50.

65. "Ittahama al-Sa'udiyya bi-l-Tawarrut fi Safak al-Damm al-Yamani," *Mareb Press*, June 13, 2008, http://marebpress.net/news_details.php?sid=11775.

66. "Hiwar al-Mu'aradha wa al-Mu'tamar Yata'aththar fi al-Qadhaya al-Jawhariyya," *al-Ahali*, July 2008.

67. See Muhammad 'Abd al-Malik al-Mutawakkil, "La Intikhabat Dun Infiraj Siyasi wa Nizam Intikhabi," *al-Nida'*, Aug. 6, 2008; or the interviews with JMP spokesman Muhammad al-Qubati in *al-Sahwa*, Aug. 7, 2008, as well as with the head of NUPO Sultan al-'Atwani in *al-Wasat*, Oct. 22, 2008. The same arguments were reiterated by the JMP in its correspondence with Salih, as repeated by *Akhbar al-Yawm*, Sept. 2, 2008.

68. "Ahzab al-Liqa' al-Mushtarak Tushakkil Lijan al-Hiwar al-Watani," *al-Balagh*, July 15, 2008.

69. "Kutal al-Mushtarak Tu'alliq Muqata'atha Jalsat al-Barlaman," *al-Wahdawi*, July 8, 2008.

70. 'Abdallah Dubla, "Al-Mushtarak Yarfa' Daraja Harara al-Muwajiha Ma'a al-Mu'tamar bi-Lijan al-Tawasul," *al-Nas*, July 14, 2008.

71. See, for instance, "Al-Barakani: Al-Ishtiraki Sharikna wa Lan Nataqasim Dawa'ir," *Naba News*, Sept. 13, 2008, http://www.nabanews.net/news/15485.

72. "Ra'is al-Jumhuriyya," *Naba News*; Nasser Arrabyee, "Opposition Cries Foul over Panel," *Gulf News*, Sept. 1, 2008, http://gulfnews.com/news/gulf/yemen/opposition-cries-foul-over-poll-panel-1.129348.

73. "Al-Mu'tamar wa al-Mushtarak Yatafiqqa 'ala Nizam al-Qa'ima al-Nisbiyya wa al-Nizam al-Gurufatayn," *Mareb Press*, Feb. 25, 2009, http://marebpress.net/news_details.php?lng=arabic&sid=15284.

74. Author interview no. 10, Dec. 19, 2012.

75. Author interview no. 9, Dec. 18, 2012.

76. "Al-Mu'tamar wa al-Mushtarak," *Mareb Press*; Muhammad Bin Sallam, "Elections Postponed," *Yemen Times*, Feb. 25, 2009, http://www.yementimes.com/print_article.shtml?i=&p=front&a=1; see also April Longley Alley, "Yemen's Multiple Crisis," 81.

77. "Al-Mu'tamar wa al-Mushtarak," *Mareb Press*; Bin Sallam, "Elections Postponed."

78. The following discussion lists all reasonable arguments concerning the coming about of the February Agreement that could be found via Yemeni and international sources. Yet given the secrecy observed by both the JMP and the regime, it was not possible to establish the parties' true motivations for the signing of the agreement beyond reasonable doubt. For a theoretical discussion of why the JMP brought itself to sign this (and later) agreements with the regime despite possible—or even probable—future breaches by the latter, see the next chapter.

79. See, for instance, Marine Poirier, "Score One for the Opposition?," *Arab Reform Bulletin*, Mar. 9, 2009, https://carnegieendowment.org/sada/22824; al-Faqih, "Al-Takattul," 168.

80. Mohammed Bin Sallam, "Opposition Confirms Election Boycott," *Yemen Times*, Feb. 15, 2009, http://www.yementimes.com/DefaultDET.aspx?i=1235&p=local&a=5.

81. "Safir Britani Yahuthth Mushtarak Ta'izz 'ala Tabanni Ru'an al-Ittihad," *Akhbar al-Yawm*, July 16, 2008; "Yemen Main Opposition Parties Meet EC Officer," *SABA*, Sept. 3, 2008, http://www.sabanews.net/ar/print163181.htm.

82. "Tawafuq Mabda'i," *al-Wasat*. According to Philbrick Yadav, too, the February Agreement was "reportedly brokered by representatives of the EU and NDI." Philbrick Yadav, *Shadow of Transition*, 71.

83. "Ta'jil al-Intikhabat wa al-Ittifaq 'ala al-Islahat Dharurat Wataniyya," *al-Balagh*, http://www.al-balagh.net/index.php?option=content&task=view&id=7043&Itemid=; author interview no. 7, Dec. 11, 2012.

84. Norton, "Making Sense of Opposition," 241.

85. "Al-Mushtarak Yaqarr Iqaf Hiwarihi Ma'a al-Ra'is Hawla al-Intikhabat," *al-Wasat*, July 16, 2008.

86. "Al-Sulta Tastawi' al-Mu'aradha fi al-Lijan al-Ashrafiyya wa al-Mushtarak Yabhath 'an Wasa'il Dhught Aqwa," *al-Wasat*, Oct. 22, 2008.

87. "San'a' Tantafidh Ta'biran 'an Rafdh al-Intikhabat wa al-Amn Yasudd wa Ya'taqil wa Ya'tadi wa Yutliq Rasas Hayy," *Mareb Press*, Nov. 27, 2008, http://www.marebpress.net/news_details.php?sid=14025.

88. Levitsky and Way, "Rise of Competitive Authoritarianism," 53.

89. Levi, "Predatory Theory of Rule," 438.

90. Holger Albrecht, "How Can Opposition Support Authoritarianism? Lessons from Egypt"; William I. Zartman, "Opposition as Support of the State."

91. Levitsky and Way, *Competitive Authoritarianism*, 23–24.

92. Tilly and Tarrow, *Contentious Politics*, 54–57, 202.

93. Despite reduced vulnerability, alliances put themselves in jeopardy, too, once they leave these official sites. In February 2009, for instance, after months of extraparliamentary action, the regime confiscated the funds of the Ba'th and banned al-Haqq. Bin Sallam, "Opposition Confirms Election Boycott." Previously, the security forces used live rounds when cracking down on JMP rallies. "San'a' Tantafidh," *Mareb Press*. On the regime's incremental repression of the JMP in the aftermath of the 2006 elections, see Philbrick Yadav, *Shadow of Transition*, 68–69.

94. Andreas Schedler, "The New Institutionalism in the Study of Authoritarianism," 331.

95. Andreas Schedler, "The Nested Game of Democratization by Elections."

96. Eva Wegner, "Islamist Inclusion and Regime Persistence: The Moroccan Win-Win Situation."

97. Randall and Svåsand, "Party Institutionalization"; Madalena Resende and Hendrik Kraetzschmar, "Parties of Power as Roadblocks to Democracy: The Cases of Ukraine and Egypt."

98. Jens Heibach and Mareike Transfeld, "Opposition Dynamism under Authoritarianism: The Case of Yemen, 1994–2011."

99. James C. Franklin, "Political Party Opposition to Noncompetitive Regimes: A Cross-national Analysis," 522, 524; Robert A. Dahl, introduction to *Regimes and Oppositions*, 13; Blondel, "Political Opposition," 473.

100. Heibach and Transfeld, "Opposition Dynamism," 600.

101. Author interview no. 9, Dec. 18, 2012.

102. Ahmad al-Zayli'i, "Ghalibiyya al-Yamaniyin La Yahtammun bi-l-Siyasa wa La Yathiqun bi-l-Ahzab," *News Yemen*, Oct. 4, 2010, http://www.newsyemen.net/view_news .asp?sub_no=1_2010_03_47636.

103. "Yasin Nu'man: Al-Mushtarak Ta'amala ma'a al-Azma bi-Mas'uliyya 'Aliyya wa Hawala 'an Yatajannab al-Ara' al-Mutatarrifa Dakhil al-Mu'tamar," *Mareb Press*, Aug. 28, 2009, http://www.marebpress.net/news_details.php?sid=15335.

104. "Qiyadi Islahi: Nata'ij," *al-Ayyam*.

105. "Al-Qadhaya al-Matruha Laysa fi-ha Sa'da wa Muhafazat al-Janub," *al-Balagh*, Mar. 9, 2009, http://www.al-balagh.net/index.php?option=content&task=view&id=7119 &Itemid=.

106. Stepan, "Tasks of Democratic Opposition," 42.

107. Marieke Brandt, "The Irregulars of the Sa'da War: 'Colonel Sheikhs' and 'Tribal Militias' in Yemen's Huthi Conflict (2004–2010)," 115.

108. "Insihab Sadiq 'Abdallah b. Husayn al-Ahmar min Jalsa Multaqa al-Tashawur al-Watani," *al-Balagh*, May 25, 2009, http://www.al-balagh.net/index.php?option=content &task=view&id=7510&Itemid=.

109. "Hamid al-Ahmar: Al-Sulta Ghayr Jada fi al-Hiwar wa Nas'a li-I'ada Hayba al-Dustur," *al-Sahwa*, Feb. 3, 2010, http://www.alsahwa-yemen.net/view_news.asp?sub_no =1_2010_02_03_75841.

110. Hamuda, "Al-Yaman fi Muwajaha," 17.

111. See, for instance, "JMP Calls Authorities for Solving South Troubles," *al-Sahwa*, May 4, 2009, http://www.alsahwa-yemen.net/view_nnews.asp?sub_no=406_2009 _05_04_70321; "Al-Mushtarak Yaqarr 'Aqd Multaqa al-Tashawur al-Watani Nihaya Mayu bi-l-'Asima San'a'," *al-Sahwa*, May 9, 2009, http://www.alsahwa-yemen.net/view_news.asp ?sub_no=1_2009_05_09_70420; "Salih al-Suraymi: Qiyadat al-Mushtarak: Al-Wahda Muhadadda bi-l-Fasidin wa 'Askara al-Hayah al-Madaniyya," *al-Sahwa*, May 10, 2009, http://www.alsahwa-yemen.net/view_news.asp?sub_no=1_2009_05_10_70445.

112. Zaid al-Alaya'a, "JMP Suspends Dialogue with GPC," *Yemen Observer*, July 31, 2009, http://www.yobserver.com/front-page/printer-10016972.html.

113. "Yemen's Army Steps up Pressure on Shiite Rebels," *al-Arabiya*, Aug. 29, 2009, http://www.alarabiya.net/articles/2009/08/29/83304.html.

114. It is important to note that the involvement of the Saudi Arabian military in 2009 was prompted by Ansar Allah's intrusion into Saudi territory, notably the strategic mountain of Jabal Dukhan in Jizan Governorate. Although there are conflicting narratives as to why Ansar Allah entered Saudi soil, Riyadh failed to dwell on direct Iranian

support for, or strategic guidance of, Ansar Allah's campaign in its official statements back then—much in contrast to 2015. In fact, such allegations were almost exclusively made by the Salih regime. However, a leaked US cable at that time found that "Despite repeated ROYG accusations of Tehran's material and financial support to the Houthi rebels in Sa'ada . . . Iranian influence in Yemen has thus far been limited to informal religious ties between Yemeni and Iranian scholars and negligible Iranian investment in the energy and development sectors." See "Iran in Yemen: Tehran's Shadow Looms Large, but Footprint Is Small (c-ne9-01257)," US Cable 04SANAA001662, Sept. 12, 2009, https://www.spiegel.de/politik/ausland/us-depeschen-zum-jemen-operation-verbrannte -erde-a-728622.html. Still, given both Yemen's geostrategic position and its proximity to Saudi Arabia, Iran did try to forge bonds with Yemeni actors already then, including not only Ansar Allah but also the Southern Movement. See Lackner, *Yemen in Crisis*, 82.

115. Christopher Boucek, "War in Saada: From Local Insurrection to National Challenge," 47, 54.

116. "Hamid al-Ahmar," US Cable 09SANAA1617.

117. "Hamid al-Ahmar," US Cable 09SANAA1617. According to another cable, the Royal Saudi Air Force was later provided with the ground coordinates of an alleged Ansar Allah position that turned out to in fact be 'Ali Muhsin's command center. The incident was widely perceived to have been an assassination plot by Salih. "Saudi Arabia: Renewed Assurances on Satellite Imagery," US Cable10RIYADH159_a, Feb. 7, 2010, https://wikileaks.org/plusd/cables/10RIYADH159_a.html.

118. Longley Alley, "Rules of the Game," 407.

119. "Hamid al-Ahmar," US Cable 09SANAA1617.

120. "Hamid al-Ahmar," US Cable 09SANAA1617.

121. Abdul-Aziz Oudah, "JMP Rejects SCER's Elections for Vacant Seats," *Yemen Observer*, Oct. 17, 2009, http://www.yobserver.com/front-page/10017408.

122. "Ittahama al-Mushtarak," *al-Masdar Online*.

123. "Tahdhiriyya li-l-Hiwar Tushakkil Fariq Qanuni li-Muqadhah Ra'is al-Jumhuriyya," *al-Sahwa*, Mar. 14, 2010, http://www.alsahwa-yemen.net/view_news.asp ?sub_no=1_2010_03_14_76726.

124. Al-Alaya'a, "JMP Suspends Dialogue."

125. "Al-Lajna al-Tahdhiriyya li-l-Hiwar al-Watani Tantakhib Basindwa Ra'isan wa al-Ahmar Aminan 'Amman," *Tashawor.net*, May 30, 2009, http://www.tashawor.net /news_details.php?sid=66.

126. Author interview no. 10, Dec. 19, 2012; author interview no. 15, Dec. 29, 2012.

127. Author interview no. 19, Jan. 6, 2013.

128. It is worthy of mention in this context that the JMP had established a Coordination Committee tasked with preparing a national dialogue already on July 14, 2008. "Al-Mushtarak Yushakkil Lijan al-Tashawur al-Watani li-Ikhraj al-Balad min al-Azma," *al-Sahwa*, July 15, 2008.

129. "Yasin Nu'man: Al-Mushtarak," *Mareb Press*; see also the remarks by 'Aydarus al-Naqib, YSP, cited in "Al-Qadhaya al-Matruha," *al-Balagh*.

130. "Lajna al-Hiwar al-Watani Tushakkil Lajna al-Musaghghara li-I'dad Muqtarahat Khutat al-'Amal," *al-Sahwa*, May 26, 2009, http://www.alsahwa-yemen.net/view_news.asp?sub_no=1_2009_05_26_70720.

131. The final statement and communiqué of the conference are to be found in "Wathiqa al-Hiwar al-Watani wa al-Bayan al-Khitami al-Sadir 'an Multaqa al-Tashawur," *al-Sahwa*, May 22, 2009, http://www.alsahwa-yemen.net/view_news.asp?sub_no=1_2009_05_22_70658; see also Mohammed Bin Sallam, "National Consultation Meeting Demands Regime Reform," *Yemen Times*, May 25, 2009, http://yementimes.com/article.shtml?i=1262&p=front&a=1.

132. "Lajna al-Hiwar al-Watani," *al-Sahwa*.

133. "Al-Ra'is Yashunn Hujuman 'ala al-Tashawur al-Watani," *al-Balagh*, May 25, 2009, http://www.al-balagh.net/index.php?option=content&task=view&id=7511&Itemid=.

134. In fact, leading JMP representatives such as al-Mutawakkil admitted that the PCND was founded "because it had become necessary to broaden the joint basis and to step up the confrontation [with the regime]." Al-Mutawakkil, "Al-Afaq," 156.

135. Al-Mutawakkil, "Al-Afaq," 156.

136. Author interview no. 3, Aug. 6, 2008.

137. David A. Snow and Robert D. Benford, "Ideology, Frame Resonance, and Participant Mobilization," 198.

138. Robert D. Benford and David A. Snow, "Framing Processes and Social Movements: Overview and Assessment," 615.

139. Snow and Benford, "Ideology," 200; Lust, "Opposition Cooperation," 431; Werner Patzelt, "Opposition," 1747.

140. Benford and Snow, "Framing Processes," 616.

141. See also Bert Klandermans, "Mobilization and Participation: Social-Psychological Expansion of Resource-Mobilization Theory," 586.

142. Benford and Snow, "Framing Processes," 617

143. Snow and Benford, "Ideology," 208; Klandermans, "Mobilization and Participation," 588.

144. Phillips, *Yemen's Democracy Experiment*, 11.

145. Glosemeyer and Sallam, "JMP Alliance," 336.

146. Yemen Polling Center, *Yemeni Citizens' Main Concerns, Perception of Human Rights and CSOs*, 9.

147. Abdulmalik al-Fuhaidi, "JMP Demands before and after February," *Yemen Times*, Sept. 16, 2009, http://www.yementimes.com/defaultdet.aspx?SUB_ID=231.

148. An English translation was published on *Yemen Vision*, the "semi-official blog of the Preparatory Committee for National Dialogue." https://yemenvision.wordpress.com/category/vision/.

149. https://yemenvision.wordpress.com/category/vision/.

150. https://yemenvision.wordpress.com/category/vision/, Section 2, II.5.

151. https://yemenvision.wordpress.com/category/vision/, Section 1, II.b, and Section 2, I.

152. https://yemenvision.wordpress.com/category/vision/, Section 2, II.3.b.

153. Yahya Muhammad al-Mawari, *'Ala Tariq al-Hiwar al-Watani*.

154. *Vision for National Salvation*, introduction.

155. "Amana al-Lajna al-Tahdhiriyya li-l-Hiwar al-Watani Tajtami' bi-l-Hay'a al-Qiyadiyya li-Lijan al-Fi'at al-Mujtama'iyya," *al-Masdar Online*, Dec. 26, 2009, http://www.almasdaronline.com/?page=news&article-section=1&news_id=3954.

156. "Amin al-Ishtiraki Yuhadhir 'an al-Tahaddiyat al-Iqtisadiyya wa Mustaqbal al-Yaman al-Ithnayn bi-Tahdhiriyya al-Hiwar," *News Yemen*, June 27, 2010, http://www.newsyemen.net/view_news.asp?sub_no=1_2010_06_27.

157. Dhi'a Assoswa, "JMP Held an Open Symposium in Ibb," *Yemen Observer*, Dec. 24, 2009, http://www.yobserver.com/local-news/printer-10017808.html.

158. "Yemenis Protest Against Surging Prices," *Daily Star*, Apr. 16, 2010, http://www.dailystar.com.lb./article.asp?edition_id=10&categ_id=2&article_id=113812#.

159. "Yemen's Opposition Demands Government to Hand over Power," *al-Sahwa*, May 1, 2010, http://www.alsahwa-yemen.net/arabic/subjects/5/2010/5/1/224.htm.

160. See table 3 and Arab Monetary Fund, *The Joint Arab Economic Report 2011: Overview & Statistical Annexes* (Abu Dhabi, 2011), 111.

161. "635 Kharqan Huthiyyan li-l-Hudna wa 445 Masiratan fi Muhafazat al-Janub," *Mareb Press*, July 14, 2010, http://www.marebpress.net/news_details.php?sid=26263.

162. "National Dialog Committee Expands Participation Base to 6,000 People," *SABA*, Jan. 10, 2010, http://www.sabanews.net/en/news202723.htm.

163. Mohammad Bin Sallam, "JMP Skeptical about Salih's Call to Dialog," *Yemen Times*, Dec. 17, 2009, http://www.yementimes.com/defaultdet.aspx?SUB_ID=33209.

164. "Ra'is al-Jumhuriyya: Musta'iddun li-l-Hiwar ma'a al-Qa'ida wa al-Huthiyin," *al-Tajammu'*, Jan. 13, 2010, http://www.attagammua.net/index.php?action=showNews&id=725.

165. "US Says Post-Salih Yemen Would Pose 'Real Problem'," AFP, Mar. 27, 2011, http://www.france24.com/en/20110327-us-says-post-saleh-yemen-would-pose-real-problem#.

166. Ronald Janse, "Counter-terrorism, Rule of Law Promotion, and the Friends of Yemen," 363.

167. Sheila Carapico, "Special Operations in Yemen," *Foreign Policy*, May 13, 2010, https://foreignpolicy.com/2010/05/13/special-operations-in-yemen/.

168. "Bayan al-Mushtarak bi-Sha'n Nata'ij Mu'tamar Lundun," Jan. 28, 2010, retrieved from *al-Islah.net*, http://www.al-islah.net/details.aspx?pagename=gen&pageid=8942.

169. Mohammed Bin Sallam, "Shura Council Delays Dialogue for the Fourth Time, Opposition to Boycott National Dialogue," *Yemen Times*, Feb. 1, 2010, http://www.yementimes.com/defaultdet.aspx?SUB_ID=33508.

170. Some individuals in the JMP and the PCND speculated that the truce would potentially open the door to national dialogue. "D. Mahmud: Al-Sulta Aghlaqat Bab al-Hiwar wa Khiyarat Ladayha 'Adida," al-Balagh, Feb. 16, 2011, http://www.al-balagh.net/index.php?option=content&task=view&id=8866&Itemid=. However, renewed regime violence against the Southern Movement soon led to them abandoning that option. "JMP Holds Authorities Responsible for Violence in the South," *al-Sahwa*, Feb. 22, 2010, http://www.alsahwa-yemen.net/view_nnews.asp?sub_no=402_2010_02_22_76239.

171. The transcript of the speech was published by *al-Masdar Online* on May 22, 2010, http://www.almasdaronline.com/index.php?page=news&article-section=1&news_id=8305.

172. Author interview no. 27, Jan. 16, 2013; "Al-Mushtarak Yurahhib bi-l-'Afw al-Ri'asi," *al-Islah.net*, May 25, 2010, http://www.al-islah.net/details.aspx?pagename=gen pageid=10099.

173. With hindsight, one is hard-pressed to account for Salih's unwillingness to make serious concessions in the negotiations with the JMP at the time—or in later months too, for that matter. While a brief discussion of the possible reasons for Salih's unyielding stance is provided in the subsequent chapter, the shortage—or indeed lacuna—of in-depth studies on one of the region's longest-serving rulers is remarkable, the more so as even his staunchest opponents would salute him for his astuteness and ability to succeed in an extraordinarily difficult political terrain such as Yemen.

174. This constitutional amendment was eventually announced in December 2010. See chapter 4.

175. For an Islahi perspective, see Yahya al-Yana'i, "Al-Tajammu' al-Yamani li-l-Islah wa al-Qadhiyya al-Janubiyya: Haqa'iq wa Mawaqif," *al-Sahwa*, May 24, 2009, http://www.alsahwa-yemen.net/view_news.asp?sub_no=1_2009_05_24_70687.

176. Author interview no. 15, Dec. 29, 2012; author interview no. 9, Dec. 18, 2012.

177. "JMP Calls Authorities for Solving South Troubles," *al-Sahwa*, May 4, 2009, http://www.alsahwa-yemen.net/view_nnews.asp?sub_no=406_2009_05_04_70321; Mohammed Bin Sallam, "Protests, Trial Continues," *Yemen Times*, June 6, 2009, http://www.yementimes.com/article.shtml?i=1265&p=front&a=2.

178. "Nass Bayan al-Mushtarak bi-Sha'n al-Tas'id al-Amni fi al-Muhafazat al-Janubiyya," Mar. 10, 2010, *al-Sahwa*, http://www.alsahwa-yemen.net/view_news.asp?sub_no=1_2010_03_10_76646; Mohammed al Qadhi, "Yemeni President 'Will Crush Activists' but Welcomes Talks," *National*, Mar. 9, 2010, http://www.thenational.ae/apps/pbcs.dll/article?AID=/20100310/FOREIGN/703099827/1002.

179. Cited in "Al-Ra'is Yashunn Hujuman," *al-Balagh*.

180. "Tahdhiriyya al-Hiwar Tunaqish Nata'ij Lajna al-Qadhiyya al-Janubiyya wa Taqarr Tawsi' al-Musharaka," *al-Sahwa*, Jan. 28, 2010, http://www.alsahwa-yemen.net /view_news.asp?sub_no=1_2010_01_28_75692.

181. Fattah Haidarah, "Preparatory Committee Ready for National Dialogue," *Yemen Observer*, June 5, 2010, http://www.yobserver.com/front-page/10018847.html.

182. Fattah Haidarah, "JMP, PDC, External Opposition Meet in Cairo," *Yemen Observer*, June 21, 2010, http://www.yobserver.com/front-page/10018980.html.

183. "Survey Made by Aden News Agency: Southern Movement Leaders Refuse Dialogues with Sanaa Except under Supervision of UN and Independence," *Aden News Agency*, Apr. 22, 2010, http://www.aden-na.com/default.asp?page=1003&NewsID=699.

184. See, for instance, "Yemen: Protests Threaten Stability," *New Humanitarian*, Apr. 27, 2010, https://www.thenewhumanitarian.org/feature/2010/04/27/protests-threaten -stability.

185. Philip McCrum, "Carrots and Sticks," 24.

186. Abu Bakr 'Abdallah, "Ittifaq Washik fi al-Yaman Yantahi al-Harb ma'a al-Huthiyin," *al-Nahar*, Feb. 11, 2010, http://www.annahar.com/content.php?table=main &type=main&priority=4&day=Thu.

187. "Al-Amin al-'Amm: 'Ardh al-Huthi li-l-Tahaluf ma'a al-Mushtarak taht al-Dirasa wa Mawqif al-Islah Huwa Mawqif al-Mushtarak," *al-Islah.net*, Feb. 7, 2010, http://www .al-islah.net/details.aspx?pagename=gen&pageid=9006.

188. Mohammed Bin Sallam, "Deputy Prime Minister Sponsors Peace Talks in Sa'ada," *Yemen Times*, Apr. 12, 2010, http://www.yementimes.com/defaultdet.aspx?SUB_ID =33866.

189. "Lajna al-Tashawur al-Watani Tu'lin Tawqi' Ittifaq ma'a al-Huthi wa Ta'tabirhu Injazan Wataniyyan Yu'azziz al-Salam fi Sa'da," *News Yemen*, Apr. 14, 2010, http://www .newsyemen.net/printn.asp?sub_no=1_2010_04_14_43057.

190. Author interview with no. 22, Jan. 8, 2013, Sanaa.

191. "Al-Sulta al-Yamaniyya Tuwaqqi' Ittifaqan Jadidan ma'a al-Mutamarridin al-Huthiyin," *Naba News*, Apr. 27, 2010, http://www.nabanews.net/2009/27974.html.

192. Author interview no. 22, Jan. 8, 2013.

193. One of the representatives of Ansar Allah in the PCND stated that Secretary-General Hamid al-Ahmar had frequently published statements in the Committee's name without prior consultation. Author interview no. 22, Jan. 8, 2013.

194. These reasons were stated in a public letter to the PCND. The letter was published by *Mareb Press* on June 3, 2010, http://marebpress.net/nprint.php?sid=25345.

195. "Yasin Sa'id Nu'man Yansahib min Ijtima' 'Asif li-l-Mushtarak wa al-Nasiriyun Ya'tadhirun," *Mareb Press*, June 20, 2010, http://www.marebpress.net/news_details.php ?sid=25775.

196. "Istighlal al-Qabila Yufqid A'dha'hu Tatallu'at Tahqiq al-Dawla al-Madaniyya," *al-Wasat*, Jan. 14, 2009.

197. "Bayan Hay'a al-Istiqlal al-Janubi Yalihu Bayan al-Mushtarak li-Kull min al-Majlis al-Watani wa Tajammu' Taij wa Ittihad Shabab al-Janub," *Aden Gulf Network News*, July 7, 2010, http://www.gulfofaden.net/index.php?page=news&news_id=3742.

198. Haidarah, "JMP, PDC, External Opposition."

199. Longley Alley, "Yemen's Multiple Crisis," 83–84; Philbrick Yadav and Clark, "Disappointments and New Directions," 86–87.

200. Al-Faqih, "Al-Takattul," 168.

201. "Natiq al-Mushtarak: Al-Mu'tamar Yatahammal Ayy Ijra' Kharij Itar al-Ittifaq," *News Yemen*, Mar. 15, 2010, http://www.newsyemen.net/view_news.asp?sub_no=1_2013_03_15_42280; Mohammed al-Kibsi, "Obama Increases Aid to Yemen," *Yemen Observer*, June 28, 2010, http://www.yobserver.com/front-page/10019028.hhtml; Mohammed Bin Sallam, "Ruling Party Calls for Dialogue, JMP Lays Out Conditions," *Yemen Times*, June 7, 2010, http://www.yementimes.com/defaultdet.aspx?SUB_ID=34204.

202. "GPC and JMP Sign Minute over February Agreement," *Yemen Post*, July 18, 2010, http://www.yemenpost.net/Detail123456789.aspx?ID=3&SubID=2420.

203. "Mahdhar Ittifaq bayna al-Mushtarak wa al-Mu'tamar 'ala Tanfidh li-Ittifaq Fabrayir," July 18, 2010, *al-Islah.net*, http://www.al-islah.net/details.aspx?pageid=10644&pagename=gen.

4. Discrediting Cooperation: The Joint Meeting Parties in the Yemeni Uprising

1. Thomas Richter, "New Petro-Aggression in the Middle East: Saudi Arabia in the Spotlight"; Blumi, *Destroying Yemen*.

2. Muhammad Ahmad Husayn Sharaf al-Din, "Nasiha li-l-Hashimiyin fi al-Yaman," *Elaph.com*, July 17, 2005, http://elaph.com/ElaphWeb/AsdaElaph/2005/7/76777.htm. The English translation is taken from vom Bruck, "Regimes of Piety," 213.

3. Al-Din, "Nasiha li-l-Hashimiyin fi al-Yaman."

4. Author interview no. 8, Dec. 13, 2012.

5. An English translation of the agreement can be found on the UN Peacemaker website, http://peacemaker.un.org/yemen-transition-mechanism2011.

6. "Mahdhar Ittifaq," *al-Islah.net*.

7. "Joint Panel Heading to Saada to Acquaint Houthis," *Yemen Post*, Aug. 1, 2010, http://www.yemenpost.net/Detail123456789.aspx?ID=2483&MainCat=3.

8. "Mahdhar Ittifaq," *al-Islah.net*.

9. "Joint Panel Heading to Saada," *Yemen Post*.

10. "Mahdhar Ittifaq," *al-Islah.net*.

11. See the joint statement of the Supreme National Body for the Independence of the South, the Higher National Council for the Liberation of the South, the Union of the Southern Youth, and the Southern Democratic Assembly (al-tajammu' al-dimuqrati

al-janubi, TAJ) on August 14, 2010, posted online at Armies of Liberation, http://www
.armiesofliberation.com/archives/2010/08/16/four-southern-groups-issue-joint-statement
-only-solution-is-independence. See also "Ru'asa' Majalis al-Hirak Yaqurrun al-Barnamaj
al-Siyasi li-l-Majlis," *News Yemen*, Dec. 12, 2010, http://www.newsyemen.net/view_news
-asp?sub_no=1_2010_12_12_49801.

12. "Ali Nasser Denies JMP's Statement," *Yemen Post*, July 21, 2010, http://www
.yemenpost.net/Detail123456789.aspx?ID=3&SubID=2435.

13. "La Tahummna Mawaqif al-Baydh wa al-'Attas wa 'Ali Nasir wa Nad'u ila Dawla
Ittihadiyya," *News Yemen*, Dec. 16, 2010, http://www.newsyemen.net/view_news-asp?sub
_no=1_2010_12_16_49987.

14. "Al-Amn Ya'taqil Ra'is Lajna al-Wasata bi-Sa'da," *al-Masdar Online*, July 28, 2010,
http://www.almasdaronline.com/index.php?page=news&article-section=1&news_id=4846.

15. "Mahdhar Ittifaq Jadid bayna al-Hizb al-Hakim wa al-Mu'aradha wa Tashkil
Lajna min 200 Shakhs," *al-Sharq al-Awsat*, July 30, 2010, http://archive.aawsat.com
/details.asp?section=4&issueno=11567&article=580319#.VjDKAyvgPIU.

16. "Fi Awwal Ijtima' li-Lajna al-Tahyi'a li-l-Hiwar al-Watani," *News Yemen*, Aug. 7,
2010, http://www.newsyemen.net/view_news-asp?sub_no=1_2010_08_07_46215.

17. "National Dialogue Preparation Committee Convened," *SABA*, Aug. 26, 2010,
http://www.sabanews.net/en/news223052.htm.

18. "Political Forums, NGOs Accept Participation in National Dialogue," *SABA*,
Sept. 27, 2010, http://www.sabanews.net/ar/news224862.htm.

19. "JMP Backs out of National Dialo-gue," *Yemen Times*, Oct. 4, 2010, http://www
.yementimes.com/defaultdet.aspx?SUB_ID=34827.

20. See the JMP statement "Nass al-Bayan al-Sahafi li-Ahzab al-Liqa' al-Mushtarak
wa Shuraka'hu 'al-Lajna al-Tahdhiriyya li-l-Hiwar al-Watani,'" Dec. 13, 2010, published
in *al-Taghyir*, http://www.al-tagheer.com/news24815.

21. Shuaib M. al-Mosawa, "Ruling Party, JMP Start Dispute Over Elections," *Yemen
Observer*, Aug. 12, 2010, http://www.yobserver.com/front-page/10019393.

22. "Al-Mutawakkil: Al-Mushtarak Yadrus Afkaran Urubiyyatan li-Naql al-Hiwar
min San'a' ila al-Qahira," *News Yemen*, Sept. 14, 2010, http://www.newsyemen.net/view
_news.asp?sub_np=1_2010_09_15_47155.

23. See "Nass al-Bayan al-Sahafi," *al-Taghyir*.

24. "Lawmakers Protest Putting 'Dropped Electoral Law' on Parliament Agenda,"
Yemen Post, Oct. 3, 2010, http://www.yemenpost.net/Detail123456789.aspx?ID=3&SubID
=2623&MainCat=3; Hamid Dabwan, "Kutla al-Mushtarak Tas'ad Fa'aliyatha al-Ihtijajiyya
dakhil al-Barlaman," *News Yemen*, Oct. 3, 2010, http://www.newsyemen.net/view_news
.asp?sub_no=1_2010_10_03_47618.

25. The JMP had just previously stressed the importance of electoral reform. See "Al-
Mutawakkil: Al-Mu'tamar Yurid min al-Hiwar al-Intikhabat wa Idara al-Harb fi al-Janub

li-Yu'id Idaratha fi al-Shimal," *al-Wasat*, Oct. 28, 2010, http://www.alwasat-ye.net/index.php?action=showNews&id=407.

26. "Ruling Party Chooses to Hold Elections on Time," *Yemen Post*, Nov. 1, 2010, http://www.yemenpost.net/Detail123456789.aspx?ID=3&SubID=2718.

27. "Approving Opposition Proposal, Saleh Orders Election Commission from Judges," *Yemen Post*, Nov. 30, 2010, http://www.yemenpost.net/Detail123456789.aspx?ID=3&SubID=2809.

28. "Al-Mushtarak wa Tahdhiriyya al-Hiwar: Ta'dilat Qanun al-Intikhabat Ijhaz li-l-Hiwar wa Inqilab 'ala Ittifaq Fabrayir," *al-Sahwa*, Dec. 11, 2010, http://www.alsahwa-yemen.net/arabic/subjects/1/2010/12/11/5469.htm.

29. "Nass al-Bayan al-Sahafi," *al-Taghyir*.

30. Longley Alley, "Yemen's Multiple Crisis," 83–84, 83.

31. Jamal Mohammed al-Ja'abi, "Ba Sondwa and the Tears of Wise Men," *Yemen Times*, Dec. 1, 2008; Saddam al-Ashmori, "Confrontations between Security and JMP Demonstrators," *Yemen Times*, Dec. 1, 2008.

32. Hamid Dabwan, "Nuwwab fi al-Mu'tamar Yuhadhdhirun min al-Tafarrud fi Iqrar al-Ta'dilat al-Dusturiyya," *News Yemen*, Jan. 1, 2011, http://www.newsyemen.net/view_news.asp?sub_no=1_2011_01_01_50533.

33. Author interview no. 27, Jan. 16, 2013.

34. For one of the few exceptions here, see Imad al-Saqqaf, "Opposition Leads Civil Disobedience," *Yemen Times*, Aug. 9, 2010, http://www.yementimes.com/defaultdet.aspx?SUB_ID=34558.

35. "Al-Mushtarak fi al-Jawf Yuhadhdhir min Tashkil Lijan al-Midaniyya," *News Yemen*, October. 4, 2010, http://www.net/view_news_asp?sub_no=1_2010_10_04_47643.

36. "Thousands of the JMP Members Protest," *Yemen Post*.

37. Fu'ad al-'Alawi, "Kutal al-Mushtarak Tumaddid Sa'at I'tisamha dakhil al-Barlaman Ihtijajan 'ala Inqilab al-Mu'tamar 'ala Ittifāq Fabrayir," *al-Sahwa*, Dec. 12, 2010, http://www.alsahwa-yemen.net/arabic/subjects/1/2010/12/12/5498.htm; "Al-Barlaman Yaqarr Asma' li-l-Lajna al-'Ulya li-l-Intikhabat min al-Qudhah," *News Yemen*, Dec. 14, 2010, http://www.newsyemen.net/view_news.asp?sub_no=1_2010_12_14_49896.

38. "Yemeni Opposition Won't Run in Parliamentary Elections, Warns of Escalation," *News Yemen*, Dec. 13, 2010, http://www.newsyemen.net/en/view_news.asp?sub_no=3_2010_12_12_40223; "Al-Barlaman Yaqarr Asma' li-l-Lajna," *News Yemen*.

39. "Al-Barlaman Yaqarr Asma' li-l-Lajna," *News Yemen*; Sahafiyyat bi-La Quyud, "Al-I'tida"ala al-Mu'tasimin amam al-Nuwwab," *YouTube*, Dec. 14, 2010, http://www.youtube.com/watch?v=tcTRPvebUHU&feature=player_embedded.

40. "Opposing Leader Calls International Community to Press on Yemen Authority," *al-Sahwa*, Dec. 19, 2010, http://www.alsahwa-yemen.net/arabic/subjects/5/2010/12/19/5662.htm; "Kutal al-Mushtarak Tuwasil I'tisamha bi-l-Barlaman wa Tad'u al-I'lam

li-l-Tafa'ulma'aha," *al-Sahwa*, Dec. 12, 2010, http://www.alsahwa-yemen.net/arabic/subjects
/1/2010/12/20/5682.htm; "Amin 'Amm al-Islah Taltaqi al-Safir al-Amriki bi-San'a' wa Yu-
naqish ma'ahu 'Adadan min al-Qadhaya," *al-Sahwa*, Dec. 12, 2010, http://www.alsahwa
-yemen.net/arabic/subjects/1/2010/12/12/5520.htm.

41. "Mushtarak Ta'izz: Ta'dilat Qanun al-Intikhabat Muhawala Ya'isa li-Himaya al-
Mashru'at al-Khassa wa al-Mutasadama ma'a Maslaha al-Sha'b wa Ruh al-Thawra wa
al-Wahda wa al-Dimuqratiyya," *al-Sahwa*, Dec. 13, 2010, http://www.alsahwa-yemen.net
/arabic/subjects/1/2010/12/13/5524.html; "Mushtarak Lahij Yad'u li-Thawra Sha'biyya
Tuzalzil al-Fasidin," *News Yemen*, Dec. 14, 2010, http://www.newsyemen.net/view_news
.asp?sub_no=1_2010_12_14_49904; "Mushtarak al-Mahra Yatadhaman ma'a al-Nawwab
al-Mu'tasimin," *al-Sahwa*, Dec. 16, 2010, http://www.alsahwa-yemen.net/arabic/subjects
/1/2010/12/16/5588.htm.

42. "I'lan 'an Tashkil Lajna Tansiq Mushtaraka bayna Lajna al-Hiwar al-Watani wa
Jama'a al-Huthi bi-Sha'n Mukhtalif al-Qadhaya al-Wataniyya," *al-Sahwa*, Dec. 16, 2010,
http://www. alsahwa-yemen.net/arabic/subjects/1/2010/12/16/5589.

43. Al-'Alawi, "Kutal al-Mushtarak;" Hamid Dabwan, "Ahzab al-Mushtarak Tad'u ila
Habba Ghadhab Sha'biyya Ihtijajan 'ala al-Tafarrud fi al-Intikhabat," *News Yemen*, Dec.
13, 2010, http://www.newsyemen.net/view_news.asp?sub_no=1_2010_12_13_49860.

44. "Al-Kutal al-Barlamaniyya li-Ahzab al-Mu'aradha wa al-Mustaqillin Tanqul
I'tisamatha ila Kharij al-Barlaman wa Tuhaddid bi-Taf'il al-Fa'aliyat al-Midaniyya 'ala
Mustawa al-Muhafazat wa al-Mudiriyyat," *News Yemen*, Dec. 25, 2010, http://www.news
yemen.net/view_news.asp?sub_no=1_2010_12_25_50301.

45. "Intishar 'Askari bi-l-'Asima Tahassuban li-Ayy Muzahara Tuqimha Ahzab al-
Mushtarak," *News Yemen*, Dec. 14, 2010, http://www.newsyemen.net/view_news.asp?sub
_no=1_2010_12_14_49888.

46. "Armed Men Attack Opposition Leaders in Sana'a," *Yemen Post*, Dec. 15, 2010,
http://www.yemenpost.net/Detail123456789.aspx?ID=3&SubID=2878&Main=3.

47. "Parliament Agrees for Constitutional Amendments; Opposition Shocked,"
Yemen Post, Jan. 1, 2011, http://www.yemenpost.net/Detail123456789.aspx?ID=3&=2934
&MainCat=3.

48. "Salih Yughliq Bab Muhawara al-Mu'aradha: Ri'asa Abadiyya wa Salahiyat Mut-
laqa," *al-Akhbar*, Dec. 31, 2010, http://www.al-akhbar.com/node/864.

49. Author interview no. 10, Dec. 19, 2012.

50. Or with the concept of conflict capability. See Schubert, Tetzlaff, and Vennewald, *Demokratisierung*, 69.

51. Anthony Giddens, *Central Problems in Social Theory: Action, Structure and Contradiction in Social Analysis*, 88.

52. Nigel Thrift, *Spatial Formations*, 69.

53. Interestingly, the major proponents of the structurationist school, such as Anthony Giddens or Pierre Bourdieu, are more prone to explaining why human action is

geared toward reproducing instead of transforming social structures. See William H. Sewell Jr., "A Theory of Structure: Duality, Agency, and Transformation."

54. Giddens, *Central Problems*, 88 (emphasis in the original). It is worth mentioning that Giddens conceives of power as a subcategory of transformative capacity (93). In political science, too, the concept of power has come to be mostly understood as a relational one following the seminal study of Robert Dahl, "The Concept of Power." See also Stefano Guzzini, "Relational Power."

55. Giddens, *Central Problems*, 149.

56. Giddens, *Central Problems*, 93.

57. Stepan, "Tasks of Democratic Opposition," 42.

58. Stepan, "Tasks of Democratic Opposition," 42.

59. While adopting a different theoretical perspective, social movement theory supports this assumption in holding that "framing processes and political opportunity structures are linked interactively." Benford and Snow, "Framing Processes," 631.

60. Author interview no. 9, Dec. 18, 2012; author interview no. 11, Dec. 20, 2012.

61. Charles Schmitz, "Yemen's Wealth Lies in Its Labour Force," 10.

62. "International Energy Statistics," *US Energy Information Administration*, http://www.eia.gov/cfapps/ipdbproject/iedindex3.cfm?tid=3&pid=3&aid=1&cid=YM,&syid=1999&eyid=2000&unit=BCF.

63. "The Joint Arab Economic Report 2011," *Arab Monetary Fund* (2011), 101.

64. "Qarar Majlis al-Wuzara' Raqm 467 li-Sana 2008," Dec. 16, 2008.

65. Raissa Kasolowsky, "Subsidies Biggest Danger to Yemen Economy," *Maktoob Business*, May 26, 2010, http://business.maktoob.com/20090000473518/Subsidies_biggest_danger_to_Yemen_economy/Article.htm.

66. "For Third Time in 2010, Prices of Oil Derivatives Rise in Yemen but No Justifications," *Yemen Post*, Sept. 21, 2010, http://www.yemenpost.net/Detail123456789.aspx?ID=3&SubID=2600.

67. "Al-'Ajz al-Mali fi al-Yaman Balagha 1.6 Milyar Dular," *News Yemen*, Mar. 8, 2011, http://www.newsyemen.net/view_news.asp?sub_no=1_2011_03_08_53162; "Al-Qirbi Urges $6 Billion in Donor Aid to Help Yemen Face Uprising," *Yemen Post*, Mar. 8, 2011, http://yemenpost.net/Detail123456789.aspx?ID=3&SubID=3256&MainCat=3

68. Larbi Sadiki, "Like Father, Like Son: Dynastic Republicanism in the Middle East," 11; Phillips, *Politics of Permanent Crisis*, 32.

69. Al-Saqqaf, "Opposition Leads Civil Disobedience"; "Security Besieging Governor House, Governmental Building in Mahweet," *Yemen Post*, July 7, 2010, http://www.yemenpost.net/Detail123456789.aspx?ID=3&SubID=2385.

70. Longley Alley, "Yemen's Multiple Crisis," 80–1.

71. "Al-Ra'is Salih Yunshi' Quwa 'Askariyya Jadida Yusallim Qiyadaha li-Najlihi al-Asghar al-'Aqid Khalid," *al-Masdar Online*, Jan. 30, 2011, http://almasdaronline.com/index.php?page=news&article-section=1&news_id=15590.

72. Author interview no. 11, Dec. 20, 2012.

73. Cited in Andrew Quinn and Regan E. Doherty, "Clinton Talks Tough to 'Stagnant' Middle East Allies," Reuters, Jan. 13, 2011, http://www.reuters.com/article /2011/01/13/us-usa-arabs-idUSTRE70C1YA20110113.

74. "Al-Barakani Yu'akkid Mudhiy Hizbhu fi Iqrar al-Ta'dilat," News Yemen, Jan. 1, 2011, http://www.newsyemen.net/view_news.asp?sub_no=1_2011_01_01_50524; "US Ambassador: We Will Support Fair and Credible Elections," al-Sahwa, Jan. 5, 2011, http://www.alsahwa-yemen.net/arabic/subjects/5/2011/1/5/6086.htm.

75. 'Abd al-Satar Bajash, "Al-Mutawakkil: Naqashna ma'a Klintun al-Awdha' al-'Amma wa Qalaq Amrika 'ala Istiqrar al-Yaman," News Yemen, Jan. 11, 2011, http://www .newsyemen.net/view_news.asp?sub_no=1_2011_01_11_50873.

76. Reiner Hermann, "Auf schmalem Grat," Frankfurter Allgemeine Zeitung, Jan. 22, 2011.

77. "Mubadara min al-Mu'tamar Tulghi Ta'bid Fatra al-Hukm," News Yemen, Jan. 18, 2011, http://www.newsyemen.net/view_news.asp?sub_no=1_2011_01_18_51091; "Ruling Party Agrees to Opposition Parties Demands," Yemen Post, Jan. 21, 2011, http://yemen post.net/Detail123456789.aspx?ID=3&SubID=3030&MainCat=3.

78. "Opposition Says Receives no Dialogue Invitation, Will Continue Struggle," Yemen Post, Jan. 29, 2011, http://yemenpost.net/Detail123456789.aspx?ID=3&SubID=3071 &MainCat=3.

79. "Ruling Party and Opposition Parties Agree to Delay Parliamentary Elections," Yemen Post, Jan. 12, 2011, http://www.yemenpost.net/Detail123456789.aspx?ID=3&Sub ID=3000&MainCat=3.

80. "Approval of Organizational Types for Monitoring Upcoming Parliamentary Elections," Almotamar.net, Jan. 30, 2011, http://almotamar.net/en/8098.htm.

81. "Al-Barakani Yu'akkid Mudhiy," News Yemen; "Massive Anti-govt. Protest Held in Yemen," Trend News Agency, Jan. 2, 2011, http://en.trend.az/world/arab/1806219.html.

82. See, for instance, "JMP Decides to Set off Protesting Activities," al-Sahwa, Jan. 2, 2011, http://www.alsahwa-yemen.net/arabic/subjects/5/2011/1/2/6001.htm; "Al-Mushtarak Yad'u ila Muwasila Ihtijajiyat al-Taghyir," al-Ishtiraki, Jan. 30, 2011, http://www.aleshteraki .net/news_details.php?lang=arabic&sid=9391.

83. "Tazaharat li-l-Hakim wa al-Mushtarak al-Mu'aridh fi San'a' bayna Mutalaba bi-Rahil Hukuma al-Tajwi' wa Mu'ayyida li-l-Ra'is Salih," News Yemen, Jan. 27, 2011, http:// www.newsyemen.net/view_news.asp?sub_no=1_2011_01_27_51425; "Protesters in Yemen Praise Security Forces," Yemen Post, Jan. 28, 2011, http://yemenpost.net/Detail123456789 .aspx?ID=3&SubID=3065&MainCat=3.

84. Mu'in al-Salami, "Fi Mahrajan Jamahiri li-l-Mushtarak bi-l-'Asima Hadharahu Qaraba Nusf Malyun," al-Sahwa, Feb. 3, 2011, http://www.alsahwa-yemen.net/arabic /subjects/1/2011/2/3/6843.htm; 'Ali Hujja, "Habba Sha'biyya Malyuniyya bi-l-Muhafazat al-Yamaniyya Ta'yidan li-l-Mushtarak wa Mutalaba bi-l-Taghyir wa al-Islah al-Shamil,"

al-Sahwa, Feb. 3, 2011, http://www.alsahwa-yemen.net/arabic/subjects/1/2011/2/3/6867
.htm.

85. Nadia al-Sakkaf, "The Politicization of Yemen's Youth Revolution," *Sada* (Carnegie Endowment for International Peace), Apr. 27, 2011, https://carnegieendowment.org
/sada/43735.

86. Today, the official starting date of the Yemeni uprising is usually considered February 11, 2011. Marie-Christine Heinze, introduction to *Yemen and the Search for Stability: Power, Politics and Society after the Arab Spring*, 3.

87. Fu'ad al-'Alawi, "Qalu in al-Sha'b al-Yamani Lan Yaqbul bi-Rahil al-Tughah wa Innama bi-Muhakamatihim," *al-Sahwa*, Jan. 16, 2011, http://www.alsahwa-yemen.net
/arabic/subjects/1/2011/1/16/6350.htm.

88. The Union of Yemeni Students was dominated by the Muslim Brotherhood. Qat chew with one of its representatives, Dec. 7, 2012, Sanaa; "Tullab Jami'a San'a' Yatazaharun li-l-Yawm al-Khamis li-l-Mutalaba bi-l-Taghyir," *News Yemen*, Jan. 19, 2011, http://
www.newsyemen.net/view_news.asp?sub_no=1_2011_01_19_51133.

89. According to one participant in this rally. Author interview no. 24, Jan. 10, 2013. See also "Al-Amn Ya'tadi 'ala Mutadhamunin Yamaniyin Qaddamu Tahni'a li-l-Sha'b al-Tunisi 'abr Sifaratihi bi-San'a'," *al-Sahwa*, Jan. 15, 2011, http://www.alsahwa-yemen.net
/arabic/subjects/1/2011/1/15/6313.htm.

90. "Al-Huthiyin Yatazaharun li-l-Mutalaba bi-Isqat al-Nizam," *News Yemen*, Feb. 21, 2011, http://www.newsyemen.net/view_news.asp?sub_no=1_2011_02_21_52405; "Ta'liqan 'ala 'Adam Iqama Fa'liyyat Ihtijajiyya bi-Sa'da," *News Yemen*, Feb. 5, 2011, http://www
.newsyemen.net/view_news.asp?sub_no=1_2011_02_05_51697.

91. Khalid al-Hamadi, "Muzaharat bi-l-'Asima San'a' 4 Ahzab al-Mu'aradha Takhruj min Hala al-Qawl li-Marhala al-Fi'l li-l-Mutalaba bi-l-Taghyir," *al-Quds al-'Arabi*, Jan. 26, 2011, http://alquds.co.uk/index.asp?fname=today\26qpt92.htm&arc=data\2011\01\01
-26\26qpt92.htm.

92. "Al-Mutawakkil li-(Niyus Yaman): Iqtarhna 'Adam al-Misas bi-l-Mada 112," *News Yemen*, Feb. 7, 2011, http://www.newsyemen.net/view_news.asp?sub_no=1_2011_02
_07_51768.

93. "GPC and JMP Exchange Lists of the Dialogue Committee," *Almotamar.net*, July 29, 2010, http://almotamar.net/en/7633.htm; "GPC and JMP Indulging in Political Bargaining," *Yemen Post*, Dec. 19, 2010, http://www.yemenpost.net/Detail123456789.aspx
?ID=3&SubID=2891&MainCat=3.

94. "Qiyadi fi Jama'a al-Huthi: La Hiwar Siyasi ma'a al-Sulta," *News Yemen*, Jan. 12, 2011, http://www.newsyemen.net/view_news.asp?sub_no=1_2011_01_11_50856; "Al-Huthi Mukhatiban al-Sulta 'Irhalu' wa Ma Yawm Masr bi-Ba'id," *News Yemen*, Feb. 15, 2011, http://www.newsyemen.net/view_news.asp?sub_no=1_2011_02_15_52111; and "Al-Mu'aradha al-Yamaniyya Tu'lin Rafdhha min Jadid Ijra' Hiwar ma'a al-Sulta," *al-Taghyir*, Feb. 19, 2011, http://www.al-tagheer.com/news26990.html.

95. "Tahdhiriyya Hiwar Ma'rib Tad'u Tahdhiriyya San'a' ila Tanfidh 'Usiyan Madani wa al-Intiqal ila Marhala Intiza' al-Mutalab," *News Yemen*, Jan. 11, 2011, http://www.news yemen.net/view_news.asp?sub_no=1_2011_01_11_50859; "Riyadh al-Adib: Mahrajan li-Mushtarak Ta'izz bi-Mudiriyya al-Masrakh Yutalib al-Sulta bi-l-Rahil," *News Yemen*, Jan. 25, 2011, http://www.newsyemen.net/view_news.asp?sub_no=1_2011_01_25_51367.

96. "Protests Intensify and Spread throughout Governorates," *Yemen Times*, Feb. 14, 2011, http://www.yementimes.com/defaultdet.aspx?SUB_ID=35560.

97. "President Saleh to Leave Office in 2013," *Yemen Post*, Feb. 2, 2011, http://yemen post.net/Detail123456789.aspx?ID=3&SubID=3091&MainCat=3.

98. "Al-Mutawakkil li-(Niyus Yaman): Al-Mushtarak Yatasallam Mubadara al-Ra'is Salih," *News Yemen*, Feb. 6, 2011, http://www.newsyemen.net/view_news.asp?sub_no=1 _2011_02_06_51727.

99. "Qiyada Ahzab al-Mushtarak fi Muhimma Kharij al-Bilad li-Ta'ziz Qa'ida al-Shiraka li-l-Hiwar al-Watani," *News Yemen*, Feb. 9, 2011, http://www.newsyemen.net/view _news.asp?sub_no=1_2011_02_09_51844.

100. "Masadir Muttali' Arja'at al-Asbab li-Khilafat: Al-Mushtarak Yu'ajjil Mu'tamar Sahafi li-I'lan Mawqifihi min Mubadara Salih," *News Yemen*, Feb. 8, 2011, http://www .newsyemen.net/view_news.asp?sub_no=1_2011_02_08_51831.

101. "Masira Mu'ayyida li-l-Thawra al-Masriyya Tatahawwal ila Muzahara Dhidd Nizam Salih," *News Yemen*, Feb. 12, 2011, http://www.newsyemen.net/view_news.asp?sub _no=1_2011_02_12_51941.

102. Cited in "Fi Mu'tamar Sahafi li-l-Mushtarak, al-Anisi: La Tazal al-Fursa Akthar fi al-Yaman li-l-Taghyir bi-l-Wasa'il al-Silmiyya," *News Yemen*, Feb. 13, 2011, http://www .newsyemen.net/view_news.asp?sub_no=1_2011_02_13_52021.

103. See the corresponding JMP statement "Nass Bayan al-Mushtarak hawla I'lanihi Qubul Mubadara Ra'is al-Jumhuriyya," Feb. 13, 2011, posted at *News Yemen*, http://www .newsyemen.net/view_news.asp?sub_no=1_2011_02_13_52012.

104. "Al-Mu'aradha al-Yamaniyya Tu'lin Rafdhha," *al-Taghyir*.

105. "Exiled Politicians Urge People to Unite against Regime," *Yemen Post*, Feb. 19, 2011, http://yemenpost.net/Detail123456789.aspx?ID=3&SubID=3159&MainCat=3; "Yemen's Former Prime Minister Accuses President Saleh of Inciting Tribes against Parties and Society," *Yemen Post*, Feb. 25, 2011, http://yemenpost.net/Detail123456789.aspx ?ID=3&SubID=3188&MainCat=3.

106. "Fi Mu'tamar Sahafi li-l-Mushtarak, al-Anisi," *News Yemen*; "Fi Liqa' bi-Shabb Ma Yusammi bi-l-Thawra al-Sha'biyya," *News Yemen*, Feb. 16, 2011, http://www.newsy-emen.net/view_news.asp?sub_no=1_2011_02_16_52155. According to an independent activist who had worked in the Media Center at the so-called Change Square in Sanaa, senior JMP representatives such as al-Mutawakkil, Yasin Sa'id Nu'man, or Yahya Mansur Abu Usba' frequently met with representatives of the Independent Youth, whereas senior

Islahis usually restricted themselves to meeting only youth groups affiliated with their party. Author interview no. 23, Jan. 9, 2013, Sanaa.

107. Khalid al-Hamadi, "Al-Shabab Yughalli Ghadhaban min Qam' al-Sulta wa Sukhtan min al-Mu'aradha wa Istiqalat Ihtijajiyya min A'dha' al-Tarafayn," *al-Quds al-'Arabi*, Feb. 15, 2011, http://alquds.co.uk/index.asp?fname=today\15qpt936.htm&arc=data \2011\02\02-15\15qpt936.htm; "Khiyarat Mudammira li-Nizam Yabdu Annahu Faqada al-Saytara," *al-Masdar Online*, Feb. 16, 2011, http://www.almasdaronline.com/index.php ?page=news&article-section=1&news_id=16448; 'Aziz al-Salwi, "Mutazahiru Ta'izz Yad'un ila 'Jum'a Ghadhab,'" *al-Taghyir*, Feb. 16, 2011, http://www.al-tagheer.com/news26 898.html; "Amana al-'Asima: Mutazahirin Yutallibun al-Mushtarak bi-Fakk al-Irtibat bi-Salih," *News Yemen*, Feb. 20, 2011, http://www.newsyemen.net/view_news.asp?sub_no=1 _2011_02_20_52331.

108. Arguably, the two most important umbrella organizations were the Coordination Council of the Youth for Peaceful Change (al-majlis al-tansiqi li-shabab al-taghyir al-silmi) and the Coalition of the Free Yemeni Youth (i'tilaf shabab al-yaman al-hurr).

109. Author interview no. 23, Jan. 9, 2013. In fact, nearly all established opposition entities had one or more affiliated youth groups. For Islah, there was also, for instance, the High Coordination (Council) for the Yemeni Revolution (al-munassaqiyya al-'ulya li-l-thawra al-yamaniyya), the Civic Coalition of the Yemeni Revolution (al-tahaluf al-madani li-l-thawra al-shababiyya) was affiliated with the YSP, the Resisting Youth (shabab al-sumud) was affiliated with Ansar Allah, and so forth.

110. Not all Bakil and Hashid tribes defected to the JMP, though. See "Masha'ikh Hashid wa Bakil Yanfun al-Maza'im Hawla Indhimamihim ila Ahzab al-Liqa' al-Mushtarak," *al-Taghyir*, Feb. 26, 2011, http://www.al-tagheer.com/news27226.html.

111. Hamid Dabwan, "Al-Barlaman Yaqarr Mukhataba al-Dhakhiliyya bi-Sha'n Maqtal al-Muwatin fi Ishtibak Musallih bayna al-Ahmar wa Duwayd bi-San'a'," *News Yemen*, Feb. 8, 2011, http://www.newsyemen.net/view_news.asp?sub_no=1_2011_02_08_51810.

112. The ROY had signed the Rome Statute of the International Criminal Court in December 2000, but never ratified it thereafter.

113. Cited in "Tahdhiriyya al-Hiwar al-Watani: Qaddamna li-l-Ra'is Kharita Tariq li-l-Rahil wa 'alayhi I'laniha 'ala al-Sha'b," *News Yemen*, Mar. 3, 2011, http://www.news yemen.net/view_news.asp?sub_no=1_2011_03_03_52878.

114. Author interview no. 17, Jan. 1, 2013; author interview no. 19, Jan. 6, 2013; author interview no. 16, Dec. 31, 2012.

115. Point three in the five-point plan jointly published by the JMP, the PCND, and senior 'ulama' on March 2, 2011. This plan summarized the JMP's preconditions to negotiations. It can be found in "Tahdhiriyya al-Hiwar al-Watani: Qaddamna," *News Yemen*.

116. Richard Bösch, "Conflict Escalation."

117. Giddens, *Central Problems*, 63, 65–69.

118. Holger Albrecht, "Contentious Politics, Political Opposition, and Authoritarianism," 6–7. See also Lisa Anderson, "Lawless Government and Illegal Opposition: Reflections on the Middle East," 225; Balqaziz, *Al-Mu'arada wa al-Sulta*, 13; I. William Zartman, "Opposition in Support of the Arab State, Revisited," 230–33.

119. Kenneth F. Greene, "Opposition Party Strategy and Spatial Competition in Dominant Regimes: A Theory and the Case of Mexico," 761. See also Holger Albrecht, *Raging against the Machine: Political Opposition under Authoritarianism in Egypt*, 37; Berker Kavasoglu, "Opposition Party Organizational Features, Ideological Orientations, and Elite Co-optation in Electoral Autocracies."

120. Greene, "Opposition Party Strategy," 756.

121. 'Abdallah Dubla, "Li-madha Yabqi al-Mushtarak Mawqifhu min 'al-Tamdid' Talmihan?," *al-Masdar Online*, Jan. 26, 2011, http://www.almasdaronline.com/index.php ?page=news&article-section=1&news_id=15442.

122. "Yemen in Most Serious Security Threat since '94—US," Reuters, Feb. 10, 2011, http://www.reuters.com/article/2011/02/10/usa-intelligence-yemen-idUSN10281269 20110210. See also "US Says Post-Salih Yemen," AFP.

123. "Al-Mutawakkil li-(Niyus Yaman): Al-Mushtarak Yatasallam," *News Yemen*; "US Urges Yemeni Opposition to Avoid Provocation," *Yemen Post*, Feb. 5, 2011, http://yemenpost.net/Detail123456789.aspx?ID=3&SubID=3101&MainCat=3.

124. Author interview no. 23, Jan. 9, 2013.

125. Author interview no. 26, Jan. 15, 2013, Sanaa.

126. Christopher Boucek and Martina Ottaway, eds., *Yemen on the Brink*.

127. Day, *Regionalism and Rebellion*, 252.

128. See, for instance, the Hasan Zayd's remarks cited in "Parliamentary System Is the Solution to Rid of the Individual Rule," *Yemen Times*, Nov. 17, 2008. See also Phillips, *Politics of Permanent Crisis*, 118, 134; and Glosemeyer and Sallam, "JMP Alliance," 341.

129. Author interview no. 16, Dec. 31, 2012.

130. See "Intizarat al-Mu'aradha al-Makasib Tafqidha Hamas al-Shari' li-l-Taghyir," *Elaph.com*, Feb. 7, 2011, http://www.elaph.com/Web/news/2011/2/630099.html (8/02/2011); Nada Bakri and J. David Goodman, "Thousands in Yemen Protest against the Government," *New York Times*, Jan. 27, 2011, http://www.nytimes.com/2011/01/28/world/middle east/28yemen.html?_r=2&partner=rss&emc=rss.

131. Author interview no. 9, Dec. 18, 2011.

132. See "Elite Thinks Dialog Is the Way Out of the Yemen Crisis," *Yemen Post*, Dec. 23, 2010, http://www.yemenpost.net/Detail123456789.aspx?ID=3&SubID=2909&=3.

133. On January 11, 2011, the paramount shaykh of the Bakil tribal confederation, Sinan Abu Luhum, presented a corresponding five-point plan to the public; on January 18, the National Solidarity Council (malis al-tadhamun al-watani), a tribal association led by Husayn al-Ahmar, followed suit; on January 20, RAY presented its dialogue initiative, which was renewed on February 13, 2011.

134. Author interview no. 11, Dec. 20, 2012.

135. See the interview with Nuʻman in *al-Sharq al-Awsat*, May 13, 2010, http://www
.aawsat.com/english/news.asp?section=1&id=20928.

136. Cited in "Qala bi-An al-Ihtijajat al-Shaʻbiyya La Tushakkil Ayy Khatar ʻala
Nizam al-Ra'is Salih," *News Yemen*, Feb. 11, 2011, http://www.newsyemen.net/view_news
.asp?sub_no=1_2011_02_10_51899. See also Nuʻman's statements during the JMP press
conference on February 13, 2011, cited in "Fi Muʻtamar Sahafi li-l-Mushtarak," *News
Yemen*.

137. Author interview no. 26, Jan. 15, 2013.

138. For a comprehensive analysis of the uprising, which is beyond the scope of
this study, see, for instance, Laurent Bonnefoy, Franck Mermier, and Marine Poirier,
eds., *Yémen: Le tournat révolutionnaire*; Durac, "Yemen's Arab Spring"; Philbrick Yadav,
Islamists and the State, 206–12; Helen Lackner, ed., *Why Yemen Matters: A Society in
Transition*.

139. Author interview no. 24, Jan. 10, 2013; author interview no. 28, Jan. 19, 2013,
Sanaa; author interview no. 23, Jan. 9, 2013; author interview no. 8, Dec. 13, 2012.

140. Durac, "Yemen's Arab Spring," 173.

141. Laurent Bonnefoy and Marine Poirier, "La structuration de la révolution yéménite: Essai d'analyse d'un processus en marche," 906.

142. Author interview no. 24, Jan. 10, 2013. Paradoxically, this distinction was adopted by the JMP itself. See here the founding charter of the JMP-initiated National
Council for the Forces of the Peaceful Revolution, which differentiates between "groups
engaging in revolutionary action and political action." "Nass Mashruʻ Tashkil al-Majlis
al-Waṭani li-Quwa al-Thawra al-Silmiyya," *al-Masdar Online*, Aug. 18, 2011, http://www
.almasdaronline.com/index.php?page=news&article-section=1&news_id=22659.

143. Author interview no. 23, Jan. 9, 2013. Particularly Hamid al-Ahmar contributed
to the financing of infrastructural facilities in Sanaa's Change Square. He also owned
Zuhayl TV, which "had an influential role in the Yemeni revolution" and often "broadcast from Change Squares around the country." Mohammed al-Samei, "Ten Private TV
Channels Compete for the Yemeni Public's Attention," *Yemen Times*, Mar. 12, 2012,
http://www.yementimes.com/en/1554/report/563/Ten-private-TV-channels-compete-for
-the-Yemeni-Public%E2%80%99s-attention.htm.

144. Bonnefoy and Poirier, "Structuration de la révolution yéménite," 907.

145. Bonnefoy, "Shabab," 98; Mareike Transfeld, "A Youth Non-Movement in
Sanaʻa: Changing Normative Geographies through Fashion, Art and Music," 246–48.

146. A copy of the letter was published in *News Yemen*, Apr. 23, 2011, http://www
.newsyemen.net/view_news.asp?sub_no=1_2011_04_23_54841.

147. One of the victims reported that only Nuʻman apologized as a private person,
insisting that he would not speak on behalf of the YSP per se. Author interview no. 24,
Jan. 10, 2013.

148. "Al-Mutawakkil li-(Niyus Yaman): Nurid Khurujan Musharrifan li-l-Ra'is," *News Yemen*, Apr. 2, 2011, http://www.newsyemen.net/view_news.asp?sub_no=1_2011 _04_02_54364. For the content of the five-point plan, see "Al-Mushtarak Yu'lin Ru'yathu li-Khatawat wa Ijra'at Intiqal al-Sulta," *News Yemen*, Apr. 2, 2011, http://www.newsyemen .net/view_news.asp?sub_no=1_2011_04_02_54365.

149. Laura Kasinof and David E. Sanger, "U.S. Shifts to Seek Removal of Yemen's Leader, an Ally," *New York Times*, Apr. 3, 2011, http://www.nytimes.com/2011/04/04/world /middleeast/04yemen.html.

150. International Crisis Group, "Yemen: Enduring Conflicts, Threatened Transition," i, 1.

151. His Facebook post was subsequently published on *ProjectYemen*, http://www .projectyemen.org/2011/03/yemeni-revolution-so-where-does-that.html#more.

152. Cited in "Fi Liqa' bi-Shabb," *News Yemen*.

153. 'Arafat Madabish, "Ishtibakat Ta'ud bayna al-Haras al-Jumhuri wa al-Jaysh," *al-Sharq al-Awsat*, Mar. 25, 2011.

154. United Nations Security Council, S/RES/2014, Oct. 21, 2011.

155. "EU to Discuss Sanctions on Yemen's Saleh Next Week in Bid to Make Him Resign," Reuters, Nov. 7, 2011, https://english.alarabiya.net/articles/2011%2F11%2F07%2 F175913.

156. Kareem Fahim and Laura Kasinof, "Yemen's Leader Agrees to End 3-Decade Rule," *New York Times*, Nov. 23, 2011, https://www.nytimes.com/2011/11/24/world/middle east/yemen-saleh-transfer-power-deal-saudi-arabia.html.

157. "Ijtima' al-Jama'iyya al-Wataniyya li-Quwa al-Thawra Yantakhib 143 'Udhwan li-l-Majlis al-Watani," *News Yemen*, Aug. 17, 2011, http://www.newsyemen.net/view_news .asp?sub_no=1_2011_08_17_57942.

158. Shatha al-Harazi, "JMP's National Council Surrounded by Confusion," *Yemen Times*, Aug. 18, 2011, http://www.yementimes.com/defaultdet.aspx?SUB_ID=36481.

159. "I'taradhu 'ala I'lanihi Qiyada al-Thawra," *News Yemen*, Aug. 21, 2011, http:// www.newsyemen.net/view_news.asp?sub_no=1_2011_08_21_58059.

160. Author interview no. 10, Dec. 19, 2012; author interview no. 22, Jan. 8, 2013; author interview no. 21, Jan. 8, 2013, Sanaa.

161. "Lajna Hamid al-Ahmar li-l-Hiwar Tad'u li-Isqat al-Intikhabat wa Ifshalahu," *Naba News*, Jan. 8, 2011, http://www.nabanews.net/2009/33024.html.

162. Altogether eight members of the al-Ahmar family were represented in the National Council. For a summary of the corresponding discussion among youth activists, see "Jadal La Yantahi bi-Sha'n al-Majlis al-Watani," *News Yemen*, Aug. 20, 2011, http:// www.newsyemen.net/view_news.asp?sub_no=1_2011_08_20_58034.

163. Radhiyya al-Mutawakkil's remarks are cited ibid.

164. Author interview no. 24, Jan. 10, 2013.

165. Author interview no. 11, Dec. 20, 2012.

166. Dresch, *History of Modern Yemen*; Robert W. Stookey, *Yemen: The Politics of the Yemen Arab Republic*.

167. Phillips, *Politics of Permanent Crisis*, 58.

168. Longley Alley, "Rules of the Game," 394.

169. Dresch, *History of Modern Yemen*, 187; Stiftl, *Politischer Islam*, 255–61; Longley, "High Water Mark," 256.

170. Author interview no. 10, Dec. 19, 2012.

171. See Ahmad al-Shamiri's interview with al-Mutawakkil in *Manar al-Yaman*, July 9, 2012, http://www.manaralyemen.com/news-10852.html.

172. See the interview with al-Mutawakkil in the *Yemen Times*, Dec. 3, 2012, http://www.yementimes.com/en/1630/intreview/1687/Former-leader-of-the-Joint-Meeting-Parties-Dr-Mohammed-Abdul-Malik-Al-Mutawakil-talks-to-the-Yemen-Times.htm.

173. Cited in Atiaf Zaid Alwazir, "Time for Hadi to Move beyond Managing Power Struggles," *Guardian*, Oct. 13, 2012, http://www.guardian.co.uk/commentisfree/2012/oct/13/hadi-power-yemen?newsfeed=true.

174. "'Ala al-Hukuma al-Yamaniyya Mu'alaja Mazalim al-Janubiyin wa Khalaq Manakh Manasib li-Itlaq al-Hiwar," *al-Thawri*, Dec. 6, 2012.

175. Author interview no. 9, Dec. 18, 2012; author interview no. 11, Dec. 20, 2012. See also Phillips, *Politics of Permanent Crisis*, 116; Longley, "High Water Mark," 256; Ghallab, *Lahut al-Nukhab al-Qabaliyya*, 210–11; al-Sharjabi, "Al-Tajammu'," 158; 'Adil Mujahid al-Sharjabi et al., *Al-Qasr wa al-Diwan: Al-Dawr al-Siyasi li-l-Qabila fi al-Yaman*.

176. James M. Buchanan, "Rent Seeking and Profit Seeking," 4.

177. Giacomo Luciani, "Allocation vs. Production States: A Theoretical Framework," 72. See also Hossein Mahdavy, "The Patterns and Problems of Economic Development in Rentier States: The Case of Iran."

178. Luciani, "Allocation vs. Production States," 76.

179. Luciani, "Allocation vs. Production States," 78.

180. This demarcation is done, first, for analytical reasons, see Raj M. Desai, Anders Olofsgård, and Tarik M. Yousef, "The Logic of Authoritarian Bargains"; Gandhi and Przeworski, "Cooperation, Cooptation and Rebellion;" Ellen Lust, "Democratization by Election? Competitive Clientelism in the Middle East." Alternatively, second, because of an assumed impact on political culture, see Ziad Hafez, "The Culture of Rent, Factionalism and Corruption: A Political Economy of Rent in the Arab World"; Douglas A. Yates, *The Rentier State in Africa: Oil Rent Dependency and Neocolonialism in the Republic of Gabon*, 22.

181. Giacomo Luciani, "The Oil Rent, the Fiscal Crisis of the State and Democratization," 132.

182. On the complexity of preference formation, see James N. Druckman and Arthur Lupia, "Preference Formation"; Aaron Wildavsky, "Choosing Preferences by Constructing Institutions: A Cultural Theory of Preference Formation."

183. This argument draws on Olson's differentiation between "exclusive collective goods" and "inclusive collective goods." Olson, *Logic of Collective Action*, 38.

184. Longley, "High Water Mark," 256.

185. For Salih's offer on May 22, 2010, see "President Saleh Delivers Speech on Unification Day," Yemen News Agency, May 21, 2010, https://www.saba.ye/en/news215024 .htm. For his offer on November 1, 2010, see "Ruling Party Chooses to Hold Elections," *Yemen Post*. On January 1, 2011, Salih renewed his offer in a letter to the JMP. See "Niyus Yaman Yanshur Nass Risala al-Mu'tamar li-l-Mushtarak wa Radd al-Mushtarak wa Shuraka'hu 'ala al-Risala," *News Yemen*, Jan. 4, 2011, http://www.newsyemen.net/view _news.asp?sub_no=1_2011_01_04_50608 (5/01/2011). For his offer on February 28, 2011, see "Saleh Meets Clerics, Talks about New Initiative for Opposition," *Yemen Post*, Feb. 28, 2011, http://yemenpost.net/Detail123456789.aspx?ID=3&SubID=3212&MainCat=3.

Conclusion

1. Particularly cross-ideological alliances are often referred to as strange bedfellows. Yet there is a reason why they become so.

2. One prime example would be the refusal of the Syrian Damascus Declaration (i'lan dimashq) to coalesce, if only tacitly, with the National Salvation Front (jabha al-khalas al-watani) founded by former vice president 'Abd al-Halim Khaddam after his defection from the Ba'th regime in 2005. As a former high-ranking regime member, Khaddam could have provided the alliance with crucial resources. Yet since he had been responsible for the crackdown on the opposition during the short-lived Damascus Spring in 2001, the Damascus Declaration declined his offer of cooperation. This decision prompted its strongest constituent, the Muslim Brotherhood, to abandon the alliance and align with Khaddam instead. See "I'lan Qiyam Jabha al-Khalas al-Watani," *al-Sharq al-Awsat*, Mar. 18, 2006, http://asharqalawsat.com/details.asp?section=4&issue=9972& article=353626.

3. Being the birthplace of the ROY's most meaningful opposition alliance neatly matched the city's image of being the national hotbed for opposition activity vis-à-vis the central government. See Maysaa Shuja al Deen, "The Endless Battle in Taiz," Atlantic Council, April 26, 2017, https://www.atlanticcouncil.org/blogs/menasource/the-endless -battle-in-taiz/.

4. Daniel Nikbakht and Sheena McKenzie, "The Yemen War Is the World's Worst Humanitarian Crisis, UN Says," CNN, April 3, 2018, https://edition.cnn.com/2018/04/03 /middleeast/yemen-worlds-worst-humanitarian-crisis-un-intl/index.html.

5. Lyse Doucet, "In the Rubble of Taiz, All Roads to Normal Life Are Blocked," *Guardian*, Mar. 15, 2020, https://www.theguardian.com/world/2020/mar/15/taiz-yemen -roads-to-normal-life-blocked-houthi.

6. René Rieger, *Saudi Arabian Foreign Relations: Diplomacy and Mediation in Conflict Resolution*, 214–16. For an analysis of the National Dialogue Conference, which as per the GCC Initiative was commissioned to, inter alia, draft a new constitution despite the inadequate representation of major societal segments as well as key political groups such as Ansar Allah or the Southern Movement, see Philbrick Yadav, *Shadow of Transition*, 131–33.

7. Blumi, *Destroying Yemen*, 188–89; Lackner, *Yemen in Crisis*, 49.

8. Laurent Bonnefoy, "Reversals of Fortune: The Islah Party in Post-Salih Yemen," 195–96; Marieke Brandt, "The Huthi Enigma: Ansar Allah and the 'Second Republic,'" 163.

9. Ginny Hill, *Yemen Endures: Civil War, Saudi Adventurism and the Future of Arabia*, 275–93.

10. An English translation of the agreement is provided online at https://peacemaker .un.org/yemen-national-partnership-2014.

11. Tobias Thiel, "Yemen's Imposed Federal Boundaries," Middle East Research and Information Project, July 20, 2015, https://merip.org/2015/07/yemens-imposed-federal -boundaries/; Philbrick Yadav, *Shadow of Transition*, 148–49.

12. Elisabeth Kendall, "Iran's Fingerprints in Yemen: Real or Imagined?"; Mareike Transfeld, "Iran's Small Hand in Yemen," *Sada* (Carnegie Endowment for International Peace), February 14, 2017, https://carnegieendowment.org/sada/67988.

13. Bushra al-Maqtari, "Al-Imarat fi al-Yaman . . . Isti'mar Ghayr Na'im," *Ta'izz Online*, July 16, 2019, https://www.taizonline.com/art428.html; Tawfiq al-Jund, "Al-Imarat fi Janub al-Yaman: Istinsakh Adawat al-Ihtilal al-Britani," *al-'Arabi al-Jadid*, Nov. 23, 2017, https://tinyurl.com/ybv6ffz5.

14. This idea was suggested early on in the war already, for instance by Hasan Zayd of al-Haqq. "Hassan Zaid: The JMP Is a Bridge on Which Political Forces Can Meet," *Yemen Times*, Oct. 21, 2016, http://www.yementimes.com/en/1875/news/5127/Hassan-Zaid --the-JMP-is-a-bridge-on-which-political-forces-can-meet.htm.

15. Nabil al-Bukayri, "Al-Yaman wa Hatmiyya al-Kutla al-Wataniyya," *al-'Arabi al-Jadid*, Jan. 18, 2017, https://tinyurl.com/2p9xt35m. See also Salim 'Abd al-'Aziz, "Al-Islah wa al-Liqa' al-Mushtarak," *al-Islah.net*, Sept. 15, 2020, https://alislah-ye.net/articles .php?id=700.

16. 'Atiq Jarallah, "Kayfa Yumkin al-Bina' 'ala Tajriba al-Liqa' al-Mushtarak fi al-Yaman ka-Hala Wataniyya," *al-Markaz al-'Arabi li-l-Abhath wa Dirasa al-Siyasat*, Aug. 4, 2016, https://www.dohainstitute.org/ar/researchandstudies/pages/art740.aspx.

17. See, for instance, Zayd's allegations in "The JMP Is a Bridge," *Yemen Times*; "What Does Yemen's New Leadership Mean for the War-Torn Country?," AFP, July 4, 2022, https://www.france24.com/en/live-news/20220407-what-does-yemen-s-new-leadership -mean-for-the-war-torn-country.

18. See the special rubric on Ansar Allah's website: https://www.ansarollah.com/.

19. "Al-Ishtiraki al-Yamani: I'tilaf al-Liqa' al-Mushtarak Tawaqqafa Mundhu 3 Sanawat," *al-'Arabi al-Jadid*, June 19, 2018, https://tinyurl.com/3pxy5rvr.

20. Heibach, "Muhammad 'Abd al-Malik al-Mutawakkil."

21. "Houthi Minister of Youth 'Assassinated' in Sanaa," *Middle East Eye*, Oct. 27, 2020, https://www.middleeasteye.net/news/yemen-houthi-minister-youth-assassinated-sanaa.

22. "Prominent Politician Mohammed Qahtan Still Forcibly Disappeared after More than Seven Years," *Alkarama*, Apr. 22, 2022, https://www.alkarama.org/en/articles /yemen-prominent-politician-mohammed-qahtan-still-forcibly-disappeared-after-more -seven.

23. Blumi, *Destroying Yemen*, 5.

24. For instance, Yemen LNG, which manages all Yemeni gas resources, is largely owned by French Total (39.62 percent), Hunt Oil (17.22 percent), and three Korean companies (SK Innovation, Ltd., 9.55 percent; Korea Gas Corporation, 6 percent; Hyundai, 5.88 percent). Yemeni shareholders, the Yemen Gas Company and the General Authority for Social Security & Pensions, own 16.73 percent and 5 percent, respectively. See https:// www.yemenlng.com/ws/en/go.aspx?c=ylng_share.

25. Lackner, *Yemen in Crisis*, 228–29.

26. Blumi, *Destroying Yemen*, 170–99.

27. For a discussion of why Ansar Allah should not be considered an Iranian proxy, see Marie-Louise Clausen, "More than a Proxy: The Huthis as a Non-state Actor with a Foreign Policy?"; Thomas Juneau, "Iran's Policy towards the Houthis in Yemen: A Limited Return on a Modest Investment."

28. Fernando Carvajal, "The Decline of Yemen's Islamist Islah Party," *New Arab*, Oct. 12, 2022, https://www.newarab.com/analysis/decline-yemens-islamist-al-islah-party. While its actual support for Islah is disputed, Turkey has reportedly tried to gain a foothold in Yemen by way of allying with Islah of late. See, for instance, "Islah Leader Calls Saudi 'Mice' and Says He Will Liberate Yemen's Mocha from UAE," *Middle East Eye*, Aug. 12, 2020, https://www.middleeasteye.net/news/islah-leader-yemen-saudi-arabia-mice -liberate-mocha-uae.

29. Gregory D. Johnson, "Yemen's Three Wars," *Lawfare*, Sept. 23, 2018, https:// www.lawfareblog.com/yemens-three-wars.

30. Michael LaForgia and Edward Wong, "War Crime Risk Grows for U.S. over Saudi Strikes in Yemen," *New York Times*, Sept. 14, 2020, https://www.nytimes.com/2020 /09/14/us/politics/us-war-crimes-yemen-saudi-arabia.html; Afrah Nasser, "US Assistance to Saudi-Led Coalition Risks Complicity in War Crimes," *Human Rights Watch*, Apr. 7, 2022, https://www.hrw.org/news/2022/04/07/us-assistance-saudi-led-coalition-risks-complicity -war-crimes. It should also be noted that Yemen's conflict parties, including Ansar Allah, have been accused of war crimes themselves. In addition, France, the United Kingdom,

and Germany have been charged with complicity in war crimes too—owing, among others, to their continued arms sales to Saudi Arabia and its allies.

31. Fred H. Lawson, "Why Foreign Military Interventions Prolong Civil Wars: Lessons from Yemen."

32. Al-Ruhani, *Al-Yaman*, 319.

33. Michael Horton, "Yemen's Emerging Political Coalitions: A First Step toward De-escalation?," 8.

34. Jamal Benomar, "Power-Sharing Is the Only Way to End the War in Yemen—If the US Supports It," *Guardian*, Mar. 26, 2021, https://www.theguardian.com/comment isfree/2021/mar/26/power-sharing-war-yemen-us-houthi-peace.

Bibliography

Abdelrahman, Maha. "'With the Islamists?—Sometimes. With the State?—Never!': Cooperation between the Left and Islamists in Egypt." *British Journal of Middle Eastern Studies* 36, no. 1 (2009): 37–54.

Abu Luhum, Sinan. *Al-Yaman: Haqa'iq wa Watha'iq 'Ishtuha*. Sanaa: Mu'assasa al-'Afif al-Thaqafiyya, 2008.

'Afif, Ahmad Jabir. *Al-Haraka al-Wataniyya fi al-Yaman*. Damascus: Dar al-Fikr, 1982.

Ahmar, 'Abdallah b. Husayn al-. *Mudhakkirat: Qadaya wa Mawaqif*. Sanaa: Al-Afaq li-l-Taba'a wa al-Nashr, 2008.

Ahram, Ariel I. *Break All the Borders: Separatism and the Reshaping of the Middle East*. New York: Oxford Univ. Press, 2019.

Albrecht, Holger. "Contentious Politics, Political Opposition, and Authoritarianism." In *Contentious Politics in the Middle East: Political Opposition under Authoritarianism*, edited by Holger Albrecht, 1–14. Gainesville: Univ. Press of Florida, 2010.

———. "How Can Opposition Support Authoritarianism? Lessons from Egypt." *Democratization* 12, no. 3 (2005): 378–97.

———. *Raging against the Machine: Political Opposition under Authoritarianism in Egypt*. Syracuse, NY: Syracuse Univ. Press, 2013.

Anderson, Lisa. "Lawless Government and Illegal Opposition: Reflections on the Middle East." *Journal of International Affairs* 40, no. 2 (1987): 219–32.

Armstrong, David, Ora John Reuter, and Graeme B. Robertson. "Getting the Opposition Together: Protest Coordination in Authoritarian Regimes." *Post-Soviet Affairs* 36, no. 1 (2020): 1–19.

Arriola, Leonardo R. "Capital and Opposition in Africa: Coalition Building in Multiethnic Societies." *World Politics* 65, no. 2 (2013): 233–72.

———. *Multiethnic Coalitions in Africa: Business Financing of Opposition Election Campaigns*. Cambridge: Cambridge Univ. Press, 2013.

Augustin, Anne-Linda Amira. *South Yemen's Independence Struggle: Generations of Resistance.* Cairo: American Univ. in Cairo Press, 2021.

Axelrod, Robert. *The Evolution of Cooperation.* New York: Basic Books, 1984.

Ayubi, Nazih N. *Over-stating the Arab State: Politics and Society in the Middle East.* New York: I. B. Tauris, 1996.

Azar, Edward. *The Management of Protracted Social Conflict: Theory and Cases.* Aldershot: Dartmouth, 1990.

Azmeh, Aziz al-. "Populism Contra Democracy: Recent Democratist Discourse in the Arab World." In *Democracy without Democrats? The Renewal of Politics in the Muslim World,* edited by Ghassan Salamé, 112–29. London: I. B. Tauris, 1994.

Baaklini, Abdo, Guilain Denoeux, and Robert Springborg. *Legislative Politics in the Arab World: The Resurgence of Democratic Institutions.* Boulder, CO: Lynne Rienner, 1999.

Balqaziz, 'Abd al-Ilah, ed. *Al-Mu'arada wa al-Sulta fi al-Watan al-'Arabi: Azma al-Mu'arada al-Siyasiyya al-'Arabiyya.* Beirut: Markaz Dirasat al-Wahda al-'Arabiyya, 2011.

Basedau, Matthias, and Alexander Stroh. "Measuring Party Institutionalization in Developing Countries." *GIGA Working Papers* (German Institute for Global and Area Studies) 69 (2008).

Bayat, Asef. "Islamism and Social Movement Theory." *Third World Quarterly* 26, no. 6 (2005): 891–908.

———. *Life as Politics: How Ordinary People Change the Middle East.* Stanford: Stanford Univ. Press, 2010.

Beach, Derek, and Rasmus Brun Pedersen. *Process-Tracing Methods: Foundations and Guidelines.* Ann Arbor: Univ. of Michigan Press, 2019.

Bellin, Eva. "The Robustness of Authoritarianism in the Middle East: Exceptionalism in Comparative Perspective." *Comparative Politics* 36, no. 2 (2004): 139–57.

Benford, Robert D., and David A. Snow. "Framing Processes and Social Movements: Overview and Assessment." *Annual Review of Sociology* 26 (2000): 611–39.

Bennett, Andrew. "Case Study Methods: Design, Use, and Comparative Advantage." In *Models, Numbers and Cases: Methods for Studying International Relations,* edited by Detlef Sprinz and Yael Wolinsky-Nahmias, 19–55. Ann Arbor: Univ. of Michigan Press, 2004.

Bercovitch, Jacob, Victor Kremenyuk, and I. William Zartman. "The Nature of Conflict and Conflict Resolution." In *The SAGE Handbook of Conflict*

Resolution, edited by Jacob Bercovitch, Victor Kremenyuk, and I. William Zartman, 1–11. Thousand Oaks, CA: Sage, 2009.

Bermeo, Nancy. "Democracy and the Lessons of Dictatorship." *Comparative Politics* 24, no. 3 (1992): 273–91.

———. "Myths of Moderation: Confrontation and Conflict during Democratic Transitions." *Comparative Politics* 29, no. 3 (1997): 305–22.

Berriane, Yasmine, and Marie Duboc. "Allying beyond Social Divides: An Introduction to Contentious Politics and Coalitions in the Middle East and North Africa." *Mediterranean Politics* 24, no. 4 (2019): 399–419.

Bidwell, Robin. *The Two Yemens*. Boulder, CO: Westview Press, 1983.

Blondel, Jean. "Political Opposition in the Contemporary World." *Government and Opposition* 32, no. 4 (1997): 462–86.

Blumi, Isa. *Chaos in Yemen: Societal Collapse and the New Authoritarianism*. London: Routledge, 2011.

———. *Destroying Yemen: What Chaos in Arabia Tells Us about the World*. Oakland: Univ. of California Press, 2018.

Bonnefoy, Laurent. "Reversals of Fortune: The Islah Party in Post-Salih Yemen." In *Yemen and the Search for Stability: Power, Politics and Society after the Arab Spring*, edited by Marie-Christine Heinze, 184–203. London: I. B. Tauris, 2018.

———. "The Shabab, Institutionalized Politic and the Islamists in the Yemeni Revolution." In *Why Yemen Matters: A Society in Transition*, edited by Helen Lackner, 87–104. London: Saqi, 2014.

Bonnefoy, Laurent, Franck Mermier, and Marine Poirier, eds. *Yémen: Le tournat révolutionnaire*. Paris: Karthala, 2012.

Bonnefoy, Laurent, and Marine Poirier. "La structuration de la révolution yéménite: Essai d'analyse d'un processus en marche." *Revue française de science politique* 62, no. 5 (2012): 895–913.

———. "The Yemeni Congregation for Reform (al-Islâh): The Difficult Process of Building a Project for Change." In *Returning to Political Parties? Partisan Logic and Political Transformations in the Arab World*, edited by Myriam Catusse and Karam Karem, 1–70. Beirut: Lebanese Center for Policy Studies, 2010. https://hal-sciencespo.archives-ouvertes.fr/hal-01041348.

Bösch, Richard. "Conflict Escalation." In *Oxford Research Encyclopedia of International Studies*. Oxford: Oxford Univ. Press, 2017. https://doi.org/10.1093/acrefore/9780190846626.013.82.

Boucek, Christopher. "War in Saada: From Local Insurrection to National Challenge." In *Yemen on the Brink*, edited by Christopher Boucek and Martina

Ottaway, 45–59. Washington, DC: Carnegie Endowment for International Peace, 2010.

———, eds. *Yemen on the Brink*. Washington, DC: Carnegie Endowment for International Peace, 2010.

Brandt, Marieke. "The Huthi Enigma: Ansar Allah and the 'Second Republic.'" In *Yemen and the Search for Stability: Power, Politics and Society after the Arab Spring*, edited by Marie-Christine Heinze, 160–83. London: I. B. Tauris, 2018.

———. "The Irregulars of the Sa'da War: 'Colonel Sheikhs' and 'Tribal Militias' in Yemen's Huthi Conflict (2004–2010)." In *Why Yemen Matters: A Society in Transition*, edited by Helen Lackner, 105–22. London: Saqi Books, 2014.

Brehony, Noel. "From Chaos to Chaos: South Yemen 50 Years after the British Departure." *Asian Affairs* 48, no. 3 (2017): 428–44.

———. *Yemen Divided: The Story of a Failed State in South Arabia*. New York: I. B. Tauris, 2011.

Browers, Michaelle L. "Origins and Architects of Yemen's Joint Meeting Parties." *International Journal of Middle East Studies* 39, no. 4 (2007): 565–86.

———. *Political Ideology in the Arab World: Accommodation and Transformation*. Cambridge: Cambridge Univ. Press, 2009.

Bruck, Gabriele vom. *Islam, Memory, and Morality in Yemen: Ruling Families in Transition*. New York: Palgrave Macmillan, 2005.

———. "Regimes of Piety Revisited: Zaydi Political Moralities in Republican Yemen." *Die Welt des Islams* 53, no. 2 (2010): 185–223.

Buchanan, James M. "Rent Seeking and Profit Seeking." In *Toward a Theory of Rent-Seeking Society*, edited by James M. Buchanan, Robert D. Tollison, and Gordon Tullock, 3–15. College Station: Texas A&M Univ. Press, 1980.

Buehler, Matt. *Why Alliances Fail: Islamist and Leftist Coalitions in North Africa*. Syracuse, NY: Syracuse Univ. Press, 2018.

Burgat, François. "Les élections présidentielles de septembre 1999 au Yémen: Du 'pluralisme armé' au retour à la 'norme arabe.'" *Monde Arabe: Maghreb-Machrek*, no. 168 (2000): 67–75.

———. "Le Yémen islamiste entre universalisme et insularité." In *Le Yémen contemporain*, edited by Rémy Leveau, Franck Mermier, and Udo Steinbach, 221–45. Paris: Karthala, 1999.

Burrowes, Robert D. "Prelude to Unification: The Yemen Arab Republic in Yemen, 1962–1990." *International Journal of Middle East Studies* 23, no. 4 (1991): 483–506.

———. "The Republic of Yemen: The Politics of Unification and Civil War, 1989–1995," in *The Middle East Dilemma*, edited by Michael C. Hudson, 187–213. New York: Columbia Univ. Press, 1999.

———. *The Yemen Arab Republic: The Politics of Development, 1962–1986.* Boulder, CO: Westview Press, 1987.

Burrowes, Robert D., and Catherine M. Kasper. "The Saleh Regime and the Need for a Credible Opposition." *Middle East Journal* 61, no. 2 (2007): 263–80.

Carapico, Sheila. *Civil Society in Yemen: The Political Economy of Activism in Modern Arabia.* Cambridge: Cambridge Univ. Press, 1998.

———. "How Yemen's Ruling Party Secured an Electoral Landslide." *Middle East Report Online*, May 16, 2003.

———. "Special Operations in Yemen." *Foreign Policy*, May 13, 2010.

Carapico, Sheila, Lisa Wedeen, and Anna Würth. "The Death and Life of Jarallah Omar." *Middle East Report Online*, Dec. 31, 2002.

Cavatorta, Francesco. "'Divided They Stand, Divided They Fail': Opposition Politics in Morocco." *Democratization* 16, no. 1 (2009): 137–56.

Clark, Janine. "The Conditions of Islamist Moderation: Unpacking Cross-ideological Cooperation in Jordan." *International Journal of Middle East Studies* 38, no. 4 (2006): 539–60.

———. "Threats, Structures, and Resources: Cross-ideological Coalition Building in Jordan." *Comparative Politics* 43, no. 1 (2010): 101–20.

Clausen, Marie-Louise. "More than a Proxy: The Huthis as a Non-state Actor with a Foreign Policy?" In *The Huthi Movement in Yemen: Ideology, Ambition, and Security in the Arab Gulf*, edited by Abdullah Hamidaddin, 273–85. London: I. B. Tauris, 2022.

Collins Dunn, Michael. "Islamist Parties in Democratizing States: A Look at Jordan and Yemen." *Middle East Policy* 2, no. 2 (1993): 16–27.

Coser, Lewis A. *The Functions of Social Conflict.* Glencoe, IL: Free Press, 1956.

Dahl, Robert A. "The Concept of Power." *Behavioral Science* 2, no. 3 (1957): 201–15.

———. Introduction to *Regimes and Oppositions*, edited by Robert A. Dahl, 1–25. New Haven, CT: Yale Univ. Press, 1973.

———. "Patterns of Opposition." In *Political Opposition in Western Democracies*, edited by Robert A. Dahl, 332–47. New Haven, CT: Yale Univ. Press, 1966.

———. *Polyarchy: Participation and Opposition.* New Haven, CT: Yale Univ. Press, 1971.

———. Preface to *Political Opposition in Western Democracies*, edited by Robert A. Dahl, xiii–xxi. New Haven, CT: Yale Univ. Press, 1966.

Dahlgren, Susanne. "The Snake with a Thousand Heads." *Middle East Report*, no. 256 (2010): 28–33.

Dahrendorf, Ralf. *Gesellschaft und Freiheit: Zur soziologischen Analyse der Gegenwart*. Munich: Pieper, 1961.

———. "Toward a Theory of Social Conflict." *Journal of Conflict Resolution* 2, no. 2 (1958): 170–83.

Day, Stephen. "The Political Challenge of Yemen's Southern Movement." In *Yemen on the Brink*, edited by Christopher Boucek and Martina Ottaway, 61–74. Washington, DC: Carnegie Endowment for International Peace, 2010.

———. *Regionalism and Rebellion in Yemen: A Troubled National Union*. Cambridge: Cambridge Univ. Press, 2012.

Desai, Raj M., Anders Olofsgård, and Tarik M. Yousef. "The Logic of Authoritarian Bargains." *Economic and Politics* 21, no. 1 (2009): 93–125.

Diamond, Larry. "Introduction: Political Culture and Democracy." In *Political Culture and Democracy in Developing Countries*, edited by Larry Diamond, 1–27. Boulder, CO: Lynne Rienner, 1994.

Dorlian, Samy. *La mouvance zaydite dans le Yémen contemporain: Une modernisation avortée*. Paris: L'Harmattan, 2013.

———. "Zaydisme et modernisation: Émergence d'un nouvel universel politique?" *Chroniques yéménites* 13 (2006): 1–22.

Dresch, Paul. *A History of Modern Yemen*. Cambridge: Cambridge Univ. Press, 2000.

———. *Tribes, Government, and History in Yemen*. New York: Oxford Univ. Press, 1990.

Dresch, Paul, and Bernard Haykel. "Stereotypes and Political Styles: Islamists and Tribesfolk in Yemen." *International Journal of Middle East Studies* 27, no. 4 (1995): 405–31.

Druckman, James N., and Arthur Lupia. "Preference Formation." *Annual Review of Political Science* 3, no. 1 (2000): 1–24.

Du Bouchet, Ludmila. "The State, Political Islam, and Violence: The Reconfiguration of Yemeni Politics since 9/11." In *The Enigma of Islamist Violence*, edited by Amélie Blom, Laetitia Bucaille, and Luis Martinez, 137–64. London: Hurst, 2007.

Dunbar, Robin I. M., and Alistair G. Sutcliffe. "Social Complexity and Intelligence." In *The Oxford Handbook of Comparative Evolutionary Psychology*, edited by Jennifer Vonk and Todd K. Shackelford, 102–17. Oxford: Oxford Univ. Press, 2011.

Durac, Vincent. "The Joint Meeting Parties and the Politics of Opposition in Yemen." *British Journal of Middle Eastern Studies* 38, no. 3 (2011): 343–65.

———. "Opposition Coalitions in the Middle East: Origins, Demise, and Afterlife?" *Mediterranean Politics* 24, no. 4 (2019): 534–44.

———. "Social Movements, Protest Movements and Cross-ideological Coalitions: The Arab Uprisings Re-appraised." *Democratization* 22, no. 2 (2015): 239–58.

———. "Yemen's Arab Spring: Democratic Opening or Regime Maintenance?" *Mediterranean Politics* 17, no. 2 (2012): 161–78.

Eriani, Kamilia el-. "Mourning the Death of a State to Enliven It: Notes on the 'Weak' Yemeni State." *International Journal of Cultural Studies* 23, no. 2 (2020): 227–44.

———. "Secularism, Security and the Weak State: De-democratizing the 2011 Yemeni Uprising." *Interventions* 23, no. 8 (2021): 1140–65.

Etzioni, Amitai. *The Active Society: A Theory of Societal and Political Processes.* 2nd ed. New York: Free Press, 1968.

Faqih, 'Abdallah al-. "Al-Takattul 'ala Qa'ida al-Dimuqratiyya fi al-Jumhuriyya al-Yamaniyya, 1990–2009." *Al-Mustaqbal al-'Arabi* 32, no. 373 (2010): 139–70.

Fawzy, Sameh. "What Is the Future of the Movement for Democratic Change in the Arab World?" *Final Workshop Report* (Cairo Institute for Human Rights) (May 2007).

Ferris, Jesse. *Nasser's Gamble: How Intervention in Yemen Caused the Six-Day War and the Decline of Egyptian Power.* Princeton: Princeton Univ. Press, 2013.

Franklin, James C. "Political Party Opposition to Noncompetitive Regimes: A Cross-national Analysis." *Political Research Quarterly* 55, no. 3 (2002): 521–46.

Galtung, Johan. *Peace by Peaceful Means: Peace and Conflict, Development and Civilization.* London: Sage, 1996.

Gandhi, Jennifer, and Adam Przeworski. "Cooperation, Cooptation, and Rebellion under Dictatorship." *Economic and Politics* 18, no. 1 (2006): 1–26.

Gandhi, Jennifer, and Ora John Reuter. "The Incentives for Pre-electoral Coalitions in Non-democratic Elections." *Democratization* 20, no. 1 (2013): 137–59.

George, Alexander L., and Andrew Bennett. *Case Studies and Theory Development in the Social Sciences.* London: MIT Press, 2005.

Ghalib, 'Umar Ahmad. *Al-Adwar al-Siyasiyya li-l-Shaykh 'Abdallah ibn Husayn al-Ahmar.* Sanaa: Awan li-l-Khidamat al-I'lamiyya, 2010.

Ghallab, Najib. *Lahut al-Nukhab al-Qabaliyya: Taqdis al-Shaykh wa La'n al-Dawla.* Beirut: Bissan li-l-Nashr wa al-Tawzi' wa al-I'lan, 2010.

———. *Al-Sira' 'ala 'Arsh al-Yaman fi Zill al-Tahawwulat al-Dimuqratiyya.* Beirut: Bissan li-l-Nashr wa al-Tawzi' wa al-I'lan, 2010.

Giddens, Anthony. *Central Problems in Social Theory: Action, Structure and Contradiction in Social Analysis.* 4th ed. Houndmills: Palgrave Macmillan, 1986.

Glosemeyer, Iris. "The Development of State Institutions." In *Le Yémen contemporain,* edited by Rémy Leveau, Franck Mermier, and Udo Steinbach, 79–100. Paris: Karthala, 1999.

———. "Wo Islamisten für Rechte von Sozialisten streiten." *Welt-Sichten,* Jan. 27, 2009. https://www.welt-sichten.org/artikel/3396/wo-islamisten-fuer-rechte-von-sozialisten-streiten.

Glosemeyer, Iris, and Hesham Sallam. "The JMP Alliance: New Political Pragmatism in Yemen?" In *Conflict, Identity, and Reform in the Muslim World,* edited by Daniel Brumberg and Dina Shehata, 327–41. Washington, DC: United States Institute of Peace, 2009.

Goldstone, Jack A. "Cross-class Coalitions and the Making of the Arab Revolts of 2011." *Swiss Political Science Review* 17, no. 4 (2011): 457–62.

Goy, Raymond. "La réunification du Yémen." *Annuaire Français de Droit International* 36 (1990): 249–65.

Greene, Kenneth F. "Opposition Party Strategy and Spatial Competition in Dominant Regimes: A Theory and the Case of Mexico." *Comparative Political Studies* 35, no. 7 (2002): 755–83.

Guzzini, Stefano. "Relational Power." In *Encyclopedia of Power,* edited by Keith Dowding, 563–66. Thousand Oaks, CA: Sage, 2011.

Hafez, Ziad. "The Culture of Rent, Factionalism and Corruption: A Political Economy of Rent in the Arab World." *Contemporary Arab Affairs* 2, no. 3 (2009): 458–80.

Halliday, Fred. *Nation and Religion in the Middle East.* London: Saqi, 2000.

———. *Revolution and Foreign Policy: The Case of South Yemen, 1967–1987.* Cambridge: Cambridge Univ. Press, 1990.

Hamidaddin, Abdullah. Introduction to *The Huthi Movement in Yemen: Ideology, Ambition, and Security in the Arab Gulf,* edited by Abdullah Hamidaddin, 1–13. London: I. B. Tauris, 2022.

Hamuda, 'Abdallah. "Hall Tahsim al-Musharaka al-Sa'udiyya Harb al-Yaman?" *Afaq al-Mustaqbal* 2, no. 3 (2010): 20–21.

———. "Al-Yaman fi Muwajaha Azmat Qadima wa Mustajidda." *Afaq al-Mustaqbal* 1, no. 1 (2009): 15–17.

Hamzawy, Amr. "Between Government and Opposition: The Case of the Yemeni Congregation for Reform." *Carnegie Papers* (Carnegie Endowment for International Peace) 18 (2009).

Harbi, Ahmad Muhammad al-. *Al-Haraka al-Wataniyya wa al-Siyasiyya al-Yamaniyya*. 2 vols. Sanaa: Markaz 'Ibadi li-l-Dirasat wa al-Nashr, 2007.

Hathaway, Will, and David S. Meyer. "Competition and Cooperation in Social Movement Coalitions: Lobbying for Peace in the 1980s." *Berkeley Journal of Sociology* 38 (1993–94): 157–83.

Hatina, Meir. "The Clerics' Betrayal: Islamists, Ulama and the Polity." In *Guardians of Faith in Modern Times: Ulama in the Middle East*, edited by Meir Hatina, 247–64. Leiden: Brill, 2009.

Haykel, Bernard. "The Huthi Movement's Religious and Political Ideology and Its Relationship to Zaydism in Yemen." In *The Huthi Movement in Yemen: Ideology, Ambition, and Security in the Arab Gulf*, edited by Abdullah Hamidaddin, 17–35. London: I. B. Tauris, 2022.

Heibach, Jens. "Contesting the Monopoly of Interpretation: The Uneasy Relationship between Ulama and Sunni Parties in Yemen." *Middle Eastern Studies* 51, no. 4 (2015): 563–84.

———. "The Future of South Yemen and the Southern Transitional Council." *GIGA Focus Middle East* (German Institute for Global and Area Studies) 2 (2021).

———. "Muhammad 'Abd al-Malik al-Mutawakkil: A Political Biography." *Middle East—Topics & Arguments* 3, no. 4 (2015): 151–58.

Heibach, Jens, and Tereza Jermanová. "Coalition Maintenance during Democratization: Comparative Insights from Tunisia and Yemen." *Middle East Law and Governance* 15, no. 3 (2023): 345–68.

Heibach, Jens, and Mareike Transfeld. "Opposition Dynamism under Authoritarianism: The Case of Yemen, 1994–2011." *Democratization* 25, no. 4 (2018): 597–613.

Heinze, Marie-Christine. Introduction to *Yemen and the Search for Stability: Power, Politics and Society after the Arab Spring*, edited by Marie-Christine Heinze, 1–23. London: I. B. Tauris, 2018.

Heydemann, Steven. "Upgrading Authoritarianism in the Arab World." *Analysis Paper* (Saban Center for Middle East Politics, Brookings Institution) 13 (2007).

Hill, Ginny. *Yemen Endures: Civil War, Saudi Adventurism and the Future of Arabia*. London: Saqi, 2017.

Hix, Simon, Abdul Noury, and Gérard Roland. "Power to the Parties: Cohesion and Competition in the European Parliament, 1979–2001." *British Journal of Political Science* 35, no. 2 (2005): 209–34.

Horton, Michael. "Yemen's Emerging Political Coalitions: A First Step Toward De-escalation?" *Terrorism Monitor* 14, no. 6 (2021): 7–10.

Hudson, Michael C. "After the Gulf War: Prospects for Democratization in the Arab World." *Middle East Journal* 45, no. 3 (1991): 407–26.

———. "Bipolarity, Rational Calculations and War in Yemen." In *The Yemeni War of 1994: Causes and Consequences*, edited by Jamal S. al-Suwaidi, 19–32. London: Saqi, 1995.

Huntington, Samuel P. "Democracy's Third Wave." *Journal of Democracy* 2, no. 2 (1991): 12–34.

———. *Political Order in Changing Societies*. New Haven, CT: Yale Univ. Press, 1968.

Huskey, Eugene, and Gulnara Iskakova. "The Barriers to Intra-opposition Cooperation in the Post-communist World: Evidence from Kyrgyzstan." *Post-Soviet Affairs* 26, no. 3 (2010): 228–62.

International Crisis Group. "Yemen: Enduring Conflicts, Threatened Transition." *Middle East Report* 125 (2012).

'Isa, 'Abd al-Malik Muhammad 'Abdallah. *Harakat al-Islam al-Siyasi fi al-Yaman*. Beirut: Markaz Dirasat al-Wahda al-'Arabiyya, 2012.

Ishiyama, John. "The Sickle and the Minaret: Communist Successor Parties in Yemen and Afghanistan after the Cold War." *Middle East Review of International Affairs* 9, no. 1 (2005): 7–29.

Janse, Ronald. "Counter-terrorism, Rule of Law Promotion, and the Friends of Yemen." In *Human Rights and Conflict*, edited by Ineke Boerefijn et al., 363–74. Cambridge: Intersential, 2012.

Jawi, Omar al-. "We Are the Opposition . . . But. . . ." In *Yemen Today: Crisis and Solutions*, edited by E. G. H. Joffé, M. J. Hachemi, and E. W. Watkins, 83–88. London: Caravel, 1997.

Johnson, Gregory. "Salih's Road to Re-election." *Middle East Report Online*, Jan. 13, 2006.

———. "Seven Yemens: How Yemen Fractured and Collapsed, and What Comes Next." *Issue Paper* (Arab Gulf States Institute in Washington) 4 (2021).

Juneau, Thomas. "Iran's Policy towards the Houthis in Yemen: A Limited Return on a Modest Investment." *International Affairs* 92, no. 3 (2016): 647–63.

Katz, Richard S., and Peter Mair. "Changing Models of Party Organization and Party Democracy: The Emergence of the Cartel Party." *Party Politics* 1, no. 1 (1995): 5–28.

Kaufman, Robert G. *In Defense of the Bush Doctrine.* Lexington, KY: Univ. Press of Kentucky, 2007.

Kavasoglu, Berker. "Opposition Party Organizational Features, Ideological Orientations, and Elite Co-optation in Electoral Autocracies." *Democratization* 29, no. 4 (2022): 634–54.

Kendall, Elisabeth. "Iran's Fingerprints in Yemen: Real or Imagined?" *Issue Brief* (Atlantic Council) (Oct. 2017).

Kibsi, Ahmad Muhammad al-. *Nizam al-Hukm fi al-Jumhuriyya al-Yamaniyya, 1990–2006.* Sanaa: Markaz al-Amin li-l-Nashr wa al-Tawzi', 2006.

Klandermans, Bert. "Mobilization and Participation: Social-Psychological Expansion of Resource-Mobilization Theory." *American Sociological Review* 49, no. 5 (1984): 583–600.

Kraetzschmar, Hendrik. "Electoral Rules, Voter Mobilization and the Islamist Landslide in the Saudi Municipal Elections of 2005." *Contemporary Arab Affairs* 3, no. 4 (2010): 515–33.

———. "Mapping Opposition Coalitions in the Arab World: From Single-Issue Coalitions to Transnational Networks." *British Journal of Middle Eastern Studies* 38, no. 3 (2011): 287–302.

Kriesi, Hanspeter. "The Organizational Structure of New Social Movements in a Political Context." In *Comparative Perspectives on Social Movements: Political Opportunities, Mobilizing Structures, and Cultural Framings,* edited by Doug McAdam, John D. McCarthy, and Mayer N. Zald, 152–84. Cambridge: Cambridge Univ. Press, 2004.

Lackner, Helen. Introduction to *Why Yemen Matters: A Society in Transition,* edited by Helen Lackner, 1–26. London: Saqi, 2014.

———, ed. *Why Yemen Matters: A Society in Transition.* London: Saqi, 2014.

———. *Yemen in Crisis: Autocracy, Neo-liberalism and the Disintegration of a State.* London: Saqi, 2017.

Landman, Todd. *Issues and Methods in Comparative Politics.* New York: Routledge, 2003.

Lawson, Fred H. "Why Foreign Military Interventions Prolong Civil Wars: Lessons from Yemen." *International Politics* 59, no. 6 (2022): 1167–86.

Levi, Margaret. "The Predatory Theory of Rule." *Politics & Society* 10, no. 4 (1981): 431–65.

Levitsky, Steven, and Lucan Way. *Competitive Authoritarianism: Hybrid Regimes after the Cold War*. Cambridge: Cambridge Univ. Press, 2010.

———. "The Rise of Competitive Authoritarianism." *Journal of Democracy* 13, no. 2 (2002): 51–65.

Lijphart, Arend. "Consociational Democracy." *World Politics* 21, no. 2 (1969): 207–25.

Linz, Juan J. "Opposition to and under an Authoritarian Regime." In *Regimes and Oppositions*, edited by Robert A. Dahl, 171–260. New Haven, CT: Yale Univ. Press, 1973.

Longley, April. "The High Water Mark of Islamist Politics? The Case of Yemen." *Middle East Journal* 61, no. 2 (2007): 240–60.

Longley Alley, April. "The Rules of the Game: Unpacking Patronage Politics in Yemen." *Middle East Journal* 64, no. 3 (2010): 385–409.

———. "Yemen's Multiple Crisis." *Journal of Democracy* 21, no. 4 (2010): 72–86.

Longley Alley, April, and Abdul Ghani al-Iryani. "Fighting Brushfires with Batons: An Analysis of the Political Crisis in South Yemen." *Policy Brief* (Middle East Institute) 7 (2008).

Luciani, Giacomo. "Allocation vs. Production States: A Theoretical Framework." In *The Arab State*, edited by Giacomo Luciani, 65–84. London: Routledge, 1990.

———. "The Oil Rent, the Fiscal Crisis of the State and Democratization." In *Democracy without Democrats? The Renewal of Politics in the Muslim World*, edited by Ghassan Salamé, 130–55. London: I. B. Tauris, 1994.

Lust, Ellen. "Democratization by Election? Competitive Clientelism in the Middle East." *Journal of Democracy* 20, no. 3 (2009): 122–35.

———. "Opposition Cooperation and Uprisings in the Arab World." *British Journal of Middle Eastern Studies* 38, no. 3 (2011): 425–34.

Lust-Okar, Ellen. *Structuring Conflict in the Arab World: Incumbents, Opponents, and Institutions*. Cambridge: Cambridge Univ. Press, 2005.

Mahdavy, Hossein. "The Patterns and Problems of Economic Development in Rentier States: The Case of Iran." In *Studies in the Economic History of the Middle East: From the Rise of Islam to the Present Day*, edited by M. A. Cook, 428–67. Oxford: Oxford Univ. Press, 1970.

Mainwaring, Scott, and Timothy R. Scully, eds. *Building Democratic Institutions: Party Systems in Latin America.* Stanford, CA: Stanford Univ. Press, 1995.

Mansur, Bilqis Ahmad. *Al-Ahzab al-Siyasiyya wa al-Tahawwul al-Dimuqrati: Dirasa Tatbiqiyya 'ala al-Yaman wa Bilad Ukhra.* Cairo: Maktaba Madbuli, 2004.

Mawari, Yahya Muhammad al-. *'Ala Tariq al-Hiwar al-Watani.* Sanaa: Markaz al-Tasmim wa al-Ikhraj al-Fanni, 2012.

McAdam, Doug, John D. McCarthy, and Mayer N. Zald. "Opportunities, Mobilizing Structures, and Framing Processes: Toward a Synthetic, Comparative Perspective on Social Movements." In *Comparative Perspectives on Social Movements: Political Opportunities, Mobilizing Structures, and Cultural Framings,* edited by Doug McAdam, John D. McCarthy, and Mayer N. Zald, 1–20. Cambridge: Cambridge Univ. Press, 2004.

McCarthy, John D., and Mayer N. Zald. "Resource Mobilization and Social Movements: A Partial Theory." *American Journal of Sociology* 82, no. 6 (1977): 1212–41.

McCrum, Philip. "Carrots and Sticks." *Middle East International* 2, no. 10 (2010): 22–24.

Melucci, Alberto. "The Process of Collective Identity." In *Social Movements and Culture,* edited by Hank Johnston and Bert Klandermans, 41–63. Minneapolis: Univ. of Minnesota Press.

Meyer, David S., and Catherine Corrigall-Brown. "Coalitions and Political Context: U.S. Movements against Wars in Iraq." *Mobilization* 10, no. 3 (2005): 327–46.

Mihklafi, Mohammad Ahmad al-. "The Electoral System in Yemen." In *Building Democracy in Yemen,* edited by Ziad Majed, 87–125. Stockholm and Beirut: International Institute for Democratic and Electoral Assistance and Arab NGO Network for Development, 2005.

Milud, Walad al-Sadiq. *Al-Inqisam al-Ijtima'i wa Atharuhu fi bayna al-Ahzab al-Qawmiyya.* Amman: Markaz al-Kitab al-Akadimi, 2012.

Mutawakkil, Muhammad 'Abd al-Malik al-. "Al-Afaq al-Dimuqratiyya fi al-Thawra al-Yamaniyya." *Al-Mustaqbal al-'Arabi* 34, no. 399 (2012): 149–58.

Newman, Edward. "Weak States, State Failure, and Terrorism." *Terrorism and Political Violence* 19, no. 4 (2007): 463–88.

Norton, Phillip. "Making Sense of Opposition." *Journal of Legislative Studies* 14, nos. 1–2 (2008): 236–50.

Olson, Mancur. *The Logic of Collective Action: Public Goods and the Theory of Groups.* Cambridge, MA: Harvard Univ. Press, 1965.

Ong, Elvin. "Opposition Coordination in Singapore's 2015 General Elections." *Round Table* 105, no. 2 (2016): 185–94.

Orkaby, Asher. *Beyond the Arab Cold War: The International History of the Yemen Civil War, 1962–1968.* Oxford: Oxford Univ. Press, 2017.

Panebianco, Angelo. *Political Parties: Organizations and Power.* New York: Cambridge Univ. Press, 1988.

Patzelt, Werner J. "Opposition." In *International Encyclopedia of Political Science*, edited by Bertrand Badie, Dirk Berg-Schlosser, and Leonardo Morlino, 1745–48. Thousand Oaks, CA: Sage, 2011.

Penner Angrist, Michele. "The Outlook for Authoritarians." In *Authoritarianism in the Middle East: Regimes and Resistance*, edited by Marsha Pripstein Posusney and Michele Penner Angrist, 221–32. Boulder, CO: Lynne Rienner, 2005.

Peterson, John E. "Tribes and Politics in Yemen." *Arabian Peninsula Background Notes* 7 (2008).

Philbrick Yadav, Stacey. *Islamists and the State: Legitimacy and Institutions in Yemen and Lebanon.* London: I. B. Tauris, 2013.

———. "Understanding 'What Islamists Want': Public Debate and Contestation in Lebanon and Yemen." *Middle East Journal* 64, no. 2 (2010): 199–213.

———. *Yemen in the Shadow of Transition: Pursuing Justice amid War.* London: Hurst, 2022.

Philbrick Yadav, Stacey, and Janine Clark. "Disappointments and New Directions: Women, Partisanship, and the Regime in Yemen." *Journal of Women of the Middle East and the Islamic World* 8, no. 1 (2010): 55–95.

Phillips, Sarah. "Evaluating Political Reform in Yemen." *Carnegie Papers* (Carnegie Endowment for International Peace) 80 (2007).

———. "Yemen: The Centrality of Process." In *Beyond the Façade: Political Reform in the Arab World*, edited by Marina Ottaway and Julia Choucair-Vizoso, 231–59. Washington, DC: Carnegie Endowment for International Peace, 2008.

———. *Yemen and the Politics of Permanent Crisis.* Abingdon: Routledge, 2011.

———. *Yemen's Democracy Experiment in Regional Perspective: Patronage and Pluralized Authoritarianism.* New York: Palgrave Macmillan, 2008.

Phillips, Sarah, and Murad Zafir. "NDI Baseline Assessment of the Joint Meeting Parties (JMP)." Yemen: National Democratic Institute for International Affairs, n.d.

Pripstein Posusney, Marsha. "Multiparty Elections in the Arab World: Election Rules and Opposition Responses." In *Authoritarianism in the Middle East: Regimes and Resistance*, edited by Marsha Pripstein Posusney and Michele Penner Angrist, 91–118. Boulder, CO: Lynne Rienner, 2005.

Ragin, Charles C. "Cases of 'What Is a Case?'" In *What Is a Case? Exploring the Foundations of Social Inquiry*, edited by Charles C. Ragin and Howard Becker, 1–17. Cambridge: Cambridge Univ. Press, 1992.

Ramsbotham, Oliver, Tom Woodhouse, and Hugh Miall. *Contemporary Conflict Resolution: The Prevention, Management and Transformation of Deadly Conflicts*. Malden, MA: Polity Press, 2008.

Randall, Vicky, and Lars Svåsand. "Party Institutionalization in New Democracies." *Party Politics* 8, no. 1 (2002): 5–29.

Resende, Madalena, and Hendrik Kraetzschmar. "Parties of Power as Roadblocks to Democracy: The Cases of Ukraine and Egypt." *CEPS Policy Brief* (Centre for European Policy Studies) 81 (2005).

Richter, Thomas. "New Petro-Aggression in the Middle East: Saudi Arabia in the Spotlight." *Global Policy* 11, no. 1 (2020): 93–102.

Rieger, René. *Saudi Arabian Foreign Relations: Diplomacy and Mediation in Conflict Resolution*. London: Routledge, 2017.

Roberts, David. *The Ba'th and the Creation of Modern Syria*. London: Croom Helm, 1987.

Rosefsky Wickham, Carrie. "The Path to Moderation: Strategy and Learning in the Formation of Egypt's Wasat Party." *Comparative Politics* 36, no. 2 (2004): 205–28.

Ruhani, 'Abd al-Wahhab Muhammad al-. *Al-Yaman: Khususiyya al-Hukm wa al-Wahda wa al-Dimuqratiyya*. Cairo: Maktaba Madbuli, 2008.

Ryan, Curtis R. "Political Opposition and Reform Coalitions in Jordan." *British Journal of Middle Eastern Studies* 38, no. 3 (2011): 367–90.

Sadiki, Larbi. "Like Father, Like Son: Dynastic Republicanism in the Middle East." *Policy Outlook* (Carnegie Endowment for International Peace) 25 (2009).

Sa'id, 'Abd al-Karim Qasim. *Al-Ikhwan al-Muslimun wa al-Haraka al-Usuliyya fi al-Yaman*. Cairo: Maktaba Madbuli, 1995.

Salamé, Ghassan. "Les dilemmes d'un pays (trop) bien situé." In *Le Yémen contemporain*, edited by Rémy Leveau, Franck Mermier, and Udo Steinbach, 37–60. Paris: Karthala, 1999.

Sallam, Hesham. "Opposition Alliances and Democratization in Egypt." *Peace Brief* (United States Institute of Peace) (June 2008).

Salmoni, Barak A., Bryce Loidolt, and Madeleine Wells. *Regime and Periphery in Northern Yemen: The Huthi Phenomenon.* Santa Monica, CA: RAND, 2010.

Schedler, Andreas. "Democratic Reciprocity." *Journal of Political Philosophy* 29, no. 2 (2021): 252–78.

———. "The Nested Game of Democratization by Elections." *International Political Science Review* 23, no. 1 (2002): 103–22.

———. "The New Institutionalism in the Study of Authoritarianism." *Totalitarianism and Democracy* 6, no. 2 (2009): 323–40.

———. *The Politics of Uncertainty: Sustaining and Subverting Electoral Authoritarianism.* Oxford: Oxford Univ. Press, 2013.

Schelling, Thomas C. *The Strategy of Conflict.* Cambridge, MA: Harvard Univ. Press, 1963.

Schmitz, Charles. "Yemen's Wealth Lies in Its Labour Force." *ITPCM International Commentary* 9, no. 32 (2013): 9–13.

Schubert, Gunter, Rainer Tetzlaff, and Werner Vennewald. *Demokratisierung und politischer Wandel: Theorie und Anwendung des Konzepts der strategischen und konfliktfähigen Gruppen.* Münster: LIT, 1994.

Schwedler, Jillian. "Can Islamists Become Moderates? Rethinking the Inclusion-Moderation Hypothesis." *World Politics* 63, no. 2 (2011): 347–76.

———. *Faith in Moderation: Islamist Parties in Jordan and Yemen.* Cambridge: Cambridge Univ. Press, 2006.

———. *Protesting Jordan: Geographies of Power and Dissent.* Stanford, CA: Stanford Univ. Press, 2022.

———. "Yemen's Aborted Opening." *Journal of Democracy* 13, no. 4 (2002): 48–55.

Schwedler, Jillian, and Janine Clark. "Islamist-Leftist Cooperation in the Arab World." *ISIM Review,* no. 18 (2006): 10–11.

Seawright, Jason, and David Collier. "Glossary of Selected Terms." In *Rethinking Social Inquiry: Diverse Tools, Shared Standards,* edited by Henry Brady and David Collier, 273–313. Lanham: Rowman and Littlefield, 2004.

Seawright, Jason, and John Gerring. "Case Selection Techniques in Case Study Research: A Menu of Qualitative and Quantitative Options." *Political Research Quarterly* 61, no. 2 (2008): 294–308.

Sewell, William H., Jr. "A Theory of Structure: Duality, Agency, and Transformation." *American Journal of Sociology* 98, no. 1 (1992): 1–29.

Shalan, Thaira. "Les organisations non gouvernementales et la société civil au Yémen." In *Le Yémen contemporain*, edited by Rémy Leveau, Franck Mermier, and Udo Steinbach, 285–300. Paris: Karthala, 1999.

Shapiro, Ian. "The Fallacies Concerning Minorities, Majorities, and Democratic Politics." In *Democracy's Place*, edited by Ian Shapiro, 16–52. Ithaca, NY: Cornell Univ. Press, 1996.

Sharjabi, 'Adil Mujahid al-. "Al-Tajammu' al-Yamani li-l-Islah: Bayna al-Barnamaj al-Siyasi wa Shi'ar al-Islam Huwa al-Hall." *Al-Majalla al-'Arabiyya li-l-'Ulum al-Siyasiyya* 24 (2009): 137–60.

Sharjabi, 'Adil Mujahid al-, et al. *Al-Qasr wa al-Diwan: Al-Dawr al-Siyasi li-l-Qabila fi al-Yaman*. Sanaa: Al-Marsad al-Yamani li-Huquq al-'Insan, 2009.

Shehata, Dina. *Islamists and Secularists in Egypt: Opposition, Conflict, and Co-operation*. New York: Routledge, 2010.

Sil, Rudra. "The Foundations of Eclecticism: The Epistemological Status of Agency, Culture, and Structure in Social Theory." *Journal of Theoretical Politics* 12, no. 3 (2000): 353–87.

Snow, David A., and Robert D. Benford. "Ideology, Frame Resonance, and Participant Mobilization." In *From Structure to Action: Comparing Social Movement Research across Cultures*, edited by Bert Klandermans, Hanspeter Kriesi, and Sidney Tarrow, 197–217. Greenwich, CT: JAI Press, 1988.

Staggenborg, Suzanne. "Coalition Work in the Pro-choice Movement: Organizational and Environmental Opportunities and Obstacles." *Social Problems* 33, no. 4 (1986): 374–90.

Stanzel, Volker. "Marxism in Arabia: South Yemen Twenty Years after Independence." *Aussenpolitik* 39, no. 3 (1988): 265–77.

Stepan, Alfred. "On the Tasks of Democratic Opposition." *Journal of Democracy* 1, no. 2 (1990): 41–49.

———. "Paths toward Redemocratization: Theoretical and Comparative Considerations." In *Transitions from Authoritarian Rule: Comparative Perspectives*, edited by Guillermo O'Donnell, Phillipe C. Schmitter, and Laurence Whitehead, 64–84. Baltimore: Johns Hopkins Univ. Press, 1986.

Stiftl, Ludwig. "Politischer Islam und Pluralismus: Theoretische und empirische Studie am Beispiel des Jemen." PhD diss., Freie Univ. Berlin, 1998.

———. "The Yemeni Islamists in the Process of Democratization." In *Le Yémen contemporain*, edited by Rémy Leveau, Franck Mermier, and Udo Steinbach, 247–66. Paris: Karthala, 1999.

Stones, Rob. *Structuration Theory*. Houndmills: Palgrave Macmillan, 2005.

Stookey, Robert W. *Yemen: The Politics of the Yemen Arab Republic*. Boulder, CO: Westview Press, 1978.

Stracke, Nicole, and Mohammed Saif Haidar. "The Southern Movement in Yemen." *Report* (Gulf Research Center & Sheba Center for Strategic Studies) (Apr. 2010).

Tansey, Oisín. "Process Tracing and Elite Interviewing: A Case for Non-probability Sampling." *PS: Political Science & Politics* 40, no. 4 (2007): 765–72.

Tarrow, Sidney G. *Power in Movement: Social Movements and Contentious Politics*. 3rd ed. Cambridge: Cambridge Univ. Press, 2011.

Thrift, Nigel. *Spatial Formations*. London: Sage, 1996.

Tilly, Charles, and Sidney G. Tarrow. *Contentious Politics*. Boulder, CO: Paradigm, 2007.

Transfeld, Mareike. "A Youth Non-movement in Sana'a: Changing Normative Geographies through Fashion, Art and Music." In *Yemen and the Search for Stability: Power, Politics and Society After the Arab Spring*, edited by Marie-Christine Heinze, 231–57. London: I. B. Tauris, 2018.

Van de Walle, Nicolas. "Tipping Games: When Do Opposition Parties Coalesce?" In *Electoral Authoritarianism: The Dynamics of Unfree Competition*, edited by Andreas Schedler, 77–92. Boulder, CO: Lynne Rienner, 2006.

Van Dyke, Nella. "Crossing Movement Boundaries: Factors That Facilitate Coalition Protest by American College Students, 1930–1990." *Social Problems* 50, no. 2 (2003): 226–50.

Van Dyke, Nella, and Bryan Amos. "Social Movement Coalitions: Formation, Longevity, and Success." *Sociology Compass* 11, no. 7 (2017): 1–17.

Van Dyke, Nella, and Holly J. McCammon, eds. "Introduction: Social Movement Coalition Formation." In *Strategic Alliances: Coalition Building and Social Movements*, edited by Nella Van Dyke and Holly J. McCammon, xi–xxviii. Minneapolis: Univ. of Minnesota Press, 2010.

———. *Strategic Alliances: Coalition Building and Social Movements*. Minneapolis: Univ. of Minnesota Press, 2010.

Wahman, Michael. "Offices and Policies: Why Do Oppositional Parties Form Pre-electoral Coalitions in Competitive Authoritarian Regimes?" *Electoral Studies* 30, no. 4 (2011): 642–57.

———. "Opposition Coalitions and Democratization by Election." *Government and Opposition* 48, no. 1 (2013): 3–32.

Wedeen, Lisa. *Peripheral Visions: Publics, Power, and Performance in Yemen*. Chicago: Univ. of Chicago Press, 2008.

———. "Seeing Like a Citizen, Acting Like a State: Exemplary Events in Unified Yemen." *Comparative Studies in Society and History* 45, no. 4 (2003): 680–713.

Wegner, Eva. "Islamist Inclusion and Regime Persistence: The Moroccan Win-Win Situation." In *Debating Arab Authoritarianism: Dynamics and Durability in Nondemocratic Regimes*, edited by Oliver Schlumberger, 75–89. Stanford, CA: Stanford Univ. Press, 2007.

Wegner, Eva, and Miquel Pellicer. "Left-Islamist Opposition Cooperation in Morocco." *British Journal of Middle Eastern Studies* 38, no. 3 (2011): 303–22.

Weir, Shelagh. "A Clash of Fundamentalism: Wahhabism in Yemen." *Middle East Report*, no. 204 (1997): 22–26.

Wildavsky, Aaron. "Choosing Preferences by Constructing Institutions: A Cultural Theory of Preference Formation." *American Political Science Review* 81, no. 1 (1987): 3–22.

Yacoubian, Mona. "Building Momentum for Reform: The Islamist-Secular Alliance in Yemen." In *The Challenge of Islamists for EU and US Policies: Conflict, Stability, and Reform*, edited by Muriel Asseburg and Daniel Brumberg, 59–64. Washington, DC: United States Institute of Peace, 2007.

Yates, Douglas A. *The Rentier State in Africa: Oil Rent Dependency and Neocolonialism in the Republic of Gabon*. Trenton, NJ: Africa World Press, 1996.

Yemeni, Ahmed A. Hezam al-. *The Dynamics of Democratisation: Political Parties in Yemen*. Bonn: Friedrich Ebert Foundation, 2003.

Yemen Polling Center. *Yemeni Citizens' Main Concerns, Perception of Human Rights and CSOs*. Sanaa: YPC, 2012.

Zartman, I. William. "Opposition as Support of the State." In *The Arab State*, edited by Giacomo Luciani, 220–46. London: Routledge, 1990.

———. "Opposition in Support of the Arab State, Revisited." In *Contentious Politics in the Middle East: Political Opposition under Authoritarianism*, edited by Holger Albrecht, 229–42. Gainesville: Univ. Press of Florida, 2010.

Zick, Andreas. "Die Konflikttheorie der Theorie sozialer Identität." In *Sozialwissenschaftliche Konflikttheorien*, edited by Thorsten Bonacker, 409–26. Wiesbaden: VS Verlag für Sozialwissenschaften, 2008.

Ziegfeld, Adam, and Maya Tudor. "How Opposition Parties Sustain Single-Party Dominance: Lessons from India." *Party Politics* 23, no. 3 (2017): 262–73.

Index

Jens Heibach is a postdoctoral research fellow at the German Institute for Global and Area Studies (GIGA) in Hamburg, Germany. His research interests include authoritarianism, opposition politics, Islamist movements, and the international relations of the Middle East. Heibach's research has received funding from the Horizon 2020 Framework Programme of the European Union as well as the German Research Foundation and appeared in journals such as the *British Journal of Middle Eastern Studies*, *Democratization*, *International Politics*, *Middle Eastern Studies*, *Middle East Law and Governance*, and *Middle East Policy*.

Printed in the USA
CPSIA information can be obtained
at www.ICGtesting.com
CBHW022341060424
6483CB00004B/17